THE HAWKHURST BRANCH

40009. The Colonnade, Hawkhurst.
J. DAVIS & SON
HOTEL
RAC
HASTINGS
A229

THE HAWKHURST BRANCH

BRIAN HART

Introduction 1

Chapter One
THE WEALTH OF THE WEALD 5

Chapter Two
THE CRANBROOK & PADDOCK WOOD RAILWAY 15

Chapter Three
BUILDING THE BRANCH 25

Chapter Four
EXTENDING THE LINE 45

Chapter Five
PROSPEROUS TIMES 53

Chapter Six
SUNNY SOUTH DAYS 77

Chapter Seven
LAND OF LOST CONTENT 103

Chapter Eight
THE HOP-PICKERS' TALE 165

Chapter Nine
SWANSONG 189

Appendices
Southern Railway Locomotive Workings 228
Distance Diagram 229
Gradient Profile 229
Track Plans 230
Signalling Plans 232
Building Drawings 236

Acknowledgements 252

WILD SWAN PUBLICATIONS

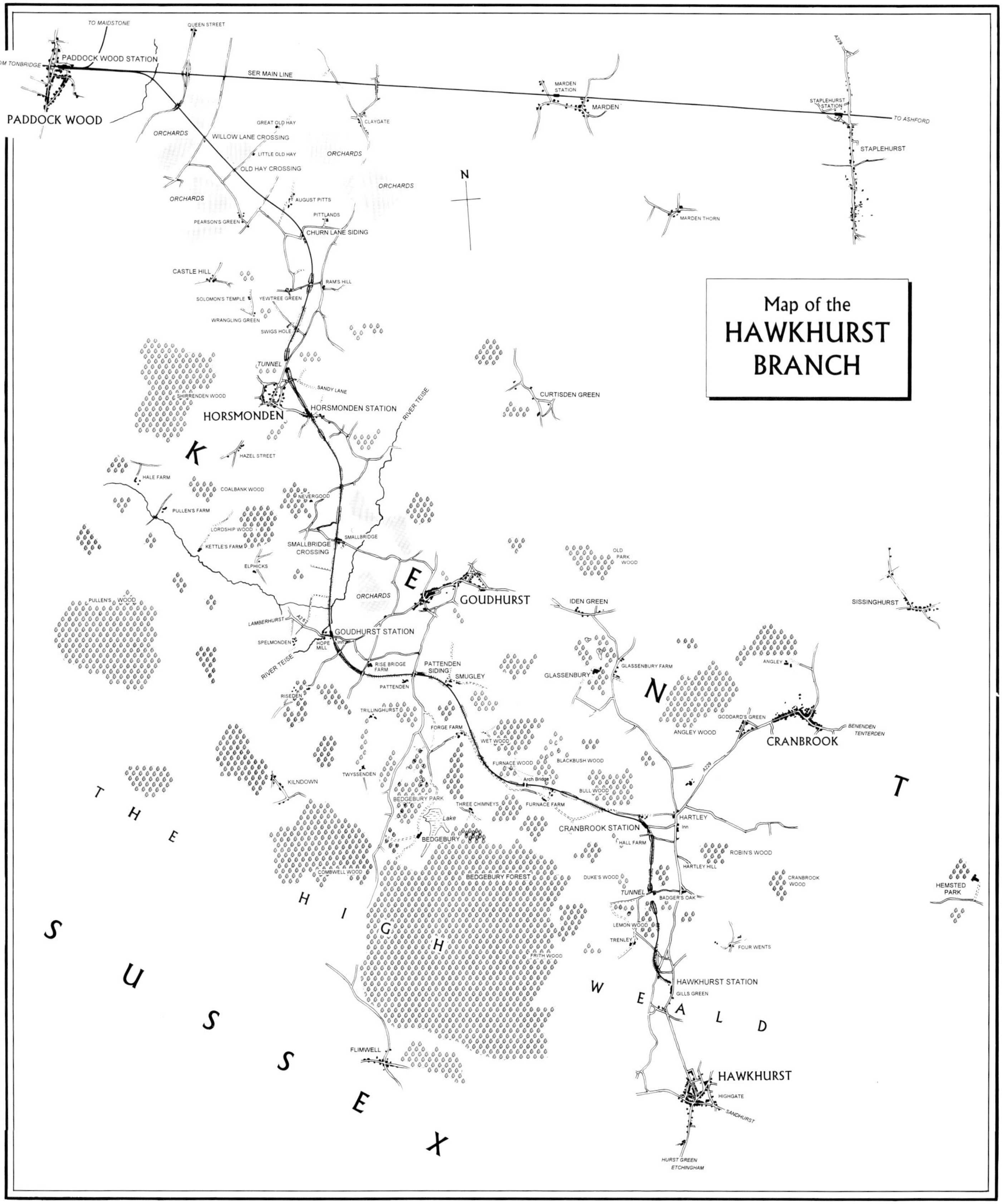

ISBN 1 874103 54 2

Designed by Paul Karau
Printed by Amadeus Press, Cleckheaton, West Yorkshire

Published by
WILD SWAN PUBLICATIONS LTD.
1-3 Hagbourne Road, Didcot, Oxon,
OX11 8DP

INTRODUCTION

AMONG the many and varied branch lines of the former South Eastern Railway, none was more characterful than the single track that penetrated the High Weald to Hawkhurst. One of the last to be constructed under the 'old order' during the final bout of fierce competition between the SER and LC&DR, its arrival on the railway map of Southern England was well overdue since plans had been put forward for a line to Cranbrook as early as the middle of the nineteenth century. The long struggle, which lasted forty years, is dealt with in the opening chapters where the intriguing story of events, both locally and on a wider scale, unfolds. It might be assumed that had the SER chairman's hostility towards the scheme prevailed, then this loveliest of single-track railways might never have been built. Certainly after 1900, or even perhaps 1895, its merits would have been insufficient to justify construction in a rapidly changing world. The eventual working union that saw the creation of the SE&CR at the turn of the century, as well as the passing of the Light Railways Act of 1897 would have likely eclipsed its attraction. In purely conjectural terms, the entire area may well have been left instead to the engineers of light railways, with branches being built from Tenterden to Ashford, Cranbrook and Tonbridge.

The line was unique in many respects, not only being controlled by Tyer's electric tablet system, but more noticeably for the signalling installed throughout by Messrs McKenzie & Holland. It is noteworthy that many of these signals, unfamiliar in the south, with their highly elaborate M&H cast-iron finials, lasted for many years, a few even into BR days. The stations, too, were quite unlike any others seen on the Southern, with distinctively gabled red-brick dwellings for the station masters. The corrugated-iron office buildings were also unusual for the SER which traditionally used weather boarding and only on the northern section of the Elham Valley Line could similar examples be found. Other structures, such as bridges and tunnels, also differed in design, contributing much to its unique charm and individuality.

Although the railway has been closed for almost forty years, I am only too well aware that I'm far from being alone in mourning the loss of this byway, for it was surely something special, a sentiment easily grasped when glancing through the photographic record. Indeed, I feel quite thankful for the quirks of fate that led to this wonderful line eventually being laid down across such a beautiful landscape.

It goes without saying that I regret never having seen trains winding their way through a district that I hold most dear, let alone having had the opportunity to ride upon its metals. Indeed, apart from a vague memory of seeing the rails of the branch curve away from Paddock Wood, the line was unknown to me until the age of about thirteen. My father came across the railway in 1963, while on a new delivery run around the district. The chance to travel with him on odd days during school holidays was often taken and it was then that my horizons began to broaden and my love of the Weald and its enchanting villages, lanes and secret corners was nurtured. Lunchtime frequently coincided with a picnic break at Hawkhurst station, enabling me to explore the derelict, vandalised offices, signalbox, engine shed etc. Everything stood so forlorn, but a later visit to Cranbrook station was more encouraging. Here there was little damage, thanks to the watchful eye of a local policeman who lived nearby and had the reputation of putting the fear of God into anyone found loitering around the place for whatever purpose. The atmosphere of this wonderful branch was still pervasive even after closure and it wasn't difficult to envisage how everyday life must have been for the railway staff who were fortunate enough to work here.

On a very damp autumnal afternoon my parents and I took a stroll south of Cranbrook to Badger's Oak tunnel. The very name conjures up all sorts of rural images, whilst the empty fields and trees in their last dying colours of summer appeared so much like the exquisite landscapes so imaginatively captured by watercolour artists such as Sutton Palmer, Wilfrid Ball and Ernest Haslehust. The wooden sleepers were covered in colourful, shiny, wet leaves, making the going slippery underfoot, whilst the air was pungent with the scents of mould and woodsmoke. On reaching the gaping mouth of the tunnel that yawned in seemingly immense blackness before us, barely a breath of wind wafted from out of the dank interior. Stepping into the cold, daunting gloom, only the sound of water greeted our ears; no more would there be the grinding, resounding rattle of the local branch train. Even though we soon perceived light at the other end, time demanded we went no further, for the business of the day was calling. On another visit we walked towards Goudhurst, the railway in a deathly hush, a silence broken only by intermittent birdsong and the sighing and whispering of trees in Bedgebury Forest. The rusty track disappeared down the discernible gradient, whilst young saplings were already gaining a firm hold between the sleepers.

It was around this time that Roger Crombleholme's *The Hawkhurst Railway* was published. I remember how eagerly I read it repeatedly from cover to cover, often taking it to school, concealed within a dreary physics or chemistry book during the long hours spent on subjects that I found tedious and barely comprehensible. Lighter studies enabled us to examine our local district when One-inch Ordnance Survey maps of East Kent were distributed. A few of the older 1947 revised editions depicted the Elham Valley Line; the stations marked as white dots denoting 'closed' with the exception of Lyminge, but the newer versions showed only a row of dashes with the legend 'Tk of Old Rly'. For one shilling I was able to buy from the school secretary one of these earlier issues of the East Kent map and it wasn't long before burning curiosity led me to seek out, in old and delightfully over-crammed, dingy and dusty bookshops, copies of adjoining maps which displayed other closed lines of Kent. The Hawkhurst branch was soon found, snaking its way across the Weald of Kent through districts and byways with such wonderfully curious and evocative names. Not surprisingly, the acquisition of these maps soon engendered a longing to visit these enticing haunts, but I was hampered by the range of my push bike. However, I did manage to reach more local places and some days I'd visit rural stations where elderly members of staff needed little coaxing to talk about their early days on the SE&CR and the Southern. Sometimes they would give me old railway mementoes, or let me hunt through the dusty luggage label racks for coloured labels pertaining to long-lost stations. Although the Hawkhurst railway was well out of my district, a trip to Paddock Wood by train one Saturday brought a surprise when the staff fished out the redundant enamelled sign which had once directed passengers over the bridge to the branch stations. This prize was excitedly taken home, where a coat of Dad's paint stripper over the obliterated lower half soon revealed those magical destinations: Horsmonden, Goudhurst, Cranbrook, Hawkhurst.

The lure of the Weald became very intense. On warm summer evenings I'd wander alone and climb the steep hill known locally as 'Caesar's Camp' at the back of my home in Cheriton. Today it is pierced by the entrance to the Channel Tunnel, whilst virtually all the favoured haunts of my childhood wanderings have since been buried beneath countless tons of concrete, the M20, gyratory feeder roads and marshalling yards. In those days, however, the view westwards was across nothing but green fields, ponds and quiet broad-leaf woodland to the hills beyond at Beachborough, upon which stood a strikingly lonesome Scot's pine. In the darkening western sky it would occasionally be silhouetted against a romantic red glow from the sun setting over the far-distant High Weald. Gradually, all became shrouded in the bluish-indigo shadows of dusk until I was left watching the evening star. These eventide reveries initiated a yearning to see as much as I could of rural, unspoilt Kent and in particular the Hawkhurst branch. This developed into an impetuously youthful decision to walk its entire length. With my schoolboy set of dividers I measured the route on my newly-acquired map of the area - eleven and a half miles from Paddock Wood to the terminus at Gills Green. This, I thought in my growing enthusiasm, should be easily walkable within a day, and so, with my younger cousin in tow, I boarded the train at Shorncliffe, armed with little more than pocket money, a map, sandwiches and a bottle of pop.

Having successfully traced a public footpath which took us onto the disused line near Queen Street bridge, we soon left the roar of the Kent Coast electrics as we began tramping from sleeper to sleeper towards those ever-beckoning wooded hilltops. Ox-eye daisies and tall grasses grew waist-high alongside the rusty-brown rails, but the tiring short steps caused by the sleeper spacing eventually led us to walk on the adjacent ash path. The idle gates at Willow Lane, rusting on their hinges, were firmly padlocked across the railway as, perspiring by now, we tramped onwards to Churn Lane. Even though we were blessed with a dry, sunny day for this grand trek, the weather soon proved hardly suitable as the last drop of lemonade was all too quickly consumed, leaving us gasping with thirst. The midday sun nearing its zenith began to sear down relentlessly, burning away the few remaining white clouds until a blue sky stretched from every horizon. Inevitably our pace began to slow as we dawdled here and there, the dull brown rails creaking in the shimmering distance, until finally we left the railway and wandered across to a nearby farm in desperate search of a drink. Here a chubby-faced farmer's wife, with a bright, cheerful laugh and ruddy cheeks, welcomed us into the cool interior of her enormous flagstone pantry. When we told her of our intention to walk to Hawkhurst, she hesitated, then smiled kindly and spoke briefly of the trains which used to rattle by so regularly at all hours of the day. In a moment's wistfulness she said she missed their presence very much indeed and, although she'd only ridden on it once or twice, it was almost as if they'd suddenly been cut off from the outside world. From a tap we were given glass after glass of water, had our empty lemonade bottle replenished and were then told to go and help ourselves to as many apples as we could carry from the wooden crates stacked high in the corner. I remember how these tasted like the crispest, sweetest and juiciest I'd ever sampled and we eagerly took half a dozen to sustain us throughout the day.

Refreshed, we resumed our walk along the line with renewed vigour and enthusiasm, but were nevertheless relieved to reach the relative coolness of Horsmonden cutting where an obsolete distant signal stood, its spectacle glass smashed. A few yards further and just around a leftward curve, we saw the tunnel before us, where a heavenly breeze wafted from out of the darkness. Inside, an intermittent dripping and plopping of water sounded somewhere in the cess as we made our way to the light at the other end. Ahead, among the large fronds of bright green ferns which graced the steep sides of the cutting, rose the elegant form of a three-arch bridge. Within a few hundred yards we came to the station, the horizontal red and white arm of the down home signal still guarding the way. I remember my cousin bravely ascended the tall iron ladder to the top and wrested this lower-quadrant relic into the 'all clear' position. Sadly, the station building had been visited by the local vandals and wandering tramps, but we peered into the derelict rooms and I remember how pleased I'd been at finding a few mouldering old tickets beneath a hole in the signal cabin floor. We wandered along to the two-way signal, just beyond the road bridge and I recollect how much I wanted to walk further into this landscape. The railway disappeared tantalisingly down gradient and I longed so much to see what was round the next bend. However, my watch warned that we'd have to retrace our steps, so, reluctantly, we turned back for Paddock Wood. Towards the late afternoon we left the branch, the sun still warm, as hungrily and with aching feet, the comforting thought of reaching home and dinner was more than an inducement. Alas, I never grasped the opportunity of walking other stretches of the line after that occasion, and, although I never achieved what I'd so ambitiously set out to do, that day remains one of the most memorable of my boyhood.

My only other real acquaintance with the line was in complete contrast to that bright, sweltering day and involved a trip to Cranbrook in the grip of winter. At that time I was a member of the Kent & East Sussex Railway Preservation Society and most Sundays I'd be engaged in cutting willows on the lonely marshes around Wittersham or involved in any number of tasks in those bleak but hopeful days. I suppose the news that the Hawkhurst branch was about to be ripped up didn't come as much of a surprise, but I greeted it with dismay in much the same way as when a fine building or old church is demolished. Fortunately for the railway preservationists, the contractors had generously consented to the K&ESRPS salvaging signalling and track equipment, as well as any other items which might be needed. On a bitterly cold Sunday, in February 1964, gangs of volunteers piled into an assortment of old cars, vans and lorries, intent on dismantling whatever might be useful. Some went to Goudhurst where the contractors had set up a base, with track piled high in the goods yard, whilst I joined the party bound for Cranbrook. On arrival at the station there were flurries of snow, but eventually the weather eased and a start was made on retrieving point rods, wire, pulleys and various signalling items. Everything was still connected, whereby from the signalbox a few of us took a last turn at pulling various levers and watching the signal arms bounce in obeyance. It felt quite wicked to be taking all this equipment to pieces, especially from a railway which had performed so well for almost seventy years. The alternative, though, was to leave it to the demolition gang whose only concern was its scrap metal value. Throughout the day the vehicles were steadily loaded with the heavy iron equipment until the light began to fade and volunteers gradually congregated on the platform.

At one stage, standing beneath the canopy, it became almost dreamlike, as though we were all waiting for a train to come steaming in from the direction of Hawkhurst and take us home. I wandered away from the group, while over to the west a leaden sunset silhouetted the gaunt branches of bare trees as an eerie hush came over the scene, the kind which heralds a fall of snow. From the end of the platform, I remember watching the lights from numerous oil handlamps flashing in the gloaming upon the railway beneath Hall Farm bridge as the last gang, cold and weary, returned to base. For an hour or so there was much activity and noise around the station as loads were secured, doors slammed, whilst from within the booking hall there drifted a buzz of voices interspersed with laughter. Inside, the roar of Tilley lamps added to the din as the last of the pies, sandwiches and lukewarm tea from Thermos flasks was hungrily consumed. The light from the lamps was reflected back from the condensation running down the grimy windows which made puddles upon the grubby green paintwork.

Then, suddenly, it was all over. Along with the others, I climbed into the back of a van, and, as we left for Tenterden and home, I couldn't resist one last backward glance at Cranbrook station, although there was little to be seen in the pitch blackness. A feeling of panic swept over me on realising that within a matter of a couple of weeks, perhaps days, the contractors would be there, ripping up the track and destroying the railway I'd known so briefly, yet which had come to mean so much. Since that day I've rarely visited what remains of the branch, preferring instead to recapture happier times with the aid of photographs and postcards.

What then, might be said in summarising the worth of the Hawkhurst branch, was it really all in vain? I think not. Admittedly, the line was never an important part of the system, but the returns did prove the SER chairman's antipathy ill-founded in regard to its usefulness. Closure in 1961 may not have caused widespread hardship, but, had the service survived, then surely, given a sensible, integrated transport policy, the railway could have acted as a useful feeder line to Paddock Wood for today's commuters. Its fate was a grim portent of things to come, when not only minor branch lines were closed, but arterial routes were recklessly axed in a misguided and reprehensible manner.

Over the years it has often been said it's a pity the line was never saved for preservation. In many ways I have much sympathy for this view, who wouldn't? The prospect of still being able to be wooed by this railway and its scenery is so very tempting. Alas, it is a matter of great regret that whilst in the south of England we have the ex-L&SWR 'Watercress' Line and the ex-LB&SCR 'Bluebell' Line, nothing to represent an SER/SE&CR branch survives. Hawkhurst would have been a perfect choice but, personally, I would have retained misgivings and scarcely welcomed the unfettered commercialism that inevitably accompanies tourist railways.

I am very well aware that it is all too easy to become sentimental about railways, branch lines in particular, since they flourished during an era of English history

This picture, taken on Friday, 9th June 1961, shows 'C' class 31256 drifting past the up distant signal near Pattenden with a solitary brake van on its way to shunt the goods yard at Goudhurst. This would be for the very last time as the locomotive would take back all the remaining empty wagons. Blowing gently in the warm summer breeze on this beautiful day, the washing on the clothes line at Risebridge Farm probably remained quite unsullied by smuts in view of such a light working. *Tony Wright*

which is viewed with much affection. Today's world seems more aggressive, noisy and hectic. It is certainly far uglier, and, whilst we may all be much better off materially, we appear to have lost so much along the way. I know I never fail to gain considerable solace from looking at old postcards and photographs, when the desire to step into the picture becomes so strong. Few photographers possessed the gift to capture this atmosphere, but the High Weald obviously attracted those who practised their art with an eye for beauty. Blessed with perfect conditions, they were able to create more than a photograph the day they opened the camera shutter. Hence, the opportunity of being able to share my favourite pictures of this enchanted land fills me with nothing less than feelings of warmth and contentment. The photographs alone make this a book to treasure, whilst the chance to write about this subject is a privilege not taken for granted.

Throughout the years I've spent researching, compiling and revising the text, I've been asked on many occasions by numerous friends "How are you getting on with Hawkhurst?", to which I've replied "Oh, it's almost finished". However, I must confess I've scarcely wanted to come to the end as it's been such an absorbing and pleasurable task. My apologies, therefore, to everyone who has been more than patient and I hope that the long wait will prove worthwhile. My great-aunt Edie's old fountain pen must have travelled a fair distance across countless pages, scraps of paper, revisions and suchlike. Now, at last, the time has come to put it down and leave my personal tribute to a vanished era and a favourite Kentish railway.

Brian Hart
Meadow Croft
Uckfield

DEDICATED TO
NORMAN RUSBRIDGE

CHAPTER ONE

THE WEALTH OF THE WEALD

ANDREDSWOLD, - ancient, mysterious, vast and barely penetrable long-lost forest of the southern counties. Once stretching a hundred and twenty miles from Kent to Hampshire, with a breadth of some thirty miles, its mighty oaks and dense thickets remained the domain of wolves, hogs, deer and birds for countless centuries. A lush green carpet of treetops covered the undulating high ground which rises from the vales between the massive chalk ridges of the North and South Downs. This secret woodland 'where nobody dwells', echoed only with the sounds of wild animals within its depths where unfurling plants struggled to complete their life cycle before summer's green mantle darkened the dappled forest floor. Birds flitted from branch to branch, their chorus of mating songs caught on the gentle breeze which wafted up from the pale indigo form of the distant downs. Deep within its hidden depths, amidst untrodden sylvan glades, springs gushed forth from damp, verdurous moss-covered banks. In numerous places rust-red trickles of oxydizing iron-rich sediment oozed from the earth, clouding and staining the many rivulets. Unknown dark pools, cool and shaded beneath the high, thick frondescence, seeped their precious life-sustaining water into the fertile soil. Noisy, unseen brooks gurgled and gushed to feed wide, languid streams which twisted and furrowed their way within the cooling forest. Joining forces, they eventually formed the rivers Eden, Teise, Beult, Medway and Rother, their silt-rich waters nourishing the plains that bordered the distant sea.

Throughout innumerable centuries this mystical forest remained undisturbed. There was no one there to marvel at springtime's burst of fresh, new life, or the autumnal amber moon which rose, full, pale-faced and of pinkish hue in the darkening eastern sky. There were no human inhabitants who might cower in fright at the freakish storms which seemingly rent a terrifying and passionate fury upon the forest's anguished trees. Groaning and creaking, the wind-tossed branches danced till they snapped, whilst for the less supple the seasonal battle was lost as they were split asunder by gales or lightning before sighing and crashing to the ground. Here, in the decades to follow, the woodland's young creatures played upon these gnarled and mossy rotting trunks as nature reclaimed its own. Pale yellow primroses, delicate celandines and quivering bluebells carpeted the sun-speckled clearings in these dells until, once more, young saplings reached high enough to close again the gap in the greenwood canopy.

Thus it remained until the marauding Saxons began to venture within its daunting confines, but they were not the first to have stood upon the chalk ridges and seen the distant thickly-wooded High Weald. The early Britons had paid scant attention to its presence, perhaps half-fearful of its dark, brooding interior. Later, the conquering Romans named it Silva Anderida, but for them it possessed little fascination other than its usefulness as a source of timber and iron-working on a very small scale. Even though its denseness hindered their roadways and subsequently the creation of any settlements, they did construct a secondary road across the Weald from Maidstone to Hastings. This ran through Staplehurst on a route now followed by the present A229, but then continued in the traditional Roman straight line, passing through Hemsted, near Benenden and on to Sandhurst two miles to the east of Cranbrook and Hawkhurst. Most of this ancient road has long-since disappeared, but its course may still be traced on Ordnance Survey maps.

The Saxons who sailed to these shores and eventually colonised the southern counties knew it as Andredswald - the forest of Andrea or Andred. Some claim the name Weald is a corruption of 'wild', implying an uninhabitable place, whilst a more plausible explanation is that it derives from the Teutonic 'wald', meaning quite literally a forest.

With the arrival in 597 of St. Augustine, whose papal mission was to establish Christianity, the heathen King Ethelbert of Kent was converted, whilst the new faith was soon embraced across the county. Even so, almost a further century elapsed before neighbouring Sussex finally relinquished paganism. The Kentish historian Frank Jessup considered this was due solely to the physical separation of these counties 'by the great and almost impenetrable forest of the Weald'.

Little by little, across these distant centuries, the early settlers began their slow, relentless exploration and clearing of parts of the forest floor. Beloved Anderida gave up its secrets as mankind gradually encroached into its quiet interior. The husbandry of hogs, which provided meat throughout the year, led to the creation of 'dens'. This Saxon word is familiar within our present-day towns and villages right across the Weald: Tenterden, Frittenden, Smarden, Horsmonden, Cowden, to name merely a few. Farms and great houses likewise denote similar origins, such as Pattenden, Twyssenden, Spelmonden, Badmonden, and so on. There are also as many 'hursts', another old term, which signifies a wooded knoll. These are similarly to be found all across this part of England: Goudhurst, Hawkhurst, Lamberhurst, Ewhurst, Staplehurst and suchlike, which began as very small settlements, but eventually grew into villages.

Initially a location virtually devoid of habitation, from the eighth century onwards the land was gradually encroached upon. Nevertheless, human impact was slight in the extreme as revealed in Domesday. The conquering Normans found the High Weald had the lowest population, not even one person per square mile, compared to the most populous area in Kent centred around Folkestone at seventeen heads per square mile.

At one time, it would have been possible to stand upon any one of the hilltop ridges of the High Weald at dusk and glance around the great expanse, to gaze upon little else but hearthside smoke slowly curling in thin wisps through the treetops. Greater and more sinister smoke was to come, however, since the streams revealed one of Anderida's most valuable treasures. A thousand years before, the Romans had made use of the ochre-coloured stone hewn from the land near Cranbrook and by the reign of Elizabeth I the industry was well-established. Having a seemingly inexhaustible supply of timber, stone from which iron could be smelted and copious amounts of water, furnaces began to spring up where the Anglicized descendants of the conquering invaders began smelting the deposits of ore being plundered from its depths. Andred's wealth of broad-leaf trees were rapaciously felled, one after another, as the demand for timber to build ships, houses and towns increased. Coppicing in the cleared woodland increased where the production of charcoal enabled the furnaces to burn bright and hot, while the clang from anvils shattered the peace of the sylvan surroundings. There were iron foundries scattered right across the Weald, including Horsmonden, Goudhurst, Cranbrook and Hawkhurst. Gradually, 'the wood where nobody dwells' was heavily ransacked to feed the desires of man. Large numbers of its stoutest oaks were felled to build merchant ships and warring galleons, while the volcanic furnaces roared and belched smoke as they created cannon and missiles. The demand for oak, ash, beech and other species in such huge quantities finally despoiled great Andredsweald, transforming it into heather and gorse-covered heathland in the high, wind-swept districts of North Sussex. In Kent, most of the cleared land was turned over to cultivation. However, not everything was entirely destroyed and pockets of woodland survived where coppicing and replanting took place. Elsewhere, there are doubtless many fine trees among the hedgerows and in copses today which are direct descendants of ancient Anderida.

Within a relatively short space of time, changes outside the district eventually caused the Wealden furnaces to become cold and derelict as the Midlands and the towns of northern England took on an industrial role. Less beligerent implements forged from Kentish iron allowed perhaps the greatest treasure of all to be found. The hoe and plough enabled the rich, well-drained soil to be tilled to bring forth an abundance of produce. In geological terms it comprises mainly the 'Hastings Beds', a clayey gravel fed with generations of woodland mulch which lies evenly across the land and up to the heights of Goudhurst. Its precious fertility is famous for its special suitability for fruit growing and has been referred to as 'a gardener's joy', whilst it was once likened to the fecundity of the Garden of Eden.

The area flourished with its valuable trade in iron, timber and foodstuffs. Cranbrook also became the centre of a prosperous cloth industry, having roots in this commercial activity as far back as the twelfth century where Flemish cloth workers had settled, bringing their skills with them. As, one by one, the forges fell silent, the hammer ponds became the haunts of wildlife and quietude returned to these lands. Just as the huge reserves of timber had once sustained its people, now the soil became all-important to the communities as cultivation and husbandry took its place. Apples, pears, cherries, soft fruit, corn, beans, hops and even the sweetest grapes grew freely and with little difficulty, whilst on the plains beneath the High Weald sheep and cattle cudded succulent pastures. While Kent earned its reputation for being the 'Garden of England', the industrious north began the revolution that would again affect not only lost Andredsweald, but all the southern counties in a way hitherto unimagined as the nineteenth century dawned.

The canal age had relatively little impact upon Kent, although the river Medway was made navigable for much of its way by the building of locks, whilst the Thames and Medway Canal provided a short cut between Strood and Gravesend. However, this last venture was relatively short-lived since the South Eastern Railway eventually used the canal's tunnel at Higham for its own purposes. In 1802 an ambitious project created quite some interest in the Weald when a system of waterways was drawn up to link the rivers Medway and Rother, running from Yalding in Kent to Rye in Sussex. Canals were also planned to branch off to Lamberhurst, by means of the River Teise, as well as Cranbrook and Headcorn. Estimated at over £100,000, the scheme failed to attract local financial support, a handicap which would similarly plague the building of the railway in the years to follow. Elsewhere, grand schemes to link Canterbury with the sea soon foundered as they came too late. The great age of the railway had begun, eclipsing the slow, tedious and time-consuming business of transporting merchandise on waterways. The creation of further wealth, power, prestige and almost limitless riches, spurred the great capitalists to invest in seemingly any scheme which came forward. This new means of efficient transportation suddenly opened up so many exciting possibilities. Nowadays we may scoff at the age of 'railway mania', but a moment's thought should be spared for just what must have gone through minds at that time. Suddenly, there was no need to rely on horses or oxen to drag small loads in wooden carts across rough tracks; no need to wait days or weeks for goods to manoeuvre circuitous canals and locks. Mercury, in the form of the railway locomotive, had arrived through the genius of a small band of men who had cleverly harnessed the terrifying power of steam into motion. As a result, it wasn't long before the maps of England's counties were being enthusiastically scrutinized by those with vested interests in the promotion and construction of 'rail roads'.

In geographical terms, much of Kent was less than inviting. The vast chalk range of the North Downs, which might well be described as the backbone of the county, stretches from Surrey to the English Channel. Where it meets the sea, between Folkestone and Dover, its ragged dizzy heights presented a formidable barrier to the railway builders, whilst its crumbling and unstable nature tested the mettle of even the most accomplished engineers. There were no easy or ready-made routes available to the surveyors who tramped the landscape. Its valleys, created chiefly by the Darent, Medway and Stour, were largely transverse to a line drawn between London and Dover. Nevertheless, such obstacles would have to be overcome since Kent was the nearest county to the continent. Up until the 1840s it was easier and often quicker to sail from London to the continent rather than endure a slow stagecoach journey along the winding, uneven roads of Kent. However, sea journeys were often disagreeable and frequently dangerous in the turbulent waters of the Straits of Dover, the notorious Goodwin Sands being the most feared among the treacherous sandbanks. As the small towns, fishing hamlets and even barren places bordering the coast, took on new importance, the people of Kent awaited the arrival of the railways with mixed feelings.

At the inception of the South Eastern Railway in 1836, the available choices before the engineers of linking the capital to the continent were scrutinized. Each option presented some difficulty, be it the expense of tunnelling for miles through the North Downs, or bridging the wide mouth of the River Medway. Finally, a decision was made in favour of driving a line from Redhill in Surrey directly along the vale of Kent to Tonbridge, Ashford and on to Dover. The scheme gained favour at the time since it made economic sense to share the London & Brighton Railway's route as far as Redhill. However, in later years this 'great way round' caused problems which were resolved only by the construction, in 1868, of a new and shorter main line via Sevenoaks.

In spite of these later shortcomings, the South Eastern's premier line to Folkestone and Dover was one of the engineering triumphs of the age. Running from Redhill to Ashford in an almost perfectly straight line, the mould was set which would dictate future railway development. Branches to Maidstone, Canterbury, Thanet and Tunbridge Wells followed during the 1840s, whilst Hastings was reached in 1851. During 1845 the railway promoters looked towards driving a railway through the High Weald when the *Kent Herald* announced the intention of building a line from Tonbridge via Paddock Wood and Cranbrook to Rye harbour. Such a line would have proved fairly difficult and expensive to construct, for, like the Tunbridge Wells and Hastings branch, the hilly countryside would necessitate sharp curves and steep gradients. It is doubtful whether the attraction of the proposed new line merely rested in bringing the communities of the Kentish Weald into direct rail communication; rather it was the development of Rye as a port. Similar proposals came forward in October 1851 for a new line branching off the South Eastern's 'railway race track' to Tenterden, Appledore and finishing up at either Dungeness, Rye or Hastings. However, the inhabitants of Tenterden were to be as disappointed as those of Cranbrook when the scheme was dismissed. Apart from the commercial interests in railway promotion, the military authorities were keen to see lines laid for strategic advantage. Just as the Royal Military Canal had been constructed as a bastion against the ambitious French, so a railway between Hastings and Ashford and bordering the vulnerable Romney Marsh, was deemed essential. Thus, in the locality of the Kentish High Weald, the SER main line skirted its northern perimeters, with stations at Edenbridge in the west, followed by Penshurst, Tonbridge, Maidstone Road, Marden, Staplehurst, Headcorn and Pluckley to the east. The Hastings branch approximately cut across its western flank and led down into the Rother marshes of Sussex, whilst the southern and eastern sides were bordered by the addition of the Hastings to Ashford line.

The establishment of these three lines roughly encircled the Kentish High Weald, yet, paradoxically, the proximity of these railways at this early date curtailed the impetus of subsequent schemes which looked to further expansion. To travel five, six or more miles to a railway station was not considered inconvenient by the companies who brushed aside the notion that every township should have its own line of railway. Indeed, there appears to have been a disdainful attitude towards those who clamoured for improvements where less than handsome profits could be expected. Railway companies frequently invited private landowners and investors to put up capital for branch lines. The gentry often sought more than what was probably a fair price to pay, whilst the railways were generally only prepared to buy acres of land at no more than agricultural value. The squabbling over land delayed and even prevented many lines being constructed, whilst those which were finally sanctioned frequently failed to be in the strategic interest of the nation. Against this background, the inhabitants of the High Weald could do little to sway the SER's directors in their opinion that the area was adequately served. Nevertheless, the people who occupied this beautiful tract of countryside were determined to continue the battle, a fight that would last for almost half a century.

It is only to be expected that full advantage was made of the railways in the Weald. The warm, fertile soil of this part of England soon germinated almost anything that was suited to its composition, whilst, weather conditions permitting, harvests were generally bountiful. The farmers soon found new outlets for their produce as

Staplehurst station on 31st October 1887, looking towards Ashford, showing hop pockets in wagons and fruit baskets stacked along the up platform. Until the opening of the Hawkhurst branch, Staplehurst was the main railhead for the High Weald. *Tonbridge Historical Society*

The Goods Clerk's house situated in the down side yard at Paddock Wood, photographed in 1871 and still occupied to this day. *Tonbridge Historical Society*

greater quantities could be grown, transported and sold to a wider populace. London was the obvious market, taking as much as could be grown in Kent's orchards and fields or grazed upon its lush pastures. Kentish produce became prized for its excellent quality, taste and freshness, but this extra trade took a heavy toll upon the primitive roads throughout the Weald. Even the turnpiked roads which had much improved the old tracks during the 1700s could become rutted and bumpy in summer, furrowed and bog-like in winter and hampering the transportation of goods. Ironically, it was the railways which had exacerbated the problem by opening up greater markets. Landowners had chalk and stone from quarries in the North Downs laboriously hauled into the district by ox-drawn carts where it could be used to pack the sodden tracks. Not surprisingly, these measures were viewed only as temporary and failed to satisfy the demands or dampen the enthusiasm for a railway directly serving the locality.

The wealth of the Weald soon found its way to the stations and depots on the South Eastern system. By August 1842 the SER had opened a station east of Tonbridge which it named Maidstone Road. There was virtually nothing there at the time, in fact the nearest villages were Brenchley and Horsmonden some three or four miles to the south east. Early maps show the station in the middle of nowhere, adjacent to a road and completely surrounded by trees known as Paddock Wood. Indeed its greenwood setting in the formative years of the SER must have been quite appealing for those who alighted here before boarding the horse and carriage for Maidstone. Two years later, in 1844, the SER completed its branch line northwards from here which ran along the Medway valley to the county town. Subsequently, Maidstone Road station was renamed Paddock Wood at the opening, although today's travellers, who gaze upon vast warehouses, supermarkets and housing estates, might well consider the name a complete misnomer.

The SER gradually improved facilities at its stations. For instance, Paddock Wood received a footbridge in 1846 which enabled passengers to cross the railway in safety. It was particularly important here as there were four lines between the platforms, whilst the brick overbridge at the western end obscured the view up the line. The SER normally favoured staggered platforms at many of its roadside stations and expected passengers to take their chances on the level foot crossings. Perhaps Paddock Wood was more fortunate, but there are indications that the station was far from complete when the main line to Dover opened. In December 1846 Mr. Barlow, the SER's chief engineer, was instructed to complete the works there, whilst in September of the following year a Mr. Mair's estimate for certain alterations was laid before the committee of works. However, by March 1848, the station master was given notice that he should 'prepare to move into the new station as soon as possible' since Mr. Barlow had finished his work. Paddock Wood was an exceptionally fine and handsome affair, built at a time when the SER seems to have had more money available to lavish on accommodation for its patrons. The down side buildings were most imposing, with the covered footbridge connecting platforms, whilst the buildings on the up side, although far simpler, boasted a handsome clock tower.

Villages in the High Weald looked to differing stations for their needs. Marden was the most easily accessible for traders from Goudhurst, whilst Cranbrook merchants drove their carts to Staplehurst. Further south, Hawkhurst folk had the alternative of using Etchingham, just over the border into Sussex and on the Hastings branch. An indication of the traffic flowing to these wayside stations is portrayed in an early view of Staplehurst where dozens of wicker fruit baskets are piled high against a row of wagons standing in the up bay platform.

The pace of railway construction on the South Eastern system slowed during the 1850s as the triangle of lines around the High Weald was completed in 1852, whilst spurs and minor branches consolidated and strengthened the SER's empire. An obvious case was the formal acquisition, in 1853, of Kent's oldest railway, the Canterbury & Whitstable, which more than justified its absorption. Alongside the geographical reasoning behind the gradually evolving railway network must be added the political diktat of Parliament, the whims of individual MPs and the military, as well as the opinions and self-interest of influential landowners. If this wasn't enough, there was also the wasteful and pointless rivalry between competing private companies. It should come as no surprise, therefore, that some curious routes were chosen for the British railway system which quite often had more to do with haphazard politics than any sensible overall strategic planning. The goad to embark upon a new era of railway promotion and construction had yet to materialize in this part of Kent. As time progressed, however, the SER began to fear the encroachment of the rival London, Chatham & Dover Railway on one side and the London, Brighton & South Coast Railway on the other. Rarely could the SER directors afford to sit back and savour any feelings of contentment with what had already been achieved. In a world where the only alternative was a horse and cart, the railways had palpable attractions. In spite of those who were always ready to oppose 'the great despoiler' and harken back to the golden age of pre-industrial Britain, most people believed railways represented progress, trade, wealth and a significant improvement in living standards.

During the 1850s the two principal towns of the Kentish Weald, Cranbrook and Tenterden, began agitating in earnest for a railway. Preliminary requests and petitions proved fruitless, as did a visit from a deputation in 1854 urging a line from Headcorn to Tenterden. Indeed, the SER would only agree to a

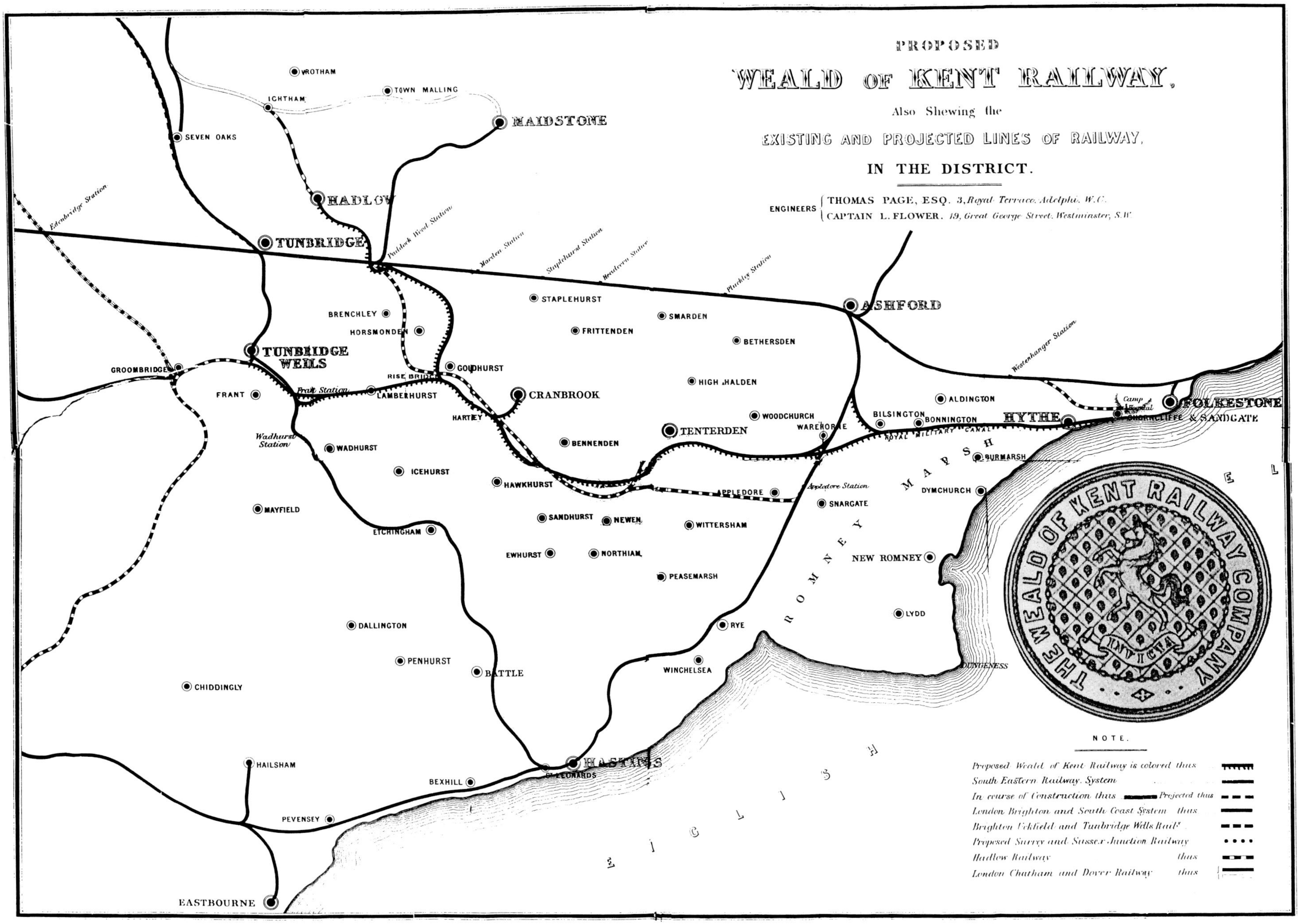

PROPOSED
WEALD OF KENT RAILWAY,
Also Shewing the
EXISTING AND PROJECTED LINES OF RAILWAY,
IN THE DISTRICT.
ENGINEERS { THOMAS PAGE, ESQ. 3, Royal Terrace, Adelphi, W.C.
CAPTAIN L. FLOWER, 19, Great George Street, Westminster, S.W.
THE WEALD OF KENT RAILWAY COMPANY
INVICTA
NOTE.
Proposed Weald of Kent Railway is colored thus
South Eastern Railway System
In course of Construction thus Projected thus
London Brighton and South Coast System thus
Brighton Uckfield and Tunbridge Wells Railʸ
Proposed Surrey and Sussex Junction Railway
Hadlow Railway thus
London Chatham and Dover Railway thus
WROTHAM
TOWN MALLING
ICHTHAM
MAIDSTONE
SEVEN OAKS
HADLOW
TUNBRIDGE
Edenbridge Station
Paddock Wood Station
Marden Station
Staplehurst Station
Headcorn Station
Pluckley Station
ASHFORD
Westenhanger Station
STAPLEHURST
SMARDEN
FRITTENDEN
BETHERSDEN
BRENCHLEY
HORSMONDEN
TUNBRIDGE WELLS
GROOMBRIDGE
FRANT
Frant Station
LAMBERHURST
RISE BRIDGE
GOUDHURST
CRANBROOK
HARTLEY
HIGH HALDEN
WOODCHURCH
TENTERDEN
WAREHORNE
BILSINGTON
BONNINGTON
ALDINGTON
HYTHE
Camp Hospital
FOLKESTONE
SHORNCLIFFE & SANDGATE
ROYAL MILITARY CANAL
BURMARSH
DYMCHURCH
Wadhurst Station
WADHURST
ICEHURST
BENNENDEN
HAWKHURST
APPLEDORE
Appledore Station
SNARGATE
MAYFIELD
SANDHURST
NEWEN
WITTERSHAM
ETCHINGHAM
EWHURST
NORTHIAM
PEASEMARSH
ROMNEY MARSH
NEW ROMNEY
LYDD
DUNGENESS
DALLINGTON
RYE
PENHURST
WINCHELSEA
BATTLE
CHIDDINGLY
HASTINGS
ST LEONARDS
BEXHILL
HAILSHAM
PEVENSEY
EASTBOURNE
ENGLISH

working agreement provided the land was not only given free of charge, but that the owners and benefactors involved paid for its construction to standards which would satisfy their engineer.

On Wednesday, 29th October 1856, a committee from 'The Cranbrook Railway' held a public meeting, at the 'George Hotel' in the town for the purpose of canvassing opinion before preliminary approaches were made to the SER. However, hopes of financial assistance were again ruled out by the SER, although the delegation received an invitation to submit details 'shewing the curves and gradients for consideration of the Directors'.

A year later the 'Cranbrook and Marden Railway', laid down plans for a line, 5½ miles in length, commencing by a junction on the SER main line and terminating in 'Mr Sharpe's Hop Garden, near the Parish Church of Cranbrook'. The cost of the line was first estimated at £38,000 which included excavating over 300,000 cubic yards of soil and sandstone, as well as constructing ten bridges. In a communication to the *Kent Herald*, Mr. Cobb, for the C & MR, commented that the SER had 'spoken of the line with great favour'. Initially, extensions to only Tenterden and Hartley were planned, but these proposals soon spawned further grand ideas which comprised:

	Miles	£
1. Cranbrook Line from Marden	5½	48,000
2. Hawkhurst Extension from Cranbrook	4	35,000
3. Tenterden Extension from Cranbrook	7	56,000
4. Wateringbury Extension from Marden	6	42,000
5. Tonbridge Extension from Wateringbury	7½	60,000
Total miles	30	241,000
Contingencies, (say £300 per mile)		9,000
Estimated Total Cost		250,000

The promoters spoke of the reductions in mileages, for example, Cranbrook to Maidstone via Marden would be only 14, a reduction by one third, whilst similar advantages applied elsewhere. The C&MR duly announced its intention to submit a bill before Parliament in 1858 whereupon, following construction, the line would be worked by the SER. Fortune, however, did not smile upon this fledgling scheme and it simply faded into history. Nevertheless, the idea for railways into the High Weald burned as strongly as ever in the minds of these Men of Kent and there could be no rest until it was achieved.

The most significant and noteworthy proposals surfaced in the early 1860s when the 'Weald of Kent Railway Company' put forward a grandiose scheme. During 1863, the South Eastern's general manager, Cornelius Eborall, was instructed to take the necessary steps leading to a Parliamentary deposit. In the meantime, the WoKR's proposals were scrutinized, as well as the implications for the SER. In its entirety, the WoKR involved the construction of a line across the High Weald of Kent, from Tunbridge Wells and Hadlow to Shorncliffe, near Folkestone. A spur near Hartley would branch off to serve Cranbrook, whilst connections would be laid into all the SER lines which were crossed. Whereas the area had once been ignored by the South Eastern, it appeared that there was now serious interest in serving the area as further ambitious and competing schemes were put forward. In January 1864, Eborall was asked to advise his directors on the best site for a station at Brenchley on an alternative proposal for a branch line from Paddock Wood to Goudhurst, Tenterden and Appledore. This particular line is understood to have been the one most favoured by the SER as best serving their interests, if not entirely those of the inhabitants of the locality.

The original scheme put forward by the WoKR sought to link up with the LC&DR, LB&SCR and SER systems in a manner that must have surely alarmed the South Eastern. This was because it risked opening up their territory to rivals and, worse still, would give access to Folkestone, even though the route was less than direct. It is, of course, difficult to conclude what went on in private behind closed doors, perhaps over tea or a Havana cigar in the smoke-filled clubrooms of London's West End. Nevertheless, the consequences for the SER are apparent and it is evident that the board of directors were not about to sanction a line which would give distinct advantages to their rivals. Accordingly, in February 1864, the SER sought to protect its interests with an agreement that the LB&SCR would not seek to work, among others, the Weald of Kent Railway, nor 'any line in the South Eastern District'. This last condition seems especially vague, for such a boundary would be difficult to identify. It would be interesting to know exactly what territory the SER considered its own, since it wandered not only across Kent and Sussex, but also parts of Surrey to Berkshire. The engineers of the WoKR were Thomas Page and Captain L. Flower and their highly-ambitious scheme might appear, on face value, vaguely absurd. However, there were obvious reasons for attempting to serve as many places as possible across the Weald, as well as inviting the active interest of both the LC&DR and LB&SCR. The art of playing off one company against another was well-practised in the nineteenth century. The engineers had clearly sought to cultivate the ambitions of the 'Brighton' with the branch via Lamberhurst which would join directly into an extension of the Lewes & Uckfield Railway, which was rapidly being projected towards Tunbridge Wells. The section to Paddock Wood seems more sensible, but the spur to join up with the proposed Hadlow Railway, and subsequently the LC&DR, must have greatly annoyed the SER. Military considerations also appear to have been in the minds of the WoKR engineers, for the easterly portion to Hythe and Sandgate bordered much of the defensive Royal Military Canal.

It must be concluded that the WoKR, the most notable of all the early schemes ever projected across the High Weald, was heavily revised by the SER before it could be considered acceptable. The branches to Tunbridge Wells (LB&SCR) and Hadlow were lopped off for obvious reasons, as was the easternmost section to Sandgate since the SER already had plans of its own for a branch from Westenhanger station. The remainder was then re-aligned to the board's satisfaction and, in doing so, conformed largely to the SER's own Paddock Wood & Appledore scheme. During the 1863/4 session, Parliamentary notices were quickly prepared for the construction of a line 27 miles in length running from Paddock Wood to Cranbrook and Tenterden before terminating at Appledore on the Hastings-Ashford line. The total cost amounted to £290,000, whilst the line was divided into four sections: Paddock Wood-Hartley; Hartley-Cranbrook; Cranbrook-Tenterden; Tenterden-Appledore. Shareholders were informed that the revised WoKR was 'necessary for the purpose of supplying the Weald of Kent with an additional amount of local railway accommodation, which the Directors think it undesirable to leave to another company to provide'. The WoKR received the Royal Assent in the summer of 1864, incidentally at the same time as the bill for the Hythe & Sandgate Railway. Locally there was much satisfaction at this news, especially when it was made known that notices were being sent out for the purchase of land. Meanwhile, the SER ordered its surveyors and engineers to prepare the plans 'without delay'.

Perhaps surprisingly, counter proposals were still coming forward. A Mr. Wythes suggested the new Paddock Wood line should terminate at Rye, whilst Mr. James Gow of Hawkhurst wanted the line to serve his town. An even grander scheme was offered by a Mr. Jeyes, of Jeyes, Bingham & Co., promoting a line from the coast at bleak Denge Ness to New Romney, through the Weald by way of Rolvenden and Hartley to Lamberhurst. From here it would skirt briefly into Sussex at Frant, before terminating at Groombridge, just west of Tunbridge Wells. Not surprisingly, Eborall declined the proposition simply on the basis of opening up the area to the 'Brighton' where the Three Bridges and East Grinstead Railway was at that time being extended to Groombridge and Tunbridge Wells. Interestingly enough, as later events proved, it appears the LB&SCR indeed harboured secret ambitions of extending even further across the Weald beyond Tunbridge Wells.

During the autumn of 1865 the SER board recommended: 'steps should now be taken to proceed with the construction of Branches to Cranbrook, Hythe, and Westerham'. Everything was going according to plan, whilst it seemed nothing could prevent the High Weald from seeing its railway. Fatefully, however, in the following year, soon after the *Sussex Express* had reported: 'Several men are now employed in surveying the branch line of the South Eastern Railway to Cranbrook', a crisis hit the financial markets, involving the collapse of companies and bankruptcies. The LC&DR was especially affected, but the result of the crash led to the immediate postponement of railway schemes and the WoKR was an immediate casualty. The course of railway history in the south changed from this point as other companies were obliged to abandon schemes. One of these, the LB&SCR's ill-fated Ouse Valley Line was already under construction and its earthworks remained uncompleted. The inevitable outcome was that railway amalgamation was talked about, even though nothing materialized. Eventually, the companies returned to their normal state of relations which, at best, ranged from suspicion and distrust to total unco-operation and even hate campaigns conducted in the press and on billboards.

In 1866 Edward Watkin took the chair of the SER from the mild-mannered James Byng. Here began the reign of a man whose time with the SER is notorious. His effusive style of brusque leadership brought him many enemies, yet somehow the SER without him is quite unthinkable. Undoubtedly he left his mark upon the company, although whether the South Eastern actually benefited from his stewardship is perhaps a debatable point.

As the effects of the financial crash of 1866 receded, matters slowly improved, but the Cranbrook and Westerham schemes remained on the shelf to collect dust. Only the Hythe branch progressed and it would be rather cynical to suggest that Watkin had something up his sleeve. Whilst it is true that he was elected MP for Hythe in 1874, the same year that the Hythe & Sandgate branch opened, the strategic importance of the line is not difficult to comprehend. Watkin was a man obsessed, for good or bad, with creating continental links. He was associated with other British railway companies, and the South Eastern was merely a link in the chain. Watkin was quite cruelly frustrated by not seeing his dream fulfilled of a more direct line into Folkestone and subsequently the continent. The Hythe branch promised far greater rewards than Cranbrook could ever hope to justify, and it is necessary to compare these lines in order to understand why the latter took so long to construct. Even so, the failure to act upon the Weald of Kent scheme at this stage sowed the seeds of widespread discontent which eventually brought the SER a bitter harvest of conflict throughout the ensuing decades.

The disinclination shown by the SER towards proceeding further with the Cranbrook line upset more people than just the ordinary inhabitants, traders and farmers of the locality. A railway into the district was much favoured by the gentry and it was at this juncture that the Rt. Hon. Gathorne Hardy MP and Alexander Beresford Hope MP became involved. Gathorne Hardy's country seat was at Hemsted Park (now Benenden Girls' School), whilst Beresford Hope resided at Bedgebury Park, near Goudhurst (nowadays also a school). Following approaches made by both gentlemen towards the SER, they were duly invited to a meeting at London Bridge headquarters where discussions took place concerning the raising of capital. However, neither was

Rt. Hon. Alexander J. B. Beresford Hope, M.P. 1874.

Watkin despised the Cranbrook project, but he was heavily involved all the same.

willing to provide any financial backing, Beresford Hope commenting: 'I do not feel, myself, able to offer you more than facilities and I must leave others to connect their fortunes with railroad enterprise in the Weald'.

It is without doubt that Watkin had no interest whatsoever in the Cranbrook scheme, due most notably to the fact that it offered little in the way of financial return or strategic advantage over rival companies. In a letter dated October 1869 to Gathorne Hardy, Watkin explained his position:

> 'My dear Sir
> I have with Mr. Eborall seen Mr Beresford Hope and Mr. Morland today and explained our position very frankly in reference to the Cranbrook line.
>
> As a mere local line it is quite impossible that it can pay, its construction at the estimated cost of £180,000 would really imply so much loss to the shareholders. Is it fair, or further, is it desirable in public interest that they should be further impoverished and rendered pro tanto [for so much] less able to give a high class service to the public at large? Considering the excessive sacrifices which we have made and the unexpected difficulties and costs encountered without any aid whatever from the owners of property, I submit that this is a case where we might reasonably ask to be allowed to abandon the project till more prosperous times.'

Watkin rambled on with more excuses, claiming that the SER was virtually in a state of complete poverty, but he did offer a glimmer of hope by saying: 'I will do my best to induce shareholders to subscribe £60,000 or £80,000 towards a modified and cheaper scheme'. Beresford Hope was sent a copy of the letter and was apparently taken in by Watkin's smooth-talking for he agreed that abandonment was probably the best solution, at least for the time being. At the end of his reply to Watkin he sought to bring attention to the demand on the Hastings branch by relating his wife's annoying experience:

> 'Lady Mildred, who went up to town yesterday, can testify to the difficulty which first class passengers by the up express on Monday from Etchingham find in getting seats.'

Having won over Beresford Hope, similar tactics were then used on Gathorne Hardy. In a sycophantic letter, the guileful Watkin penned:

> 'I beg to acknowledge very gratefully your note of the 30th which, I am sure, our shareholders will cordially appreciate and I should be much obliged if you would allow me to communicate it to them in the ordinary case of our reports. What you propose is not only reasonable, but what we shall do with alacrity. And also as you will see by the report which I will send you, our shareholders are already advised to subscribe capital in aid of any future scheme. That scheme can quietly mature and as soon as I can again raise the dividend to 5% I will cordially and personally co-operate and consider myself pledged to do so. No one outside knows the difficulty and anxiety which attended the completion of the large stations and of the short Tunbridge line [the recently opened main line via Sevenoaks, avoiding Redhill] and we are entitled to that sympathy which your note is the first generous expression of which I have yet received from the district - always excepting the invariable kindness of Mr. Hope.
> I am, my dear sir, very faithfully yours,
> Edward Watkin'

The letter obviously worked, whereby the cunning Watkin had both MPs eating out of his hand, for in a subsequent reply Gathorne Hardy concluded: 'We both desire that the district shall be as well supplied as your present lines will allow and from what you say I am sure we may rely upon such being the case.' At this time, November 1869, Watkin was off on the business which motivated him most of all. This included a trip to Paris to meet the directors of the French Northern Railway to collaborate on the plans for the new harbour facilities at Boulogne. Being a politician, he was well-versed in the tactics of diplomacy, while at the same time holding his cards closely to his chest. However, Watkin's true intentions towards the Cranbrook line are revealed in a hasty and heavily-underlined note passed quietly to his colleague James Byng who took the chair during his visit to France.

> 'As regards our abandonments -the letters from Hardy and Hope are so good that I have recommended Mr. Eborall to

try for powers of abandonment through the Board of Trade. If we could quietly get the Appledore & Cranbrook killed in this way, while we have friends in court, we shall have gained a great point. Let us do so.'

Perhaps someone had a quiet word in Gathorne Hardy's ear at Westminster, or maybe he simply became suspicious of Watkin. Whatever the reason, Gathorne Hardy picked up his pen a few weeks later and wrote of his deep regret on hearing of the Cranbrook line's abandonment. He reminded the SER board that no pecuniary aid had been demanded when they had been urged to support the SER against a rival company which had proposed to serve the Weald. He spoke of the difficulties his constituents experienced in buying in coal, lime, manures and other vital commodities, as well as the hardship faced over moving cumbersome loads of produce out of the district. Commenting on the need for a connection with Maidstone, the county town, Gathorne Hardy considered this important for jurors and witnesses - 'a class which elsewhere has great facilities of locomotion'. He also voiced his suspicions as to why they were being asked to wait 'till more prosperous times' and considered that a guarantee should be given that facilities at Staplehurst should at least be maintained. He then abruptly reminded them that Mr. Hodges, his predecessor at Hemsted Park, had only given his hearty support to their Dover line on the understanding that Staplehurst should always be a 'first class station with all the best trains stopping there'. In conclusion he warned: 'Many people in Cranbrook would be glad of a cheap single line to Staplehurst, but I would not be interested in what would practically be a mere tramway'.

Two months later, in February 1870, the blow came to the hopes expressed at that time of a having a railway through the Weald. A dream that had been nurtured for a quarter of a century was ended when the SER applied to Parliament to abandon all the proposed railways running to Cranbrook, Tenterden and Appledore. Thus, the SER was subsequently absolved from any commitment to seeing the Weald of Kent Railway laid down across this beautiful part of England.

Charles Pannett & Son, the Hawkhurst saddlers, were well known for their fine craftsmanship. Their shop, on the corner of Highgate Hill, was next to the Royal Oak Hotel.

Ebenezer Williams

CHAPTER TWO

THE CRANBROOK & PADDOCK WOOD RAILWAY

WHEREAS the ill-fated Weald of Kent Railway disappeared into history, the calls upon the SER to construct a line into the Kentish High Weald continued unabated. From time to time it was likely the main topic of conversation among the farmers and tradesmen who, over pints of local ale, complained about the difficulties in moving goods over the district's primitive roads. Cranbrook was the main centre of supply, being a market town where agricultural fairs were held regularly throughout the calendar.

In the 1870s most of its 4,000 inhabitants were reliant on Bixley's omnibuses to Staplehurst which ran four times a day, whilst two carriers each operated a horse van twice a day. There was also a run to Tenterden on Wednesdays and Saturdays. Similarly a pair-horse omnibus from Tenterden ran to Hawkhurst, via Rolvenden, Newenden and Sandhurst, where it connected with Samuel William's 'bus from Cranbrook. This took passengers on to Etchingham station to meet the late afternoon express trains. There were also half a dozen other operators of vans and 'waggons', mainly serving Etchingham, but also travelling as far afield as Rye, Maidstone, Hastings and Tunbridge Wells. The post from London to Hawkhurst arrived via Staplehurst station just after midnight, where it was sorted and despatched at 7am. Within the pages of *Kelly's Directory* for 1871 will be found all the numerous trades which thrived in almost every township throughout England at that time. The wealth of saddlers, blacksmiths and wheelwrights is striking and illustrates just how dependent this country once was on horses. In an age that had yet to witness the invention of the internal combustion engine, these gentle animals were truly faithful friends, even though many were over-worked and sometimes ill-treated by a few heartless individuals. Goudhurst was also served by carriers, mainly to Tonbridge, Tunbridge Wells and Maidstone and there was even a coach to London on Wednesdays. Here there were also many 'farmers and hop growers' listed in 1871, which says something about the fertility of the land. Horsmonden, the smallest of these four parishes, seems to have been especially blessed: 'The soil is rich, and produces large quantities of hops, fruit and corn. The forest trees, consisting of oak, chestnut, elm, beech and ash, are of remarkably luxuriant growth'. The area is described as undulating 'with beautiful sylvan scenery', whilst the privileged rector could enjoy 'a magnificent view over a vast expanse of the counties of Kent and Sussex' from the lofty tower at his rectory.

In attempting to understand the reasons for the SER's initial disinterest and complete lack of action over the Cranbrook line, it is necessary to look briefly at what was happening on a wider scale. By the 1870s the SER's monopoly in Kent was being increasingly threatened by the rival LC&DR which had established main lines from London into North Kent, the Medway towns, Thanet, Canterbury and Dover. Penetration deeper into SER territory continued with an extension from Otford to Sevenoaks, whilst there were alarming proposals to reach Ashford, the very hub and heart of the SER empire. By 1872 the LC&DR's contractors were busily engaged on a new line between Otford Junction, near Sevenoaks, and Maidstone where advantage was taken of the vale at the foot of the North Downs. This new line opened on 1st June 1874, but it wasn't until a decade later that the LC&DR was in a position to open its rival station at Ashford.

The lack of a direct SER route between Maidstone and Ashford was already a cause of discontent since passengers had to make a circuitous journey via Paddock Wood. However, the SER was not blind to this woeful state of affairs. In 1872 various schemes came forward to build a branch line through the Loose Valley, from Tovil, just south of the county town, to either Headcorn or Pluckley. In turn, these led to suggestions for further extensions to Tenterden, the High Weald and the coast.

While the SER dithered over the Loose Valley Railway, the inhabitants of the Weald gathered together yet again to pursue their cherished dream. Arriving on the desk of the SER's Tooley Street headquarters in September 1876 were particulars for a light railway between the centre of Cranbrook and Paddock Wood. Disinterest persisted, but the directors were eventually obliged to receive the deputation of influential advocates who travelled up by train to arrive at two o'clock in the afternoon of 30th November. They were represented by Mr. John Stewart Hardy, the eldest son of Gathorne Hardy. Accompanying him were such notaries as Col. Lloyd, the High Sheriff of Kent; William Courtenay Moreland, JP, of Lamberhurst; Major Hartnell of Hawkhurst; William Neve Esq and William Sharpe Esq of Cranbrook. There were also representatives from Brenchley, Goudhurst, Lamberhurst, Cranbrook and Hawkhurst who came to add their support to the new company which was being formed under the title of the 'Cranbrook & Paddock Wood Railway'.

They proposed that a cheap, light railway should be constructed, with an 8-ton axle loading and a maximum speed of 25 mph. The line would be worked by the C&PWR company until the traffic developed, at which point it would be taken over by the SER. Since they considered their line would be 'valuable to the SER', one third of the capital cost, about £25,000, should be

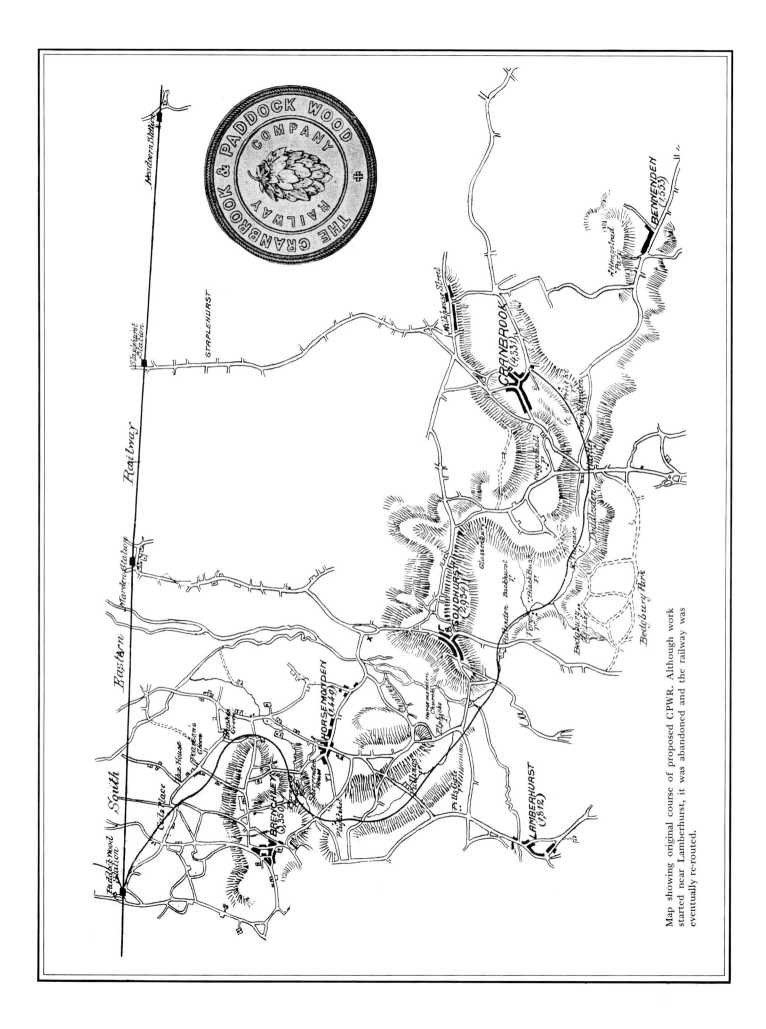

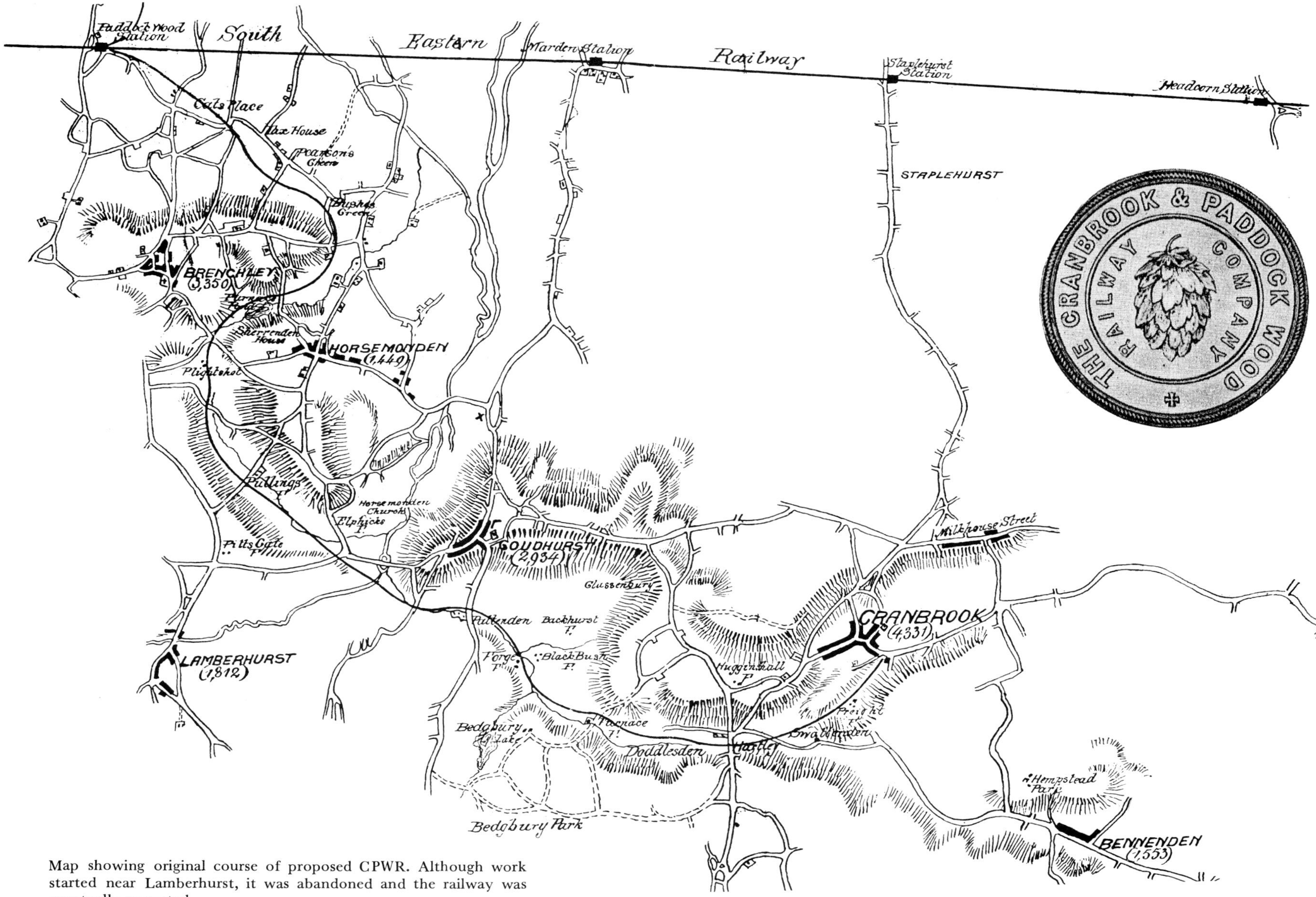

Map showing original course of proposed CPWR. Although work started near Lamberhurst, it was abandoned and the railway was eventually re-routed.

Paddock Wood Junction station in 1872, looking east to Ashford, with its handsome Italianate building on the down side. This view shows the station master on the platform in his top hat, in front of the nameboard which advised passengers that this was the 'Station for Maidstone Branch'. Of interest is the original SER signal cabin perched above the up platform track; the clock on the brick footbridge tower, and the workmen beneath the signal cabin, which probably explains the presence of the trolley on the up fast through line. *Tonbridge Historical Society*

The Railway Hotel, formerly the Maidstone Road Inn, at Paddock Wood advertised itself as 'Commercial and Family Hotel, two minutes from the station. Good stabling, and motor accommodation. Telephone No. 3, Paddock Wood'.

contributed by the South Eastern. However, the C&PWR would find their own rolling stock and would work the line throughout. They also sought facilities at Paddock Wood station for interchange, as well as a dock for their passenger trains. Through booking was considered essential, although the C&PWR would look upon Paddock Wood station 'as its own' and set independent station-to-station fares.

Predictably, Watkin remained quite unimpressed, but he did promise to consult with James Byng. He subsequently told Byng he had grave doubts over the policy of building light railways and considered that an ordinary line would be 'infinitely preferable'. Accordingly, the promoters of the Cranbrook railway secured the provisional backing of the SER, albeit with certain conditions. These included a single line of standard railway being adopted; landowners selling plots at moderate prices; and level crossings in place of bridges. If these could be secured, the SER directors would recommend to their shareholders the subscription of one third the cost of construction, not exceeding £50,000, and working it at 50% of gross receipts. Accommodation for the line would be provided at their Paddock Wood station, whilst 'liberal through rates' would apply. Subsequently, in August 1877, the Cranbrook and Paddock Wood Railway Company gained Parliamentary authority to proceed. One of their first actions was to request that Francis Brady, the SER's competent chief civil engineer, should be engaged as consulting engineer to the C&PWR. Brady was happy to oblige and informed his colleagues on the board that he reckoned a 'good workable line to connect Paddock Wood with Cranbrook, with all necessary intermediate stations and sidings etc.' might be achieved for around £140,000. As a result, Brady travelled down to Paddock Wood on 12th March in the following spring, where he accompanied Messrs. Harcourt and Butler, engineers to the C&PWR, on a tour of the district. However, in a letter to John Shaw, the SER's manager and secretary, Brady admitted:

> 'I can give no opinion as to the probable cost of the works until I obtain the amended plan and section and a copy of the earthwork quantities. Mr. Butler has promised these shortly. The Parliamentary deposit is no guide in this matter, as the line has been deviated outside the Parliamentary limits of deviation in several places, and roads which were originally intended to be crossed on the level have now, under the act, to be carried either under or over the railway by means of bridges and approaches of a somewhat heavy character. I think it would be well to reserve in the agreement power to the South Eastern Company to deviate

The High Street, Cranbrook, looking south, about 1893, with canvas awnings stretched across the pavement to wooden poles, and slipper baths and other galvanised ware stacked outside the shop which boasts 'Cottage furnished throughout for ten pounds'.

the line between Paddock Wood and Goudhurst as they may think fit. This would enable us to shorten the line and improve it.'

Two months later, the joint agreement between the SER and the C&PWR was eventually finalised with the participating company seals being affixed. Watkin and Byng were both elected onto the board of the latter, a move which must have been seen as the ultimate gesture of approval. Even so, matters did not proceed quite so smoothly as anticipated and there were difficulties in finding people willing to subscribe. This forced the C&PWR to seek further powers for an extension of time to purchase the land.

During 1879 the SER board was told 'some progress may now be made in the commencement of the works of this railway'. In September, Watkin was able to report that the promoters had purchased almost all the land required at agricultural value, whilst 'alterations were being made as to the position of Cranbrook station in order to save costs'. A month later a highly-sceptical Sir Edward grudgingly toured the route with Mr. Perks, the C&PWR's solicitor, where the latest plan to divert the line at Cranbrook was briefly discussed. From his office at 5 St. Thomas' Street, London Bridge, Francis Brady responded to the request for a deviation scheme and came up with a plan which terminated the railway in the centre of Cranbrook. This was at a point 'where convenient approach roads could be made to the passenger and goods stations without disturbing any important trades'. Although the deviation shortened the route by approximately 10 chains, the gradients remained almost the same.

In the spring of 1880 the long-awaited construction of the railway commenced when Mr. George Furness, the contractor, began excavating a cutting and building an embankment near Lamberhurst. The tenant farmers in the district, who were affected by the route of the line, received compensation for those crops which had been planted, but which it was expected they would not be able to gather. In June an initial payment of £200 9s 6d was made to Furness as matters slowly progressed and by August, at a meeting of C&PWR shareholders, John Gathorne-Hardy* was pleased to report 'everything is progressing favourably'. He went on to say that since construction had commenced, the calls to subscribe were now being met. In even more confident tone he revealed that the SER had spent £12,000 on the project so far and were 'not likely to let the line remain uncompleted, especially as they seem to have the construction of a line from Hartley to Dungeness in contemplation (hear-hear)'. He further announced that negotiations were in hand for the purchase of crops on the intended route to Hartley and expressed his satisfaction that the SER was seeking to purchase land between Hartley and Cranbrook so that the railway should run into the centre of the town.

On hearing that the route of the C & PWR would terminate in Cranbrook town centre, the inhabitants of Hawkhurst became very alarmed over this unexpected development. Subsequently, they petitioned the SER to alter their plans, suggesting they should instead continue southwards from Hartley whereby Hawkhurst would then be placed on the railway map.

It is quite probable that at this perilous stage, indecision over where the line should terminate did little to help matters along. Soon after, all work on the line faltered before coming to a complete standstill. However, the underlying reasons which were most likely responsible are to be found elsewhere. As previously hinted, the SER's chairman remained steadfastly hostile towards the whole Cranbrook project. Indeed, his only interest was likely confined solely to the vague notion of an extension to Appledore. That in itself rested upon the idea of extending further to Dungeness where he dreamed of creating a new port. In the event, the Dungeness scheme was attempted a few years later but it did not embrace the Cranbrook line. Instead, the Loose Valley Railway was revived; commencing at Maidstone, then running to Headcorn, Tenterden, Appledore and Dungeness where its terminus would have been established upon the bleak and isolated, windswept and inhospitable shingle spit-head of Denge Marsh.

Watkin's enthusiasm for all things connected with continental traffic seemingly drove him to pursue any plan which came his way. It was therefore most unfortunate for the C&PWR that just at that time he should be off in pursuit of yet another of his cherished dreams. He had recently suffered a series of frustrating setbacks, throughout which he had been publicly humiliated over his personal ambition to see the Hythe & Sandgate branch reach its intended goal of Folkestone Harbour. Watkin, however, was resolutely determined not to be entirely thwarted in his grand scheme. Thus, his efforts were directed elsewhere. At that time the Hundred of Hoo Railway was quietly being plotted to run along the North Kent marshes, near Gravesend, to terminate at the equally desolate, howling wilderness of the Isle of Grain which bordered the mouth of the Medway. It was a direct counter-attack against the hated LC&DR's rival port of Queenborough. In order to build the branch railway to Port Victoria, as it was eventually imperiously titled, Watkin seems to have seen to it personally that nothing stood in the way of its progress. In July 1880, just a couple of months after work had, at long last, begun on the C&PWR, John Shaw reported that the Hundred of Hoo bill had passed the committee stage of the House of Lords. Immediately, the SER ordered: 'No time will be lost in proceeding with the works'. Whether there were contractors unable to begin work immediately is not known, but what is

*Gathorne Hardy was elected to the House of Lord in May 1878 where he took the title of Viscount Cranbrook of Hemsted. At this occasion his family of four sons and five daughters changed their surname to Gathorne-Hardy.

certain is that George Furness was swiftly and peremptorily taken off the C & PWR for in September he was busily engaged at Cliffe on the first stage of this latest route to the continent.

During the period that the sites on the C & PWR lay idle, the residents of Hawkhurst grasped the opportunity to gather support for their argument to bring the railway further south. The outcome of this activity successfully culminated on 12th July 1882 when the Royal Assent was given to the Hawkhurst Extension bill. Even though the Hundred of Hoo Railway progressed rapidly, with Port Victoria opening that September, work on the Cranbrook line failed to resume. It seems that Watkin's attention could still not be focused upon this branch and the hapless subscribers to the High Weald railway. All along, the Cranbrook project was persistently hampered by events and sudden crises taking place elsewhere in the county. Just when it seemed as though the works might recommence, more trouble began brewing with the LC&DR whose directors were now promoting a bill to drive a line from Kearsney, on their Canterbury-Dover line, through the Alkham Valley and right into the heart of fashionable Folkestone. It is a wonder that Watkin ever found any sleep at night as he laid his head on the pillow, tussling with the day's problems racing around in his brain. Rarely were the SER and LC&DR in peaceful co-existence, whilst so much energy and resources were wasted in trying to constantly outwit each other.

The inhabitants of the Weald viewed the squabbling with degrees of despair and annoyance. Their only concern rested on the resumption of work on their railway. Accordingly, a public meeting was held at Cranbrook in February 1883 when a memorandum was sent to the SER. In championing the cause of the common folk, Gathorne Gathorne-Hardy, now Lord Cranbrook, wrote directly to Watkin. Once again, plenty of excuses were forthcoming in the reply:

'Dear Lord Cranbrook,
I entirely admit the forbearance which you have shown in the matter of the Cranbrook line. We have had so dreadful an half year owing to the utter failure of the hops and the fruit that it has taken a good deal of the heart out of us. I had hoped certainly, to have made a vigorous commencement of the works as soon as the days get a little longer and I shall move my board on my return from Cannes (where I am going for a fortnight) to take the matter into immediate consideration, embarrassed as we are by the failure of our income.

Believe me, dear Lord Cranbrook, very faithfully yours,
Sir Edward Watkin'

In spite of this assurance, the SER did not discuss the Cranbrook line until July when it amounted to just that, with no further action deemed necessary. Of greater concern to the SER at that period was the LC&DR's latest extension, from Maidstone to Ashford, which was rapidly approaching completion. Worse still, if the 'Chatham' gained approval for the Alkham Valley Line they suspected they would complete a loop by extending from Folkestone to Ashford. With these developments in mind, the SER had been busily promoting new lines for which they had won Parliamentary support. These comprised Appledore to Lydd (1881); Appledore to Headcorn (1882); Headcorn to Loose (Maidstone) (1883). If this wasn't enough, they hurriedly took up the powers of the ailing Elham Valley Light Railway Company and promptly set about building a double-track main line from Canterbury to Cheriton in order to keep the LC&DR out of Folkestone.

On hearing of the likelihood of the Loose Valley Railway commencing, and thus linking Dungeness, Appledore, and Tenterden to Maidstone and London via the North Kent line, the C&PWR's secretary wrote to his counterpart on the SER board:

C&PWR
147 Leadenhall Street
London EC
24th October 1883

'Dear Mr. Shaw,
Cranbrook Railway
Will you kindly remind your Directors tomorrow that the time for purchase of land expires on 27th May 1884 and for construction of the railway on 2nd August 1884, so that if these periods are to be extended it will be necessary this session to apply to Parliament.

As it seems pretty evident that the £100,000 or more which the Company would have to expend on making the line to Cranbrook (13½ miles) will be almost wasted, and the line, when made, most unsatisfactory, I would suggest for the consideration of your Board that a short line might be made from the Headcorn and Tenterden line which would meet all the needs of Cranbrook and save at least £65,000.

The Directors would find that they would be able to construct a line from Maidstone to Tenterden at very little beyond the cost of the Cranbrook line - with the advantage that the former would be useful and probably remunerative, whilst the latter would entail a permanent yearly loss.
Yours truly,
Robert William Perks'

Perks' suggestion was evidently dismissed since, on 24th January 1884, it was reported that a further six acres of land costing £2,762, had just been purchased for the Cranbrook line. On that day, a letter was also read out from Lord Cranbrook which sent a warning salvo across SER bows:

Hemsted Park
15th January 1884

'Dear Sir Edward,
I certainly expected an earlier reply as the time approaches for the meeting of Parliament and my move to London. We have been kept so long in a state of suspense in this district that there is naturally a considerable amount of feeling at the idea of losing a railway for which pledges have been over and over again given.

When the South Eastern Company voluntarily took up the scheme a second time it was natural to suppose that it was done with deliberation, and that we might rely upon the promises held out, nor, so far as I am aware, did the Maidstone and Ashford line prevent them being renewed up to the latest period.

I feel myself placed in a very disagreeable position which may compel me to take steps in Parliament to prevent the abandonment of a line which I think so valuable to this part of the country.

I hope that you will kindly let me know your decision as early as possible.

Yours very faithfully 'Cranbrook'

Watkin replied immediately, explaining to his lordship the very grand nature of the schemes before the SER in the probable hope that it might mollify him:

'Dear Lord Cranbrook,

I had an ordnance map prepared to show you the alternative railways for the accommodation of the county of Kent, but it is so big that probably the enclosed will indicate, just as well, the powers existing. I repeat that Parliament has changed the face of things by allowing the Chatham Company to extend to Ashford. We think the South Eastern, who cannot be expected to do everything at once, should at present concentrate their efforts in shortening the line between London, via Northfleet and Snodland, in completing the line from Maidstone to Headcorn for Ashford and beyond and extending it to Tenterden. All this could be done in a couple of years. But on the other hand to make the line from Paddock Wood to Cranbrook in the round about route which has unfortunately been selected would, I think, be a very great mistake. It must be remembered that lines have to be worked as well as made - and when made - I am sure this Cranbrook line, dealt with as it must be, could never be worked with satisfaction to the public. Certainly it could never be worked on main line principles

What is shown on the enclosed map would give the county of Kent two main through routes and would put into communication with the agricultural parts of it, all those large populations - Strood - Gravesend - Woolwich etc., etc., which hug the river.

What I recommend is that this important work be done first and that the Cranbrook works stand over, at all events until the main line works be opened. I am quite ready to recommend my colleagues to withdraw their powers for extension of time for the Cranbrook line, and although I think it would be a mistake - and if you say that the Cranbrook line - mistake as I consider it - must be made, in advance of anything else - then I will bring the question in that shape before my proprietors next Thursday - and ask them to decide.

Believe me, dear Lord Cranbrook, faithfully yours,

Sir Edward Watkin'

Lord Cranbrook was quite unimpressed with Watkin's blustering and eloquently expressed the sense of betrayal and deep dissatisfaction felt by himself, his colleagues and locals:

'Dear Sir Edward,

I have considered carefully the projects which you bring before me, and however beneficial they may prove to certain districts of Kent, it seems to me they can be of no advantage to ours, but rather tend to exclude it permanently from any chance of a through line. That chance was probably a small one, and I presume that the South Eastern Directors took up a railway not suited for a main line under the belief that it would always be only a branch. Whether it has been properly laid out is a question into which I have not personally entered, but have accepted what was also accepted by your Board. To me the shortest route, the easiest gradients and the best adapted for working in harmony with the South Eastern system would be the most advantageous. I assume however that other considerations affected the plan, and in adopting the line sanctioned, the SER Directors were willing to give them effect. On the whole I cannot but come to the conclusion that in the interest of Cranbrook and neighbourhood I am bound to hold fast by the promises made to us and to the Parliamentary position which we have obtained. I shall much regret being brought into antagonism with the company of which I am a shareholder and more so with officials to whom I owe so many personal civilities and conveniences. I sincerely hope that this may be avoided.

'Cranbrook'

Yet two more years passed by during which time Watkin oversaw the commencement of the Elham Valley Line, but nothing came of the Loose Valley Railway nor, for that matter the Cranbrook project. Eventually, in December 1885, it seems Lord Cranbrook's patience finally ran out, whereby a terse communication was delivered to SER headquarters in Tooley Street:

Privy Council Office

'Dear Sir Edward Watkin,

Mr. Hope, like myself, is uneasy at the prospect of further delay in making the Cranbrook line. The promises given to us were so specific and express that I can hardly imagine the possibility of further procrastination and I hope you will reassure us on the point.'

As already mentioned, Watkin's attitude towards the whole idea of a railway across the High Weald, be it a terminus at Cranbrook, or a through line to Appledore, was made plain in 1869 on that hurriedly scribbled piece of paper to James Byng. Lest there still be any doubt, it is only necessary to read what he said to a meeting of the SER proprietors in January 1886 when his personal hostility was made abundantly apparent:

'Gentlemen, I believe we have redeemed in one shape or another every honourable pledge which the shareholders of the past authorized their directors to give with regard to that local accommodation. There is the Westerham Branch; the Hythe Branch; the Lydd and Dungeness Branch; the Branch to New Romney; the line to Port Victoria; the Bromley Branch and more than all, the extension of the Greenwich line right away through to the main line which cost over half a million pounds. These arose from pledges from the past. Well, now we are pressed very much by Mr. Beresford Hope and Lord Cranbrook to make that Branch between Paddock Wood and Cranbrook. I do not want, and do not like to do it; with me it would be almost like having a tooth drawn (hear, hear) but I am very much afraid that you are pledged

Goudhurst village, showing the Vine Hotel, built around 1600, with Burgess Stores on the opposite corner.

to a further outlay of some £600,000 to make a branch line which will be a great local accommodation, and which may have a gradually growing traffic, but which is not one of those commercial speculations that I should advise you to enter upon its merits (hear, hear).'

In spite of Sir Edward's antipathy, it seemed that at last the long saga of the securement of the Cranbrook line might be coming to a conclusion. Just a few months later, in the spring of May 1886, the general manager of the SER, Myles Fenton, toured the district and met the directors of the C&PWR. The yellowed, dusty plans were taken along and scrutinized; however, the SER board remained distinctly uneasy over the chosen route. Accompanying Myles Fenton on his trip into the High Weald were two of Lord Cranbrook's sons, John Stewart Gathorne-Hardy, chairman of the original C&PWR Co., and Alfred Erskine Gathorne-Hardy, MP for East Grinstead. Francis Brady, the SER's engineer, also went along in the horse-drawn carriage as they toured the proposed route and compared it to the plans and sections already drawn up. Brady's subsequent report commented:

'The line for the greater part of its course presents no features distinguishing it from an ordinary cross country line. Near Lamberhurst, however, it takes a detour through the property of William Moreland Esq., which we understand was in consequence of a desire on his part at the commencement of the undertaking to develop his property and lay out a portion in building ground. The detour in question, besides lengthening the line by a mile and a half, involves much heavier work than the natural course of the line. We were all of opinion that it is desirable that the line should be straightened at the portion referred to viz: between Yew Tree Green and Hope Mill, which would effect a saving in distance of 1 mile 41½ chains. Mr. Gathorne-Hardy expressed his willingness to negotiate with landowners on the spot and to assist in every way in obtaining all necessary powers for the desired alteration, whether by consent or by taking the voice of public meetings, provided the work was commenced without unreasonable delay. We are informed that he has since informally sounded out some of his landowners and has reason to suppose that even those who would have preferred the original line will not interpose any vexatious opposition to the desired improvements.'

The original route of the C&PWR followed a more meandering path than that which Brady was subsequently asked to shorten and which was eventually built. At Yew Tree Green, just north of Horsmonden, the line had been planned to continue its south-westerly curve, passing through Shirrenden Wood and running to the west of Horsmonden and Hazel Street. It then continued southwards, passing to the west of Hale Farm, Pullens

Farm, Kettles Farm and Elphicks, where it followed a natural valley formed by a tributary of the river Teise to Hope Mill. The old C&PWR map also shows the extension into Cranbrook, running level from Hartley, then descending at 1 in 86 before levelling out again to terminate very conveniently behind the High Street. This section was carefully measured out as '1 mile, 3 furlongs, 5 chains, 56 links'. It is also noteworthy that the extension to Tenterden had, by that time, been crossed out. Accordingly, an application was made to Parliament to deviate the line, bringing it to the east of Horsmonden and following a more direct route to Hope Mill which was on the road between Goudhurst and Lamberhurst. The proposed deviation caused some minor upset in the locality, as reported by Alfred Thompson of the estate department, who canvassed opinion in November 1886. The rector of Horsmonden, the Rev. Hugh Smith-Marriott, admitted he was 'not personally desirous of having the railway' but agreed not to 'offer any opposition if his tenants and parishioners were generally in favour of it'. Thomas Buss, a farmer and hop grower of Lower Rams Hill, regretted that the new line would cut right throught his principal hop gardens which, he claimed: 'would render them much more difficult and expensive to work and let in draughts which do much mischief'. He didn't think the best route had been chosen and thought the most important question must be where the station should be sited. He said he'd be satisfied if 'Mount Pleasant' was the spot selected. He then went on to criticise the SER for not having a booking office on the up side at Paddock Wood - 'people have to go over the bridge first, or pay the porter to perform that service'. Elaborating, he claimed the station master agreed with him and had told him: 'fifty passengers come from districts on the up side for every one who comes from the other side'. The villagers of Horsmonden wanted to know where their station would be located, whereupon Myles Fenton confirmed they were looking at a site in the vicinity of Spring Cottage, on the Goudhurst Road.

Mr. Clementson, the miller at Hope Mill, considered that the railway was 'very much wanted'. However, he remained suspicious of the SER, like many others in the district, and doubted whether they had any serious intention to construct the railway. He thought they were simply talking about it yet again 'in consequence of the proposed new line from Tunbridge Wells to Tenterden which is ascribed to the Brighton company'. Indeed, here was a thought, and it demonstrates how the South Eastern had to guard its western flank from the LB&SCR.

There were many unfortunate shareholders who, for a number of years, had seen their capital tied up with a project that was entirely moribund. At a meeting in November 1887, a resolution was passed that the SER should honour its pledges. Taking up their cause yet again, Lord Cranbrook, who was also tired of the SER's endless dallying, wrote to Watkin in somewhat bitter terms:

'Dear Sir Edward,
I write to you with an almost despairing feeling about the Cranbrook Railway which personally I can hardly expect to see completed. A little more than three years ago the Board of Directors made a promise which the late Mr. Hope and I accepted in good faith; that the railway should be finished in three years, i.e. last August. During the intervening period nothing so far as I know was done in that direction and although an Act was obtained this year for an improvement of a portion of the line I have heard nothing of any step towards the commencement of the works. The solemn engagements made and communicated to the shareholders ought surely to be now fulfilled and the cheapness of labour and material offer special inducements to undertake the work. So far as I am concerned this is the last letter I shall write to urge it, but I hope that the directors generally will take the question into immediate consideration.
Faithfully yours, 'Cranbrook'

Watkin remained as disinterested as ever, but offered little resistance and subsequently he initiated moves to begin work, as revealed in his reply:

Charing Cross Hotel

'Dear Lord Cranbrook,
I read your letter to our Board on Thursday and the directors ordered that a valuation should be made of what would be fair and just to pay each landowner and also as to what would be reasonable and sufficient communications on such a line, and that then offers be made to each person accordingly and further that if the proposals were accepted - the works be let by tender. It will, now, remain for the landowners and others to expedite, or delay, the works, as they may be disposed to deal fairly or unfairly. At the same time I must say for myself, that in the present state of the traffic and the times I think it would have been better to have waited.

I have the honour to be, dear Lord Cranbrook, very faithfully yours,
E. Watkin
P.S. Last year we found it impossible to get anything definite from the owners and occupiers. Evidently many wanted their pound of flesh - or more.'

Lord Cranbrook replied to say that he did not consider land would be a burdensome problem and he hoped his fellow landowners would not 'stand in their own light' by demanding unreasonable terms. He wished the railway would be coming nearer to Hemsted Park for he would certainly not ask a high price for the land. Quite how much Lord Cranbrook really trusted Watkin will never be known, but there is good reason to believe that, behind the scenes, strings were being pulled. Perhaps tired of the interminable struggle, his lordship used his influence among his Parliamentary colleagues since the SER was finally forced into building the railway into the High Weald. In order to explain this fully, it is necessary to momentarily jump forward several years to a shareholders' meeting held at the Cannon Street Hotel on 25th January 1894. In the chair was the 74 year-old Watkin, serving his last few months at the helm of the South Eastern. One of the company's eminent directors, Sir George Russell, defended the SER's recent actions and went on to explain the circumstances surrounding the construction of the line:

> 'It is stated that in the last ten or eleven years we, of this Board, have constructed competitive and useless lines to the benefit of no one but the landowner. That is an absolute misstatement. I don't want to be technical and I will take a wider range of time than is named in the circular, but the only two cases that can be found in the approximate limit of time relied upon are those of the Elham Valley Line and the Cranbrook Line. The case of the Elham Valley Line I know well. [Sir George cut the first sod in August 1884.] Originally it was a line independently promoted in the interests of the Chatham, with the object and intention of bringing the Chatham from Canterbury into Folkestone. It was essential to the interests of this company that the ground should be occupied and it was solely with that intention and with that object that the Elham Valley Line was constructed, the Bill for which was obtained by the South Eastern in 1881. With regard to the Cranbrook Line, although it is true that the Act under which the line was ultimately constructed was passed in 1881, the original Bill had passed as early as 1864. We were under an obligation to construct that line, and we could not have gone to Parliament to obtain powers in other matters unless we had fulfilled that obligation.'

Hence, the SER eventually had little alternative but to press ahead with the railway. Then, at long last, it all suddenly began to happen. In December 1889 notices of compulsory purchase were sent out to obtain the remaining plots required. Six weeks later, the *Kent & Sussex Courier* reported:

> 'Cranbrook & Paddock Wood Railway:
> Considerable activity has suddenly shown itself in connection with the above project. Two engineers have been in the district surveying and a large land owner has received a letter from a director of the South Eastern Railway Company stating that the line will be commenced at once. We advise our readers, however, to accept the last paragraph *cum grano salis*.'

Happily, no pinch of salt was necessary, as material evidence of the SER's intentions was soon apparent. At the beginning of March, W. R. Stevens, the SER's secretary, told the board that Mr. J. T. Firbank was willing to construct the line. This included stations, a passing place, telegraphs, signals and everything necessary for the railway with the exception of the permanent way for a price of £6,000 a mile, or £5,000 a mile excluding stations, signals, etc. The board of the C&PWR, which remained an independent company, was strongly urged to accept Firbank's offer. They were also advised to engage Mr. E. P. Seaton as the line's engineer. Edward Seaton was a competent engineer, beginning his career in 1870 at Crewe with the London and North Western Railway. In 1881 he was taken on by the Metropolitan Railway, of which Sir Edward Watkin was also chairman. Seaton agreed to the C&PWR's invitation and seems to have readily taken on the challenge of building a line which was not going to be without some difficulties. After an extraordinarily arduous and protracted battle, the patience and fortitude of the inhabitants of Horsmonden, Goudhurst and Cranbrook had finally paid off. Hawkhurst, however, had yet to convince the C&PWR and SER that the line should continue southwards to include them. For the time being though, it was a period for contemplating the benefits that would be coming with the new branch railway. No longer could they be denied the sweet fruits of victory.

MR. E. P. SEATON

CHAPTER THREE

BUILDING THE BRANCH

MORE than forty long years had passed since the idea of a branch railway into the High Weald of Kent had first been mooted. After so many hollow promises, false starts and bitter disappointments, it seemed scarcely believeable that the railway would become a reality within a few years. The *Kent & Sussex Post* summed up the general feeling in one sentence:

> 'The leaps and bounds which to the imagination of a great many the Cranbrook and Paddock Wood Railway is making is little short of marvellous'.

On the 26th April 1890 the same newspaper reported that an 'important step' had been taken a few days earlier when some of the land was formally handed over to Mr. Firbank, the contractor. It wasn't long before tangible evidence of the new line began to appear as, towards the end of May, building materials and the contractor's plant began arriving at Paddock Wood. For J. T. Firbank, the Cranbrook project followed on from the Metropolitan Railway's extension from Aylesbury to Quainton Road. According to contemporary newspaper accounts, Firbank is reported as using four locomotives during the construction of the C&PWR, however, the identity of only two has been recorded. One was a Manning Wardle 0-6-0 saddle tank, built in 1863, numbered 81 and named *Wrexham*. Prior to the Kent contract it was working on the building of the Metropolitan's Rickmansworth to Chesham branch. The other locomotive was also an 0-6-0ST, younger by just one year, but constructed by Fox, Walker & Co. of Bristol. Named *Fox* and numbered 41, its next known duties after the completion of the Cranbrook line were in 1898 on the Basingstoke and Alton Railway which was also a Firbank contract. *Fox* is understood to have ended its days on the GWR's Fishguard Harbour line in 1907.

Throughout the summer and autumn, work progressed at a rapid rate as surveyors pegged out the route while gangs of navvies began the task of excavating the deep cutting at Horsmonden and building the embank-

C&PWR surveying team with their graduated poles and theodolyte during the construction of the branch. Holman Stephens, resident engineer, is second from left. *Colonel Stephens Railway Museum*

ment near Yew Tree Green. However, while they were engaged on the Paddock Wood to Hope Mill section, it is apparent that the question of the terminus had not yet been decided upon. At the beginning of November a site meeting was arranged at Cranbrook for those on the board of the C&PWR Co. to view the locality. On reading of this in the *Kent & Sussex Post*, which was published at Hawkhurst, a resident of that town, Mr. Francis Heath, decided prompt action was needed. Accordingly he organized a public meeting, calling upon the residents of the town to support him in his efforts. A lively and well-attended gathering heard the usual complaints of having to travel long distances to the nearest SER stations, of high charges demanded by road carriers and the difficulties experienced in getting commodities into and out of the town. Following much heated discussion, a memorial was sent to the SER:

Hawkhurst, November 1890

'Gentlemen, - We the undersigned inhabitants of Hawkhurst and neighbourhood respectfully beg to urge on your attention the great want of railway accommodation, from which this district suffers. We hail with pleasure the commencement of the line from Paddock Wood, and we most earnestly entreat your Honourable Board to bring this line into the town of Hawkhurst, without further delay: from whence considering the nature of the ground, it could, at some future date, be extended through a wide district, which seriously requires railway accommodation. A line from Paddock Wood to Hawkhurst is urgently required, and offers more advantages to the District, as a whole, than any of the schemes that have hitherto been put forward, and we beg to subscribe ourselves.
Your Obedient Servants'

Work on the railway slowed during December in consequence of the adverse weather conditions which hampered the men. This period began with violent thunderstorms which darkened the sky while brilliant displays of lightning arcked across the heavens above the Weald. Some of the storms were quite frightening in their ferocity, much as if the old gods and sprites who were once imagined to live in ancient Andredsweald had returned to wreak a terrible vengeance. The night sky was equally spectacular with peculiar showers of meteors, or 'comets' as they were referred to by the *Post* which described them: 'very brilliant, lasting for half a minute or so'. However, the worst of the weather came just before Christmas when intensely low temperatures turned the ground rock-solid, making matters extremely difficult for the navvies. Even so, the scene was one of indescribable beauty, with water droplets crystalized on the bare trees, whilst the fields were white with hoar-frost. For a few days the temperature plummeted to such a depth that at Hope Mill the River Teise froze over, an occurrence that hadn't taken place for half a century. It must have been a trying time to work through, with numb fingers and toes, when even a watery, pale yellow, midday sun failed to warm the frozen country-side. The conditions persisted for some weeks with no improvement, whilst during March the county was swept by blizzards which virtually blocked all roads and railways.

In the meantime the boards of the SER and C&PWR were looking favourably at extending the branch to Hawkhurst, not at some vague future date, but as part of the current contract. The C&PWR directors therefore asked Edward Seaton to come up with some engineering details and plans. Seaton must have had a difficult time tramping around the frozen, snow-bound countryside between Cranbrook and Hawkhurst, but at the end of February 1891 he was able to forward his proposals:

'Gentlemen,
In accordance with your instructions, I have walked over the ground from Hartley to Hawkhurst, accompanied by Mr. Beresford-Hope. I find that there are no engineering difficulties in the proposal to make an extension of the C&PWR to Hawkhurst from Hartley and I have laid down a line on the accompanying plan and prepared a section of the ground and laid down the gradients.

The line leaves the Paddock Wood railway by a curve of 20 chains radius and then runs in an almost straight line due south and curves again to the east at its termination near to Gills Green. The sharp descent of the main road prevents the station being placed nearer to the town. The station at Hartley will be situate near to Bishop's Farm, a short distance west of the High Road, but this road being placed on a ridge of the hill will not permit without great additional cost of the station being placed nearer to it.

The length of the line is 1 mile 57 chains and passes through the estate of Mr. Beresford-Hope for a distance of 1 mile, then through that of Mrs. Gow Steuart and Mr. Hayhurst. Hartley station will be about 1½ miles from Cranbrook, and Hawkhurst about 7/8ths of a mile from the centre of town. The gradient at the commencement is 1 in 500, the steepest is on a gradient of 1 in 60. Four roads are crossed but none of an important character. I estimate the cost at £11,500 but should the line not be made between Hartley and Cranbrook, a length of about 1 mile 70 chains, the total cost of the whole undertaking will be somewhat decreased. The Hawkhurst extension could be taken on to join the Tunbridge Wells and Hastings branch at Etchingham, a distance of some 6½ miles, without any very heavy works as shown on the trial section, or a very cheap line could be formed following the course of the river Rother to Rye or Winchelsea, passing about 4 miles of Tenterden and 2 miles of Rolvenden. This, I should like to explain on the small ordnance map.

The Hawkhurst extension should be proceeded with at the same time as the line from Paddock Wood as the excavated material must go into the bank west of Hartley.
I have the honour to be, gentlemen, your obedient servant,
E. P. Seaton.'

Following consultations between the SER and the C&PWR, it was agreed that Mr. Seaton should proceed with the extension to Hawkhurst, whilst the Hartley to Cranbrook section, which would have terminated behind Stone Street and the High Street, should be abandoned. Alfred Gathorne-Hardy said he'd already spoken to the landowners affected by the proposed extension and had received their approval to go ahead. Edward Seaton's estimate for extending the line to Hawkhurst was as follows:

Cranbrook & Paddock Wood Railway:
Extension to Hawkhurst:- 1 mile, 4 furlongs, 6 chains, 8 links.

Earthworks:		Cu. yards	Price per yard	Total
Cuttings:	Rock	47,206	2s 6d	£5,900 15s 0d
	Soft Soil	99,733	1s 3d	£6,233 6s 3d
	Roads	11,230	1s 3d	£701 17s 6d
Including diversion of road				
Total		158,169		£12,835 18s 9d

Embankments inc. Roads, bridges, public roads	£1,350
Accommodation bridges and roads	£500
Tunnel	£3,350
Culverts and drains	£300
Metalling on roads	£132
Permanent way, including fencing	£3,520 15s 8d
Permanent way for sidings and junctions	£1,100
Station	£1,000
Contingencies	£2,408 17s 6d
Land, (21 acres, 2 rods, 13 perches)	£2,158 2s 6d
Grand total	£28,655 14s 5d

In March, the *Kent & Sussex Courier* reported:

'KILNDOWN - The new railway:
Mr. Philip Beresford-Hope is responsible for the pleasing announcement that within two years the long-looked-for railway would come past where he then stood. There will be one station at Horsmonden, a second at Hope Mill (Goudhurst), accommodating Lamberhurst folks and a third at Hartley, near Cranbrook. From this last-named high point the line could some day be extended to Hawkhurst or to the sea coast. He [Beresford-Hope] has given up his own right to have a station at Pattenden, but there will be a siding at that place.'

Following the delays brought about by the previous winter, full advantage was made of the lengthening days and the work was hastened, so much so that by the middle of June 1891 the *Courier* revealed:

'The total cost of this line is estimated to be £100,000, and at the present time some 400 navvies are employed. Already the neighbourhood presents a busy aspect and the value of the land is said to be going up.

The contractor's workshops are at Paddock Wood and the stables, powder magazine, and so on, at Horsmonden, and a brick field has been started on Mr. Beresford-Hope's estate. Huts for the navvies have been erected along the line and a galvanized iron mission room, the latter being provided with an evangelist by the inhabitants of Horsmonden, thanks to Col. Courthope, and the Salvation Army pay an occasional visit. The plant includes four engines, a steam crane and some 200 trucks. The line is estimated to cost £6,000 per mile exclusive of purchase of land and compensation.'

At the beginning of July the 'Navvies Mission Room' was opened at Horsmonden when 'a number of men sat down to a substantial tea and afterwards listened to evangelistic addresses'. These establishments, as well as the Temperance coffee stalls, were provided in an effort to prevent the worst excesses of drunken behaviour for which the navvies were notorious.

The remaining land as far as the terminus at Gills Green was purchased during the summer. Meanwhile, Edward Seaton wrote to the SER board in July to say that Mr. Firbank was now ready to begin laying the permanent way between Paddock Wood and Hope Mill stations. Fifteen hundred tons of steel rails were required for the new branch, but this was not inclusive of the fifteen thousand tons which was needed over the next three years for renewals on the whole system. The SER, therefore, duly invited tenders from their regular suppliers.

Whereas there had followed much satisfaction in Hawkhurst with the good news of the railway continuing southwards, such was not the case at Cranbrook. Many of the residents and traders here were understandably aggrieved that, seemingly at the very last moment, they were to be deprived of their railway and a station right in the heart of the town. It was little consolation that a station at Hartley, nearly two miles away to the south west, was now proposed. Accordingly, a deputation from Cranbrook was received during July by the C&PWR directors, but Gathorne-Hardy could offer little hope of improving the railway accommodation on offer. He retorted that there were two outstanding reasons why the extension into the town had been dropped. Firstly, 'in consequence of the excessive cost' and, secondly, 'the demands for compensation made by landowners'. Nevertheless, he offered a glimmer of hope in that if reasonable terms could be agreed, it would be considered. All the same, it is not necessary to point out the difficulties in working two separate spur lines which would be the end result now that work had begun on the Hawkhurst extension. Thus, in reality, Cranbrook lost out in favour of Hawkhurst.

Throughout September and October, work on the railway south of Hope Mill station progressed at a rapid rate. The *Courier* spoke of several gangs of men employed on the section near Forge Farm where cuttings and embankments were being made. Further south, near Hartley, other workmen were busily engaged in clearing woodland and surveying the land, whilst over 200 hundred men were reported to have been working on the branch at that time. Each morning, as autumn's mists covered the low-lying fields and valleys, the men would emerge from their huts in preparation for the day's work. The heavy dew upon the grass and chilling air would slowly dissipate as the rays from a weak sun gradually grew stronger. By noon it was often one of those delightfully warm autumnal days, pungent with the smell of damp leaves and woodsmoke from the fires which were lit to brew tea.

During November 1891, a reporter from the *Courier* penned the scene before him:

All the spoil from cuttings at Badger's Oak was carried southwards once the tunnel had been completed, and used to build the huge embankments necessary to carry the railway to Gills Green, its terminus north of Hawkhurst. Here, in the summer of 1892, the contractor's locomotive was engaged in making up the embankment near Slip Mill Road bridge.

> 'CRANBROOK: The Coming Railway.
> Considerable progress is being made at Cranbrook with our railway. At Badger's Oak Farm two sets of navvies, under Messrs. John Clarke and W. Williams, gangers, are busily engaged, one party making a deep cutting in the direction of Goudhurst, and the other party driving a tunnel towards Gills Green, Hawkhurst, the earth being utilized in filling up the valley between which will require many thousands of tons. The tunnel, we understand, will go under Mr. Eaton's oast house at a depth of about 60ft. At the commencement of the tunnel hard rocky substances are met with which defy the use of the pick and shovel and therefore considerably retard the progress and necessitate 'blowing up' operations. Deep cuttings have to be made before Gills Green is reached where another gang is shortly to commence work.'

Three weeks later, on 4th December, Badger's Oak tunnel was reported under construction:

> 'CRANBROOK: C&PWRly.
> The second section of this line has now been fenced in as far as Hartley where temporary sheds and offices have been erected. The construction of a third section - extending from Hartley to Gills Green has also been commenced, but will not be completed for a considerable time as it is necessary to tunnel Hartley Hill. The tunnel, which has just been started, is in a direct line and adjacent to the buildings at Badger's Oak.'

It is not surprising to learn that accidents occurred during construction, but, happily, the Cranbrook railway did not take a heavy toll of life. Cuts, bruises and fractures were commonplace, but more serious incidents did take place from time to time. There was a narrow escape at the beginning of December which almost cost one workman his life while assisting to move a six-ton steam crane. Without warning the machinery suddenly toppled, only missing him by a whisker as it crashed onto its side. Less fortunate was Leonard Bartholomew, just twenty years of age, who was at work in early February 1892 in the cutting near Furnace Farm, between Hope Mill and Cranbrook. It was a fairly deep cutting, of some thirty feet, when around four o'clock on a Friday afternoon several tons of earth suddenly slipped and completely buried him. It took a frantic quarter of an hour for his workmates to extricate his body, by which time, of course, the poor chap had been asphyxiated. It was reported he'd also received 'a dreadful wound in the lower part of the body', so even if his colleagues had reached him in time he may well not have survived in view of the limited medical skills available. A few days later a further mishap occurred when a chap named Smith fell under a truck and had his leg run over. He was carted off to the Cranbrook Infirmary with a suspected broken leg. These incidents led to calls for the line's contractor, Mr Firbank, to provide a 'hospital hut' for his navvies. Firbank, however, wrote to the Cranbrook authorities saying that he was quite unable to pay for such facilities at present, but enclosed a cheque for five pounds towards the local infirmary funds.

On enquiring of the progress of the line in February, the SER were told that the complete line to Hawkhurst was proceeding in a satisfactory manner, whilst an opening throughout could be expected early in the following year.

Having set the direction of the railway towards Hawkhurst where it would terminate at Gills Green, almost a mile north of the town, further suggestions for extension began to filter through. Mr. F. W. Parker of

Rolvenden wrote to the SER as head of a local committee set up to argue the merits of continuing their new railway across the Weald:

Rolvenden, Kent

'Sirs,
I am directed to inform you that a public meeting was held in this parish on Saturday 16th January 1892, at which a resolution was passed unanimously on the motion of William Pomfret Esq., MP, that 'having regard to the great distance of any railway from the district (which comprises the country lying between Hawkhurst, Gills Green and Appledore) it was imperatively necessary to have railway accommodation for that district' and a committee of gentlemen interested in the district was subsequently appointed with the object of expediting, if possible, the continuation to Appledore of the line of railway from Paddock Wood to Gills Green which is now in formation by the C & PWR Co. It is hoped, with much anxiety, that it is intended to continue the line from Gills Green to Appledore and I am further instructed by the above named committee to ask the directors of the C&PWR if they will be so good as to grant them an interview.....'

The committee found itself cold-shouldered by both the SER and C&PWR in a brusque reply which retorted that there was 'no intention on the part of this company, nor the Cranbrook Company to expend further capital at present on any extension of the authorized lines and therefore it was hardly necessary for the deputation to wait upon the Directors'. Quite undaunted, however, another member of the Rolvenden committee wrote personally to Sir Edward Watkin:

'Dear Sir Edward,
As it is rumoured that the representatives of the SER Co are coming into this district to inspect its position as regards railway accommodation, I have been requested to ask your careful consideration of the comparative merits of the existing two suggested lines, namely:

1. Cranbrook to Appledore
2. Headcorn to Appledore

I beg leave to call to your attention the fact that a continuation of the line from Gills Green to Appledore (or from Hartley to Appledore) would pass through a district which is mostly from about 8 to 12 miles distant either from the main SE line or its branch from Tonbridge to Hastings and that the population which it would benefit is considerably more numerous than would be served by a line from Headcorn to Appledore and that the length of railway to be made Cranbrook to Appledore or Headcorn to Appledore is much the same. It occurs to those who are in such urgent want of a continuation of the C&PWR to Appledore that it may be a principal object to have direct railway communication from the dockyards at Woolwich and Chatham to Dungeness and that a continuation of the C&PWR will effect this object without in any way encumbering the main line of the SER as the traffic between these places would in that case pass across the main line at Paddock Wood instead of passing over it from Paddock Wood either to Headcorn or Ashford on its way to Dungeness via Appledore. This is no doubt argumentative, but most probably a point that has not been overlooked by the directors of the SER. Either of the above routes should serve Tenterden well, but I am aware of the objections raised as I think with very good cause to a station at Small Hythe (on the route from Cranbrook to Appledore) for Tenterden as being not only too far from the town, but at the foot of a very steep hill.

I submit that the country along the line from Gills Green to Appledore would admit of a railway being made as easily and perhaps even more easily and supply a much larger amount of passenger and goods traffic than the line from Headcorn to Appledore, irrespective of Tenterden, the traffic of which would be secured by either line.'

Watkin passed the letter on to the SER board as he felt unable to personally involve himself. Aged 73, his time with SER was drawing to a close and, besides, he had never had much interest in these local lines. As for his colleagues on the board, they declined taking any action on the Tenterden line until after the Cranbrook branch had been finished and opened.

An uncharacteristically cold snap heralded the start of April, but this was nothing compared with the end of the month when heavy snow fell to a depth of five inches. For a few days work was delayed, but a welcome thaw enabled a return to normal and a fortnight later beautiful spring weather was being enjoyed.

In an effort to make the navvies' life a little better, as well as improve their behaviour, a mission hut was set up near the tunnel between Cranbrook and Hawkhurst:

'THE RAILWAY: - A room for the Navvies: Through the exertions, we believe, of Colonel and Mrs. Ready, assisted by ladies and gentlemen of Hawkhurst and Cranbrook, a building has been erected close to the navvies dwellings at Badger's Oak, where they can enjoy recreation in games &c., which have been provided; and later on, it is understood, Mr. Niedermann, the missioner, will hold services there and probably some musical entertainments will also be arranged.'

The habitual drunkenness of some of the men employed by the railway contractors is common knowledge, but it would be unjust to brand them all as hopeless inebriates. Quite often there was nothing else to do but spend a few hours at the local inn, especially during the summer and following a long, hot and exhausting day's work on the railway. The heavy and extremely demanding labouring was tedious and backbreaking work and only the most pious could have denied the men their reward of a few pints. There was also much humbug that 'sin' was the exclusive preserve of the lower echelons of society. No doubt, though, most navvies were happy to allow the missioners to feel they were accomplishing something in the way of spiritual renewal and guidance. Singing hymns and listening to sermons was likely viewed as a small price to pay in order to enjoy the rare company of womenfolk and sample their dainty teas and refreshments.

This view, looking north towards Cranbrook station, shows workmen excavating the cutting near Badger's Oak in the late autumn of 1891.

It is not too difficult to conjure up the scene at Badger's Oak during that period. At the end of yet another glorious day the surrounding countryside would be at its most verdant loveliness. The sweet evening air would be filled with birdsong, while somewhere, within the nearby woods might come the distinctive call of the rarely-seen cuckoo. Huge mounds of soil from the open wounds created in the gently undulating landscape scarred the view until nature's own healing process could invade. The contractor's locomotive and trucks would stand idle upon the temporary tracks laid at the site of Cranbrook station, while up at their huts on the hillside the men would sit outside smoking tobacco and enjoying the chance to rest. Nearby, perhaps, the mission hut would be entertaining a few of them as, in the stillness, the sound of a piano and a young lady's voice might hold them momentarily spellbound and pensive. By all accounts such establishments were a success, for later that summer the *Kent & Sussex Post* informed its readers:

> 'HAWKHURST: - Badger's Oak Mission Room.
> On Wednesday evening the Temperance friends from Hawkhurst gave another entertainment to the navvies, who attended in fairly good numbers, and seemed interested in the programme, giving their attention to various readings and recitations and joining heartily in the singing.'

As the earthworks progressed on the section to Hawkhurst, so further accidents occurred. In the early summer of 1892 a workman had the misfortune to fall and break a number of ribs. Patched-up, he resumed working in a cutting, loading barrowloads of spoil into wagons. A scaffold and ramp arrangement enabled the wagons to be filled before the locomotive propelled them to the sites where embankments were under construction. While tipping out a barrow he missed his footing and fell into the wagon below, sustaining a very severe head wound which at first was feared might prove fatal. Fortunately, police constable Bradford happened to be there and with his skills of first aid was able to patch up the poor fellow so he might be conveyed to Cranbrook Infirmary. A few days later another navvy suffered serious injuries to one of his feet when it was somehow crushed by the buffers of the contractor's locomotive. The next day, there occurred another foot injury at the same cutting to another labourer.

While the heavy earthworks were under way south of Hope Mill, the track and signalling were nearing completion on the first section of railway from Paddock Wood. There were still many labourers, track gangers, carpenters, builders and others on this section who were all employed by Firbank. At the end of each week around three hundred men gathered in the station yard at Horsmonden where they would be paid off at the timekeeper's office. Ordinarily it was an unremarkable event, but on 30th July an incident took place which resulted in a navvy by the name of James Sullivan being brought before the Cranbrook magistrates charged with stealing £9 10s 0d - 'the monies of Joseph T. Firbank, railway contractor'. George Hildred, pay clerk, stated he'd had £75 in sovereigns, with an equal amount in half-sovereigns and silver. Sullivan had come up to the window two or three times seeking payment, but Hildred had told him he could not be paid there as he didn't belong to that section. The pay clerk eventually went off on his rounds to the other sites, but it was only at six o'clock, when he had finished, that he found himself short by £9 12s 1d. Unknown to Hildred, who'd been momentarily distracted, Sullivan had put his hand through the window and grabbed a bag containing the missing amount. He was, however, heard to say to his accomplice, 'Come on, I've got it'. During the day Sullivan rather foolishly decided to spend his ill-gotten gains in the village where he bought himself a new pair of trousers which he was wearing when arrested by the local constable. At the police station he was made to remove his new clothes which were held up and shaken whereupon nine incriminating half-sovereigns rattled out onto the floor. When quizzed on how he came by the money, Sullivan protested he'd won it at cards. The magistrates remained unimpressed and promptly sentenced him to six months hard labour which, on reflection, seems vaguely absurd for a man well-accustomed to gruelling manual work.

On 6th August, the *Post* was able to relate some exciting news:

> 'GOUDHURST: The Railway - Long looked for, come at last! The railway is being pushed on with vigour. The station master's house and the waiting rooms at Hope Mill are in course of erection and the permanent way is laid down, so that it looks as if the directors' promise to have the line opened to Hope Mill (and possibly to Pattenden) by the 1st September is likely to be fulfilled.'

It was also reported that on Friday, 5th August, the first trial trip had taken place with a special train running the complete length of the new line, from Paddock Wood to the temporary terminus.

Charles Sheath, secretary to the SER, had already written to the Board of Trade announcing their intention to open the railway from Paddock Wood to Hope Mill Station by the beginning of September. During the first week of August, Edward Seaton advised that everything would be ready for inspection by the end of the month. At a meeting of the SER board on 25th August, Sheath revealed that Major Marindin from the BoT had been delegated to inspect the route as far as Hope Mill and that it was planned to open the line to passenger and goods traffic in a week's time, on Thursday, 1st September. The testing of the equipment and signalling was going ahead, with everything performing satisfactorily. Messrs. Mackenzie & Holland were responsible for providing the signalling apparatus on the branch. This included new works at Paddock Wood in association with the branch for which a contract worth £572 15s 0d had only recently been awarded.

Towards the end of August it became apparent that the deadline of 1st September would not be met. Unforeseen delays with the works at Paddock Wood subsequently led to the postponement of the intended inspection date. Sir Myles Fenton was therefore obliged to telegram the BoT:

> 'We wrote and telegraphed Major Marindin yesterday that inspection of Cranbrook & Paddock Wood Line could not take place today but they appear to have missed him. Please inform him impossible for inspection to take place today.'

Every effort was now being made to have the first portion completed as quickly as possible, as revealed by the *Courier*:

> 'Strenuous efforts are being made to ensure the opening of this line for goods and passenger traffic as far as Hope Mill in the course of this month. On Sunday the workmen were employed on the completion of the permanent way up to this station and the work is being actively pushed forward in furtherance of the expected opening.
>
> On the afternoon of Sunday it was found necessary to convey one of the workmen to the West Kent General Hospital at Maidstone, there to be operated upon for a case of strangulated hernia.'

On Saturday, 3rd September, Major Marindin arrived at Paddock Wood station where he commenced his tour of inspection. His subsequent report and recommendations read as follows:

> 'I have inspected the completed portion of the Cranbrook & Paddock Wood Railway, from Paddock Wood to Hope Mill, a distance of 6 miles, 27.27 chains.
>
> The line is single throughout, with sidings at Churn Lane and Horsmonden Station, and a loop at Hope Mill Station. Land has been purchased for a double line, but all the works are constructed for a single line line only which has been made wide enough for a double line, except the cutting from 3 miles 38.50 chains to 3 miles 50 chains.
>
> The gauge is 4′ 8½″ and the width at formation level is 14 feet in cuttings and 18 ft on embankments.
>
> The permanent way is of the standard South Eastern type, and the line is well-ballasted with broken stone and shingle, and fenced with post and wire fencing.
>
> The steepest gradient has an inclination of 1 in 66 and the sharpest curve has a radius of 28 chains.
>
> There are two embankments 30 ft and 35 ft in height and one cutting, partly through rock with a depth of 48 ft, but all the other embankments and cuttings are of comparatively small dimensions, and for half of its length the line is nearly a surface line.
>
> There are six underbridges and four overbridges all with abutments of brickwork. Two of the underbridges have brick arches with spans of 18′ 2″ and 12′, and the other four, with spans of 26′ 3″, 21′2½″ and 8′ 6″, have longitudinal girders under each rail. Three of the overbridges, with spans of 15′ 3″, 14′ 9″ and 13′ 10″, have wrought iron girders and jack arches and one has 3 arches of 18′ span. There are also eight brick culverts from 3′ to 8′ in width and a brick-lined tunnel 85 yards in length.
>
> All the works are of a substantial construction and, with the exception of the culvert at 4 miles 76 chains which, owing to a slip on the embankment, will require watching, are standing well and the line is well finished. The girders have sufficient theoretical strength and those under the line were satisfactorily tested.
>
> There are 4 public road level crossings and 14 field or occupation crossings

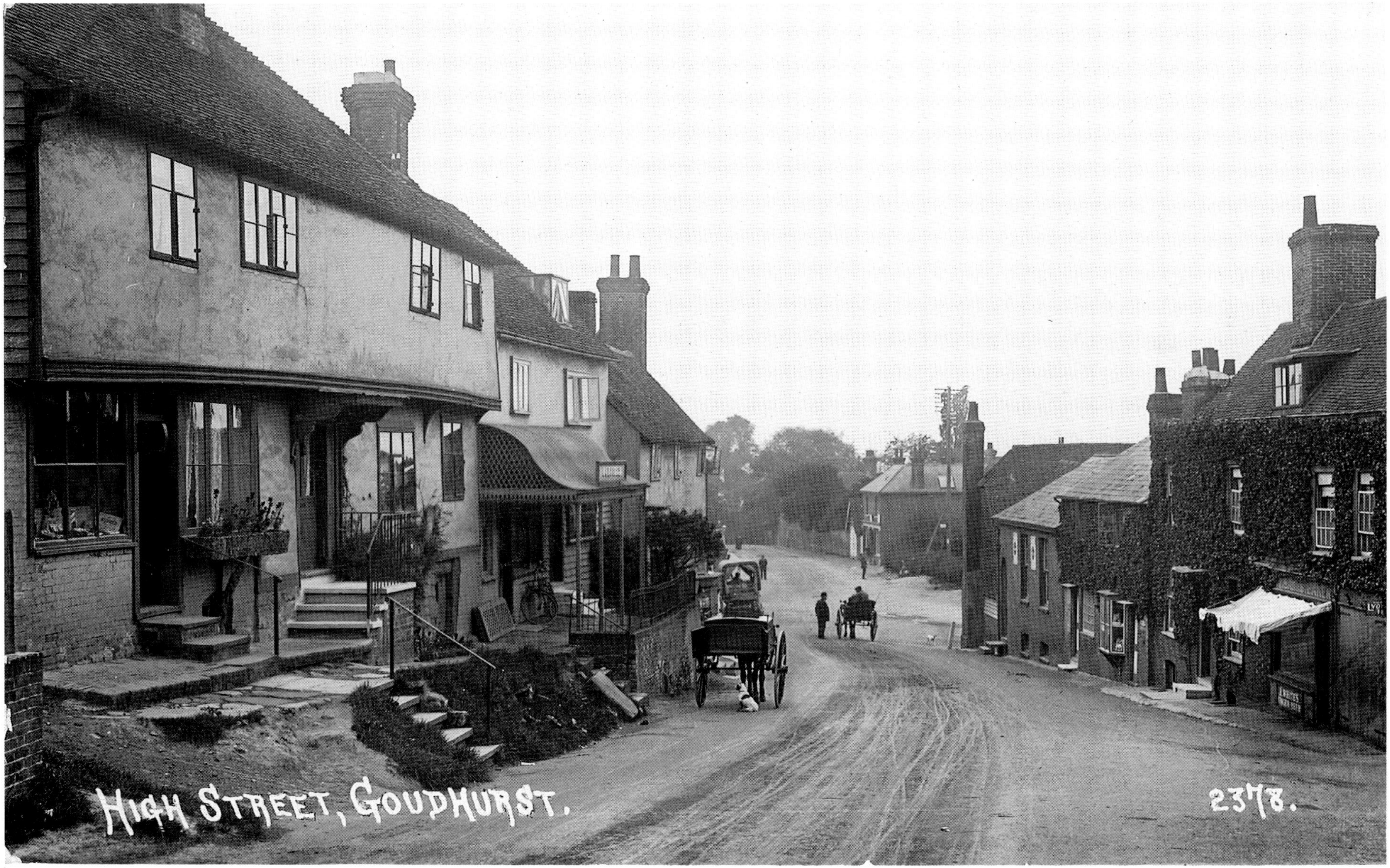

A most enchanting view of a sunny day in Goudhurst, taken about a hundred years ago and not long after the opening of the railway. *Goudhurst and Kilndown Local History Society*

One of the public road crossings, that at 5 miles 26 chains [Smallbridge], is an unauthorized crossing; but although it is not one of those specially authorized in the Company's Act of 1887, it is shown on the deposited plan as a level crossing of a public road. It is a very unimportant road and is stated, and appears, to be very little used, and a lodge and proper gates have been provided at it. I think that the Company might be allowed to endeavour to obtain parliamentary sanction for this crossing next year, failing which they must construct a bridge in lieu of it. There are stations at Horsmonden and Hope Mill, with sufficient accommodation for passengers. The former station has one platform only, but the latter, which for the present will be the terminus, has a loop and two platforms and has both lines signalled for arrival and departure

At Paddock Wood the new line runs into a dock behind the platform of the SERly's station, but up branch trains can also run out on to the SE up platform line. There is, however, no running junction for down trains, and all branch trains have to start from the dock line. This station has adequate accommodation and the signalling arrangements are mostly very modern, but I am informed that, very shortly, the station will be re-modelled. Although not yet completed, arrangements have been made for the signalmen in Paddock Wood East Yard cabin, which contains 26 levers, to have control of the points leading from the new line and a new siding on to the up platform line, bolting them by a properly interlocked lever.

Upon the new line the signalling is carried out in the following cabins:

Paddock Wood Junction Cabin, containing 16 working and 8 spare levers.

Horsmonden Cabin, containing 6 working levers and an Annett's Key

Hope Mill Cabin, containing 14 working levers and an Annett's Key.

There is also a siding at Churn Lane with points locked by the Train Tablet and there is a 2-lever frame at Churn Lane level crossing working the signals in each direction and both of the gates. The gates at the level crossing at 1 mile 14 chains [Willow Lane] are worked from the ground and there are no signals, and the gates at the level crossing at 6 miles 14 chains [Hope Mill station], also worked from the ground, are bolted by a properly interlocked lever in Hope Mill Cabin.

The following are the requirements which I noted:

1. At Paddock Wood: Safety points at A siding; detectors at facing points; gauge ties at facing points; connections to be made; and the bolting of points from the SER's Cabin to be completed.
2. At several crossings, the crossings to be fenced up to the line.
3. Handrails at the sides of the underbridges.
4. Some fishplate bolts to be made good.
5. At Hope Mill Cabin No. 9 lever to lock Nos. 2 and 5.
6. The bank and culvert at 4 miles 76 chains to be watched.
7. Undertakings to be furnished:

(a) To stop all trains at the intermediate station, there being no turntable at Hope Mill.

(b) To work the line under the Electric Tablet System, rules for which working must be submitted for approval.

Both these undertakings must be made under the seal and the signature of both the owning company and the SER company, who are to work the line.

Subject to the satisfaction of all these requirements within a fortnight and of Nos. 1, 4, 5 and 7 before the opening, I can recommend that the opening of this new line for passenger traffic may be sanctioned.

I have the honour to be, etc.

[signed by] Major Marindin.'

Quite apart from the foregoing official information, a report in the *Courier* provides a useful insight into the day's proceedings during Major Marindin's visit:

'The official inspection by Major Marindin (of the Board of Trade) of such part of the new Paddock Wood and Cranbrook Railway as extends from Paddock Wood Junction to Hope Mill station (between Goudhurst and Lamberhurst) a distance of a little over six miles took place on Saturday with a satisfactory result. Two engines were used to test the strength of the bridges (nine in number). This portion of the line passes chiefly through Hastings sand, very little clay having been met with, but the largest cutting, - that at Horsmonden, 48 feet deep at the deepest part - is made mostly through the solid rock. There is a tunnel under the road (from Horsmonden to Maidstone) nearly 100 yards long. The longest and largest embankment is the one at Swiggs Hole which averages about 42 feet in height and is half a mile in length. The steepest gradient is 1 in 66 and this extends for a mile. There are three gate houses at the public road level crossings and two stations, one at Horsmonden and one at Hope Mill. The latter is a 'passing station' and therefore has two lines of rails, so that a train for the Hartley end can here pass another for the Paddock Wood Junction. At Churn Lane, Horsmonden, a farmers' siding has been constructed. A considerable amount of labour has had to be employed in diverting the course of the river in several places.'

The necessary undertaking was duly forwarded to the Board of Trade:

'The Cranbrook and Paddock Wood Railway hereby undertake that all trains running on the line shall be stopped at the intermediate station at Horsmonden, there being no turntable at Hope Mill station. They further undertake that the line shall be worked under the electric tablet system; rules for which workings are attached to this undertaking.'

Watkin personally fixed the company seals of the C&PWR and SER to the document before its despatch to the BoT.

Throughout the following week the outstanding works and requirements were attended to with all possible speed. Subsequently, the first section of the Hawkhurst branch railway was opened for passenger and goods traffic on Monday, 12th September 1892. The honour of hauling the ceremonial train to Hope Mill fell to one of James Cudworth's '118' class of 2-4-0 locomotives, No.112. It came straight from Ashford works in gleaming condition, having recently been reboilered. Appropriately bedecked by the SER men with garlands of fresh local hops and the Union flag, the engine glided into Hope Mill amidst much cheering. The scene was one of much excitement and jubilation, as witnessed by a reporter from the *Post:*

'The event was observed as a holiday by many persons, more especially as passengers on the opening day were allowed to

One of James Cudworth's '118' class locomotives, No. 112, is shown here at Hope Mill station on Monday, 12th September 1892, appropriately decorated with hop bines for the occasion, with Driver Frank Martin, accompanied by fireman G. F. Cheal on the footplate, Holman Stephens standing next to them, and, on the tender, guard William Hollingsworth. The down home signal, which features above the roof vents of the third carriage, originally had two arms, one beneath the other. Its shape is slightly distorted due to the habit of Victorian photographers painting out the sky on glass plate negatives. *Colonel Stephens Railway Museum*

Beautifully lined-out and well-groomed, No. 112, with driver Martin and fireman Cheal, posing for the cameraman. No one seems to have noticed that the Union Flag was upside-down. *Collection H. C. Bassett*

dispense with the usual formality of obtaining tickets bearing a fixed and well-understood money value. Flags were displayed from Mr. Clementson's premises, Hope Mill, and at least one enterprising photographer attended to take a view of the first train, which was arranged to leave Hope Mill at 8.52 am - a very convenient time, passengers by this train being enabled to join an up train at Paddock Wood. We understand that Mr. Field, the station master, has been transferred to rural Goudhurst from the important station of Reading. There can be no two opinions as to the advantages to be derived from having a railway station within a mile of the village instead of its being, as was formerly the case, five miles distant to us. Our inhabitants will be enabled to get out of the village more conveniently than before and what is very important, visitors will be enabled to get into Goudhurst much more easily than has hitherto been the case. Just now, Goudhurst is an especially busy little place, being full to overflowing with hop-pickers, navvies and mechanics working at several places, in addition to its usual population.'

The *Courier* provided an equally illuminating account:

'The first section of this line is at last open and the hopping season is a very opportune time for the event. No little excitement has been caused in the neighbourhood and on the opening day when all the passengers were for once conveyed free it is stated that several took advantage of the trip who had never before been in a train in their lives and had in fact hardly stirred from their native villages - a fact that is not easily grasped in these days of locomotion. But the engine garlanded with the fragrant hop bine and surmounted with the Union Jack will do far more wonderful things for the district, and this was the general opinion expressed at the dinner in celebration of the long-looked-for event which was held at the Gun Inn, Horsmonden. The train service at present is not an extensive one. There are five trains daily, the first leaving Paddock Wood at 9.42am and the last from Hope Mill at 5.30pm. The four Sunday trains, however, extend over a wider range, the first leaving Paddock Wood at 7.43am, the last returning from Hope Mill, which is within easy distance of Goudhurst, at 8.25pm.'

The celebratory dinner at the 'Gun Inn' on that Monday evening was a thoroughly enjoyable occasion. Around fifty guests crowded into the function room, sitting down to a large table where a splendid dinner was placed before them. Mr. Throssel, the agent for J. T. Firbank, presided over the evening's events which included numerous toasts to Her Majesty, the new railway and those involved in its creation. A hearty, rousing and well-received sing-song rounded-off the celebration.

Hope Mill station at the opening of the first section of the Hawkhurst Branch in September 1892. *Colonel Stephens Railway Museum*

Holman Stephens, seated on the left, beneath the beautifully-painted station nameboard with its heavy blended shade to the serif letters. Unfortunately, the signwriter's work lasted barely four months when the name changed to simply 'Goudhurst' on New Year's Day 1893. *Colonel Stephens Railway Museum*

SOUTH-EASTERN RAILWAY.

PADDOCK WOOD AND CRANBROOK LINE.

TIME TABLE.

Down.	Week-days.					Sundays.			
Paddock Wood dep	9.42	12.35	2.8	4.48	6.35	7.43	9.5	7.6	8.3
Horsmonden ...arr	9.52	12.45	2.18	4.58	6.45	7.53	9.15	7.16	8.13
Hope Mill..........	9.58	12.51	2.24	5.4	6.51	7.59	9.21	7.22	8.19

Up.	Week-days.				Sundays.			
Hope Mill ....dep	8.52	12.10	1.32	5.30	8.35	9.30	7.30	8.25
Horsmonden ....arr	8.58	12.16	1.38	5.36	8.41	9.36	7.36	8.31
Paddock Wood	9.8	12.26	1.48	5.46	8.51	9.46	7.46	8.41

For the next three weeks the railway began to establish itself as business gradually built up. It was also the hop-picking season, so traffic was especially brisk. However, the autumn of 1892 was particularly wet, most noticeably at the commencement of October when heavy rain persisted for a few days. On the night of Tuesday, 4th October, the embankment near Nevergood Farm, between Horsmonden and Hope Mill stations, gave way and slipped for some length into the adjoing fields. Efforts to re-open the line to Hope Mill were quickly put in hand as revealed in a letter from Holman Stephens, the resident engineer, to his father:

Cranbrook,
11th October 1892

'My dear Dah,
I am very sorry I missed the post wishing you very many happy returns of the 10th. But last Tuesday night we had a bad slip and the traffic was quite stopped till this afternoon. We have been working night and day at it to get it opened. I hope to be up soon and trust you are quite well. With much love to you and Mam.
Yours, H.'

In a little over a month after opening, the telegraph system was installed at Hope Mill station, with the first testing of the equipment taking place on Wednesday, 19th October. It seems to have been quite an occasion, being greeted with much pride by the locals when Mr. E. Beech of the 'Chequers Inn' at Lamberhurst had the honour of sending an inaugural message that morning to Mr. W. Gurr.

With the opening of the new railway to Hope Mill, it became necessary to put in hand the fairly major alterations at Paddock Wood alluded to by Major Marindin in his report. Over £5,000 was authorized to be spent on re-modelling the track layout, providing a new siding, as well as purchasing ten acres of land for extending the goods yard. The early buildings on the up side were demolished, together with the distinctive clock tower and the original footbridge. More substantial station offices, as well as canopies with familiar SER valancing, were duly erected, whilst M. J. Shaw & Co. provided a new iron footbridge costing £695. Most of this work was completed in time for the opening of the completed branch to Hawkhurst.

Traffic upon the line was apparently well beyond expectations, but there was less contentment over the name of the station at the temporary teminus:

'GOUDHURST - The Railway:
We understand that the amount of traffic, both passenger and goods, on this new line has somewhat surprised everybody, so much so that additional siding accommodation will have to be provided to prevent blocking of traffic in subsequent years.

Our village station - much to the chagrin of many of our people, was named Hope Mill after the name of the part of the parish in which it was erected. A petition was presented to the Railway Company, pointing out that it would be much more convenient if the name of the station could be made the same as that of the parish, and we are pleased to report that this reasonable request has been granted, and henceforth our station will be known by the name of 'Goudhurst' instead of 'Hope Mill'.'

The change of name subsequently took effect from New Year's Day 1893.

At a board meeting of the SER in mid-February, it was reported that the work on the remaining section was progressing sufficiently well to expect an opening in early summer. However, these predictions proved to be over-optimistic.

Further accidents marred construction when, during January, two men were badly cut about the head in a distressing but unspecified incident at Hartley, but a fatality in March brought the second recorded death. The 38 year-old man, named Squires, came from Watford and had only been working on the line for four days. At half-past eight in the morning he'd been shovelling in the cutting near Badger's Oak tunnel when an overhanging mass of earth, weighing about two tons, suddenly collapsed. Here it is sufficient to say that he was crushed, without repeating the ghoulish details luridly reported in the press. The poor chap's remains were taken to the 'Duke William Inn' at Hartley where an inquest subsequently recorded a verdict of accidental death.

On 19th May, Mr. Sheath announced to the board that he intended to arrange an inspection by the Board of Trade during June. Nevertheless, there was still much to be done, whilst on the section already opened the problems of under-capacity were hurriedly being addressed:

'GOUDHURST - The Railway: The much-needed additional siding accommodation at our station has now been supplied and there is ample room for wagons to pass and repass between the two additional lines of rails which are capable of accommodating some thirty trucks.'

It soon became apparent that Sheath's aspirations for an early inspection would not be possible. Landslips,

The railway station at Cranbrook nearing completion. The contractor's wagons loaded with spoil were being moved with the aid of the saddle-tank locomotive, *Fox*.
Collection Charles Evernden

both in the cuttings and along the new embankments, were still being experienced while the spoil settled. The slips in the cuttings were of no great consequence and were quickly dealt with; however, the embankments between Goudhurst and Cranbrook required some serious re-engineering. Two miles south of Goudhurst, near Forge Farm and adjacent to the appropriately-named Wet Wood, the embankment gave way for some considerable length. A remedy involved lessening the weight of the earth, while the opportunity was taken to ease the gradient from the authorized 1 in 50 to 1 in 60. A similar exercise was carried out a couple of miles further towards Cranbrook, near Furnace Farm, with an identical alteration to the gradient.

By the end of June the SER felt confident enough to propose an opening to Hawkhurst on 1st September. Even so, it was not until Wednesday, 30th August that a representative from the BoT was able to visit the completed extension. The subsequent report reads as follows:

> 'I have inspected the extension of the Cranbrook & Paddock Wood Railway from Goudhurst to Hawkhurst, a single line 5 miles 73.73 chains in length.
>
> Land has been purchased for a double line, but all the works, with the exception of one overbridge, have been constructed for a single line only.
>
> The gauge is 4′ 8½″, the widths at formation levels in cuttings and banks are 14 feet and 18 feet respectively. The permanent way is in all respects similar to that between Paddock Wood and Goudhurst and, with the exception of some few portions, is better ballasted.
>
> The steepest gradient has an inclination of 1 in 60, 1 in 50 having been authorized, and the sharpest curve (close to the terminus) has a radius of 18 chains. The country through which the line passes is very undulating and there are consequently several deep cuttings and high embankments, the deepest cutting having a depth of 44 feet, and the highest embankment a height of 49 feet. Some trouble has been experienced with slips, both in cuttings and on embankments; these slips appear to have been successfully dealt with hitherto, though with a recurrence of wet weather they will need careful watching.
>
> The new stations are Cranbrook and Hawkhurst which have been provided with sufficient accommodation and goods loops. Goudhurst station has been altered and provided with a second platform and shelter shed, and signalled as a passing place for passenger trains. An agricultural siding has been put in at Pattenden. The works on the line consist of
>
> 1. Four overbridges, one of 26 feet, one of 15 feet and 2 others of 14 feet and 14′ 8″ span, all constructed with brick abutments, that of 15 feet span having a brick-arched top and the others tops composed of wrought iron joists with brick arches turned between them.
> 2. Four underbridges of spans varying between 11′ 8″ and 27 feet, two constructed with brick abutments and two with concrete ones carrying wrought iron girders.
> 3. A tunnel in brickwork 181 yards long.
> 4. Four brick culverts, widest 5 feet.
>
> The works appear to have been substantially constructed and (with the one exception of the culvert at 9 miles 18 chains) to be standing well. The girders have ample theoretical strength and those under the line gave very slight deflection under test. The culvert at 9 miles 18 chains is out of shape in its southern half. It is stated not to have altered its present shape for a length of time, but it should be carefully watched. There are no level crossings of public roads. The fencing is principally post and wire with some short lengths of post and rail.
>
> The signal arrangements are carried out in raised cabins at:
> *Goudhurst*; (old cabin new frame) containing 16 working levers, 0 spare levers.
> *Cranbrook*; containing 16 working levers, 0 spare levers.

Hawkhurst; containing 12 working levers, 2 spare levers. The siding connection at Pattenden is provided with a one-lever frame, locked by the train tablets in use or the tablet section between Goudhurst and Cranbrook.

No engine turntable has been provided at Hawkhurst, which is about 11¼ miles from Paddock Wood but an undertaking is to be furnished that the trains should stop at all stations.

The line is well-finished and the following are the requirements which I noted:

1. Goudhurst Station: No.8 signal should work only with No.6 points. A catch point has to be removed before the line is opened.

2. Cranbrook Station: No.11 lever should lock No.10 in both positions. No.12 lever should lock No.9 in both positions. The safety points at the Hawkhurst end of the Goods Line is too near to the main line and should be moved so as to afford a clear 6 feet space.

3. Hawkhurst Station: If the line at the back of the platform is to be used for passenger traffic it should be provided with arrival and departure signals and facing point appliances and the siding leading to it supplied with safety points. If it is to be used only as a goods line or siding, the back of the platform should be fenced and a safety point put in on No.9 crossing at about 6 feet from the main line.

4. The ballasting should be completed.

In consequence of the falling gradient on the Goudhurst side of Cranbrook station, goods trains before commencing to shunt should in all cases be placed on the goods loop and no shunting should be allowed on the main line.

The line is to be worked by the South Eastern Company, the safety of the single line being secured by the use of the Train Tablet, instruments for working which have been provided at Goudhurst, Cranbrook and Hawkhurst stations. The secretary handed to me an undertaking to this effect and

A Stirling 'O' class, with a single six-wheeled coach on an inspection special, pausing at Cranbrook just prior to opening. This is another picture featuring Holman Stephens, who is shown sitting on the left. The wooden board fixed across the buffers had been secured with the rope passing around the smokebox handrail. *Colonel Stephens Railway Museum*

as to trains stopping at all stations, it is satisfactory except that it is not signed by the chairman of the two lines and I returned it to him for these signatures to be obtained.

Subject: (1) to the above requirements, which should be met within a month; (2) to the undertaking as to the mode of working; (3) to the remarks as to shunting at Cranbrook station; (4) to a moderate speed being observed on the embankment, where slips have occurred, until these embankments have become solidified and; (5) re-inspections at the first convenient opportunity after the requirements have been met, I can recommend the Board of Trade to sanction the opening of the line between Goudhurst and Hawkhurst stations for passenger traffic. Unauthorized gradients of 1 in 60 have been introduced between 7 miles 76 chains and 8 miles 21 chains and between 8 miles 75 chains and 9 miles 52 chains. These are not steeper than, or indeed so steep as some others authorized but still they are illegal and a certificate should therefore be applied for us to authorize them.

[signed]

Major General C. S. Hutchinson R. E.'

Responding to Hutchinson's criticism of the unauthorized gradients, engineer Edward Seaton considered that the railway had been 'much improved' by easing the acclivity of these inclines, especially on the approach to Cranbrook station. However, Hutchinson duly expressed his satisfaction on a subsequent visit to the branch, noting that his requirements had been faithfully carried out. He told the BoT:

'The siding at the back of the [Hawkhurst] platform has been adapted for passenger traffic and the signal cabin contains 14 levers all in use. The line is now well-ballasted.'

The *Post* commented upon the very up-to-date nature of the new line:

'This line is worked on the electric tablet system, which absolutely prevents a collision, and is the only line in the south of England on which this system is worked. The signalling is on the most improved system, and telephonic communication exists between each station.'

The cost of the Hawkhurst railway approximated £160,000. Actual expenditure up to June had been £148,585 18s 7d, with a sum in the region of £10,000 needed for completion. All that remained was the ceremonial opening of the line to the public and this was arranged for Monday, 4th September. The *Post* gave a very full account of the day's proceedings and the more salient points provide a valuable glimpse into the events of a century ago:

'The completion of this line, so long looked for, is now an accomplished fact, and the slow and laborious work of excavating and platelaying has given place to the iron steed, which glides along with sturdiness and alacrity through the lovely undulating country and well-wooded land, which, in other parts, is under high cultivation, and belonging to an enterprising and fairly successful class of agriculturalists, while here and there are signs of new industries cropping up. Though - as Lord Medway informed his hearers, at the dinner to celebrate the opening - the Parliamentary name is the Paddock Wood and Cranbrook Railway, still we think the public will soon follow the suit of 'Bradshaw' and give it the terminal title of Hawkhurst, - the Paddock Wood and Hawkhurst Line. Already the route and gradients have been given, and we have but little to record, save that the Time Service was carried out in its entirety on Monday, and, as might have been expected, there was a crowd of persons at the Hawkhurst station all day who indulged in the mild excitement of a return journey from Cranbrook or Goudhurst Stations; three-halfpence to Cranbrook, return ticket 2d. The engines were decorated with flags, but the free rides, which some expected, did not come off, for it was thought it would be difficult to work them with the through traffic. Several enterprising people have already set about catering for the conveyance of goods, parcels and passengers, and there is no lack of conveniences for getting to and from the station. Under the courteous management of Mr. Clark, the Station Master, *pro tem*; the numerous inquiring folks are satisfied as far as possible, but of course it will take some time to get everything into regular working order, and a month's experience on all sides will no doubt show that the new line has many advantages over other routes. At present, a pretty good train service is put on, but possibly this may be improved upon, as experience will be the best test. At all events we are assured that Sir Edward Watkin and the Company are well satisfied with the traffic returns made at Goudhurst and Horsmonden Stations, and we doubt not but that in time both Cranbrook and Hawkhurst will prove equally good.

Having got so much, we must be asking for more. A continuation of the line to Appledore or Dungeness would make this branch much more important and convenient. And there is some prospect of this, for speaking at this dinner, on behalf of the SER Company, Mr. Seaton said that now this, the first line in the Weald of Kent was opened, he hoped it would go on extending North, South, East and West. We can only expect them to be influenced by the sordid motives of pecuniary gain, but still that would result in the benefit of both the private and trading community, so that we sincerely hope the new line will be given a fair trial and then be judged upon its merits.'

At 7pm on the evening of the opening day, sixty guests sat down to 'a most sumptuous repast' at five shillings per head in a marquee at the rear of the Queen's Hotel in Hawkhurst. The interior had been artistically draped and was brilliantly illuminated for the event for which Mr. Clements, the caterer, had 'exerted himself to place a first class spread before the guests'. Following the loyal toasts and a brief musical interlude, Lord Medway asked the gathering to raise their glasses for 'Success to the Paddock Wood and Cranbrook Railway'. In his speech he begged to remind everyone that the Cranbrook railway had been the brainchild of Sir Edward Watkin. This was an extremely generous, if highly untruthful compliment, especially as Watkin could not even be bothered to attend the dinner. His lordship reflected upon the long struggle throughout the years leading up

The opening of the railway to Hawkhurst on Monday, 4th September 1893, with a Cudworth class '118' bedecked with flags, and, standing on the footplate, the driver, holding the key token loop in his hand. Hawkhurst's longcase platform clock can be seen already fixed to the wall, whilst the early oil lamps are of interest. The new porters' barrows and platform seats are just some of the items which had been supplied prior to opening.

Collection Brian Piper

The up starting signal at Cranbrook standing at 'all clear' as preparations were being made to restart the inaugural trip back to Paddock Wood on 4th September 1893.

Colonel Stephens Railway Museum

to the line's commencement but, he added, he was now looking forward to reaching London by eleven o'clock without having first to drive to Etchingham or Staplehurst. His address was, however, tinged with some regret at not having the line continued into Cranbrook itself as he believed it would have been a 'valuable adjunct'. In jocular mood he recalled how he'd been invited to discuss the siting of Cranbrook station: 'Sir Edward came down to Cranbrook on this occasion and telegraphed to meet me, yet though I had a pair of horses put in, so great was his impetuosity that before I could get there, he had fixed the site and had gone away again!'. This comment caused much raucous laughter and serves as a measure of the extent of Watkin's interest in this particular railway. In concluding, Lord Medway thanked the contractors and all those who had been connected with its construction. Raising his glass to the toast, he said he would like to 'couple the names of Messrs. Seaton and Stephens for they were much indebted to them for their services'. The *Post* then reported the comments made by the engineers and contractors:

> 'Mr. Seaton in responding, said it was now 30 years since the first Act of Parliament was obtained for making this railway, but he had only been connected with it for four years. If the working of the line went on in the same successful way as the first half had done, it would be one of the most successful branches of the S. E. Company. Sir Myles Fenton and Mr. Light had both been down, and expressed themselves highly satisfied with the way the returns were coming in. Goudhurst had perhaps done more than most small branches, and the traffic there had been so great that the accommodation had to be enlarged. At Horsmonden and Cranbrook they had deemed it necessary to increase the accommodation for goods traffic, and he believed the Company had spent their money wisely and well in making ample provision for the requirements of this large and prosperous neighbourhood. He hoped the line would go on extending as he should like to be present at many meetings like this when branch lines were opened (applause).
>
> Mr. Stephens said the line had not been constructed without some engineering difficulties to overcome, but now that it was completed he hoped it would be a great convenience to them all. The engineers were very much indebted to the contractors and others who carried out the work
>
> Mr. Heath proposed the toast of 'The Contractor', remarking that Mr. Firbank had established a name for good work. He hoped their friends at Benenden, Rolvenden, Northiam and other places, would agitate for their line to be connected with Dungeness, and that Mr. Firbank might be the Contractor.'

Finally, the health of Lord Medway was toasted 'in hearty fashion, being followed by rounds of Kentish Fire and cheers raised for Lady Medway'. Thus, ended the celebrations that evening on the first day of regular services to Hawkhurst.

The Hawkhurst branch was unmistakeably a product of the South Eastern Railway, built by J. T. Firbank and engineered throughout by Edward Seaton. It is only necessary to emphasise this for the simple reason that, over the years, railway authors have unwittingly blurred the distinction by simply stating that the branch was engineered by Holman F. Stephens. This is bending the truth and it is necessary to attempt to clarify his precise involvement. In later years Stephens engineered and managed a number of light railways across Britain, which he was able to progressively create through personal contacts, commissions and fees from various projects. In Kent, though, he was indeed wholly responsible for the Rother Valley Railway (later the Kent & East Sussex); the Sheppey Light Railway (always operated by and eventually bought out by the SE&CR); and the East Kent Light Railway. These lines came about following the passing of the 1896 Light Railways Act and bore no semblance whatsoever to the Cranbrook & Paddock Wood Railway.

Holman Fred Stephens, (not Frederick), was born in 1868 and from an early age displayed a keen interest in practical pursuits such as the sciences, the military and railways. At the age of 14 he began a five year term studying engineering at University College, London, before entering the service of the Metropolitan Railway in 1888. He was based at Neasden under the company's chief engineer E. P. Seaton for almost three years, during which he also had experience of firing on locomotives. When Edward Seaton was approached by Watkin (who was also chairman of the Metropolitan) and asked to take on the Cranbrook project, it was a fortuitous opportunity for Stephens since the scheme offered useful training in railway civil engineering, as well as valuable practical experience on site. The only detrimental aspect associated with this employment appears to have been that it offered little in the way of financial remuneration; however, his father managed to send him a regular if small allowance to help him along. As a hard-working and extremely ambitious person, Stephens seems to have been far more concerned with making contacts, since in his letters home he frequently begged his father to use his influence in the social and business circles in which he moved in order that it might be advantageous to his career. This was important in Victorian society where introductions, social as well as business, could open doors when qualifications and honest skill sometimes made little impression. Initially, it may only be assumed that Edward Seaton and Holman Stephens enjoyed a close and amicable working relationship, but, sadly, it was not destined to last.

At the commencement of the Hawkhurst branch construction in 1890, the 22 year-old Stephens was appointed resident engineer by Seaton. Being a position of some considerable responsibility, it involved him lodging in the locality and remaining on site virtually from dawn to dusk. It was also around this time that Stephens met up with 13 year-old William Austen who lived with his grandmother in Cranbrook. The young lad, taken on by J. T. Firbank, was allocated to work for Stephens as a 'chainman' which entailed holding the graduated poles during surveying. Stephens was obviously impressed by Austen and eventually offered him proper salaried employment when the Rye and Camber

Tramway contract came his way in 1895. Stephens' role on the C&PWR would have been to ensure that the designs and specifications from Seaton's Westminter offices were properly carried out and to schedule by the contractor's builders and navvies. All the original drawings for stations, bridges and tunnels bear the authoritative signature 'E. P. Seaton', although it is documented that Stephens 'assisted in the design of 20 small bridges, 2 short tunnels, 6 stations, etc'.

The Hawkhurst branch was heavily engineered, a fact plainly manifest to anyone who knew the railway or is acquainted with the hilly terrain around this part of Kent. Some very substantial earthworks were necessary in order to drive the line through the High Weald. Laid to standard specifications, it would be quite wrong to associate this line with any of Stephens' charming, but by comparison, extremely lightly-laid railways. The line's gradients, the steepest of which was 1 in 60, have often been misleadingly cited as 'hallmarks' of Stephens' work, but this is misrepresenting the facts. All over the SER system there are steeper and longer sections, for instance, the Sandgate branch ranged from 1 in 54 to 1 in 59 for almost its entire length. Similarly, the radii of the branch's curves were not especially remarkable and sharper examples could certainly be found elsewhere on the SER. Unquestionably it was Seaton who determined the necessary gradients and civil engineering projects, whilst photographs depicting Stephens with the surveying team show that he was entrusted with setting out the line. As resident engineer, he was also given sole supervision of the works, whilst Seaton allowed him to assist on other projects during this period, mostly associated with the Metropolitan Railway.

Responsibility for the stations has also been rather unthinkingly and erroneously credited to Stephens, simply because the exterior walls of the station offices were clad in corrugated iron. The Hawkhurst branch buildings were substantially constructed in a fashion that was far stouter and more sophisticated than anything ever seen on his subsequent railways built at minimal cost. Perhaps it is only to be expected that Stephens should go on to imitate this pattern in later projects, but in a more lightweight and cheaper form. Horsmonden, Goudhurst, Cranbrook and Hawkhurst owe their pedigree to the South Eastern Railway which had first used this method of economic fabrication only three years earlier, in 1889, on the Elham Valley Line. Whereas the cost of a 'standard' SER weatherboard station building appears to have amounted to approximately £350 in the 1880s, these corrugated steel prototypes could be provided for less than half that amount, around £140. This saving was understandably viewed desirable by the directors in regard to these two less-important lines which Sir George Russell freely admitted the SER was 'obliged' to construct. Messrs. Humphreys of Knightsbridge were responsible for providing the stations at Canterbury South, Bridge and Bishopsbourne and the almost identical design suggests that Francis Brady, the SER's engineer, passed over the drawings to Horsmonden builders Mancktelow Bros., for use on the Hawkhurst branch. However, it might be mentioned that the C&PWR station offices were larger than the three Elham Valley examples, differing slightly in appearance, most noticeably by having the wooden awning stanchions set back a few feet, which added much to their aesthetic appeal.

In conclusion, Stephens' role as resident engineer was undoubtedly a position of considerable responsibility and importance, but one in which he acted according to the chief engineer's specifications. His involvement entailed overseeing the wide variety of engineering projects since it is recorded that Seaton visited the sites only on special occasions and relied upon his deputy to report back and, possibly, make decisions in his absence. Edward Seaton, unlike Stephens, would certainly not have dirtied his clothes on site. On the other hand, Stephens appears to have earned the respect of his fellow workmen, whilst ably carrying out what was asked of him by Seaton. His superior was evidently well-pleased with the young man's progress for he wrote in praise to Stephens' father saying: 'I cannot speak too highly of the way he has conducted himself'. Unquestionably, 'Colonel Stephens' as he later became in his military career, was a truly remarkable man and although his achievements in the ensuing years were considerable, it cannot be claimed that he was responsible for the Cranbrook and Paddock Wood Railway. The Hawkhurst branch was thoroughly well-engineered and soundly-constructed to the highest standards required by the parent South Eastern Railway Company. Such an achievement was primarily due to the combined efforts and professionalism of its chief engineer, Edward Seaton, and its contractor, J. T. Firbank.

Kent and Sussex Post.

SATURDAY, SEPTEMBER 16th, 1893.

SOUTH-EASTERN RAILWAY.

PADDOCK WOOD AND CRANBROOK LINE.

TIME TABLE FOR SEPTEMBER.

DOWN.

Paddock Wood, dep—	Weekdays.	8.52	10.10	12.35	2.20	4.48	6.55	7.55
	Sundays.—	7.48	9.7	6.41	8.3			
Horsmonden—		9.2	10.20	12.45	2.30	4.57	6.5	8.5
	Sundays.—	7.58	9.17	6.51	8.13			
Goudhurst—		9.7	10.25	12.50	2.35	5.1	6.10	8.10
	Sundays.—	8.3	9.22	6.56	8 18			
Cranbrook—		9.16	10.34	12.59	2.44	5.10	6.19	8.19
	Sundays—	8.12	9.31	7.5	8.27			
Hawkhurst—		9.21	10.39	1.4	2.49	5.15	6.24	8.24
	Sundays—	8.17	9.36	7.10	8.32			

UP.

Hawkhurst—	Week-days.	8 20	9.32	11.52	1.19	4.2	5 20	7.7
	Sundays—	8.22	9.45	7.17	8.40			
Cranbrook—		8.25	9.37	11 57	1.24	4.7	5.25	7.12
	Sundays—	8.27	9.50	7.22	8.45			
Goudhurst—		8.33	9.45	12.5	1.32	4.15	5.33	7.20
	Sundays.—	8.35	9.58	7.30	8.53			
Horsmonden—		8.39	9.51	12.11	1.38	4.21	5.38	7.26
	Sundays.—	8.41	10.4	7.36	8.59			
Paddock Wood, arr—		8.48	10.0	12.20	1.47	4.30	5.46	7.35
	Sundays.—	8.50	10.13	7.45	9.8			

Paddock Wood station, about 1905, showing the canopies erected over both platforms, whilst the up side buildings had been extended to the rear. Another signal box, 'Paddock Wood West Yard Cabin', brought into use on 3rd March 1895, is seen on the left, whilst the very tall SER signals were typical of the period.

The large East Yard cabin which contained 90 levers (3 spare), was similarly built astride the Hawkhurst branch at Paddock Wood, being brought into use on Sunday, 26th June 1898. It replaced the original signal box on the right, which was pulled down, along with the early SER signal gantry. *A. H. Curd (Southern Railway Magazine)*

CHAPTER FOUR

EXTENDING THE LINE

WITH the opening of the line to its eventual terminus overlooking the High Weald, the SER retimed the trains to accommodate the longer run. In its first week the *Post* noted that business had been brisk, with trains well-patronized, but there was still a deep-seated sense of resentment in Cranbrook. The effect of this resulted in further calls for some form of rail connection with the heart of the town. During the week the railway had opened, the *Courier* reported that a surveyor had been taking measurements from the town to the station, while the *Post* revealed to its readers:

'CRANBROOK: The SER are willing to construct a branch line which will really be a continuation of the main line, and start from the left hand side of the station, to continue up the valley, across the main road, and pass at the back of the town to a field close to Baker's Cross Brewery, - on condition that interest at the rate of about 3 per cent be paid on the cost per annum, which will be about £400 p.a. This is already practically guaranteed, and the work will be commenced as soon as the necessary formalities can be gone through. It only remains to give the names of the principal officers of the [extension] company and they are as follows: Contractor, Mr. J. T. Firbank; Engineer, H. F. Stephens; Secretary, Mr. Sheath; Solicitor, Mr. Willis; and the chairman of Directors, The Hon. A. E. Gathorne-Hardy, MP.'

The proposals, however, were still rather vague and no one knew whether to expect a standard railway or a light tramway. In an effort to clarify the position, a meeting was held at the Vestry Hall where 'Mr. Seton [sic] the engineer' gave outline details of a steam tramway. Commencing opposite the booking office at Cranbrook station, the line would run along the centre of the new approach road, then on the western side of the highway to Goddards Green. From here it would gradually deviate to the centre of the road, continuing to the 'Carriers Yard' where a depot was proposed. The trams would meet all trains and run intermediately for goods. The gradients were rather severe, ranging from 1 in 19 to an average of 1 in 25. Electric traction was deemed too expensive, whereas it was reckoned that the cost of laying the rails, along with two 'steam traction engines' and two carriages would amount to £12,700. Since the average tonnage of goods coming into Cranbrook had been 1,400 tons per week, it was concluded that revenue on the tramway would amount to £3,500 for goods traffic per annum. With around eighty passengers using the station daily, they estimated receipts of £364 a year by charging an average of sixty tram passengers 4d from the station to the town. The residents who filled the hall that evening were not impressed by this idea and Dr. Thomas Joyce who practised in Cranbrook proposed the following motion which was easily carried:

'That this meeting representing the inhabitants of Cranbrook, view with extreme disfavour the construction of a steam tramway down the centre of the town, but consider a light line of railway between Hartley and the town very desirable.'

The well-heeled of Cranbrook were able to be driven to Cranbrook station in their own 'fly' or trap, whilst the less well-off had to make do with the horse-drawn conveyances which were put on by private operators to run almost two miles each way. Matters were little better at Hawkhurst since the station at Gills Green was over a mile away from the crossroads in the centre of the village. Messrs. Clout and Drake each operated vans for passengers and goods, but on busy days these often filled up quickly with little alternative than to wait for a return visit of the van or walk. Goudhurst, perched upon a hilltop, was also a mile away from the station which nestled in the valley at the bottom of a steep and winding road. Only Horsmonden could boast a station within the village, yet even this would not have been the case had the SER abided by the C & PWR's original chosen route.

Further work on improving the facilities did, however, continue. A steam roller was engaged in putting down the loose gravel on the road up to Hawkhurst station; the *Post* welcoming this deed by claiming that it was: 'now much more suitable for vehicular traffic which at one time had great difficulty in getting in and out'. Then, at the end of September, the Postmaster General issued a notice saying that telegrams could henceforth be dealt with at Hawkhurst station, whilst postal services would be improved now that it was no longer necessary to use Etchingham station. The most sought-after benefit, though, was a 'cheap' express to London, for five shillings return, to take people to London by 10.30am.

Having seen the Hawkhurst branch completed, the inhabitants of Tenterden took the opportunity of sending a memorial to the SER, urging them to consider a new line which would give them railway communication with London and the coast. The SER approached Seaton, who readily agreed to survey the land and come up with proposals. On 17th October he was in a position to present them with schemes which included extending the railway from either Cranbrook or Hawkhurst:

'Gentlemen,
Agreeable to your instructions, I have pleasure in laying before you three schemes for affording Tenterden and the surrounding villages Railway accommodation.

Scheme 1 is a continuation of the C&PWR from Hawkhurst to Appledore station on the Rye & Hastings branch. This line passes near to the villages of Benenden, Newenden, Sandhurst and Rolvenden and within about 1½ miles to the south of Tenterden and forms a junction with the Rye & Hastings branch at Appledore and so forming a connection with the Lydd line. The length of the line is 14½ miles. For the first three miles the works are somewhat heavy as a deep ravine has to be crossed, the gradients being 1 in 80 and 1 in 100. The other 11½ miles is practically a surface one and few roads of any importance have to be crossed.

I estimate the works at	£75,000
Permanent Way	£18,850
Land	£14,000
Obtaining Act	£7,000
Total	£114,850

The works are estimated for a single line, but the land is taken for a double line. The principal landowners are Viscount Cranbrook; Mrs. Gow Steuart; Mr. Kemsley; Mr. Pomfret MP; and Miss Brokett.

I propose to place the stations at Furnace Mill, Henden Bridge for Rolvenden, Tenterden, Redhill Bridge and the enlargement of Appledore station. On January 16th 1892 a public meeting took place at Rolvenden when Mr. Pomfret MP moved a resolution in favour of this scheme which was passed and many of the landowners were present. I also understand that most of the owners have been written to and are anxious for the construction of the line and have promised to sell their lands at agricultural prices.

The second scheme is from Headcorn to Appledore. This line has already been authorized by Parliament and forms part of the Loose Valley Railway. After leaving Headcorn, the line takes a southerly direction passing through Lashenden, Biddenden to Tenterden. Near Redhill Bridge the line turns westwards and then takes the same course as the first scheme. The length from Headcorn to Appledore is 13 miles 5 furlongs. The gradients on the deposited plans are steep, but I have altered them so that no gradient is worse than 1 in 100. The line for the first 5 miles is almost on the surface, but after this, through Tenterden, the line is very heavy, necessitating the constructing of 2 tunnels, one of 330 yards and the other of 220 yards, and also a short viaduct. A great deal of this work could be saved if the line was diverted to a yellow centre line on a map]. The saving would be some £30,000. The remaining portion is almost on the surface. The stations would be at Biddenden, Tenterden, Reading Street, and Appledore station enlarged.

I understand that all the landowners along the route are in favour of the line and would sell the land for agricultural value – in some cases as low as £30 per acre. I estimate the line, including permanent way and land for a double line, excavations and underbridges for a single line, with tunnels and overbridges being estimated for a double line at £154,000. I also estimate that the cost of the line from Headcorn to Tenterden would be £72,000. The distance from London to Appledore is 59 miles 1 furlong by this route. This would be an alternative route to Hastings, over the Hastings & Rye branch and although the distance is 12 miles longer, yet the gradients are very much better.

The third scheme commences with a junction with the C & PWR at Cranbrook station and following very nearly the original centre line of that railway, crossing the main Cranbrook and Tenterden road near the Brewery, passes close to Sissinghurst, taking a westerly direction to the south of Biddenden and so to Tenterden, Reading Street to Appledore where a junction is formed with the SER. Stations would be placed at Cranbrook Town, Sissinghurst, Biddenden, Tenterden and Reading Street.

This route appears to be an easy one to construct, at the commencement there would be a short tunnel bridge under the Hartley Road. There would be a short cutting of the greatest depth of 30 feet at 2 miles and for the next 5 miles the line is nearly on the surface. At Tenterden there is a long cutting, but from 11 miles to the end of the line, is again almost a surface one.

The length from Cranbrook to Appledore is 16½ miles and London – Appledore 61 miles. The steepest gradient is at the commencement and is 1 in 80, all the other gradients are very flat. I estimate the overall cost at £126,000 and land for a double line at £14,000, making a total of £140,000.

I have the honour to be, gentlemen, your obedient servant,
E. P. Seaton'

At this time the directors were evidently uninspired by the thought of extending the Hawkhurst branch, or affording Tenterden railway facilities. Undoubtedly the costs of extending or building a new line must have been weighed carefully against projected income. It is also probable that they were mindful of the impending Light Railways Act which could be used at a later date to serve Tenterden and provide a much cheaper line. More likely, they wished to wait a while longer to see how traffic would develop on the Hawkhurst branch.

From what may be gleaned from contemporary records, it appears that the business on the branch continued at a brisk pace. George Drake of Hawkhurst, who advertised himself as 'SER Carrier', had commenced running his horse-drawn vans five times a day from 4th September between the town and the station. His main competitor, Charlie Clout, left the moor, about a mile to the south of Hawkhurst, at 7.45am to meet the first up and down trains, carrying passengers, parcels and light goods. Mr. T. Miles operated a van from Cranbrook to Hartley for all up trains and remained at the station for fifty minutes to meet the down service. No doubt the staff invited him in for a cup of tea on many occasions.

With the railway it was possible to convey with relative ease all manner of merchandise into the area and heavy loads no longer had to be laboriously carried in portions by carts over long distances. A consignment comprising two tons of marble in six wooden cases, ordered by Mr. Edwards, a local builder, arrived at Hawkhurst with the morning goods train on 29th January 1894. Requiring careful handling onto carts, it unfortunately brought the first known accident since the opening of the line, with a young man named James being injured. The railway truck had been shunted into a siding where each case was to be unloaded, but, on moving the first, the remainder toppled, trapping the hapless workman. It took several men to shift the load, but, happily, their colleague escaped with only broken ribs. The cause of the accident was attributed to the wagon not being level due to some subsidence in the new siding.

Perhaps it was as a result of this accident that during the spring the SER ordered a 10 ton travelling crane specifically for use on the new branch. Costing £370, the firm of T. Smith & Co. of Rodley, near Leeds, provided the staff with this useful piece of equipment. Even so, it eventually proved inadequate due to the volume of goods traffic that was being handled.

In spite of the line being open for business throughout, there was still much work to be completed. According to a Special Traffic Notice dated the week ending 7th July 1894, remedial track repairs were being undertaken between Pattenden and Cranbrook. This involved lifting and slewing the 'road' between mileposts 7¾ and 8¼, whilst, a little further south, ballasting and draining works were in hand as far as milepost 9¾. Drivers were warned to keep a good look-out for any hand signals which might be exhibited. The same notice reveals that the Tank House, adjacent to the signal box at Hawkhurst, was under construction at this time. Both 'Engine Shed and Coke Stage Roads' are reported as being closed while this was under way. A plentiful supply for the water tank was found near Badger's Oak tunnel where a pump and housing shed was erected. Drivers were ordered to loudly sound their whistles on approaching milepost 10 to warn these workmen.

All this work was carried out by Firbank's men who were to be found at Horsmonden, Pattenden and Gills Green on associated projects, such as making up the roads where the railway was crossed. They were also required to be on hand to attend to minor slippages in the formation and deflections in the track as the railway settled. A rock fall in Horsmonden cutting during June 1894 needed swift attention whilst drivers were notified to: 'keep a sharp look-out and be prepared to stop by Hand Signal if necessary'. During this same period the contractor's engines and his ballast trucks were still working between Paddock Wood and Hawkhurst each day, in between the normal service trains operated by the SER.

The gradual increase in traffic necessitated the provision of much greater siding accommodation at Horsmonden. Edward Seaton supplied plans which included a 400 yard-long loop adjacent to the running line through the station. A 625 yard-long siding connected into this on the down side in the Paddock Wood direction. However, a similar siding on the up side, together with a '25ft-wide metalled roadway' running alongside, was not pursued. Accordingly, on 23rd July 1894, the following letter from Charles Sheath was despatched to the Board of Trade:

> Secretary's Office
> Cranbrook & Paddock Wood Railway
> London Bridge Station
>
> 'Sir,
> I am directed to forward you the enclosed plan shewing the alterations which have been carried out at our Horsmonden station, and shall be glad to hear that the Board of Trade sanction the loop line being opened for traffic.
>
> If any information is required, our Engineer, Mr. Seaton, whose address is Abbey Buildings, Princes Street, Westminster, will be glad to attend at the Board of Trade after receiving a notice to that effect.'

Three weeks later, on Monday, 13th August, Major General C. S. Hutchinson, R. E. inspected the works and filed his report which revealed the following information:

> 'I have inspected the new connection of a loop siding with the Cranbrook & Paddock Wood (Single Line) Railway at Horsmonden station.
>
> These connections are worked from two dwarf frames, one (from which an old connection is also worked) containing two levers, and the other one, both worked by an Annett's key in the signal cabin, which contains 6 levers all in use.
>
> The arrangement being satisfactory, I can recommend the Board of Trade to sanction the use of these new connections.'

Earlier in the year Holman Stephens had written to his father, saying that 120 men remained working on the line. He mentioned that he was 'looking about' for any work that might be offered, adding:

> 'I shall know soon if the Tenterden line is going on or not, and if not shall try for something else, but do not want to risk the loss of 4 years work which now, in the present state of trade, is hard to get'.

However, in the middle of April, Stephens had to tell his parents that Edward Seaton's scheme for a Cranbrook to Tenterden line had just been rejected by the SER. By now Stephens' relationship with Seaton had soured even further and in a resentful frame of mind he complained bitterly to his father:

> 'It is the greatest rubbish Mr. Seaton talking about me wasting my time as there is work going on which requires much constant supervision, only last Sunday I was on the work all day and had to walk nearly eight miles, - all he wants to do is get off paying me'.

He continued:

> 'The best thing I can see is to stay on till I can get something else, I don't want to cut myself adrift all together. He [Seaton] gives up the line in about 15 weeks and I should very much like to see it finish. I hear privately that the company may apply for powers to extend the line on from Hawkhurst, if so there would be at least a winter's work preparing the plans etc.'.

A couple of weeks later a further letter read:

> 'My dear Dah,
> Many thanks for your kind letter, also for causing a ticket for the R. A. to be sent to Sir Myles Fenton. I saw Mr. Seaton on Saturday and had a talk with him. I shall see him in a day or so and will come up to have a chat with you at an early date. When you come through here, as I hope you will in a day or so, you will be able to judge for yourself as to the respective capacities for architecture of Mr. Seaton and Myself. There are 13 houses I designed here and 3 he did, you can see which in your opinion look best.
> Love to Mam and yourself, yours H.'

Sir Myles Fenton, general manager of the SER, had paid a visit to the Hawkhurst branch during early May

BALDWIN'S EXCURSION

FROM

Hawkhurst and Cranbrook

TO

Canterbury, Ramsgate, and Margate,

ON MONDAY, 18TH SEPT,

BY TRAIN LEAVING		RETURN TICKETS.
HAWKHURST	8.20	3/-
CRANBROOK	8.25	
GOUDHURST	8.33	
HORSMONDEN ...	8.39	
PADDOCK WOOD ...	9. 0	2/6

Returning at Night by Special Train. Children half-price.

Passengers may break the journey at Canterbury, to visit the world-renowned Cathedral, Dane John, and some of the most historic churches, proceeding to Ramsgate or Margate by later trains.

The Special Train will return from Margate at 7.10, Ramsgate 7.25, and Canterbury 7.55 p.m.

The Tickets will be available to return the following day by ordinary trains, on payment of 1/6 excess fare

Tickets may be had at the Railway Stations previous to the Excursion, or of Mr A. K. Baldwin, Tunbridge Wells.

Thomas Miles & Son,

Proprietors of the

GEORGE HOTEL, CRANBROOK.

COMMERCIAL & POSTING HOUSE.

GOOD BEDS AND LOCK-UP COACH-HOUSES

Wines and Spirits of the best description.

Bottled Ales and Stout;

PARCELS FORWARDED TO ALL PARTS.

OMNIBUSES,

On and after September 4th, and until further notice, will leave the George Hotel, for Staplehurst Station as follows:—8.40 a.m to meet the 9.52 down train, 9.53 up train, 10 11 up train, returning off these trains.—4.0 p.m to meet the 5.1 down train and 5.7 up train, returning off these trains.

OMNIBUSES

Will also leave the George Hotel for CRANBROOK STATION, commencing September 4th, and until further notice, as under:—

Week-days.

8.0 a.m to meet 8.25 up, returning off 9.16 down
9.10 „ 9 37 (Express) „ 10.34 „
11.30 „ 11.57 up, returning off 12.59 „
1.0 p.m „ 1.24 „ „ 2.44 „
5.0 „ 5.25 „ (Express) 6.19 „
6.45 „ 7.12 „ returning off 8.19 „

Sundays.

8.0 a.m to meet 8.27 up, returning off 9.31 down
7.0 p.m „ 7.22 „ 8.27 „

FARE 6d.

at which he promised Stephens he would raise the matter of extending the line to Appledore at the next board meeting. Stephens also approached Charles Sheath, who was destined a few years later to become the SER's secretary, as well as one of the directors, Lord Medway, in the hope of being employed by the SER on a permanent basis. Fenton promised Stephens that he would ask Francis Brady, their chief civil engineer but, sadly, nothing came of it. Eventually, Stephens returned home to live with his parents, probably through financial necessity, whilst some time was spent at Seaton's London office. However, during 1895 he was back in Cranbrook, this time working for the local Water Company. Finally, a dispute over his claim for payment in settlement for work done on the Hawkhurst branch sadly led him to make a rather spiteful suggestion in a letter to his father which reads:

> 'I can see Mr. Seaton's hand in this; it is a rather nasty piece of work and if you see Mr. McClaren you might tell him, as he is a director of the Met. and Seaton is working for them.'

Thus Stephens' association with the C&PWR came to a bitter and unhappy end. In many ways it was a great pity that it should have culminated in this fashion, since Stephens was a brilliant man in many respects and eventually went on to prove himself. Whilst his connection with the Hawkhurst Branch might have been brought to a peremptorious conclusion by the SER, it was not the end of his participation in the creation of railways in the South East, for very soon he was working on the Rye & Camber Tramway.

With the summer of 1894 there came the first opportunity for the inhabitants of Hawkhurst and Cranbrook to make good use of Baldwin's popular excursions. Even though Goudhurst had had a station for two years, special excursions had not been arranged until then, so the villagers there were equally pleased at being able to take advantage of the novelty. On this first occasion the Goudhurst choirboys were treated to a day out at Hastings, travelling by way of Tonbridge Junction and Tunbridge Wells. There must have been considerable excitement that morning as they assembled on the platform, awaiting the arrival of the train which came steaming around the bend from Cranbrook. Almost none had ever set foot inside a railway compartment before, so the journey was understandably as great an experience as their first glimpse of the sea.

Another excursion involved a party of workers from Hawkhurst who visited Wembley Palace for an event which went on so late that they had to return by way of Etchingham on the last train from London. Similarly, 'Mr. Baker's Excursion' which ran from Dartford to Hastings by way of Strood, Maidstone and Tunbridge Wells, picked up excited travellers all along the way, conveying 700 adults and children to the seaside. Excursionists from Hawkhurst branch stations were taken to Paddock Wood on the ordinary 7.50am service train, whilst special arrangement was made for their collection in the evening. This involved an engine leaving Hawkhurst at 8.30pm to take the branch stock to Paddock Wood to await their arrival. A homeward journey calling at all stations brought them back, after which the locomotive came off and returned light to Tonbridge. This arrangement was evidently standard procedure for at the close of the season the *Post* announced:

> 'The Last Excursion:
> On Wednesday, 10th October Special fast excursions will run to Tunbridge Wells, Hastings and Eastbourne, leaving Hawkhurst at 7.50am and returning by special train from Paddock Wood. By this time hop-picking will be over and no doubt a great many families will avail themselves of this last trip to the seaside before the long winter nights set in.'

Whereas it is probably true to say that most people were satisfied with the railway communication provided by the SER, there remained a hope that the line might yet be extended. Cranbrook residents once again petitioned for an extension into the town during the late summer of 1894, whereas Tenterden set about obtaining an Act of Parliament for a railway. In spite of the inconvenience faced by people stepping onto the platform at Cranbrook station with yet a two-mile road journey to go, it obviously didn't deter that many, as reported in the *Post* during the 1895 season:

> 'CRANBROOK - Visitors: Cranbrook has never been so full of visitors as during this season. Apartments &c have been in full demand since the commencement of the season. The opening of the new railway has certainly been of much good to many people.'

The branch line was undoubtedly a great attraction, not only for the local people who were able to get out and about, especially with the aid of cheap fares, but also to the youngsters of the villages along the way. Perched upon stiles, or peering over the parapets of the bridges, they could frantically wave to the crews as the gleaming locomotives rolled by. Playing in the woods and meadows, a shrill whistle would cause them to race to the fence bordering the track where, moments later, the train came thumping past. Shouting and waving to its occupants, the sound from its resounding wheels grew fainter, while the engine's steady beat would often grow more earnest if a gradient made it work that much harder.

Such popular childhood pastimes were not always entirely innocent, whilst instances of children wandering onto railway lines and being killed or maimed was, and still is, fairly commonplace. Nowadays, any child found trespassing can expect to receive little more than a ticking-off, but such actions, especially where malicious acts were involved, were once dealt with far more harshly. Such an incident took place on 1st December 1895 when a couple of boys were brought before the Cranbrook magistrates. Ten year-old Eddie Ward and nine year-old Sammy Roberts were both orphans belonging to the Dr. Barnado's Home at Hawkhurst. Having absconded from their lessons, they wandered onto the railway at Gills Green and decided to play with the signals until they were spotted. Running off along the line, they continued as far as the daunting black gape of Badger's Oak tunnel. Probably fearful of venturing into its foreboding depths, they instead set about placing pebbles, pieces of stone and drainpipes left in the cess, and anything else they could find upon the rails. In the meantime the station staff had alerted the local constabulary who caught up with the young culprits. It transpired that both boys had managed to place obstructions on the rails for a distance of thirty feet, and when these were bagged-up they weighed half a hundredweight. For their misdemeanour, both lads were each given five strokes of the birch.

In February 1896 Edward Seaton received his final payment from the SER for his services as engineer of the C&PWR, while the business of tying-up all the loose ends also began. In due course an advert appeared in *The Engineer:*

> 'FOR SALE: On Paddock Wood Railway - Two 6-wheel locomotives. - apply J. T. Firbank, London Bridge.'

They apparently failed to find a purchaser since Firbank later used *Fox* on the Basingstoke-Alton contract in 1898, whilst *Wrexham* remained in his ownership until 1904. His 'pumping engine' at Goudhurst was, however, purchased by the SER for £100, whilst £40 was spent on 'certain sanitary improvements' in the station master's house and railway cottages at Horsmonden. Precisely what these arrangements comprised is not known, but by all accounts they were needed since the SER was obliged to pay five pounds compensation to a Mr. Harry Brabon of Goudhurst who had unwittingly drunk the contaminated water at the station well and subsequently contracted typhoid.

As the sites were gradually cleared of building materials the appearance of the railway improved. Already the embankments and cutting sides were being invaded by flora and grasses which helped heal the scars and blend the line into its surroundings. There was also an opportunity, too, for the station staff to create and tend their traditional platform flower beds which were once such a common and much-appreciated feature.

More substantial improvements during the autumn of 1896 came with cattle pens being installed in the goods yard at Goudhurst, whilst an extension to Churn Lane siding had to be made to cope with ever-rising demand.

The fledgling scheme to build a steam tramway from Cranbrook station to the town centre failed to make any progress, whereby it merely faded away. Horse-drawn omnibuses and vans continued to ply along the Hartley road and it was on one of these that a rather alarming incident took place in February 1896. A gentleman by the name of Rivers had travelled down the line on his way to Cranbrook on a fine spring morning. The weather was evidently pleasant enough to encourage him to travel upon the open top deck of the horse-drawn omnibus waiting in the approach road. While enjoying the fresh air and the expansive views across the countryside, he was suddenly hit by an overhanging branch from a tree, which managed to knock him completely off the vehicle. Remarkably, he suffered only a dislocated wrist which was soon attended and bandaged by a Miss Smart of Marden, a fellow passenger and member of the St. John Ambulance Association.

The Hawkhurst branch continued to prove a success, in spite of the early disinterest and scepticism of the SER. Cheap excursions became an established feature, especially during January and February when special trains were put on for the London pantomime season. By travelling on the 7.48am from Hawkhurst, London could be reached for 3s 6d (three shillings from Goudhurst and Horsmonden), with children under 12 half fare. A busy day spent in the noisy, bustling capital, followed by a pantomime at one of the many theatres or music halls must have made a truly unforgettable day's outing for lucky children. The special train didn't depart for home until midnight so there cannot have been many who didn't doze all the way home in the train which rattled and raced over the rooftops of London and out across the cold, quiet fields of Kent.

Such outings were normally the preserve of the middle classes, but occasionally the less fortunate were able to travel somewhere for at least one day in the year. Sunday school outings provided the one opportunity for poorer children to experience something of a holiday, even if it was only for one day. Attendances to the Sunday gatherings would always increase prior to the event, but charitable teachers did not judge and welcomed all who came along. A regular and popular event was the annual Goudhurst Church of England Temperance Society's excursion. The weather was especially kind in 1896 when, on 15th July, the long road leading down to Goudhurst station was crowded with children, marching along in orderly rows on this beautiful summer's morning. The sky was blue, the sun warm, while the hedgerows and wayside banks were full of air-swept scent from the flowers and grasses which nodded in the breeze. The pungence of oil and creosote from the railway must have excited them as they filed over the level crossing before gathering upon the platform. When the signalman in his cabin emerged to shut the gates across the road before setting his signals, the anticipation must have been unbearable as ears strained for the tell-tale sounds of their train. Then, a whistle would be heard as their excursion, the 8.05am train, came steaming around the bend from the direction of Cranbrook. The ride to Horsmonden, across the cultivated fields and through hop gardens, must have been a wonder as they watched their village home, straddling its glorious hillside setting, slowly disappear from view. Leaving Horsmonden, they experienced the unique thrill of a railway tunnel before joining the main line to 'pause briefly at the big station of Paddock Wood'. Onward they rode, to Tonbridge Junction, where there were many steam locomotives at the shed and in the sidings, while fast expresses came pacing through at speed on their way with the continental services to Folkestone and Dover. Travelling down the Hastings branch, they must have thought they were miles from home until, after 'a very comfortable ride down', everyone spilled out onto the platforms at this most popular of Victorian seaside resorts. The marvel of the sea and shore, it was later reported, particularly excited many of the children who had never seen it before, let alone experienced the joys of wavelets running in to wash over their toes. The tide was out, so there was plenty of sand for building castles and playing games of ball. Treated to a 'quite splendid tea', followed by a tour around the pier, where the numerous attractions delighted them, they finally left Hastings station by the 7.15pm train. After 'a lively journey home' they were all thoroughly weary by the time Goudhurst was reached. One of the children subsequently wrote: 'We had a long way to walk home from the station and if everyone was as tired as myself, then they were glad to get home to rest'.

The circuitous route to Hastings gave rise to suggestions that the Hawkhurst branch should be extended to Etchingham, or some such convenient point. Furthermore, as had been proposed by the town clerk of Hastings during that year, such a line would improve communication between Hastings and Maidstone, Chatham, etc. A similar scheme in 1898 envisaged a line running from Hastings, through Doleham, Brede Bridge, Mill Corner, Bodiam Mill, Conghurst and Hawkhurst, where a station would be nearer than the terminus at Gills Green. The SER board declined any involvement since both schemes were 'unlikely to happen'. However, it appears there was yet again renewed interest at that time in extending the Hawkhurst branch to Tenterden. On 19th July 1897 the SER met the newly-formed Tenterden Railway Company where five proposals were made. These included the SER promoting the Parliamentary bill to authorize construction of a line from Cranbrook to Tenterden and Appledore, as envisaged by Edward Seaton, and that the railway should pass as near as practicable to Tenterden. It was suggested this should be somewhere between Pick Hill and Summer Hill on the Wittersham road. By December, the SER company seal had already been affixed to an agreement with the Tenterden company, while petitions were arriving at London Bridge for stations to be built at Rolvenden and Reading Street, the latter a hamlet just to the west of Appledore.

Perhaps engendered by the Light Railways Act, the closing years of the nineteenth century appear to have given rise to a minor outbreak of 'railway mania'.

The earliest-known view of Cranbrook station, probably taken around 1905, and featuring the McKenzie & Holland signals, most prominently the up home, as well as the ringed-arm controlling the loop siding. *Lens of Sutton*

Certainly the Weald, especially in the Tenterden district, was gripped by much speculation and debate as to where lines ought to be laid and who should construct them. However, not everyone was quite so convinced that building more railways was desirable. The Victorian traveller who toured the district preparing a discourse for Black's 1904 *Guide to Kent* observed:

> 'A branch is in view by Cranbrook to Tenterden (9 miles by road) that would open up a now out-of-the-way district, which active tourists might prefer to keep as a preserve of quiet, lovely nooks. Another line is talked of to join Tenterden to Ashford.'

It would be correct, nonetheless, to say that a majority were in favour of seeing a railway brought to Tenterden whereby, ostensibly, the SER began taking serious steps towards this goal. In February 1898, two quite individual bills were put forward. The C&PWR, which still existed as a separate company, promoted the Appledore extension, while the SER, rather astoundingly, applied to convert the Hawkhurst branch to double track. Such a notion is a little difficult to comprehend, not only coming so soon after the completion of the line, but in view of the obvious requirement to rebuild tunnels and bridges all along the route. Could the South Eastern have genuinely been seriously intending to embark upon such a major scheme, or was it merely a ruse to fend off the independent competition which, in the form of the Rother Valley (Light) Railway, was about to build a line from Robertsbridge to Tenterden?

Opposition to the C&PWR's extension bill came from the Misses Appach of Swattenden, whose land to the south-east of Cranbrook would have been bisected by the new line. A petition against the C&PWR was laid before the SER board on 9th March, at the same time that the solicitor reported that the bill for doubling the Cranbrook line was expected to receive the Royal Assent at the end of the month.

Whilst work is understood to have begun on the Rother Valley Railway that spring, the SER lost all interest in pursuing this last grand fling with developing or extending the Hawkhurst branch any further. On a wider scale the warring SER and LC&DR were moving rapidly towards a working union, whilst the emergent SE&CR committee clearly had no desire to build such a line. There was no need to reach Appledore, or even Dungeness, especially since Watkin had finally retired as chairman in 1894. It was only natural that resources for continental traffic would henceforth be concentrated on Folkestone and Dover.

At the end of July 1898, the C&PWR bill was withdrawn and the proposals abandoned, but the directors found it difficult to extricate themselves from the aborted scheme. Subsequently, the chairman of the

C&PWR, Alfred Gathorne-Hardy, wrote to Albert Dixon of the Tenterden Railway Company with a palliative:

> 'My dear Sir,
> As you are aware, we had intended to give your district suitable railway accommodation by means of an extension of the Cranbrook line, but when it became obvious that this was practically impossible, I at once suggested that your powers should be preserved in order that accommodation should be secured to you. We are now prepared to undertake to make the Headcorn and Tenterden line with such variation as is necessary to make it a part of a first rate through line when it is completed.'

In spite of this offer, which also spoke vaguely of the SER coming up with a working agreement if they preferred an independent line, there seems little else to suggest there existed any serious proposals to embark on enlarging the South Eastern system. Indeed, it is plainly evident from the meetings between the SER directors and their shareholders, that there was never any genuine intention to build a branch from Headcorn to Tenterden. Watkin's 'well-known ingenuity', which he cunningly used to deter deputations, had always been brought into play under his stewardship, whilst any hope of a Tenterden branch had quite honestly expired with the failure of the Loose Valley Railway scheme.

No doubt all this activity was probably watched on the sidelines with a degree of interest and detached amusement by the railway staff employed on the Hawkhurst branch. It must surely have cropped up in conversations between the signalmen, booking clerks and station masters who, over a cup of tea, might have mused whether their relatively quiet backwater might one day become a busy through route. Business on the branch remained buoyant and was still increasing, for in May 1898 the SER introduced two extra mid-morning trains. One left Paddock Wood at 10.40am, while the other left Hawkhurst at 10.54am, passing each other at Goudhurst. At that time there were eleven trains each way with four on Sundays. The extra trains, as well as a revision of the timetable, probably came about as a result of the (unspecified) improvement to the five electric train tablet instruments, costing £15 each, which was authorized in April.

The summer season was again a busy time for the branch and there were numerous attractions on offer which easily tempted the traders, farmers and ordinary locals to take a day ticket for London. Baldwin's cheap excursions enabled them to purchase return fares at 3s 0d for one day, 4s 0d for two days, or 5s 0d for three days 'in town'. The Dairy Show at the Agricultural Hall undoubtedly attracted many to make a trip, while others flocked to the Kennel Club's Dog Show at the Crystal Palace, with crowds swarming to an exciting 'Grand Naval Display' on Trafalgar Day at Earls Court.

During the winter of 1898-99, the talk in the village shops once again included the possibility of new railways being built in the area. *The London Gazette* spoke of a new line intended to run from Cranbrook, through Tenterden and on to Ashford. The engineer behind this latest proposal was none other than Holman Stephens whose scheme, estimated at £120,925, was making use of the Light Railways Act of 1896. Almost immediately, opposition to the Tenterden-Ashford portion came swiftly from the SER because it competed with the Tenterden Railway Company's Headcorn-Tenterden line which the South Eastern revealed would be worked 'in the same manner as the C&PWR's Hawkhurst branch'. Stephens, therefore, had little alternative but to drop the Ashford section 'at the instance of the SER' and was grudgingly obliged to limit his grand scheme to the 'Cranbrook and Tenterden'. The press, however, gave notice that: 'the Rother Valley Railway and Headcorn & Tenterden Railway shall be completed within the next two to three years', but went on to quantifiy this statement by adding: 'Mr. Stephens' lines will connect up with the SER system at Cranbrook, Tenterden and Robertsbridge'.

Any progress on the anticipated SER Tenterden branch from its main line at Headcorn was certainly difficult to detect. Then, surprisingly, in June 1899, the SER's chief engineer, Mr. Peter Tempest, unexpectedly received instructions to confer with Edward Seaton concerning the construction of the branch, and prior to submitting his plans and estimates. Nevertheless, interest suddenly and rapidly waned, followed by a tactical withdrawal from any obligations. Finally, it was left to Stephens to serve Tenterden with an extension from Rolvenden on the RVR. This eventually managed to reach Headcorn in 1905, whereupon it became known as the Kent and East Sussex Light Railway. As for the Cranbrook & Tenterden, its tale of fruitless endeavour belongs with the history of the Rother Valley Railway, and its association with the Hawkhurst branch ends here.

CHAPTER FIVE

PROSPEROUS TIMES

COME 1900 the nominally independent Paddock Wood & Cranbrook Co. was finally absorbed by the South Eastern Railway Company which itself remained a separate legal entity until the railway grouping of 1923. The absorption made little difference to the branch where there were no tangible signs of any change as the line had always been worked as part of the SER system. However, the Managing Committee, set up under the general title of the South Eastern & Chatham Railway, anticipated bringing about improvements to the SER and LC&DR systems. It is evident, too, that the public expected to witness something better, although many seemed to be of the opinion that their union would be for the worse. Across the county there followed complaints that with competition removed, all incentives to serve those in trade had disappeared. Hawkhurst was no exception as revealed by a letter in the *Post*:

> 'HAWKHURST: The Railway Companies amalgamation:
> - No one knows when goods will be delivered:
> Dear Sir,
> Having had several reasons during the last six months to woefully complain of the dreadful delay in the delivery of goods, (more especially perishable articles) both here and in London, I would ask if a letter in your valuable local paper would be likely to do anything to arouse the trading part of our district to move in the matter and publicly show how the amalgamation of the two lines have benefited the public. Showing what I complain of, I have had ice down during the hot weather take 15, 16 and 17 hours from Bricklayers Arms to Hawkhurst, and last week I sent some carcasses of mutton for sale in the London Market, put on the SE&C Railway at Hawkhurst Station on Wednesday afternoon before 6 o'clock and were delivered at the Central Meat Market, London, on the following Friday, making a day and a half doing under 50 miles.
> Yours faithfully,
> H. Goldfinch,
> The Moor, Hawkhurst.'

Such malcontent wasn't solely restricted to tradesmen and goods traffic. It may also have been the case that the railways were victims of their own success and enterprise. The SE&CR was undoubtedly a marked improvement on the state of affairs which had existed during the nineteenth century when railway passengers were often treated quite appallingly. The Managing Committee soon set about the tasks before it with sleeves rolled up, so that by the end of the Edwardian era the SE&CR was one of the smartest and best-run railways. Nevertheless, the effects of improvements were frequently slow to filter through, especially in the backwaters which had to make do with what had been cast-off from elsewhere. This was especially noticeable in the matter of rolling stock and locomotives, although in fairness the latter were always impeccably maintained by the cleaners and engine crews who took great pride in their job.

The handsome, two-road engine shed at Hawkhurst was used for stabling the regular branch locomotive overnight. While most people were still in their beds, the fireman would already be preparing his engine for the day's business. This involved either 'lighting-up' or stoking the small fire left in the back of the grate overnight. The boiler and tender would have been filled at the end of the previous day's turn, while coal would be readily stacked for use.

Having shunted the engine out of the shed siding and onto the stock left in the platform overnight, there was usually time for a brew-up and a railway breakfast, cooked on the shovel held in the firebox. On frosty mornings the warmth of the cab was most welcome, while from above the buffer stops at Hawkhurst a pale sun drearily peered over the horizon. The sound of horses' hooves upon the gravelled approach road heralded the arrival of passengers who would rub their stiff hands and momentarily warm themselves by the glowing coals in the booking hall grate. Behind his little window, the clerk would busy himself exchanging crisp card tickets for the cold coins dropped by numb fingers onto the wooden, cupped shelf. Meanwhile, the guard might well be checking the parcels and consignment dockets with the station master. Across the track, the signalman kept an eye on the clock from within his warm cabin as he took pride in burnishing every piece of brass on the instruments perched upon the shelf above his lever frame. Shortly before departure time, the Hawkhurst signalman would use his Tyer's No.6 electric train tablet instrument to contact his colleague in Cranbrook cabin. Having gained permission for the train to enter the section between stations, he would withdraw the tablet from the machine, place it in the leather pouch and hand it to the engine driver. As the arm of the starting signal at the end of the platform obediently dropped into the 'off' position, the last person to arrive would run panting and hurrying into a compartment just as the guard blew his whistle. Emitting great white plumes of condensing steam into the cold, crisp air, the engine would coax the line of elderly six-wheelers into motion as the train slowly pulled away from the Wealden terminus and headed off around the bend towards Cranbrook.

During the early years, the first departure was scheduled for twenty past eight, but this was later altered to leave thirty-five minutes earlier. Some through running to Tonbridge was eventually introduced by the SE&CR which proved far more convenient since Hawkhurst branch trains could also connect with services on the Hastings line. Throughout most of the day, however, the line was operated purely as a branch from Paddock Wood with one train running up and down. Goods trains were often shunted into the yards at

A. J. Sims' grocery stores and Post Office at Gills Green. The steps leading up to Hawkhurst station were at the point where the cart stands in the road.

Horsmonden or Goudhurst while the local service passed through. Goudhurst was also used as a passing place for passenger trains, generally during the time which, nowadays, is described as the evening peak. The working timetables during the early 1900s show the presence of three trains there on a regular basis at certain periods in the day, since the 'up' goods was also in the yard waiting to follow behind on its way to Paddock Wood.

A revision of the old SER working brought later evening trains to Hawkhurst, an undoubted bonus for the residents of the High Weald. The regular branch engine came off duty around six thirty, whilst two further arrivals brought people home. The last train out left shortly before 10pm, whereupon it continued through to Tonbridge. Since there were so many minor revisions throughout its life, the selection of timetable examples can only illustrate a broad picture.

At the opening of the line in 1893, the well-to-do who required an annual season ticket for London would have to pay £42 if they used Goudhurst station. Weekly, fortnightly and various monthly rates were also advertised, but these were only available to first and second class passengers. An office or banking clerk who, for instance, travelled second class from Horsmonden, would have to find £30 from an annual salary, but, if this was too much to pay in one lump sum, a weekly ticket costing two guineas (£2 2s 0d) was obtainable. All these rates were suffixed as being 'Exclusive of Government Duty'.

It was only possible for the Hawkhurst branch to be worked in such a manner by providing housing for the locomotive crews at the terminus station. Early starts and late finishes made it necessary for railwaymen to live relatively close to the sheds. Accordingly, it was not uncommon for their families to move into new rented accommodation, often provided by the railway company, whenever it became necessary to transfer to another depot. However, it is difficult imagining any spouse complaining of the prospect of living at so delightful a Kentish village as Hawkhurst, yet they probably mourned the loss of having so many neighbours if they'd moved from much larger towns. A row of six terraced cottages was erected at Hawkhurst adjacent to Mill Road bridge. They were very substantial and cosy, with small gardens at the rear for growing vegetables and perhaps keeping a few chickens, whilst at the bottom of the plot loomed the rear wall of the engine shed. A footpath from the rear of these cottages led across rough ground, giving access to both engine shed and station for the men, whilst a fork continued eastwards, past the station master's house to the main road at Gills Green. Here the local stores enabled provisions to be purchased without a mile-long traipse along Station Road to the shops in The Colonnade.

Unlike the other three stations, for some reason there was no station master's accommodation provided at Hawkhurst. Initially, a rented dwelling in the village was made available, until such time as the SE&CR began constructing houses where required. The station master at Hawkhurst was eventually fortunate in having a large detached house, set in its own grounds and just to the south of the track. Given that its style is virtually identical to those erected about 1909 at other locations, such as Elham and Bishopsbourne, it seems probable that it, too, appeared in the Edwardian era. As for the very distinctive three-storey houses at the other stations, these were, of course, built at the same time as the railway. Those at Cranbrook and Goudhurst were adjacent to the station offices on the platform, whilst at Horsmonden it was decided, for some undiscovered reason, to situate it next to the approach road.

With Goudhurst, Cranbrook and Hawkhurst stations being quite far from the villages and towns they served, it isn't surprising that a sense of community built up around these railway hamlets. Like beads on a necklace, the railway strung them all together. In spite of the long hours worked by the men, there was the sense of satisfaction at a good day's job well done. Uncoupling from the stock left in the platform overnight at Hawkhurst, a blackened, weary crew would stable their engine, their thoughts dwelling on the hot dinner in the oven and a warm hearthside only a few minutes walk down the garden path.

It seems almost certain that throughout the early years James Stirling's '118' class were given virtually exclusive charge of the passenger trains. Furthermore, it is likely that No. 112, which hauled the inaugural train to Hope Mill in September 1892, continued working the branch for many years, since it was based locally at Tonbridge shed. According to Don Bradley, in his book *The Locomotives of the South Eastern Railway* (RCTS 1963), other '118's rostered for the Hawkhurst duties included Nos. 68, 108, 145, 191, 244, 247 and 252. Tonbridge locomotive depot (of which Hawkhurst was a sub-shed), also sent out these particular engines to work the relatively light duties on both the Maidstone and Westerham branches.

Advances in locomotive development were being made all the time as improvements to design and efficiency led to sleeker and more powerful types. Greater comfort for the engine crews was initiated by James Stirling and enhanced by H. S. Wainwright in later years. However, the '118's, which once enjoyed the reputation of being the mainstay of the SER's express passenger services, were gradually succeeded by Stirling's faster and more robust engines which took pride of place. Even so, a use was found for these displaced 'old-timers', although, with their roofless cabs, there can have been little pleasure in battling up Cranbrook bank in the teeth of a sou-westerly squall.

The war with the Boers in 1900 brought about a patriotic call to arms and the Weald was no exception with many local lads encouraged to leave their homes to fight in South Africa. During February, those who were selected as being suitably fit and able were cheered off from the villages and towns as they dutifully marched along the winding roads leading to Cranbrook station. Small children peered through wooden garden gates, waving their tiny hands at all the 'brave boys' who tramped down these lanes. It was reported that many people crowded excitedly onto the station platform at Cranbrook where the last tearful farewells were made before the train, bound for Southampton, finally steamed out amidst much cheering and waving. It is difficult to imagine what must have gone through the minds of these young men who set off that day to answer this particular call to protect British interests overseas. Undoubtedly, many of them had probably never ventured far from their villages, or been further than, say, Tonbridge, Ashford or Maidstone. It must have seemed quite an undreamt-of adventure, racing across the southern counties to a strange city where huge steamships, bound for a foreign land, crammed the many docks. The tales of daring escapades so glibly portrayed in the press, rarely matched the grim and bloody reality which awaited most of them. As with all wars, the enthusiasm for the campaign gradually seeped away as casualty lists rose among those who bore the brunt of the conflict. The 'Heroes of Ladysmith' eventually returned, many of them jaundiced, crippled and dispirited, while comfort was taken with the news which came through in mid-May on the railway telegraph that Mafeking had, at last, been relieved. One of the first casualties of the Boer War to be sent home badly wounded was William Bellingham of Horsmonden who had previously been employed by the SER as a porter at the village station.

During this unhappy time, a rather strange incident took place on the branch. The train involved was the 1.15 afternoon service from Hawkhurst which had just left Goudhurst. Driver Rofe, who was based at Tonbridge, suddenly spotted a man walking alongside the track ahead, at which he opened his whistle as a warning. However, the trespasser took no notice, by which time the train had almost caught up with him. In a trice the man hurled himself across the rails whereby the driver immediately applied his brakes, brought his train to a shuddering halt and braced himself for the worst. Miraculously, the injured jaywalker had suffered only a blow to his face, but the wound was bleeding very badly and he was almost unconscious. Luckily, on board the train, travelling as a passenger, was guard Richardson who had honours in first aid and, even more fortuitously, just happened to be carrying his kit. With the assistance of train guard Cripps, they quickly bound

June, 1901.

SERVICE OF TRAINS ON PADDOCK WOOD AND CRANBROOK LINE.—Single Line, Worked by Train Tablet System.

STATIONS.	A Goods.		a m	a m	a m	Goods. arr. F	Goods. dep.	p m	p m	p m	p m	Goods. arr. B	Goods. dep.	p m J	p m NS X	p m S X	p m				SUNDAYS. a m	a m	p m	p m	
DOWN TRAINS—Week Days.																									
Tonbridge ....dep.	..	6 30	..	8 35	9 38			..	..	4 0	..						..	..	..	..	7 15	..	6 10	..	..
Paddock Wood ....arr.	6 40	...		8 45	9 48	...	...	...	...	4 10	...	...	...	...			...	...	...	...	7 25	...	6 20	...	...
Paddock Wood ....dep	–	6 45	7 8	8 55	10 15	..	11 2	12 35	2 25	4 15	4 35		4 50	5 58	6 50	6 55	7 52	..	..	..	7 32	9 7	6 23	8 32	..
Horsmonden ....arr.	7 0	7 5	7 18	9 5	10 25	11 16	11 20	12 45	2 35	4 25	4 44	5 5	5 15	6 8	7 0	7 5	8 2	...	...	...	7 42	9 17	6 33	8 42	...
Goudhurst .... „	7 15	7 30	7 22	9 9	10 29	11 30	11 44	12 49	2 39	4 29	4 48	5 25	5 40	6 12	7 4	7 9	8 6	..	..	..	7 46	9 22	6 37	8 46	..
Cranbrook .... „	7 40	7 52	7 31	9 18	10 38	11 54	12 6	12 57	2 48	4 38	4 57	5 50	6 26	6 21	7 13	7 18	8 15	...	...	...	7 55	9 31	6 46	8 55	...
Hawkhurst .... „	8 0	..	7 36	9 23	10 43	12 12	..	1 3	2 53	4 43	5 2	6 32	..	6 26	7 18	7 23	8 20	..	..	..	8 0	9 36	6 51	9 0	..

STATIONS.	a m	a m	a m	D Goods.		a m	p m	Goods. G		p m	p m	Empty p m	NS	S	Goods. *		p m	Eng.		SUNDAYS. a m	a m	p m	p m	
UP TRAINS—Week Days.																								
Hawkhurst ....dep	7 46	8 15	9 32	..	9 0	11 50	1 15		1 30	3 0	5 18	6 0	6 50	6 55		7 35	9 0	..	..	8 12	9 42	7 5	9 15	..
Cranbrook .... „	7 51	8 20	9 37	9 5	9 19	11 55	1 20	1 35	2 15	3 5	5 23	J	6 55	7 0	7 40	7 50	9 5	...	...	8 17	9 47	7 10	9 20	...
Goudhurst .... „	7 59	8 28	9 45	9 28	9 51	12 3	1 28	2 25	3 0	3 13	5 31	6 13	7 3	7 8	7 57	9 15	9 13	..	..	8 25	9 55	7 18	9 28	..
Horsmonden .... „	8 5	8 34	9 51	...	...	12 9	1 34	3 8	3 28	3 19	5 37	...	7 9	7 14	9 21	9 25	9 19	...	...	8 30	10 1	7 24	9 34	...
Paddock Wood ....arr.	8 14	8 43	10 0	10 8	..	12 18	1 43	3 38	..	3 28	5 46	6 27	7 18	7 23	9 38	..	9 27	..	..	8 39	10 10	7 33	9 43	..
Paddock Wood ....dep.	8 15	...	...	...	...	...	...	...	...	...	...	...	...	...	...	9 45	...	9 46	...	...	10 11	...	9 44	...
Tonbridge ....arr.	8 25	..	..	..	..	..	..	..	..	..	..	..	..	..	10 0	..	..	9 56	..	..	10 21	.	9 54	..

A Goods and Passenger Engine. The Goods Shunts at Goudhurst for the 7.8 a.m. Down Passenger to pass and at Cranbrook for the 7.46 a.m. Up Train to pass. **B** The 4.50 p.m. Down Goods to shunt at Goudhurst for the 5.18 p.m. Up Passenger Train to pass and at Cranbrook for the 6.0 p.m. Up and 5.58 p.m. Down Trains to pass. **D** This Train will convey H.B. and C.K. Traffic also Cattle on Market Days. **D** Shunts at Cranbrook for 8.35 a.m. Down and at Goudhurst for 9.32 a.m. Up Passenger Trains to pass. **F** Shunts at Cranbrook for 11.50 a.m. Up Passenger Train to pass. **G** The 1.30 p.m. Up Goods Shunts at Goudhurst for the 2.25 p.m. Down Passenger Train and at Horsmonden for 3.0 p.m. Up Train to pass. **J** The 6.0 p.m. Up Empty Train shunts at Goudhurst for the 5.58 p.m. Down to pass. **NS** Not on Saturdays. **S** Saturdays only. **X** Passes the 6.50 p.m. Up Passenger Train at Goudhurst. ***** The 7.35 p.m. Up Goods Shunts at Goudhurst for 7.52 Down and 8.25 p.m. Up Trains to pass.

up the poor fellow's wounds and lifted him aboard where they restarted for Horsmonden and a doctor. Unfortunately, none could be found here or at Paddock Wood, so the brake van in which he was lying was hurriedly detached and coupled up to the rear of the Maidstone train where, eventually, he was attended at the West Kent Hospital. The injured man was later identified as George Golding, a labourer from Claygate, near Marden, but his reasons for such a desperate act remain a mystery.

Attempted and successful suicides upon the railway system were fairly commonplace, whilst unintentional accidents happened from time to time. Happily, the Hawkhurst branch wasn't connected with many tragedies, but minor incidents occurred as part of everyday life. For example, during April 1902 a Mr. Worthington of Ditchells, Hawkhurst, arrived at the station in his dog-cart to await the 4.46pm train. Unfortunately, just as the locomotive coasted in to the terminus, the safety valves lifted on the boiler and the sudden noise frightened the horse which reared and bolted. In its terror, the animal broke both shafts of the cart before careering away from the station and towards the flight of steps leading down to the main road. Here it fell at the fence, but mercifully was uninjured and after a while was calmed before being led away following the ordeal.

Another minor incident around this time involved a chap by the name of Golbey who, during December 1903, was engaged in unloading a coal truck in Horsmonden yard. Unknown to the engine crew, he was still on the wagon when the train was shunted, whereby he was thrown some ten feet to the ground, breaking his arm in the fall.

The Hawkhurst branch continued to prosper as further improvements and increased facilities were gradually brought into use. Churn Siding was proving to be a useful railhead for the local growers for in May 1899 an additional siding had been authorized for farmer Taylor of Pitlands.

Further down the line, permission was granted during November 1901 to the Anglo American Oil Company to erect a fuel depot on company land at Hawkhurst station. The SER received a yearly rent of £7 10s 0d for this site which was later leased to the British Petroleum Company in April 1913. It is, perhaps, ironic that this business served only to contribute to the eventual demise of the railways and the Hawkhurst branch in particular in favour of the mass-polluter.

Elsewhere on the line, the rise in goods traffic demanded the erection of a fixed 5 ton crane in the yard at Goudhurst. The general manager reported that the travelling crane was normally sent down when required, but that it was a far from satisfactory arrangement. Accordingly, a cheque for £154 10s 0d was drawn for Messrs. Jessop & Appleby who were instructed to supply all the machinery, whilst the SE&CR's engineering department built a brick base. The new crane was completed and subsequently in use towards the end of 1902.

All manner of goods, merchandise and odd items were once handled by the railways, but nowadays the purpose of some of these commodities is obscure to say the least. For instance, a Mr. Taylor of Victoria Villas, Brighton, wrote to the station master at Horsmonden:

> 'Dear Sir,
> I enclose a cheque value £3 7s 6d for enclosed account. Will you order me another truck of smokebox ashes, or shall I order it from store keeper myself?'

Whereas the tradesmen were apparently well-catered for, discontent among ordinary patrons surfaced during the summer of 1902 at a shareholders' meeting of the SER. A Mr. J. L. Thomas complained that the SE&CR seemed interested only in continental, seaside and excursion trains whereby 'residential traffic' was neglected. He went on to cite a particular irksome example:

> 'The service is not sufficiently quick or what it ought to be and you are inviting opposition from various quarters. Let me mention my own experience. I like to spend a day in the country sometimes and the other day I thought I would go to Hawkhurst. The most convenient train for me at that time was a little after 10 o'clock; now it is a little before 10 o'clock. That train was timed to take three hours on a journey of 47 miles [from London]. Is that a railway rate? It is not even a decent donkey rate (laughter). You go to the expense of making that branch line and you do not use it. It is a beautiful country serving Goudhurst, Cranbrook and other places - a beautiful country that would accommodate an enormous residential traffic - why not use it?'

In the chair was Henry Cosmo Bonsor who defended the SE&CR by saying:

> 'I very much regret that it took Mr. Thomas so long to travel to Hawkhurst, but he was not then a residential traveller. We bring our passengers up from Hawkhurst and take them down again much more quickly than he mentioned, but he got into a very slow train - I forget what he actually called it (laughter).'

Mr. Thomas also wanted to know why the SE&CR wasted resources by operating branch line trains of six carriages or so, with only half a dozen passengers on board. He then enquired why they could not 'adopt the system of the North Eastern Railway of auto-motor carriages holding, say, fifty people - only one carriage, but carrying a very much larger percentage of living load'. He continued:

> 'Again, why do you not make the little line from Hawkhurst to Robertsbridge? That would give you a through communication from Gravesend, Maidstone and those places down to Hastings, and would give you, in case of accident on your other line, a double road to Hastings. Its cost, too, would be infinitesimal, and I feel sure that if it was properly worked it would be a success.'

Another shareholder, Mr. C. A. Case, was more aggrieved with the way the existing system was operated and its poor connections:

> 'I have not come here to ask you to make a new line, but to ask you to use the lines that you already have. I am in business at Maidstone, but I happen now to be living at Dover. I am constantly travelling between Maidstone and Dover, and the junction is used just in the same way as when the competition existed between the two Companies. I refer to certain trains arriving at Ashford from Dover and Margate. There is no more communication between Maidstone, with 35,000 inhabitants, and Dover with 35,000 inhabitants, than there is between Dover and Hawkhurst with its 2,000 inhabitants. There are also more trains between Tonbridge and Hawkhurst than there are between Maidstone and Tonbridge.'

Such inadequacies in respect of connecting services were evidently well-known, for instance, Black's 1904 edition of its *Guide to Kent* spoke of:

> 'Paddock Wood Junction: - a place of interest chiefly to railway travellers, since it makes the central knot of SER lines - with Tonbridge to the west and Ashford to the east and here going off branch lines north to Maidstone and south to Hawkhurst, so that this is one of the places where Kentish men spend a certain proportion of their lives in waiting for trains, and discussing the agricultural prospects of the fine green country around, watered by the Medway and its tributaries the Teise and the Beult, to the east, about whose courses lies, praised by cyclists, the lowest and flattest part of the Weald of Kent.'

Indeed, in some circumstances it seems that both Kentish Men and Men of Kent might have reached their destinations quicker had they taken to their bicycles!

In spite of bitter complaints from ordinary travellers who faced frustrating delays, the SE&CR remained popular with excursionists who evidently patronised every conceivable special that was laid on. Fifty local people from Hawkhurst boarded the train on a cold day in February 1904 for a half-day excursion, joined by seventy more at Cranbrook, so that by the time the train had reached Paddock Wood it was reported as 'packed out'. Travelling by way of Otford and Swanley Junction, London was reached at three in the afternoon, where entertainments went on till late in the evening. Although the return trip was accomplished in good time, most of them didn't reach their beds until well after two in the morning.

The cold snap continued and a fortnight later, during early March, snow fell to a depth of several inches, but it soon thawed as spring approached and another prosperous season began. Even though the Sunday train service had, for some years, been halved from its original four trips each way, the SE&CR increased it to three for the duration of the summer period. This catered for seasonal visitors who came to Cranbrook and the High Weald for its renowned health-giving atmosphere, as well as locals

A signalman's view of Paddock Wood station from the East Cabin. The water column on the left was for Hawkhurst branch trains. The redundant M&H signal post features next to the gentleman on the platform, whilst the SER bracket signal just behind him enabled trains for the 'Cranbrook Line', as it was still called, to start away from either the bay or up platform. The siding on the extreme left continued across the approach road to the West Yard whilst the West Yard Cabin can be seen above the footbridge.

who were able to afford the occasional day at the seaside. On weekdays the ordinary service comprised ten trains each way so the tranquil stillness of Bedgebury Wood, between Goudhurst and Cranbrook, was regularly disturbed with echoes of railway trains clanking and clattering through its glades.

During May 1905 a rather pleasing little ceremony took place when Mr. Bowyer, the station master at Hawkhurst, retired after twelve years in this, his last posting. Having moved here when the station had been opened, he'd witnessed its growth and prosperity, while earning the respect of his local community in Gills Green, as well as all his regular travellers. In gratitude for his 'unfailing courtesy and service' he was presented with a beautiful illuminated address and a handsome purse containing a gift of twenty guineas (£21) from the SE&CR.

Whereas the railway companies always rewarded dedication and honesty, employees who fell foul of company regulations or engaged in criminal activities could expect swift retribution. In September of that year, a goods porter and a goods clerk were both charged with breaking open a vending machine at Cranbrook station. Vanilla chocolate and cigarettes worth £1 8s 4d, comparable to more than a week's wages, had been stolen, whilst the goods clerk was found to be in possession of a pair of leather boots reported missing from a suitcase. The goods porter confessed to breaking open the machine with a point cleaner after red paint had been noticed on the implement. Even so, he protested: 'I was straight enough till I came to Cranbrook station. I've been led astray'. The clerk was fined £4, the porter £2 and each received a month's suspended sentence. The greatest punishment, however, was not only the disgrace and instant dismissal from the company's service, but the prospect of unemployment with no means of financial support.

With the SE&CR having established itself during these first half-dozen years, great progress had been made in locomotive development under the genius of locomotive superintendent H. S. Wainwright. He produced some formidable classes of engines that were very powerful, yet elegant in the extreme, as anyone who has gazed upon the graceful lines of his 'D' class 4-4-0s will surely testify. However, the Hawkhurst branch was far too lowly to see these elegant machines during the 'good old days' of Edwardian England, although many years later the 'D's did venture along this delightful railway into the High Weald. Throughout these very early years of the SE&CR, James Stirling's 'Q' class 0-4-4 tank locomotives were commonly used and were doubtless preferred by the crews to the last remaining '118's which were sometimes sent out. It might appear that the SE&CR was reluctant to dispose of anything that might yet be repaired, but it was merely prudent housekeeping. Certainly, the Hawkhurst branch during this period would have been an attraction to those who regularly subscribed to *The Railway Magazine* and ardently followed locomotive development. Whereas the more ancient locomotives of the SER, such as the '118's, had all but disappeared from the rest of the system by this time, it was still possible to see these relics from the Victorian era sauntering through the hop gardens and undulating landscape to Hawkhurst. These old 2-4-0s, with their outside coupling rods pacing in time to the beat of the exhaust, must have made a fine spectacle on a spring morning when traversing the high embankment at Yew Tree Green, or working for all their worth up the 1 in 60 climb to Cranbrook. The line's most famous '118', No.112, had gone to the scrap road in March 1901, but its boiler had been retrieved for use on another member of the class where a few more years working life might be extracted. The last documented appearance of a '118' on branch duties took place during the winter of 1903/4 when No.92 ended its days rostered for Hawkhurst and Westerham services before scrapping occurred in the following April.

Most of the goods services appear to have been hauled by Cudworth's 'Standard Goods' 0-6-0 engines, until suitable replacements were found. These capable locomotives had proved themselves a worthy design, handling heavy loads with relative ease over the demanding gradients on the system. Even though most of the class had been withdrawn by the time the Managing Committee was formed, a few survivors remained at Tonbridge where they worked the Tunbridge Wells goods and shunted the sidings. No.100 was often rostered to run light to Paddock Wood for shunting, before taking the late afternoon goods train down to Hawkhurst. Incidentally, it was this engine which disgraced itself in February 1902 by leaving the rails at Paddock Wood. Shortly after this escapade it went to the scrap yard, being followed by the remaining members of the class during 1903/4. Their place was filled by Stirling's handsome 'O' class 0-6-0s which were a distinct all round improvement.

As well as the 'thoroughbred' SER engines, there were occasions when unusual and interesting visitors made an unexpected appearance. During 1907 No.546 (formerly LC&DR No.87 *Ulva*) a Martley 0-4-2 well tank built in 1886, was sent down to work the line for a time. It was

Cudworth 'Standard Goods' No. 100 in the down platform at Paddock Wood. The noticeboard beneath the canopy reads 'Passengers are not allowed to cross the lines under any pretence', but it did not deter hop-pickers from risking their lives.

A quiet corner of Horsmonden. The shop on the left advertised itself as a 'Commercial and Cyclists' Tea Room'.

evidently no match for the regular 'Q', which it probably replaced for the duration, since it was to be seen lying idle in February 1908 at the rear of Tonbridge shed. It is indeed a pity that the opinions of the long-gone SER crews cannot be sought as to the suitability and capabilities of these various locomotives. Intimate knowledge such as this has regrettably gone to the grave.

Each summer season brought trainloads of visitors to Cranbrook, for it remained a popular place with those who sought recuperation without the need for seaside 'cures'. The unrivalled beauty of the surrounding countryside proved a great magnet, whilst those fortunate enough to have relatives here were probably glad of a break from the noise and smoke of bustling Edwardian London. Outward business also remained buoyant, especially on excursion days which were greatly looked forward to and well-organized. Many local societies arranged annual outings as the high spot of their calendar. Just one example was the local congregationalists' 'Band of Hope' trip to the seaside in July 1905. Around 250 juvenile members clambered aboard the train at Cranbrook, accompanied by an equal number at Goudhurst, with yet more joining at Horsmonden. After journeying via Ashford, Canterbury and Ramsgate, a most enjoyable day was spent at Margate where the numerous attractions at the popular resort delighted and entertained them all.

Apart from these busy times, there were also occasions which created much fuss and pomp and which allowed the railway staff to decorate the station with patriotic bunting. The most notable event took place in 1906 when Princess Christian of Schleswig-Holstein, came by the Royal Train to Cranbrook. The platform was covered in scarlet cloth upon which were gathered the local dignitaries and churchmen who nervously awaited the arrival of Her Royal Highness. At the scheduled time the Royal Train came pacing up the bank before drawing slowly into the platform to stand precisely at the appointed spot for the honourable reception. The occasion was the dedication of a commemorative window in Cranbrook church to the late and much-lamented Queen Victoria. Later that same day, the princess was driven to Benenden where she laid the foundation stone for the sanatorium. A similar visit occurred in the following year, during May, when yet again there was an excuse to decorate the station. Flowers and flags were festively draped about the platform, the floor covered again with rich crimson, whilst the canopy supports were each gaily entwined with numerous brightly-coloured flags. The SE&CR timed the day to perfection with tea being served on the gleaming train which mirrored the festooned station while it waited in the platform. Afterwards, Princess Christian was driven in a motor car to Benenden.

Towards the close of 1907, the SE&CR decided to set about altering the office accommodation at Hawkhurst station since it was considered inadequate. The existing porters' room was therefore converted into an office for the station master, whilst an old carriage body was brought down for use by the displaced staff. The cost of this work amounted to around fifty pounds, with an additional £14 15s 0d being spent on a corrugated iron lamp room, ordered from Messrs. T. Ash & Co, for which the engineering department provided a concrete base close to the buffer stops.

As already mentioned, the coming of the railway engendered a small community at Gills Green. Similarly, although to a lesser extent, the station at Cranbrook

Station Approach, Horsmonden, with the road to Goudhurst passing beneath the bridge. The building in the centre belonged to T. Maylam & Co., 'Millers & Corn Merchants, Paddock Wood & Horsmonden', whilst the roader shed and weigh bill room feature to the left of the picture.

Poster boards with the SE&CR heading display a selection of excursion offers, timetables, as well as illustrating the delights of a day trip to Dover. Unusually, the platform facing was built of stone.

The young lad by the gate was evidently watching the village postman free-wheel down the hill, while the shopkeeper at C. Styles' general stores was talking to the woman in black. The station buildings and waiting shelter can be seen at the bottom of the hill.

Goudhurst and Kilndown Local History Society

A wonderful view of Goudhurst, about 1910, with a typical train of the period hauled by a well-maintained 'Q' class waiting alongside the down platform. The little lad standing by the wicket gate was obviously anticipating the train's departure. All the signals were original McKenzie & Holland examples, whilst the crossing gate with red diamond banner and oil lamp is of special interest. The window frames of the signal box were painted white, whilst the rest of the woodwork was at this time, one uniform colour. The waiting shelter, supported on stilts and the wooden loading gauge are also depicted.

required nearby dwellings to be erected upon the hillside behind the station for use by the staff. There was also a local inn, the 'Railway Hotel', at the commencement of the approach road at Hartley, with a post office and general stores a little further towards Cranbrook.

Unlike today, it was needful for most people to grow their own vegetables in back gardens as a means of making the weekly wage stretch further. Allotments were once a familiar feature of the railway scene and the staff were graciously allowed to take into cultivation any available and suitable strips of lands bordering the track. George Goldsmith, a platelayer at Cranbrook, had quite a sizeable patch of sun-trapped land on the gentle slope between the down starting and up home signals. During the hop-picking weeks of early September 1909, he was mystified by repeated pilfering of potatoes from his

An up train coasting into Goudhurst, watched with interest by some youngsters hanging over the platform fence.

The approach to Goudhurst station from the Lamberhurst road. The sign above the cart advertised the Railway Hotel which stood on the other side of the level crossing, whilst the large sign at the entrance to the yard reads 'The Seaborne Coal & Coke Co., also at Paddock Wood and Yalding'. The jib of the yard crane also features in the left foreground.

This fine Edwardian view of the railway and the station at Cranbrook features a motor car rumbling along the approach road. *Collection Tony Riley*

A sunny morning in Cranbrook in the days before popular motoring.

cherished plot. Consequently, he asked for half a day's leave from his normal trackside duties in order that he might dig-up and bag what remained. Having unearthed the entire crop, he loaded into sacks almost three-quarters of a hundredweight for his larder, but decided he'd complete the task after a break. On his return, however, he found to his dismay that one bag had gone missing, whereupon a brief search in the immediate area brought to light its careful concealment under a bush. Rather than retrieve it there and then, he fetched the local constable, whereupon they crouched in hiding until eight o'clock that evening when their attention was alerted. Three men came stealthily creeping along the railway track from the direction of Badger's Oak and headed straight for the bush, at which moment out sprang George and the policeman. They grappled with two of the miscreants, but the third immediately fled back down the line towards Hawkhurst, never to be seen again. James Finn and John Fox, both hop-pickers from East London, were subsequently hauled before Cranbrook magistrates and charged with stealing the potatoes, for which they each received a sentence of a month's hard labour.

The annual spell of hop-picking, which usually took place around the end of August and beginning of September, was always a busy period for the SE&CR. Apart from the exodus of hundreds of Londoners to the hop fields of Kent and eastern Sussex, there was also extra traffic during this season as the huge quantities of fruit and other produce had to be packed, loaded and transported to the markets. Numerous instructions were handed out to railway staff in order that the goods trains, particularly on market days, should be worked as efficiently as possible. On the Hawkhurst branch it was the duty of the crew of the mid-day goods train to perform all the shunting at stations and sidings along the line so that the evening freight had only to attach on the return run to Paddock Wood. For example, specific instructions were given that the mid-day goods should take out the empty wagons at Churn Lane siding and shunt in the market trucks in readiness for the 7.50pm up goods. All work was required to be finished by 4.50pm, whilst it was necessary not to interfere with the normal passenger timetable. Most freight trips were scheduled to be in the yards at any of the four stations while a passenger train passed through, but delays sometimes occurred. It was often difficult to load livestock wagons if there were stubborn or troublesome animals, whilst other disruptions to the timetable occurred through extra heavy loads, late arrivals of wagonloads from nearby farms, not to mention inclement weather.

Tow-roping, by which means a wagon was moved in a siding by a rope attached to an engine on an adjacent line, was abolished in January 1910 at Churn Lane when a new siding connection was provided. The Board of Trade had distinctly disapproved of this practice since it was considered positively archaic and even dangerous.- Major J. W. Pringle inspected the new works on 20th April, whereby his subsequent report reads as follows:

> 'I made an inspection today of the new works at Churn Lane Siding, between Paddock Wood and Horsmonden on the Hawkhurst Branch of the South Eastern & Chatham Railway.
>
> A new connection with the single line, facing trains from Paddock Wood, has been provided at this siding with the object of doing away with the necessity of tow-roping. The points are fitted with an economical facing point lock and bar. They, as well as the old connection, are worked from a new ground box situated near the adjoining level crossing. The frame in the box contains 6 levers, all in use, and the point levers are controlled by tablet for the single line section. Home signals in each direction are provided, interlocked with the gates of the level crossing.
>
> The interlocking is correct, and, provided that down trains working at the siding stand on the level gradient on the north side of the level crossing, the arrangements are satisfactory.
>
> Subject to this promise, I recommend the Board of Trade to approve these new works.'

The siding frame, which was housed in a neat wooden hut, was connected by electric telegraph to Horsmonden and Paddock Wood signal cabins whereby notice of approaching trains was received by means of a warning bell. The requirement for the engine to leave its wagons on the north, or Paddock Wood side, of the road crossing while shunting took place, was to avoid the risk of runaways on the rising 1 in 66 gradient south of the crossing which would have posed a danger for road users at Churn Lane.

There were four public level crossings on the branch: Willow Lane; Churn Lane; Smallbridge; and Station Road, Goudhurst. These were protected by traditional wooden gates which could be locked in both positions. Only Goudhurst and, originally, Churn Lane crossings were provided with home signals. In later years the Southern Railway dispensed with those at Churn Lane, considering instead that sufficient protection would be afforded with distant signals. However, it is evident that engine crews had subsequent cause to rue this particular decision. At Willow Lane and Smallbridge the railway provided gate-keepers who lived nearby and were paid a wage to man the crossing. Here, warning bells installed in the cottages were rung by the relevant signalman a few minutes before the train was due.

There were also a few other crossings, mainly for the use of farmers, where small gates opened away from the railway to enable carts and livestock to reach the adjacent fields. In earlier days the farmhands and traders were expected to be acquainted with the times of trains and observe the accepted practice of crossing the line in safety. Unfortunately, the rules were periodically broken and this sometimes led to needless accidents. During September 1909 a drayman, employed by a Mr. Wickham of Yalding, opened a gate at one of these crossings between Horsmonden and Paddock Wood and led his horse and van onto the railway before undoing the opposite gate. He'd probably acted in this way many times before, breaking the rules by not bothering to open both gates prior to crossing the line. However, on this occasion a goods train was well on its way and his panic can easily be imagined on suddenly hearing its approach as he frantically struggled to move the obstruction. Unable to pull up in time, the goods train struck the body of the van, scattering its load of heavy oak barrels in all directions and seriously injuring the drayman. Miraculously, the horse was quite unharmed, but understandably terrified, escaping from the broken shafts before bolting down the line. No doubt the incident served as a lesson to other careless individuals who were too idle to observe rules laid down for their own welfare.

Disruptions to normal working, either through accidents or unusual circumstances were, and still are, fairly commonplace on the railways. Extremes of weather can also be responsible for widespread chaos and often there is little that can be done until such spells are over. Winter's picturesque mantle of snow invariably blocks most of Kent's railway system during cold climatic phases since the county is particularly prone to catching the full force of icy blasts from Arctic winds off the North Sea. Accumulated snow and a sudden thaw will burst riverbanks, flood fields, wash out culverts, erode embankments and cause serious slips in cuttings. These problems were all experienced to some degree on the Hawkhurst branch and the track gangs were obliged to keep an ever-watchful eye on their allotted sections. During October 1909, heavy and persistent rain brought widespread flooding to many parts of the Weald. The Rother broke its banks and quickly washed out the Kent and East Sussex Railway, but fortunately the Hawkhurst branch escaped being damaged by the river Teise. However, this tributary of the Beult rose to an alarming degree and for a time it seemed as though the bridge just to the north of Goudhurst station might be swept away, but Edward Seaton's engineering held fast. The meadows surrounding the station and railway were all under many feet of water, while Hope Mill was reported as being 'swamped'. Eventually the deluge ceased, the rivers subsided and mopping-up began.

With such copious quantities of water around, it might seem ironic that piped water was so valued. Wells existed in numerous places, but many of these were unsatisfactory as they occasionally became contaminated and poisoned the user. In fact, it wasn't until 1908 that Goudhurst station was fitted-up to the supply already connected to the station master's house by the Cranbrook & District Water Company.

Other improvements worth mentioning at this time involved Paddock Wood station, as revealed in a company memorandum: 'The time has come when this important junction station should be lighted by gas'. The cost of providing the supply, piping and mantles etc., amounted to £335. Although it was more expensive to burn, with a charge of £210 a year for gas compared to £147 for oil, it was a significant improvement in illumination. The station staff, too, must have heartily welcomed the changeover, whereby the laborious task of filling countless reservoirs, trimming and lighting wicks was replaced by simply operating a chain by means of a pole and hook. Such up-to-date convenience could not, of course, be provided at the remote stations on the Hawkhurst branch which remained oil-lit and pungent with the smell of burning paraffin for almost the entire seventy years.

Throughout the last years of peace in the run-up to the Great War, life continued much as always. This mean-

A delivery van with its tail-board lowered while collecting goods from the station. The other vehicle had probably arrived to pick up passengers from the train standing in the station. The locomotive had been detached from its train, its chimney featuring behind the man carrying the suitcase.

'Q' class No. 173 on arrival at Hawkhurst in 1909. The headcode for the branch, i.e. a solitary board on the top lamp iron of the locomotive, appears to be a white diamond on a black board, rather than a white cross which was the official branch headcode.

'Q1' class No. 366 (rebuilt 1906) at Paddock Wood with the Hawkhurst branch train in 1910, featuring on the front of the engine with an oilcan fireman Frederick Mercer, his driver watching from the cab, and the guard at the door of his van with flag unfurled.

dering railway, which toured hop-gardens, fertile fields, pleasant valleys and wooded hillsides, had been open for twenty years, during which time it had justified its construction and become part of life for the descendants of those who had settled in ancient Andredswold. Outwardly, there was little evidence that anything could ever change to any marked degree. Excursions to London were still organized during the seasons, but the increasing popularity of motor coach and charabanc outings could not be ignored. When, in 1885, Herr Benz had successfully perfected a motor which ran on alcohol, it is doubtful whether anyone envisaged the changes that would come with the internal combustion engine. As this technology developed, so the railways became vulnerable where they were unable to compete. The residents of Hawkhurst could hardly be blamed for showing more interest in an open charabanc trip to Hastings, running through the leafy lanes of Sussex, rather than a roundabout railway journey via Tonbridge. The position of the stations, notably at Goudhurst, Cranbrook and Hawkhurst, proved to be part of the undoing of the line as soon as the first motorized omnibuses arrived on the scene. Various private operators found easy pickings in this part of the county, serving the centre of the villages with a more convenient if less frequent service. The Maidstone & District Motor Services Company soon established a regular timetable with 'buses running from Maidstone to Hastings via Staplehurst, Cranbrook and Hawkhurst, as well as from Maidstone to Hawkhurst via Goudhurst. Nevertheless, the Hawkhurst branch was fortunate in many other ways since it was boosted by an ever-increasing and developing agricultural trade, as well as providing a train service for longer distance journeys, for which 'buses cannot replace railways. However, the standard of service offered still provoked many people into picking up their pens, as revealed in a letter to *The Times* in October 1910:

'Sir,
On Saturday, travelling from Dover to Hawkhurst with my maid, I had a new experience in exaction on the part of railway officials. My hand baggage, consisting of a small bundle of rugs, a handbag and a cardboard box, was weighed along with my heavy luggage. Thinking that this was a vagary of the Dover porter, I wrote to the Managing Director of the South Eastern Railway to inform him of what had occurred, and I have received the following letter in reply.

'Madam, the General Manager has handed me your ladyship's letter of the 8th inst., and I have to inform you all luggage, whether conveyed with the passenger in the compartment or labelled and placed in a guard's van, is weighed in order that the excess weight, if any, may be ascertained. Trusting this explanation will be acceptable to you,
I am, Madam,
your ladyship's obedient servant,
- Thomson.'

This weighing of hand baggage is unique in my experience, although we who live in this part of England have learned to expect anything of the South Eastern Railway Company, which seems to devise every possible means for keeping people from travelling.
I am, Sir, yours &c,
Violet, Lady Cecil.'

It was not only the numerous societies and members of the general public who used the railways for a jamboree or special excursion. In May 1914, Hawkhurst was the chosen venue for the annual 'Railway Managers' Outing' when two dozen officials of the SE&CR travelled down by train into the depths of rural Kent. On arrival at the 'Queen's Hotel' they were served a splendid cold luncheon, served by Mrs. Clements. During the afternoon they played bowls upon the green and strolled around the gardens, enjoying the fresh air and scenery. A sumptuous tea was served, after which the assembly returned to the station and the waiting special direct train to London, whilst everyone agreed that it had been an 'immensely enjoyable' day.

The collision involving a goods train and the drayman's horse van is thought to have taken place at Old Hay crossing, between Willow Lane and Churn Lane. It is possible that there were other mishaps or close shaves since, in 1914, instructions were sent out that the whistle boards at this particular crossing should be repositioned to stand 500 yards distant in both directions. The drivers of up trains had complained of difficulties in obtaining a clear view of the crossing, by which time they were almost upon it. Accordingly, all drivers running towards Paddock Wood were required to hold the engine's whistle continuously open from the board to the crossing, a distance of over a quarter mile. In the opposite direction, whistles were required to be opened immediately the board was passed and held down for about ten seconds.

The outbreak of the Great War had a limited effect on the branch. Such would not have been the case had Watkin's more fanciful ideas of extending the line to Dungeness and building a new port come about. This line, however, saw little of the drama that began to unfold on the rest of the system as the Government's war machine rolled into action. Britain was now at war with the country whose roaming people had, centuries earlier, conquered impenetrable Andredswold, settled here and whose descendants considered themselves thoroughly English. The natural bonds which had once existed between the nations were quickly broken when suddenly everything German became something to be despised. Politicians, who had once described Germany as Britain's greatest ally, together with a slavish press, helped to whip public opinion into hysterical hatred as columns of young men queued up to enlist. The local lads of the Wealden towns and villages were no exception and hundreds dutifully joined up in the earnest belief that they should 'do their bit for King and Country'. All the stations along the line became synonymous with anxious farewells, in spite of reassurances from those in uniform that they'd 'be home by Christmas'.

The war brought shortages of all sorts, not only in merchandise, but also manpower. For the first time, women stepped into jobs normally held only by men, and many signalboxes and stations became staffed by female employees or young lads waiting until they were old enough to 'pick up the King's shilling'. It was imperative that the annual harvest was gathered without fail, so the Hawkhurst branch remained almost as busy as ever, but the passenger services, not unexpectedly, began to suffer. From the outbreak of war in August to the following June of 1915, there were ten down trains, with nine in the up direction. During 1916 these were slightly reduced to nine down, with seven running up to Paddock Wood. The Sunday service remained unaltered with just two trains both ways, one morning and evening. This was worked from Hawkhurst, using the engine stabled there in the shed from Saturday night. Returning at 9.13pm on Sunday evening, the locomotive was put away until required a few hours later to work one of the two first up trains on Monday morning. The other up train was a return trip to Paddock Wood made by the first down train of the morning. Throughout the day a solitary train ran to and from the terminus to Paddock Wood, but by the evening two trains operated the branch, passing each other at Goudhurst. This catered mainly for London office workers and those who were still employed in the larger towns of Tonbridge and Maidstone. At this time the SE&CR was ordinarily using set 252 for the branch services. This comprised two six-wheeled third class carriages, each containing fifty seats, an ordinary composite bogie (used only Monday to Friday) and a brake van. Morning and evening trips are revealed in a 1917 carriage working notice as being worked with three-coach sets. Other trains consisted of an ordinary composite bogie coupled to a tri-composite bogie and a bogie carriage with brake compartment.

The freight service began each weekday with the 6am departure from Paddock Wood. Swinging away from the main line, the train headed southwards towards the distant, bluish hills of the Weald, not calling at Churn

Taken from Bradshaw for May-August 1913.

RAILWAY MAP OF GREAT

Miles		mrn	mrn	mrn	mrn	mrn	mrn	aft	aft	aft	aft	aft	a	aft	aft	aft	Saturdays only	aft	Saturdays only	Sun. mrn	Sun. aft
	Maidstone West ... dep.	6 19	6 43	8 10	8 48	10 3	11 12	12 42	1 18	2 32	4 1	4 54	6 27	7 11	8 29	9 33		10 49		8 18	7 8
1	Tovil	6 22	6 46	8 13	8 50	10 7	11 14	12 45	1 22	2 35	4 5	4 57	6 30	7 14	8 26	9 37		10 52		8 21	7 11
1¾	East Farleigh ¶	6 26	6 50	8 17	8 54	10 11	11 18	12 49	1 26	2 39	4 9	5 1	6 34	7 18	8 30	9 41		10 56		8 25	7 15
4¾	Wateringbury	6 35	6 59	8 26	9 3	10 20	11 27	12 58	1 35	2 48	4 18	5 10	6 41	7 27	8 39	9 50		11 5		8 34	7 24
6¼	Yalding ¶	6 40	7 4	8 31	9 8	10 25	11 32	1 3	1 40	2 53	4 23	5 15	6 47	7 32	8 44	9 55		11 10		8 39	7 29
10	Paddock Wood 244 arr.	6 50	7 13	8 40	9 17	10 34	11 41	1 12	1 49	3 2	4 32	5 24	6 54	7 41	8 53	10 4		11 19		8 48	7 38
	Paddock Wood dep.	7 0	7 23	8 54	9 21	10d52	11 43	1 26	2 2	3 5	5 19	5 37	6 58	7 43	9 5	10 6		....		8 57	7 40
15¼	Tonbridge Junc. 248 arr.	7 11	7 32	9 3	9 30	11d1	11 52	1 36	2 11	3 14	5 29	5 45	7 8	7 52	9 14	10 16		....		9 6	7 49

TONBRIDGE JUNCTION, PADDOCK WOOD, and HAWKHURST.—South Eastern and Chatham.

Miles	Down.	mrn	mrn	mrn	mrn	aft	Except Sats	aft	Sats only	aft	Except Sats	aft	Sats only	aft	aft	Fridays only	aft	aft	aft	Sun. mrn	Sun. aft
	Tonbridge Junction .. dep.	7 6	9 23	10 35	11 55	2 5		2 30		3 8		3 31		4 21	....		5 40	6 50	8 55	9 37	8 26
5¼	Paddock Wood arr.	7 16	9 32	10 43	12 4	2 15		2 40		3 17		3 40		4 30	....		5 49	6 59	9 5	9 48	8 35
	Paddock Wood dep.	7 27	9 40	10 50	12 13	2 30		2 43		3 26		3 50		4 35	5 35		5 54	7 5	9 8	9 52	8 42
9¼	Horsmonden	7 36	9 49	10 59	12 22	2 39		2 52		3 34		3 59		4 48	5 43		6 8	7 14	9 17	10 1	8 51
11¾	Goudhurst	7 40	9 53	11 3	12 27	2 44		2 57		3 38		4 4		4 47	5 47		6 13	7 19	9 22	10 5	8 56
15¼	Cranbrook	7 49	10 2	11 12	12 36	2 53		3 6		3 47		4 13		4 56	5 55		6 22	7 28	9 31	10 14	9 5
16¾	Hawkhurst ... arr.	7 54	10 7	11 17	12 41	2 58		3 11		3 52		4 18		5 1	5 59		6 27	7 33	9 36	10 19	9 10

Miles	Up.	mrn	mrn	mrn	mrn	aft	aft	Sats only	aft	Except Sats	aft	aft	aft	aft	Sun. mrn	Sun. aft
	Hawkhurst ... dep.	8 1	9 6	10 11	11 37	12 54	3 19		3 27		5 5	5 50	8 14	9 57	8 24	6 55
1	Cranbrook	8 6	9 11	10 16	11 42	12 59	3 24		3 32		5 10	6 4	8 19	10 2	8 29	7 0
5¼	Goudhurst	8 12	9 17	10 22	11 48	1 5	3 30		3 38		5 15	6 13	8 25	10 10	8 36	7 8
7¼	Horsmonden	8 17	9 22	10 27	11 53	1 10	3 35		3 43		5 20	6 19	8 30	10 15	8 41	7 14
11½	Paddock Wood 244 arr.	8 27	9 32	10 37	12 3	1 20	3 45		3 53		5 30	6 28	8 40	10 25	8 50	7 24
	Paddock Wood dep.	8 34	10 12	10 52	...	1 26	3 58		3 58		5 37	6 58	9 5	10 26	8 57	7 31
16½	Tonbridge Junc. 248 arr.	8 43	10 24	11 1	...	1 36	4 7		4 7		5 45	7 8	9 14	10 35	9 6	7 40

a Do not call at the Halts.

d Leaves Paddock Wood at 10 35 and arrives at Tonbridge Junction at 10 45 mrn. on Saturdays.

¶ "Halts" at Beltring and Branbridges, between Paddock Wood and Yalding; and at Teston Crossing, between Wateringbury and East Farleigh.

For other Trains

BETWEEN	PAGE
Tonbridge Junc. & Paddock Wood	244

[Maidstone West.] 268

Lane, and arriving at Horsmonden at 6.15am. A ten minute pause allowed parcels and post to be unloaded before setting off once again where Goudhurst was reached at 6.35am. Twenty minutes were allocated here, after which a ten minute stop at Cranbrook followed before arrival at Hawkhurst at 7.23am. The return working left at a quarter to eight, after having shunted the empties and picked up loaded wagons from the goods shed and yard. Cranbrook was not booked as a stop on the up journey, whilst Pattenden siding was only dealt with on request. Arriving at Goudhurst at 8.05, the yard was sorted and the goods held there to allow the 8.15am from Hawkhurst to pass through the station at 8.25am. Afterwards, the goods continued its journey north to Horsmonden, where it was again held out of the way while sorting the yard in order to allow the 9.40am passenger train from Paddock Wood to run south to Hawkhurst. The goods was booked to arrive at Paddock Wood at 10.10am, calling at Churn Lane siding only on request.

During the early years, three goods trips were regularly scheduled, but, by the Great War, two were normally sufficient. The second freight trip of the day left Paddock Wood at 1.30pm, calling at Churn Lane for ten minutes, then twenty-five minutes at Horsmonden, three-quarters of an hour at Goudhurst, an hour at Cranbrook, before arriving at 4.25pm at Hawkhurst. Two hours were allowed for sorting the yard there, before setting back up the branch at 6.45pm. Ten minutes were allowed at each station, including Churn Lane siding, to call and pick up wagons left ready earlier on the down journey, with arrival back at Paddock Wood due around 8.20pm. On Sundays there was one goods train only, running to the same weekday schedule, but returning from Hawkhurst at 11.10am. A working timetable for the summer of 1916 shows that half an hour was allowed at Cranbrook, ten minutes at Pattenden siding, forty minutes at Goudhurst and ten minutes at both Horsmonden and Churn Lane before arriving back at Paddock Wood at 1.20pm.

Reading old timetables and relating the schedules once worked can be a very dreary exercise, and, besides, these endless columns of figures portray nothing of the experience which demanded a certain amount of skill. The whole business of loading and unloading all manner of goods, merchandise and awkward consignments had to be well-organized and efficiently handled. On busy days it was frequently a very tight operation and no train could afford to be delayed since its slot in the timetable would be lost, whereby disruptions to other trains would ensue. Once the train had been loaded, secured and was steaming off into the distance, it is no small wonder that the staff were glad to reach for the kettle, safe in the knowledge of yet another job well done.

As the war effort increased, so severe cuts to the Hawkhurst timetable followed with the railways coming under Government control. The Sunday service appeared in the published timetables as 'temporarily suspended', however, 1916 proved to be the last year for Sunday trains as they were never reinstated throughout the life of the branch. The *Kent & Sussex Courier* of 12th January 1917 told its readership:

> 'HAWKHURST: Railway Facilities: Now that this branch is being taken over, the railway travelling has been cut down tremendously, as only four trains come in and four trains depart during the week days, whilst on Sunday there are no trains either in or out. Still, the people do not go without their Sunday papers, as motors have been requisitioned for that purpose.'

Only three months later unsubstantiated rumours began to suggest that the Hawkhurst service was to be yet further curtailed, but the *Courier* was unable to find any official confirmation

Throughout this period, as well as the years leading up to the Great War, passenger services were ordinarily worked with 'Q' 0-4-4Ts based at Tonbridge, as well as a member of the same class shedded at Hawkhurst. Tonbridge also supplied the 'O' class 0-6-0s which, by and large, formed the motive power for the goods, although on occasions they worked a passenger train, standing in for an absent 'Q' class engine.

During 1913 the SE&CR had faced a critical shortage of locomotives, a problem which was only to be exacerbated by the conflict in Europe. It became a case of beg, borrow or buy anything that was available from other British railway companies. The Great Northern Railway loaned ten 2-4-0s and one of these, No. 995, worked the Hawkhurst branch in place of a displaced 'Q'. In his book, *The Locomotives of the South Eastern & Chatham Railway* (RCTS 1961), Don Bradley commented that this engine was 'kept particularly well-cleaned by its elderly driver and youthful fireman'.

By far the most extraordinary locomotive ever recorded on the branch was SE&CR No. 752. This 0-6-0 saddle tank was constructed in 1879 by Manning Wardle, originally numbered 725 and previously owned by Joseph Firbank, the father of the contractor engaged to build the C&PWR. He named it *Grinstead* whereupon it was sent in the early 1880s to work on his contract for building the Lewes and East Grinstead Railway in Sussex. During 1899, No.725 was sold to another contractor, William Rigby of Yorkshire, who painted it dark blue, named it *Middleton* and used it on the Folkestone Harbour improvement scheme. The little engine presumably proved itself very useful on the quays at Folkestone, for it was sold to the SE&CR during 1904. Following repairs at Ashford works, it was specially treated nonetheless to the full resplendence of the company's Brunswick green livery, complete with lining and gilt lettering. New cast brass plates bearing its modified number of 752 were affixed to the cab sidesheets, whilst even the copper cap upon its chimney was burnished. Permanent employment was found at

Manning Wardle 0–6–0ST No. 752 in the drab, dull paint applied during the Great War – a far cry from the resplendent SE&CR livery in which it was originally out-shopped by Ashford. It also lost the burnished copper cap from its chimney.

Folkestone, but, shortly after the outbreak of the Great War, its place was taken by a far more powerful 'R' class 0-6-0T exchanged with Tonbridge shed. Unfortunately, No.752 was unable to manage the tasks previously handled by the Tonbridge 'R', whereby it was eventually sent down to Hawkhurst. Don Bradley stated that during the hop-picking season of 1915 it was to be seen shunting the yard there. Mention might also be made here of the fact that it has often been intimated that this diminutive engine worked the branch goods, but such a proposition seems scarcely likely in view of the demanding gradients and the heavy loads at that period. In later years No.752 was known to the crews by the delightfully appropriate nickname of 'Thumper' in consequence of the noise it emitted when speeds over 5mph were attained. With this in mind and making the reasonable assumption that it must at least have made the odd journey up and down the branch running light, numerous images spring to mind. In his book *The Hawkhurst Railway* (NG&LRS, 1961), Roger Crombleholme admitted a 'certain fascination for the thought of this little contractor's engine, far from her native Leeds, "thumping" through Horsmonden cutting'. Equally intriguing is the daydream of being a platelayer at that time and standing at the southern portal of Badger's Oak tunnel. This was was on a falling 1 in 80 gradient to Hawkhurst, and its cavernous walls must have echoed loudly to the curious sounds of this characterful engine as it came noisily and gaily bounding out on its way to the terminus. As a brief postscript, No.752 was returned to Tonbridge shed in 1916 and eventually despatched once more to Folkestone Harbour until sold in 1926. Further adventures followed this plucky little engine until, sadly, it was broken up for scrap in 1945. Thus came the end for one of the most remarkable and unusual locomotives ever to run over the Hawkhurst branch.

Another equally interesting development came about during the closing months of 1914. This involved the SE&CR fitting ex-LC&DR 'R' class No.675 and 'R1' No.703 with the necessary equipment to operate three six-wheeled sets as auto trains. A detailed account is found in D. L. Bradley's incomparable histories on SE&CR locomotives. Here, though, it is sufficient to record that trials proved very successful, including the pioneering trips over the Hawkhurst branch. In later years auto-trains became the normal method of working the Paddock Wood-Hawkhurst service, but the inaugural runs must have proved quite a novelty. The apparatus allowed the train to be driven from either end, with the locomotive sandwiched in the middle, as well as pulling or pushing at one end. It isn't difficult to imagine the surprise among uninformed locals standing on Cranbrook platform as a string of carriages came up the bank from Goudhurst, followed in the rear by great clouds of steam from an unseen locomotive working hard on the 1 in 60 gradient.

The push-pull trains, as they were more commonly known, were designed to effect economies in working services, especially on lines where passenger receipts were light. However, the war disrupted conversions of further locomotives for this purpose and the Hawkhurst branch soon reverted to normal methods of operation.

Apart from the usual 'Q', 'O' and the 'Q1' and 'O1' rebuilds, there were occasional visits from far more lordly engines such as Stirling's elderly 'B' class. These handsome 4-4-0s graced any train and in their heyday were regularly used to haul the Royal Family to the lonely and secluded Port Victoria, as well as the SER's prestigious 'Granville Express'. Nevertherless, the days of many of these grand and elegant locomotives were soon numbered as H. S. Wainwright's more powerful designs for the SE&CR replaced them. Even so, useful work on

'O1' No. 390 standing in the platform road at Hawkhurst with an up service. The presence of men ir military uniform seems to indicate this picture was taken around the end of the Great War.

Lens of Sutton

An 'O1' shunting the yard at Cranbrook, seen here in the platform road with a couple of wagons. The down starting signal had been replaced with a new SE&CR specimen, whilst the original M&H up home signal perched at the top of the embankment had also gone. This photo also provides a glimpse of more wagons in the yard between the trees on the left.

lowlier duties could still be found for many Stirling engines since the Hawkhurst branch was still forbidden territory for many of the newer classes. Common visitors in later years were as yet prohibited, since a working timetable of 1917 disallows the running of 'C' class 0-6-0s; 'D', 'E' and 'L' 4-4-0s; as well as the robust 'J' class 0-6-4Ts. A revision of the rules eventually led to the 'C's and 'D's being permitted over the branch, which was just as well in view of the heavy trains which sometimes needed to be worked. It is also worth mentioning that at this time instructions were in force that tender engines running from Hawkhurst to Paddock Wood should only run smokebox first, a rule later rescinded.

In spite of the war, the everyday business of agriculture and feeding the nation could not be allowed to be interrupted. Indeed, there was an even more urgent need to ensure that harvests were plentiful and gathered on time. In July 1917 it became necessary to extend the siding at Churn Lane, a task undertaken by the engineering department and following an agreement with local farmer Mr. Esau Taylor. In view of the way in which the Hawkhurst branch had proved itself so vital to the local agricultural community, it would appear that the late Sir Edward Watkin had woefully misjudged the potential of the C&PWR.

A slight disruption to normal working occurred during the wet autumn of that year when, in October, two fairly

An allotment holder gathering potatoes from his patch at Cranbrook. This picture shows the shunt arm of the SE&CR signal in the 'off' position. *R. F. Roberts*

serious landslips blocked the line between Cranbrook station and Badger's Oak tunnel. The engineers sent down to clear the obstruction noted that 'other movements were in evidence'. In order to prevent the adjoining land slipping and causing further disruptions, the SE&CR purchased this extra ground from Mr. Isaac Lewis for £10, whereby the opportunity was taken to strengthen the formation.

With the end of the war, the railway companies began tackling the accumulated log of repairs and renewals. A resumption to somewhere near the pre-war level of service would take many months to achieve and during the winter of 1920/21 there were still only four trains each way being advertised for this part of the High Weald. By the following summer, however, the SE&CR was in a position to increase the service to six down and

PADDOCK WOOD AND HAWKHURST BRANCH.

Down Trains— WEEK DAYS.							SUNDAYS and Good Friday.
		a.m.	a.m.	p.m.	p.m.	p.m.	
Tonbridge Junction..	dep.	8 8	10 50	1 28	5 48	6 37	.
Paddock Wood	arr.	8 17	10 58	1 37	5 57	6 46	...
	dep.	8 33	11 5	1 50	6 8	7 25	.
Horsmonden	arr.	8 42	11 14	1 59	6 17	7 34	... SERVICE SUSPENDED.
Goudhurst	,,	8 46	11 18	2 3	6 22	7 39	.
Cranbrook	,,	8 55	11 27	2 10	6 34	7 48	...
Hawkhurst	,,	9 0	11 32	2 15	6 39	7 53	.

Up Trains— WEEK DAYS.								SUNDAYS and Good Friday.
		a.m.	a.m.	a.m	p.m.	p.m.		
Hawkhurst	dep.	7 49	9 14	11 49	5 4	6 47	.	
Cranbrook	,,	7 54	9 19	11 54	5 9	6 52	...	
Goudhurst	,,	8 0	9 24	12 0	5 15	6 58	.	
Horsmonden	,,	8 5	9 30	12 5	5 20	7 3	...	SERVICE SUSPENDED.
Paddock Wood	arr.	8 15	9 40	12 15	5 30	7 13	.	
	dep.	8 28	9 48	12 18	5 35	7 27	...	
Tonbridge Junction ..	arr.	8 37	9 57	12 27	5 48	7 36	.	

For General Notes see page 16.

Taken from Public Timetable for 1919.

PADDOCK WOOD AND HAWKHURST BRANCH.

Down Trains— WEEK DAYS.						*Sats. only.*		Not Sats.		*Sats. only.*		Not Sats.	SUNDAYS (Christmas Day and Good Friday).
		a.m.	a.m.	p.m.	p.m.	p.m.		p.m.		p.m.		p.m.	
Charing Cross	dep.	.	.	12 15	3 0	*3 43*	.	.	.	*5 35*	.	6 0	
Waterloo Junction	,,	...	...	...	...	...	...	...	...	...	...	...	
Cannon Street	,,	6 53	LL	.	.	.	.	4 35	.	.	.	.	
London Bridge	,,	6 57	9 33	12 20	3 8	*3 52*	...	4 38	...	*5 41*	...	6 5	
Tonbridge Junction	arr.	8 14	10 52	1 24	3 50	*5 7*	.	5 26	.	*6 50*	.	6 50	SERVICE
	dep.	8 17	10 55	1 30	4 3	*5 45*	...	5 45	...	*7 8*	...	7 8	SUSPENDED.
Paddock Wood	arr.	8 26	11 3	1 39	4 12	*5 54*	.	5 54	.	*7 17*	.	7 17	
	dep.	8 30	11 8	1 50	4 30	*5 58*	...	5 58	...	*7 32*	...	7 32	
Horsmonden	arr.	8 39	11 17	1 59	4 39	*6 7*	.	6 7	.	*7 41*	.	7 41	
Goudhurst	,,	8 43	11 21	2 3	4 43	*6 12*	...	6 12	...	*7 46*	...	7 46	
Cranbrook	,,	8 52	11 30	2 12	4 52	*6 25*	.	6 25	.	*7 55*	.	7 55	
Hawkhurst	,,	8 57	11 35	2 17	4 57	*6 30*	...	6 30	...	*8 0*	...	8 0	

Up Trains— WEEK DAYS.													SUNDAYS (Christmas Day and Good Friday).
		a.m.	a.m.	a.m		p.m.		p.m.		p.m.		p.m.	
Hawkhurst	dep.	7 49	9 5	11 44	.	3 39	.	4 57	.	6 1	.	6 44	
Cranbrook	,,	7 54	9 10	11 49	...	3 44	...	5 2	...	6 6	...	6 49	
Goudhurst	,,	8 1	9 17	11 58	.	3 51	.	5 9	.	6 13	.	6 56	
Horsmonden	,,	8 6	9 22	12 4	...	3 56	...	5 14	...	6 20	...	7 1	
Paddock Wood	arr.	8 16	9 32	12 14	.	4 6	.	5 24	.	6 30	.	7 11	
	dep.	8 31	9 43	12 16	...	4 31	...	5 30	...	6 33	...	7 22	SERVICE
Tonbridge Junction	arr.	8 40	9 53	12 25	.	4 42	.	5 39	.	6 42	.	7 31	
	dep.	8 45	10 8	12 49	...	4 58	...	6 0	...	7 20	...	7 36	SUSPENDED.
London Bridge	arr.	9 32	10 58	1 46	.	5 46	.	7 0	.	8 29	.	8 54	
Cannon Street	,,	9 36	11 2	...	...	...	...	...	...	...	...	9N 1	
Waterloo Junction	,,	Stop	Stop	1 56	.	5 54	.	7 10	.	.	.	Stop	
Charing Cross	,,			2 4	...	5 59	...	7 14	...	8 37	...		

N—Terminates at London Bridge on Saturdays.

16

JULY 11th, 1921, and until further

Taken from Public Timetable for July 11th 1921.

seven up trains. The irregular working involved more than just one engine operating on the branch and is partly explained by the fact that as one train arrived at Hawkhurst at 4.57pm, so another departed from the bay platform road. The last passenger train of the day was the 7.32pm from Paddock Wood (6pm connection from Charing Cross), so whoever commuted to London couldn't afford to leave the office late. At 8pm the evening train glided into Hawkhurst station where the engine uncoupled from the stock before returning to the nearby shed for the night and the next morning's departure at 7.49am.

Improvements to the London suburban services during 1922 created a shortage of suitable locomotives for this work. Many of the 'Q's and the 'Q1' class rebuilds were suddenly in heavy demand with the result that the normal Hawkhurst branch engines were reallocated. Their place was largely taken by the 'O's which were still around in sufficient numbers, as well as those rebuilt to 'O1' by Wainwright. Tonbridge shed duly received 'O's Nos.170 and 171 for the Hawkhurst and Maidstone branch duties, whilst 'B' class No.458 turned up from time to time to help out.

The restriction on the 'C' class engines working the branch goods appears to have been lifted around this time for a serious accident involving a member of the class took place early one morning. A reporter related the story in the local press:

'An accident occurred to a goods train at Goudhurst station on the Paddock Wood and Hawkhurst branch of the S. E. and C. Railway on Tuesday morning. One of the heaviest locomotives running on the line was completely overturned, but fortunately no one was injured and owing to the prompt measures taken by the railway officials very little inconvenience was caused to the passenger traffic. In the course of the afternoon the line was cleared for the resumption of goods traffic.

The accident occurred to the 6.30am goods train from Paddock Wood. By an error the points were open to a siding and shortly after leaving the station on the Cranbrook side the train turned off on to the siding. Immediately on discovering the mistake the driver shut off steam, the guard applied the brakes, but the train had gained too much momentum to avert an impact with the buffer stop at the end of the siding. The heavy engine (No. 244) crashed into the stop, and the wheels, mounting the bank, the engine, with a tremendous crash, was overturned on to the permanent way immediately in front of the bridge over which passes the roadway leading from Blue Coat Farm to Finchcocks. The driver and the stoker jumped as the locomotive overturned and their escape uninjured is little short of miraculous. The front of the engine tender struck the bank and the remainder of the train was uninjured. The driver and stoker immediately raked out the fire from the engine. The station master telegraphed for a steam crane and breakdown gang from Tonbridge. The operations of clearing the line were at once commenced and about 3.30 the engine was got on her wheels again and an hour later the line was clear of the obstruction and the engine having been lifted on to the siding, was attached to another engine and started on its way to Ashford works. During the day the train service was continued by trains running up to the obstruction from either end and the only inconvenience to passengers was a short walk of about 200 yards, which intervened between the scene of the accident and the station. At dusk the line was clear for traffic as usual.'

The appalling effects of the Great War served only to change the world even more as the pace of social and economic upheaval increased. Apart from the financial crises and depressions, there was an ill-wind blowing for the railways and one which would bring about many casualties. However, the natural wealth of the Weald protected the Hawkhurst branch from becoming one of those lines which suffered either rationalization or total closure. Thanks to the locality's fertile soil and hard-working inhabitants, the railway continued to thrive as carrier of local people, hop-pickers, schoolchildren and a variety of agricultural and domestic goods.

Throughout the twenty-odd years under the managing committee, there was little tangible evidence of any great change on the branch. The SE&CR had, however, renewed certain aspects of the fabric of the railway, including some of the signalling. Many of the original Mackenzie & Holland examples had been replaced with standard SE&CR posts and fittings, perhaps thus removing a little of its individual status. Even so, a few remained to intrigue the railway archaeologist and help retain something of its sense of identity. The surrounding glorious countryside thankfully stayed the same, enabling the branch to hold on to its uniquely special rural character which endeared it to everyone who knew it. By and large, it was a completely different world once the train had left Paddock Wood Junction, before heading towards those dreamy, hazy, wooded hilltops of the High Weald. Nevertheless, tangible signs of 'progress' could be detected in that extra land was leased out in 1922 to British Petroleum, Anglo-American and Shell-Mex oil companies for the erection of storage tanks. Even so, despite the increasing threat from motor vehicle traffic, station master Langridge, who had charge of Hawkhurst and Cranbrook, together with A. J. Heath who looked after Goudhurst and Horsmonden, could rest content that their livelihood was not being threatened. As they left their comfortable railway homes each morning and gazed across this patch of English heaven, the branch line they had come to know so well still had a bright and secure future as the Southern Railway took control on New Year's Day 1923.

William Saxby handing over the Tyer's key token to the driver of engine No. 458. This 'B' class locomotive, along with No. 34, were the only two out of a total of 29 members of the class not to be rebuilt to 'B1'. Only five years later, in December 1931, it was withdrawn for scrap. *H. C. Casserley*

CHAPTER SIX

SUNNY SOUTH DAYS

FOLLOWING the amalgamation of the SER into the Southern Railway, it became clear that the prospects for the Hawkhurst branch were far brighter than that of many other minor or secondary routes which came under investigation. Fortunately, this particular Kentish railway could look forward with confidence to the decades that stretched ahead.

Hawkhurst signalman William Saxby, chatting to the driver of the 6.30 evening train for Paddock Wood on Saturday, 24th July 1926. The signal box had recently been repainted in the smart Southern Railway livery of buff, dark green and white, but it still retained its original SER enamelled iron nameplate 'Hawkhurst Station Signals'.
H. C. Casserley

The Southern Railway was a well-organized company and quickly established its identity, along with a publicity department which led to its slogans becoming familiar rhymes. In the years hence, everyone knew the couplet 'Live in Kent and be content' from the posters which accompanied the spread of suburban electrification. This helped engender the exodus of the middle classes to the leafier climes of London's neighbouring counties.

The villages and small towns of the High Weald were still mainly populated with people who worked locally, but there followed a gradual increase in the number of season ticket holders. It can only be presumed that the joy of living in this exquisite landscape was adequate recompense for the rather long and sometimes tedious journey.

During its twenty-five years existence, the Southern Railway monitored the income and prospects of all its numerous lines. Routes which had come about through historical quirks of fate, or had been laid down to stem competition from rivals, quite naturally began to be heavily scrutinized. Economies in working some of these lines were gradually introduced, either through singling, closure to passengers, or in some cases, complete abandonment. The healthy financial state of the Hawkhurst branch and its usefulness to the Southern may be readily assessed in knowing that it was never threatened in this manner. Indeed, it is perhaps ironic that a branch which Sir Edward Watkin tried so much to kill off in the 1860s survived, when other projects which he personally and passionately pursued quickly succumbed.

Another welcome facet of the Southern was its ability to bring about widespread improvements to the fabric and operation of the railways within its charge. Numerous committees effected significant changes which were generally for the better, although it is a pity that the SR invested so heavily in 'bus company shares to the detriment of its many rural branch lines. Far from complementing railway services, these road hauliers merely siphoned off valuable traffic.

Through the detailed logging of operation and incidents, it is possible to gain something of an insight into the everyday working of the Hawkhurst branch during the ensuing decades. Every irregularity or minor upset had to be reported and investigated, so it is fortunate that the company operated in this way. It should not be misconstrued that, up until 1923, occasional derailments, single-line tablet irregularities, train fires and suchlike did not occur. This is certainly not the case and, generally speaking, it was only the tragic incidents which made the newspaper columns or the records of the old SER. One of the first such known mishaps under the Southern took place on the evening of 2nd October, during the very first year of the new administration. Just after eight o'clock, the 6.55pm goods train from Hawkhurst to Paddock Wood arrived at Horsmonden where it was required as normal to proceed into the loop siding. This was in order that the 8.5pm passenger train from Hawkhurst, which followed, could pass through. Drivers of goods trains entering the southerly end of the loop were instructed to come to a stand at Horsmonden's two-way home signal which, for this operation, was left at 'danger'. Only then should the train proceed at the command of the signalman, who was required to show a green flag or green handlamp, while standing by the points. On this occasion, signalman Wood had set the points for the loop and was waiting in the 'six-foot' (between the loop and running line), waving a lamp displaying a white, or clear, aspect. Driver Batchelor, in charge of the goods, therefore passed the up home signal without stopping, whereupon Wood indicated that he should pull up. Before the driver could do so, his engine collided in the darkness with a loaded wagon which had been left in the fruit-packing dock awaiting collection. Such was the impact that the wagon was knocked off the rails. Wood hurriedly went back to his signal cabin on the platform to give the code 'obstruction danger' to Goudhurst, since the tail end of the goods train was fouling the running line. In order to clear the line as quickly as possible, the engine of the passenger train at Goudhurst uncoupled, before running light to Horsmonden where it drew back the stranded goods. This was drawn back down the line and put away in Goudhurst yard before resuming the 8.5pm service. The breakdown gang was eventually requisitioned, arriving at half-past ten, where re-railment was achieved by one o'clock in the morning. Subsequently, both signalman Wood and driver Batchelor were cautioned over the incident.

Further improvements were introduced as time progressed. In February 1924 Hawkhurst became the first station on the branch to be connected to the national GPO telephone network. Many passengers must have found this a great convenience when it was necessary to call relatives to come and collect them. Less well-off inhabitants either walked the mile into the town, or made use of the motor omnibus, from the Royal Oak Hotel, which bumped and whined its way up the long hill to meet all trains.

On Sundays, Hawkhurst station was closed and locked between 11.40am and 5.55pm. Outside these hours it was opened by the staff for goods traffic only and the two freight trips which were normally operated. This information was evidently known to a burglar who gained entry during a quiet afternoon in September 1925. Forcing open a window and wrenching off the grille of the Booking Office ticket window, the thief crawled through the small opening where he ransacked the room. Breaking open a suitcase, he made off with most of the contents, including a pair of flannel trousers, which resulted in a claim for £26 16s 0d being preferred against the SR. Unlike most petty thieves, no railway items were stolen, although the staff immediately summoned the local police. A month later, the culprit was eventually traced and arrested, whereupon he duly received a quite staggering sentence of five years imprisonment.

The efficient operation of any railway required team effort and the SR employed many people at differing grades to ensure that the company's business was conducted smoothly and efficiently. Responsibility for the four stations was, at this time, down to two station masters. There were also signalmen, booking clerks, porters and ancilliary staff engaged at the stations, whilst added to this were the platelaying gangs and the train crews. Finally, the SR relied on its gatekeepers, who were paid a weekly wage and lived in adjacent railway cottages, to man the level crossings. It was not a demanding job, but it required a certain degree of diligence and attention to duty. Quite often, the wives of railway employees were engaged for this task and they were expected to arrange their household chores around the timetable. It was a pleasant enough way of earning a few extra shillings to supplement the weekly household budget, since the train crews were invariably a friendly lot who would cheer the day along with a wave and a grin. In some instances, the daily newspaper, milk and other commodities would be dropped off along the way.

In December 1925, the gatewoman at Willow Lane Crossing, just 1¼ miles south of Paddock Wood, was probably tucked up in her bed at the end of another demanding day when a loud crash shattered the still night air. Due to the fact that there was very little traffic along these lanes at night, the gates were normally bolted and padlocked across the road after 6pm. It had been a particularly foul night and it seems she had been in a hurry to return to the warmth of her hearthside once she'd fixed both gates. Unfortunately, she'd failed to properly bolt down one of them, which was subsequently blown foul of the line by the high wind later that evening. As a result, at just after eleven o'clock, the 10.40pm goods train from Goudhurst ran into the gate, instantly reducing it to splintered wreckage. No signals were provided at this crossing, the train crews relying solely on their knowledge of the 'road' and the red lamps upon the barriers. Had the gate been blown entirely shut across the line, its glaring bull's-eye light might have been seen, but being half-closed there was no chance of the driver or fireman spotting it in time. 'Miss Williams has been admonished' noted the subsequent report, but she wasn't the first person, and wouldn't be the last, held responsible for wrecking the level crossing gates on the Hawkhurst branch.

A few months later it was the turn of the gates at Churn Lane to be run through. Towards the end of August 1926, a 6.7am 'special' was being operated to Hawkhurst and, although not specifically stated, must have been a hop-pickers train. Checker J. Bailey, who had responsibility for the crossing, was blissfully slumbering in his bed, so the gates were still across the railway, as was the practice on this minor road, whilst the protecting signals were at 'danger'. It was also unfortunate that a thick autumnal mist was hanging heavily in the quiescent, cold air above the surrounding fields and hop gardens. As soon as driver Peckham observed Churn Lane's home signal was still 'on', he

A delightful photograph, taken about 1927 by John Kite, depicting 'O1' No. 48 pulling out of Hawkhurst, having just crossed Slip Mill Road bridge, at the start of the 1 in 80 climb to Badger's Oak tunnel. The spoked wheels of the engine, tender and wagons are strikingly silhouetted against the skyline. *John Kite, cty. John Minnis*

hurriedly applied the locomotive's brakes, but because the line curved to the right in the down direction, guard Dykes at the rear didn't act accordingly until he'd also seen the danger. By this time it was far too late to stop the heavily-loaded train which ran a further 54 yards beyond the signal, before ripping through both gates. Bailey was rudely awoken by this exceptionally noisy alarm call at 6.14am, whilst the exchange of words between himself and the engine crew may best be left to the imagination! Driver Peckham was later reprimanded for assuming the way ahead would be clear, whilst checker Bailey had a ticking-off for being less than attentive in his duties through over-sleeping.

As a probable consequence of this accident, the Southern Railway accordingly revised the signalling arrangements at Churn Lane. On 1st December 1926, the protecting home signals were abolished. They were replaced by new distant signals, both just over 200 yards further out from Churn Lane crossing. The precise details, given in the official signalling records, show that from this date forward, a new down distant was brought into use at 743 yards, and a new up distant at 1,122 yards from the crossing box. These new distant signals continued, of course, to be interlocked with the gate locks on the existing frame.

Accidents involving trains were not always the fault of the operating staff. All number of other factors were frequently responsible, such as the occasion, just two months later, which occurred at Cranbrook. At seven in the morning, on 1st November, the 5.5am goods train from Paddock Wood came steaming up the bank with a wagon, belonging to the LNER, well ablaze. The train pulled up adjacent to the goods yard, where the station staff assisted the engine crew in isolating the truck which was loaded with ninety bales of straw. The fire had gained such a hold and was so fierce, that it took them twenty minutes to extinguish the flames, which by then had destroyed not only the cargo but seriously damaged the wagon. The reasons behind the fire were attributed to a number of co-acting factors. Because of the General Strike, the locomotive was burning imported American coal, which apparently sent out brittle splinters and sparks, whereby the straw was easily ignited. The bales, loaded at the forwarding LNER depot, were protected only by tarpaulins with the ends exposed. With the locomotive working a heavy train, on the 1 in 60 gradient through Furnace Wood, rogue sparks were flying everywhere and it was just unfortunate that one should find the tinder-dry straw.

The mid-1920s witnessed a marked improvement in the level of service, with a pattern of eight trains each way being introduced. Perhaps surprisingly, the journey time of approximately twenty-seven minutes in both directions remained unaltered, even though faster running was feasible. A decade earlier, for example, the 6.40pm from Hawkhurst completed the trip, calling at all stations, in just twenty minutes. Theoretically a speeding-up of services should have been possible, in spite of the prevailing general speed restriction of 40mph throughout. In later years this was altered to a leisurely 30mph, whilst 10mph at Smugley Farm crossing, south of Goudhurst, remained unaltered.

Motive power, besides the 'O1's, the last 'O's and the occasional 'B' class engines, was ordinarily provided by 'Q's and 'Q1's, many of which had been released to the country depots following the rapid spread of suburban electrification. However, by the start of the 1930s, almost every single member of this once-ubiquitous class had disappeared. From then onwards their place was taken by ex-SE&CR 'R' and 'R1' 0-4-4Ts, as well as ex-LB&SCR tank locomotives.

A rationalization of some of the signalling at Paddock Wood took place in 1928 when 'C' cabin was abolished and its work transferred to 'B' cabin, the elevated box astride the Hawkhurst branch at the eastern end of the station. An additional ground frame was provided, whilst a staffing economy of £475 per annum was anticipated as a result of the alteration. While mentioning signalling matters at Paddock Wood, one curiosity was the original Mackenzie & Holland wooden-posted signal, complete with elaborate iron finial, which stood on the platform at the exit of the Hawkhurst bay. It must

202 **JULY 10th, 1927, and until further notice.**

HAWKHURST BRANCH.

(SINGLE LINE—ELECTRIC TABLET.)

Distances.	*DOWN TRAINS. WEEK-DAYS.*	7.22 a.m. Tonbridge.								SO				NS		SO	
		a.m.		a.m.				a.m.		p.m.				p.m.		p.m.	
M. C.		arr.	dep.	arr.	dep.			arr.	dep.	arr.	dep.			arr.	dep.	arr.	dep.
5 21	Paddock Wood	7 31	7 40	.	9 35	.	.	.	10 40	.	*1 15*	.	.	.	1 30	.	*4 0*
9 49	Horsmonden	7 48	7 49	9 43	9 44	...	...	10 48	10 49	*1 23*	*1 24*	...	...	1 38	1 39	*4 8*	*4 9*
11 50	Goudhurst	7 53	7 58	9 48	9 49	.	.	10 53	10 54	*1 28*	*1 29*	.	.	1 43	1 44	*4 13*	*4 14*
15 16	Cranbrook	8 5	8 6	9 57	9 58	...	...	11 2	11 3	*1 37*	*1 38*	...	...	1 52	1 53	*4 22*	*4 23*
16 58	HAWKHURST	8 10	.	10 2	.	.	.	11 7	.	*1 42*	.	.	.	1 57	.	*4 27*	.

DOWN TRAINS. WEEK-DAYS.	NS																	
	p.m.		p.m.				p.m.				p.m.							
	arr.	dep.	arr.	dep.			arr.	dep.			arr.	dep.						
Paddock Wood	.	4 18	.	5 51	.	.	.	7 22	.	.	.	10 5	.	.	.	.	.	.
Horsmonden	4 26	4 27	5 59	6 0	...	...	7 30	7 31	...	...	10 13	10 1	...	...	...	...	...	...
Goudhurst	4 31	4 32	6 4	6 5	.	.	7 35	7 36	.	.	10 18	10 1	.	.	.	.	.	.
Cranbrook	4 40	4 41	6 13	6 14	...	...	7 44	7 45	...	...	10 27	10 2	...	...	...	...	...	...
HAWKHURST	4 45	.	6 18	.	.	.	7 49	.	.	.	10 33	.	.	.	.	.	.	.

Distances.	*UP TRAINS. WEEK-DAYS.*									Mixed.				SO		NS	
		a.m.		a.m.				a.m.		a.m.				p.m.		p.m.	
M. C.		arr.	dep.	arr.	dep.			arr.	dep.	arr.	dep.			arr.	dep.	arr.	dep.
—	HAWKHURST	.	7 44	.	8 35	.	.	.	10 8	.	11 43	.	.	.	*3 15*	.	3 32
1 42	Cranbrook	7 48	7 49	8 39	8 40	...	...	10 12	10 13	11 47	11 48	...	...	*3 19*	*3 20*	3 36	3 37
5 8	Goudhurst	7 55	7 56	8 46	8 47	.	.	10 19	10 20	11 56	11 57	.	.	*3 26*	*3 27*	3 43	3 44
7 9	Horsmonden	8 0	8 1	8 51	8 52	...	...	10 24	10 25	12 2	12 3	...	...	*3 31*	*3 32*	3 48	3 49
11 37	Paddock Wood	8 10	.	9 1	.	.	.	10 34	.	12 12	.	.	.	*3 41*	.	3 58	.

UP TRAINS. WEEK-DAYS.	SO		NS															
	p.m.		p.m.				p.m.				p.m.							
	arr.	dep.	arr.	dep.			arr.	dep.			arr.	dep.						
HAWKHURST	.	*5 5*	.	5 10	.	.	.	6 30	.	.	.	8 9	.	.	.	.	.	.
Cranbrook	*5 9*	*5 10*	5 14	5 15	...	...	6 34	6 35	...	...	8 13	8 14	...	...	...	...	...	...
Goudhurst	*5 16*	*5 17*	5 21	5 22	.	.	6 41	6 42	.	.	8 20	8 21	.	.	.	.	.	.
Horsmonden	*5 21*	*5 22*	5 26	5 27	...	...	6 46	6 47	...	...	8 25	8 26	...	...	...	...	...	...
Paddock Wood	*5 31*	.	5 36	.	.	.	6 56	.	.	.	8 35	.	.	.	.	.	.	.

Paddock Wood, 23rd April 1927, with 'O1' No. 48 once more, this time propelling a string of wagons back out of the up platform road. Note the shunt signal in the 'off' position. The large nameboard is prominent, with its cast-iron letters advising passengers that this was the station for 'Cranbrook & Hawkhurst Line and Maidstone Branch'. Compared to previous pictures, the signalling had been slightly simplified, whilst the old M&H starting signal post can be seen above the 'O1's tender. *H. C. Casserley*

have been intended to signal trains out of the platform at the opening of the branch in 1892, but from all the evidence it seems to have been made redundant very early on. Even the earliest postcard views depict this old signal having been replaced with a bracket signal of SER design which had turned wooden finials. Unusually, the original post, which bore all the signs of once having been fitted-up for carrying a signal arm, counterweight etc., outlasted the branch itself, even though for almost all its life it was a useless artefact. Up until Sunday, 26th June 1932, some of the signalling at Paddock Wood was also controlled by 'A' cabin, situated at the western end of the station and adjacent to the overbridge. After that date, 'A' was closed, with all functions being transferred to the other box, which was simply renamed 'Paddock Wood'. The opportunity was also taken to abolish 'Tudeley Intermediate', its functions henceforth being shared by Paddock Wood and Tonbridge East cabins. A degree of stamina was required by all those who worked at Paddock Wood signalbox. Not only was a considerable amount of armwork required in pulling heavy levers at all hours throughout the day, but three flights of wooden steps had to be negotiated each time the branch tablet was handed over.

A rather amusing incident involving the train tablet took place on 15th February 1928, although it would not have appeared so at the time. The early morning goods, commencing from Paddock Wood at 6am, rumbled into Goudhurst station platform where signalman Reeve was waiting to exchange the Goudhurst-Cranbrook tablet for the Horsmonden-Goudhurst one in the possession of the train crew. In his willingness to be of assistance with the unloading that morning, Reeve laid the Cranbrook tablet on a platform seat, but forgot about making the switch-over when the time came. It was only when the train was merrily steaming around the bend that the blunder dawned on him, whereupon he immediately rang through to his colleague at Cranbrook. Once the train had arrived, driver Luck surrendered the erroneous token to the station porter who set off on his trusty bicycle in the direction of Goudhurst. Meanwhile, signalman Reeve was puffing and panting as fast as he could pedal through the twisting lanes and byways to a hurried rendezvous. Having made the switch and replaced the correct tablets in the instruments, all was well and no delay to the goods occurred. However, they were obliged to report the matter, the result of which led to Reeve being suspended for one day due to inattentiveness, whilst driver Luck lost two days for not checking his tablet before setting off.

Another train fire took place during July 1929 when the 5.50am freight from Paddock Wood was on its way down to Hawkhurst. The guard spotted smoke while the train was in Horsmonden tunnel after the engine had been working quite heavily on the 1 in 66 rising gradient from Churn Lane. Pulling up near the station, buckets of water were used to quickly extinguish the flames which had already succeeded in destroying four bundles of wicker fruit baskets.

The variety of duties, which the staff were generally obliged to carry out, often resulted in human error when normally attentive minds were distracted. Such was the case on the morning of 30th October that year when the second up train of the day, which included a through carriage for London, pulled into Cranbrook at 8.34am. It was common practice for this particular coach to be marshalled at the front of the train, but on this occasion it had been coupled at the rear, at the instruction of Paddock Wood. Signalman Russell was already waiting at his usual spot on Cranbrook platform, ready to exchange tablets as the train came drifting under Hall Farm bridge and into the station. However, driver Bristow pulled up short of the recognized position, owing to the fact that there were some heavy parcels and a perambulator waiting to be loaded into the guard's van which, this morning, was immediately behind the engine. Russell, therefore, placed the iron hoop, to which was affixed the tablet in its leather pouch, upon his shoulder, while he obligingly assisted in the loading of the pram and parcels. His attention was further diverted by several passengers who enquired if they were in the correct carriage for London. It was only after the train had departed, and he'd returned to his cabin, that his oversight suddenly dawned upon him as he opened the pouch. The mistake had also been realized by driver Bristow, who brought his train to a halt near Furnace Farm and sent his fireman running back along the line to make the exchange. This resulted in a delay of twenty minutes, so the error had to be reported. In view of Russell being distracted, he was let off lightly with a caution. However, the driver was ticked-off for failing to check his tablet before starting away from Cranbrook and, as a result, lost two days' pay.

Incidents such as these serve to illustrate the responsibilities faced by the operating staff in running a railway and the joint effort required simply to transport people from one place to another. It was not a case, as the public might well have imagined, of merely pulling a signal lever so the train could set off just as it pleased. The rules governing the movement of trains had evolved over many years in the previous century, providing Britain with the safest possible system. It is

This delightful picture from Hall Farm bridge shows passengers from the 9.7 a.m. (see opposite) strolling up the approach road from Cranbrook on a warm summer's day. *H. C. Casserley*

With the 9.7 a.m. service from Paddock Wood, 'D1' No. 2234 is seen here, pulling away from Cranbrook with plenty of steam to spare on Saturday, 22nd July 1933. *H. C. Casserley*

fortunate that the irregularities in working the Hawkhurst branch never brought about any serious accidents or injuries to passengers, but the SR had a duty to see that its rules and regulations were strictly observed.

An incident, similar in many ways to that at Cranbrook, took place at Hawkhurst only a few months later, on 24th January 1930. On this particular afternoon, signalman Saxby withdrew the tablet from his Tyer's instrument, placed it in the pouch and prepared to hand it over to the driver of the 5.5pm passenger train. However, just at that moment his attention was diverted by the shunting operations going on in the goods yard, where the engine was making up the 5.25pm freight. In his usual manner, he lowered the up platform starting signal, saw the train away and only then spotted the iron hoop and tablet still propped up inside his signalbox. His heart must have sunk into his boots, since he had a remarkable and enviable thirty years unblemished record of duty. It was indeed a pity it should have been tarnished in this way but, in the light of this, he was let off with only a caution. Driver Pope's conduct, on the other hand, was deemed to be inexcusable, whereupon he duly lost three days' pay.

Oddly enough, relief-signalman Hemsley made exactly the same mistake later that year when, on 22nd August, the 8.30am left Hawkhurst without the tablet. Again, it was released from the instrument, placed in its pouch and then, due to a last minute distraction, failed to be handed over to the train crew. The driver noticed this latest blunder only on arrival at Cranbrook, whereby a member of staff from Hawkhurst had to walk up the line with the tablet so the train might proceed. Hemsley lost a day's pay, but the driver, who could offer no reasonable explanation, was harshly dealt with and disgraced by being reduced in rank to a shunting driver.

In May of the following year it was the turn of the Goudhurst signalman to once more forget his procedural duties. The train from Horsmonden had just arrived on its journey to Hawkhurst, whereby signalman Reeve had already taken out the tablet in readiness for the exchange with driver Goldsmith. At the time, Reeve was busy collecting tickets from passengers and, in the confusion, the same tablet was inadvertently accepted by him. Thus, the train went off with the Horsmonden-Goudhurst tablet, an error noticed only when Reeve opened the pouch in his cabin. Once again, arrangements were made to meet the Cranbrook porter halfway. For their lack of attention, driver Goldsmith and signalman Reeve received suspension from duty for three and two days respectively.

This particular spate of irregularities culminated in March 1932 when signalman Saxby withdrew the tablet for the 8.30pm departure from Hawkhurst and was

An ex-LB&SCR 'D1' 0–4–2T No. 2234 sauntering alongside the Kent Coast main line with a train for Hawkhurst about to be overtaken by the Wainwright locomotive hauling a Folkestone express in the summer of 1933. *G. A. Stickler*

again distracted. On this occasion he was, for some reason, required to couple up the engine to the train and, while doing so, placed the pouch on the footboard of the leading coach. It was dark at the time, but the driver should have noticed he hadn't the authority to leave. On arrival at Cranbrook the crew realized they'd nothing to exchange, but were quite unaware that the tablet they so desperately needed was still lying, only a few feet away, where Saxby had left it. If they had only known this, then the matter might have been hurriedly resolved, with no one else any the wiser. Instead, the driver accepted the Cranbrook-Goudhurst tablet and reported he'd obviously omitted to pick up the first one at the commencement of his journey. In the meantime, signalman Saxby, anxious to locate the missing piece of equipment, rang through to Goudhurst cabin asking his colleague to check and see if it was still on the footboard. Although it was too late to hush up the incident, a quick search thankfully revealed it perched in exactly the same position. Matters could have been considerably worse had it fallen off somewhere between stations, thus necessitating a night-time search with handlamps. In spite of its return to Hawkhurst by the next down train, driver Johnson was suspended for three days, whilst Saxby lost two days.

As already mentioned, during these early years of the Southern Railway, minor revisions were made to the signalling. In regard to the actual signals themselves, it was a pity that many of the original C&PWR's signal posts had rotted through, as had some of the replacements put up by the SE&CR. Therefore, the SR set about erecting steel latticed-posts with standardized L&SWR pattern lower-quadrant fittings. Although far more durable, to the railway archaeologist they lacked the aesthetic appeal of the highly-distinctive McKenzie & Holland signals, which were quite unique in the south. Happily, though, given the backwater nature of the Hawkhurst branch, a very small number of these old signals remained for many years, most notably Cranbrook's up starter, whilst some elderly examples from SE&CR days also managed to escape renewal.

In 1933 serious proposals were made, to introduce long and short section working in order to simplify operating the branch at periods during the day, as well as economise on staffing. The long sections were planned to be Paddock Wood-Goudhurst and Goudhurst-Hawkhurst. During such times, the cabins at Horsmonden and Cranbrook would have been switched out. However, in spite of detailed plans being drawn up by the signalling engineers, for some undiscovered reason it was eventually decided not to pursue the idea.

The mile-long climb at 1 in 66 from Churn Lane to Horsmonden cutting is thought to have been partly responsible for a further train fire, which happened during June 1931. As the early-morning freight emerged from the tunnel, the seventh wagon from the engine was well ablaze. The truck, containing empty fruit baskets and bags, was isolated from the rest of the train and pushed into a siding at Horsmonden station. The hose from the locomotive was used to extinguish the flames,

'O1' No. 1041 pausing on the down through line at Paddock Wood whilst a 'C' class was waiting by the up through starting signal. A number of workmen, watched by other staff on the platform, were obviously engaged in some kind of activity in this atmospheric glimpse of life on the Southern at this time.
Lens of Sutton

but not before the contents had been almost destroyed and the truck badly damaged.

Agricultural traffic continued to be the mainstay of the branch, as witnessed by the extra facilities required at sites other than the stations. Thirkell's siding, near Paddock Wood, was situated on the down side, controlled by a small ground frame. Beyond, were the more extensive Churn Lane sidings, on the up side, whilst a mile south of Goudhurst on the down side were sidings at Pattenden. Further accommodation was under review during 1932, following an application from two local landowners, Mr Herbert Coleman and Mr Whitehead. They farmed land along the south side of the railway between Goudhurst and Cranbrook and were keen to have a single track laid in for their business. The SR duly provided a plan to show how a connection, siding and ground frame could be installed, for £351 which included truckloads of ash to form a roadway to the site. A gate across the siding entrance was also allowed for, whilst locking of the points would be provided by Annett's key. Rates would be charged as those from Cranbrook for the acceptance and delivery of goods. However, the scheme was not taken up and it may be assumed that the tradesmen continued using either Cranbrook station or Pattenden.

The Hawkhurst branch is probably most renowned for the hop traffic it carried during the late summer and early autumn. However, equal business came through other seasonal trade, such as Horsmonden's regular lamb sales each July. This event not only necessitated considerable organization by the traffic department, but also extra shunting manoeuvres by the train crews.

The fruit and flower crops were also very valuable to the SR, especially the former, which saw a hectic time for all concerned during harvest. The business, quite naturally, depended heavily upon the weather, whereas fluctuations in quantity and quality were only to be expected. The cherry crop, for which Kent is traditionally famous, was especially vulnerable to late frosts which could scorch and ruin the blossom. Cold winds were another problem, although the valleys of the Weald tended to offer greater protection to trees than in the more exposed orchards in the north of the county. Apples and pears of many varieties grew in abundance and generally proved to be a more reliable crop. On average, around 40,000 crates and packages were loaded and railed out of the district each season from Horsmonden alone, representing over a hundred tons of freight and between £300-£400 worth of business to the Southern Railway

The beautiful weather of 1933 proved to be an exceptionally good year for fruit growers when bumper crops were gathered, packed and loaded into trucks for the London markets. Derek Reader remembers, as a boy, helping out with the loading of soft fruit during July and August in 1937/8. The baskets were taken by lorry from the fields to Goudhurst station where a special train, comprising two or three box wagons and in charge of a 'C' class, would be waiting in the up platform. He recalls that it was necessary to arrive punctually at four o'clock, in order that the cargo could be loaded and promptly despatched

Whilst freight traffic helped sustain the railway, the branch was not unaffected by the growing social trend towards private motor cars and public 'buses. It is doubtful whether regular users would have been especially aware of a decreasing number of passengers on the trains, but it was happening all the same. Nevertheless, the line still provided a valuable service to locals, bound for Maidstone market, or the normal journey to work or school each day.

By comparing the receipts of 1925 with those of 1938 it is possible to detect the drift to competing road transport. Throughout this thirteen year period the sales

The platform starting signal had already 'given the road', as Bill Saxby was strolling along the platform with the tail lamp of the push-pull unit, whilst the driver of the 'D3' class 0–4–4T No. 2367 (formerly LB&SCR *Norwood*) can be seen standing on the left of the engine. Like the 'D1s', a few 'D3s' were similarly allocated to Tonbridge shed during the 1930s. *Lens of Sutton*

of ordinary tickets at Horsmonden and Goudhurst were almost halved. Cranbrook witnessed a drop of around two-thirds, whilst at Hawkhurst a dramatic decline approaching three-quarters took place. Horsmonden and Goudhurst, which suffered least from the drop in ordinary passengers, remained virtually static in season tickets sales, with 31 and 24 regular users respectively. Cranbrook, however, doubled its number to 45 and, perhaps surprisingly, so did Hawkhurst with almost 50 people using the station on annual tickets. It is apparent, therefore, that although the trend towards 'buses continued for short journeys, there was a simultaneous increase in the number of people willing to live this far out in Kent and travel to work by train every day.

Unfortunately, the financial picture as a whole in regard to passenger traffic was not entirely encouraging as receipts were in decline. Nevertheless, this fashion was not confined to the Hawkhurst branch alone, and the drop of approximately one third across the board at this time was far less than experienced on many other lines which eventually closed.

More apparent changes took place during the early years of the 1930s. In line with the company's general policy of economies on branch lines, rationalization, and re-organization of working, the SR closed a number of its sub-sheds. Hawkhurst was officially shut in 1931, whereby all motive power was henceforth supplied and housed at Tonbridge.

Following the complete withdrawal of the entire 'Q' and 'Q1' classes by 1930, the Eastern Section of the SR looked further afield for suitable replacements. Tank engines had obvious advantages over 0-6-0 or 4-4-0 tender locomotives which were sometimes rostered for passenger duties simply because nothing else was available. Eventually, a number of ex-LB&SCR tanks were brought 'over the border' for use on the Westerham, Hythe and Hawkhurst branches, where they performed with complete success. One of the locomotives most regularly seen during the mid-30s was a Stroudley 'D1' 0-4-2T, No. 2234, which trundled up and down all day from Paddock Wood to Hawkhurst on what was a leisurely duty. The 'D3' 0-4-4Ts are also known to have put in an appearance from time to time, but whether they were truly suitable replacements for the old SER tanks they displaced is not recorded. Push-and-pull working was operated more and more due to its efficiency and greater flexibility. Nevertheless, it appears that greater care had to be taken when running with the engine in the rear since trains often ran very quietly. This could be hazardous for those at the farm crossings, particularly during the hop-picking season when youngsters were warned to stay away from the railway. With a train coasting downhill and heading into the wind, the public had to exercise extreme caution when crossing the line.

Generally speaking, the operation of the push-pulls caused few problems once the crews had mastered the foibles of the machinery. However, mechanical faults did occur from time to time, whilst drivers' errors sometimes caused minor accidents. For instance, in the late afternoon of 18th March 1933, the 5pm from Hawkhurst had just completed a smart and punctual half-hour run up the branch, but, in pulling into the bay platform at Paddock Wood, the driver misjudged his speed. As a result the train, with the engine at the rear, hit the buffer stops with a hard jolt, but only superficial damage was caused. One of the passengers, standing up ready to alight, was thrown back onto his seat and complained of being knocked about. No real harm was caused, though, and the driver was let off with just a caution.

Two months later a further incident on the branch had to be reported, but this time it involved a train fire. It occurred at around half-past three on the afternoon of 18th May, during a particularly hot spell of weather that heralded a pleasant summer. In fact, the day was so warm that the creosote in fourteen telegraph poles, loaded into two wagons, had begun to ooze out of the wood. The afternoon goods was marshalled in the ordinary way with the wagons, NE twin timber trucks Nos. 12794 and 72816, positioned fifth and sixth behind the engine. Along with the new poles were fifteen lengths of timber and eight stay blocks. The rest of the train comprised a fairly heavy load, with the result that the engine was working hard on the 1 in 60 Cranbrook bank. Stray sparks ejected from the smokebox soon ignited the flammable liquid seeping out of the poles, whereby flames hungrily took hold as the crew pulled up their train at the down home signal. Both wagons were quickly uncoupled from the rest of the train, which was then drawn forward into the platform, while buckets of water were thrown into the blazing pyre. After managing finally to extinguish the flames, the train proceeded to Hawkhurst, suffering a delay of 33 minutes. Extensive damage was caused to the two trucks and their consignment, and in fact the blaze had been so fierce that adjoining wagons were scorched and seared by the heat. Subsequently, the SR had to pay compensation of £28 15s 3d for the charred poles and sundry items destroyed.

Minor calamities such as this were all part and parcel of railway life and were only to be expected. Other occasional mishaps included derailments, such as the upset caused during mid-morning shunting on 20th June at Paddock Wood. An empty two-coach train, left in the up bay from an earlier working, was being drawn out before stabling for the day in the up siding. Due to a misunderstanding between the acting shunter and the signalman, one of the carriages ended up astride No.50 points, obstructing the Hawkhurst branch where it entered the bay. The Tonbridge breakdown train arrived at 11.42am and within two hours the damage was made good, with normal working resuming at 2.20pm. For the duration, though, the Hawkhurst services were switched to the up local line.

A month later, on 24th July, another derailment necessitated the summoning of the Tonbridge breakdown crew, but this time all the way down to Hawkhurst. Considerable chaos was caused in this instance when, at 8.25 in the morning, a brake van left the road at the points leading into the yard. The brake had come down coupled to the rear of the 7.40am push-pull service from Paddock Wood. After passengers had alighted, the train was shunted out of the platform where the brake was uncoupled, the intention being to gravitate it into the siding. In the meantime, the push-pull unit was drawn back into the platform in readiness to form the 8.30am return working. Porter Bright, who was aboard the brakevan and conducting the operation, saw the points set for the yard, whereupon he released the automatic brake, intending to work the hand brake when necessary. However, as his vehicle trundled over the points, the leading wheels derailed due to the blades not being properly closed. As a result, the 8.30am could not make its exit from the platform road, which sent the 'phone wires buzzing for alternative arrangements to be quickly organized. Tonbridge hurriedly arranged for a fresh engine and coaches to be sent down to Cranbrook, while a bus was hired to take stranded passengers to meet it. Once the replacement train had cleared the branch, the crane was sent down and re-railment was achieved by half past ten. At a subsequent investigation into the matter it was suggested that the reason for the point blades not being properly closed was an obstruction lying between the stock and switch rails. Nevertheless, both porter Bright and signalman Saxby were reprimanded when it emerged that the protecting shunt signal had not been pulled 'off', nor even observed. Quite clearly, the rules and procedures of the railway were there for a definite purpose.

Incredibly, a year to the day, on 24th July 1934, signalman Saxby was involved in yet another derailment at Hawkhurst. Waiting in the bay platform with seven schoolchildren on board was the 7.40am, comprising a two-coach unit and the locomotive from the early morning goods working. It appears that it was the usual practice for the points to be set and the corresponding starting arm on the signal bracket to be lowered in readiness for a prompt departure. However, on this fine morning, driver Burbidge found the signal still at 'danger', so guard Kemp began walking down towards the station to see Saxby who, at that time, happened to be in the booking office. As he approached, Saxby appeared at the booking hall door, whereupon 'All right' hand signals were exchanged. Therefore, the guard returned, giving his driver the signal to start while shouting: 'The signalman says its all right', indicating that the points had been set, even though the signal remained against them. Assuming this would save Saxby a walk back to his cabin, solely in order to lower the signal arm, the crew promptly took the train out, whereupon, seconds later, the engine and leading wheels of the first coach promptly left the track. Apart from a bumpy ride, no one was the worse for wear and the children were able to transfer to the 8.30am service which was on its way down and not affected by the derailed train. It is not difficult at all to imagine the language that probably flew around, nor the sick feeling in the pit of the stomach experienced by those responsible. At 7.55am Hawkhurst had to ring through to Tonbridge to summon the breakdown crew and report the incident. On arrival at 9.30am, work commenced, but the re-railing took all morning and it wasn't until 1.40pm that everything was back on the rails once more. The SR took a very dim view of this instance of slack behaviour. For their lack of vigilance, the signalman and guard were each suspended from duty for four days, whilst the driver was extremely lucky in losing only a day's pay. His fireman also received a ticking-off, being cautioned for failing in his duties in 'not keeping a look-out on the route ahead'.

It is true to say that all railway staff were obliged to be attentive at all times, not only in their own duties, as laid out in the company rule book, but as a matter of course. Fortunately, such was the case in most instances and more serious accidents were often averted. One of the most common hazards on the branch appears to have been freight train fires, brought about by a combination of factors such as dry summers, the nature of the merchandise, heavy loads and steep gradients. During the tinder-dry weeks of late summer and autumn, the crews were required to keep a special look-out, not only for train fires, but also lineside blazes which could quickly spread uncontrolled. The vulnerable stretches were the notorious climb up to Cranbrook from Goudhurst and the long gradient from Churn Lane to Horsmonden tunnel. On 10th August, the engine on the 12.50pm midday goods to Hawkhurst had been working particularly hard on the run up to Horsmonden with a heavily-loaded train which included a string of empties. As the train echoed through the short tunnel, the guard observed a fire in the third vehicle from the engine, a NE wagon, No.70519. On arrival at the station the staff assisted in dowsing the flames which had already succeeeded in destroying 28 of the 40 half-sieves on board. A Southern Railway box truck, No.46672, immediately behind, was also badly scorched.

A year later, on 15th August 1935, an indentical incident took place, but this time in a wagon belonging to the Great Western Railway. Eighty empty fruit baskets destined for the packing station at Horsmonden were completely destroyed, whilst the wagon itself was badly burnt.

One other fire known to have occurred during this period was on Thursday, 23rd September 1937, at 6.50am when the early morning freight was running between Goudhurst and Cranbrook. Smoke suddenly began issuing forth from the sixth wagon, whereupon the crew quickly brought the train to a stand. Assisted by members of the engineering department, who happened to be working nearby, they managed to pull apart the load of timber destined for Hawkhurst, thus saving much of the consignment. However, the LNER wagon, originating from Silvertown, was seriously damaged in spite of attempts to dowse the flames with water taken from the locomotive's tanks. It was assumed that a quantity of straw left on the floor of the wagon had been ignited by a rogue spark, which had then started this latest conflagration. The stranded train led to the 7.35am passenger service from Paddock Wood to Hawkhurst being terminated at Goudhurst, while two up trains were cancelled with passengers conveyed by motor coach.

Apart from the occasional fires, derailments and irregularities, there were often other incidents which required investigation. An unusual state of affairs led to a rather curious accident which occurred on 30th October 1934. This involved the ten o'clock freight from Hawkhurst to Paddock Wood which had been sent ahead early due to a light load. With only a box wagon of fruit and a brakevan, 'O1' class No.1437 started away from Horsmonden at 10.18am, instead of the normal booked time of 10.55am. Meanwhile, checker Bailey at Churn Lane siding who, it may be recalled, had responsibility for operating the gates, was attending to a line of wagons being prepared for the evening freight. He heard the bell code 'is line clear?' and assumed this meant the train he was expecting was just about to leave Goudhurst. Thinking he had at least another ten minutes to spare, he carried on working in the sidings. Worse still, though, he failed to hear the 'train entering section', sounded on his bell by the Horsmonden signalman as the 'O1' steamed out of the platform and into the cutting. Four minutes later, to his sudden amazement, he heard the sound of a train approaching on the breeze, whereby he dropped what he was doing and ran towards the crossing. On the footplate of the Stirling 0-6-0, driver Kinchen had been surprised to see the Churn Lane distant still 'on', so he and guard Kemp reduced speed. Due to the curvature of the line, the position of the gates couldn't be seen until quite late, especially when the sidings were full of wagons. Seeing the barriers still across the railway, a full application of the brake was made, but it was too late to stop No.1437 sliding through both gates. Even though no other damage was caused, the driver was reprimanded for failing to sufficiently check the speed of his engine after passing the distant signal. The SR also took steps to see that the relay bell at the crossing keeper's hut was made to ring more loudly.

Communication between all the signal boxes and the branch stations was, of course, already established, but up until then only Hawkhurst had an outside connection into the GPO's telephone system. This meant that local traders either had to conduct their business by letter, or visit the stations in person if they wished to make enquiries or arrangements. Not surprisingly, in view of the large amount of fruit and other agricultural traffic handled at Horsmonden, representations were made to the SR to have the station wired up to the public telephone. The SR agreed, whereby an instrument was duly installed by the GPO in the booking hall for an annual rent of £6 8s 0d.

Throughout the 1930s the Hawkhurst branch was regularly used each summer by ramblers who would either travel down separately, in couples, or sometimes in well-organized parties. The Southern Railway published its own popular guide books for those who wished to explore the countryside around London which laid within easy reach of both steam and electric trains. The more adventurous, however, took to the branch lines that led deep into the countryside where new development, arterial roads and suburbia weren't known. Many came to tramp the empty lanes and winding roads of the High Weald, with its breathtaking scenery and unspoilt villages, as yet untouched by so-called improvements. Here, little had changed in decades as each trackway led past whispering woods, across scented meadows and through secret valleys. Of course, the English weather was often typically unpredictable, but 22nd July 1934 was a perfectly beautiful day when 'H' class 0-4-4T No.1553 and 'C' class 0-6-0 No.1291 were coupled together to rumble into Cranbrook with a specially-chartered Ramblers' Excursion.

The 'C's and 'H's were still very rare visitors to the branch since at that time there were still enough 'O1's around to handle most of the freight trips, whilst ex-LB&SCR 'D1's and 'D3's were often given charge of passenger duties. These were increasingly augmented by ex-LC&DR 'R' and SE&CR 'R1' 0-4-4 tanks, a class known affectionately to the crewmen as 'Bobtails'. Based at Tonbridge, they were also sent out to work the Westerham and Maidstone branches, as well as the Redhill service on the old SER main line. Specifically, 'R's Nos.1666/8/9/70/75 and 'R1's Nos.1700/3/4/7/10 were used, but 1666 and 1704 appear to have been principally rostered on the runs to Hawkhurst.

A spell of wet weather towards the end of 1935 brought trouble to the line when, on the night of 2nd/3rd January, part of the embankment near Forge Farm, south of Goudhurst, subsided. A ganger discovered the slip at 5.30 that morning, whereupon he raised the alarm, while arrangements were put in hand to make good the damage. All trains terminated at and returned from Goudhurst, with emergency 'bus services substituting. The gangs worked all through the morning and were able to have the line open for use by 2 o'clock in the afternoon. Even so, a speed restriction of 15mph remained in force for seventeen days.

As spring turned to summer once more, the warm spell being enjoyed by everyone settled in and 1936 turned out to be a better year to get out and about. The long,

Even though the branch was normally closed on Sundays, occasional specials were operated. Here, a Ramblers' Excursion, hauled by 'C' class No. 1291 and piloted by 'H' class No. 1553, was photographed leaving Cranbrook on 22nd July 1934 as eager hikers were making their way up the approach road, no doubt intent on discovering the charms of the High Weald on this sunny morning.

G. A. Stickler

The diminutive signal box at Horsmonden may be seen in this unusual view of the station and goods yard. The curiously windowless rear wall of the station master's house is seen above the open wagons. These belonged to various railway companies, private owners, as well as the Midland Colliery. *H. A. Vallance*

The station master at Goudhurst had a rose arbour over his door, and ivy making its way up the walls. It must have been a rather idyllic posting, living here as station master, away from the hectic life at the busier places, with the branch trains drifting past the windows as regularly as clockwork. The down side waiting shelter was still in place, but the up starting signal had been replaced with a concrete post one. *H. A. Vallance*

sunny days were also welcomed by the SR, not only for the increase they brought in passenger receipts, but also the rise in goods traffic. Bumper crops created more business for the railway and, in spite of the growing competition from road vehicles, Horsmonden, for example, was able to maintain its share of the market, with no decrease whatsoever in trade over a decade. Even allowing for the increase in rail charges, which had risen by approximately 25% during this period, the returns were most encouraging. Unfortunately, though, this welcome bonus was wiped out in the following year due to poor weather in spring which reduced outgoing produce by as much as a quarter.

Later on, in the summer of 1936, a distressing accident took place on the morning of 8th August. In a field, quite some distance from the railway, a horse belonging to Fred Russell of Pullen's Farm was being moved to fresh pasture. Without warning, the animal suddenly took off, but, since it wasn't wearing a bridle or headstall, the task of recapture was difficult. After a considerable chase, the horse jumped a number of hedgerows into adjoining fields, before leaping over the boundary fence and onto the railway. Just at that moment the 9.43am push-pull from Hawkhurst, with the engine at the rear, had left Goudhurst and was approaching Smallbridge. The driver immediately made a full application of the brake, but the unfortunate creature went straight underneath the train and was instantly killed. The undergear of the unit was damaged, whilst the train crew had the gruesome task of assisting farm hands in removing the poor animal's remains. Such incidents were understandably upsetting and on this occasion it was one of those unavoidable rare moments when fate brings about circumstances which lead to a tragedy.

Smallbridge was yet again in the news during 1938 when two accidents involving the level crossing were reported. During this period the SR employed Mr. and Mrs. Capeling as keepers. They lived in the railway cottage on the eastern side of the line, adjacent to the minor road which twists its way down from the heights of Goudhurst, past Trottenden Farm and on to the Horsmonden Road. On the evening of 28th February Mrs. Capeling was on duty, since her husband was having his normal two-hour break. At a quarter to eight, the block repeating bell in their porch announced 'train entering section', but since Mrs Capeling had already closed the gates across the roadway, she felt there was no need to go out into the dark and windy night. Moments later, they were both startled as 'R1' class No.1704, leading a two-coach push-pull set, smashed through the down side gate. Pulling up, the crew found that the automatic brake pipe and lamp bracket on the locomotive's buffer beam had been damaged in the collision. It was therefore necessary for the train to carry on to Goudhurst, under the control of the hand brake only, where the fractured vacuum pipe could be temporarily repaired, probably by stuffing with oily rags. At a subsequent investigation into the incident, it

A quiet moment between trains in this 1930s view, showing the western end of the loop and catch siding.

When Hugh Vallance visited the line in the mid-1930s, he found well-tended rural stations. The roses at Cranbrook were always a much-admired feature, as was the remarkable and wholly appropriate hop bine which is seen adorning the side of the signal box and scrambling up the adjoining telegraph pole. A repaint seems imminent, whilst, unlike Hawkhurst, the signal box originally had just 'CRANBROOK' painted onto its front panel. *H. A. Vallance*

Cranbrook's smock mill, dating from 1814, is perfectly framed in this Edwardian view looking eastwards along Stone Street. This charming old Wealden town, with its delightful mixture of old buildings and varied selection of shops, rarely failed to provide something of intrigue for those who wandered hereabouts.

emerged that the keeper and his wife were not in the habit of padlocking the gates, as required by the regulations and had, instead, relied solely upon the bolts being dropped into the road. It was assumed that an unknown person had used the crossing after Mrs. Capeling had closed them and hadn't bothered to fix the gate securely. Consequently, the strong wind that evening had driven the gate back to stand in the path of the approaching train. The SR warned them both to be more vigilant in future.

Oddly enough, the second accident took place only months later and involved the loss of both gates when another train ran through them. This time it happened very early on a Sunday morning, on 19th June, and must surely have awoken the slumbering occupants inside the keeper's cottage. The train formed a connection off the 1.45am Aldershot to Rye special, which had left Paddock Wood at 3.25am. Mr. Luck, the Goudhurst station master, had been previously informed of its running, but had completely forgotten to advise Smallbridge crossing, a foolish error, since at night the gates were always bolted and padlocked across the railway. Driver Smith was in charge of 'O1' class No.1432, which was running tender first, as dawn began to break on a rather cold and drizzly midsummer morning. Visibility was very poor, partly owing to the dim light and the heavy mist hanging about the adjoining fields and across the railway. As a result, he didn't notice the red glare from the gates' bull's-eye lamps until he was about a hundred yards away. He immediately made a full application of the brake but, on a falling gradient with a heavy train, it had limited effect and there was little time to do much else. The 'O1' broke through the wooden gates, smashing the remnants beneath its wheels before finally coming to a stand some fifty yards the other side. Yet again, the vacuum pipe had been fractured by a blow from the obstruction, so, once more, the train was taken on to Goudhurst with only the hand brake. Fortunately, the crew's ingenuity effected a temporary repair, utilizing oily cloths rammed into the pipe and thus enabling the vacuum to be restored. Only eleven minutes lost time was recorded as the train left Goudhurst for its destination. In due course, station master Luck was ticked off for failing in his duties, whilst the engine crew were held free from blame in view of the weather conditions.

Two further tablet irregularities during 1938 appear to have exasperated the SR so much that they revised the signalling arrangements. The first occurred on Saturday, 28th May, after the 9.7am from Paddock Wood to Hawkhurst had just left Goudhurst. The signalman returned from the down platform, walked up the steps into his cabin, placed the tablet on the Tyer's instrument and returned the down starting signal to danger. He then carried on with some pressing station business,

A smiling young woman (Hugh Vallance's wife?) posing by one of the station lamps at Hawkhurst. The porters' room near the buffer stops is seen with both its top sashes pulled right down – presumably it was a very warm day. This wooden building was provided in place of the old railway carriage body which proved inadequate when the porters were ousted from the main station building. Behind this we can see a gangers' trolley hut, and a corrugated-iron oil store. *H. A. Vallance*

completely forgetting to put the tablet in the instrument, as well as sending on the 'Train out of section' message to Horsmonden. In due course, he returned to his cabin to exchange bell codes with Cranbrook for the down train, before accepting entry into his section of the 9.43am up train from Hawkhurst. Having done this, he returned to the other matters on his mind. At around 9.52am he left what he was doing and made his way down to the road where he shut the level crossing gates before lowering his signals. As the train came steaming into the station, he sent 'Train entering section' to Horsmonden. He then picked up the tablet and, after opening the crossing gates behind the train, went up to the driver and exchanged tablets. Presumably, he had entirely forgotten that he'd omitted to pass the tablet through the Tyer's instrument as required. Nor had he received acceptance of the up train from Horsmonden in the authorized manner. When he'd sent 'Train entering section', the Horsmonden signalman had not been in his cabin and, although he'd heard the bell, he wasn't sure what number of rings had been given, i.e., 2-pause-1 (Train out of section), or 2 (Train entering section). He therefore attempted to contact Goudhurst on the railway circuit, but by that time the Goudhurst signalman was absent from his cabin. He then tried the office telephone, with success, but it was too late since the train was already on its way. The SR viewed this incident with some disapproval and suspended the Goudhurst signalman for two days, whilst his colleague was let off with only a stern caution.

The final straw for the SR was obviously the incident which took place on Saturday, 5th November, involving the 7.35am to Hawkhurst. On arrival at Horsmonden the tablets were correctly exchanged in the normal fashion, after which the signalman went along to the van to assist the guard in unloading the large number of parcels. Incredibly, the signalman then returned to the engine and exchanged tablets once again, all concerned completely forgetting they'd already fulfilled this duty. The error was only realized after the train had left and the tablet was about to be entered into the instrument. A taxi-cab was hurriedly summoned, whereby the Horsmonden booking clerk made the correct exchange at Goudhurst. The mix-up resulted in the train being delayed by six minutes. The driver subsequently acknowledged his failure, but escaped being disciplined as he was due to retire at the end of that week. The signalman, however, was not quite so lucky and lost a day's pay.

Following these half-dozen incidents in the space of eight years, the SR spent £400 on altering the locking arrangements on the branch. Attention was drawn to the fact that the starting signals at stations weren't interlocked with the relative tablet instruments, in accordance with what was standard practice elsewhere.

The revision ensured that the starting signal could not, henceforth, be lowered until the correct tablet had been passed through the Tyer's electric instrument. It is worth mentioning that before the work was authorized, Mr. Ellson, the chief engineer, commented: 'This single line has been in operation for many years without this locking and the amount of traffic over the Branch is comparatively small. I presume you have taken this into consideration and are satisfied that the circumstances justify this expenditure?'. Before the go-ahead was received, the SR perused the cash receipts of the line which, in themselves, provide a useful insight into its economic performance:

Cash Remitted	1925	1938
	£	£
Paddock Wood	14,252	9,688
Horsmonden	3,724	1,214
Goudhurst	2,727	983
Cranbrook	6,366	1,884
Hawkhurst	4,303	2,088

The above table clearly indicates the gradual loss of income to the railway over a thirteen year period, with matters worsened by the fact that the pound sterling was also worth rather less in 1938.

It would appear that the revision to the Tyer's instruments put an end to the spate of irregularities for the time being. However, they were not eradicated entirely as later events would prove. These incidents, as well as minor derailments and other upsets, inevitably took place at odd intervals throughout the line's history. It may also be concluded that these had happened right from the opening of the line in the days of the old SER, even though such reports have not come to light. It would be wrong to imagine that the branch was, in any sense, unsafe or especially prone to these unfortunate circumstances. Indeed, the Hawkhurst branch certainly does not stand out as exceptional in this respect. It is simply that every irregular matter had to be reported and investigated, while for most of the time the railway operated safely, efficiently and according to schedule. No record of any passenger fatality has been found, which is creditworthy, although one or two might have been jostled about on occasions!

Most of the drivers on the Hawkhurst branch were well used to the foibles of the push-pull units, for instance, knowing exactly when and how to apply the Westinghouse brake. Unfortunately, for newly-passed drivers, no amount of theory, or even guidance by experienced men, could help when it came to being 'up front' in the driving unit, all by yourself and responsible for your train. One new driver, recently rostered to the units on the Hawkhurst branch found this out when, on Friday, 15th October 1938, he was bringing the 9.43am from Hawkhurst into Paddock Wood. The engine was, of course, propelling at the rear, but it seems apparent that he misjudged his speed for he found there wasn't quite enough room left between his unit and the buffers by the time he'd applied the brakes. No real damage was caused, but the journey was ended rather too abruptly for one passenger on board who promptly tore the staff off a strip for being thrown about. No doubt a cup of tea afterwards in the station offices did wonders and restored his composure. The young driver, in view of his inexperience, was let off with only a warning to be more careful in future.

From 1934 onwards, the timetable of eight trains each way on weekdays had been revised and reduced to form an imbalanced working of seven up and six down trains. This continued for the duration of the 'thirties, up until the outbreak of war in 1939. The first departure from Hawkhurst was at 7.45am. This train passed a down service at Goudhurst which, incidentally, had to be held there for nine minutes while the section cleared. The down train for Hawkhurst then made a further journey up and down the branch, before arriving back at Paddock Wood at 10.15am. It was normal practice for the early crew to come off around midday, their place being taken by the late shift who would book on before taking out the 12.30pm, returning from Hawkhurst an hour later. No further trips were made during the afternoon on Mondays to Fridays, the stock being left in the bay at the main line station, until 4.20pm when three runs were made to cater for schoolchildren, commuters and other workers returning home. The last train arrived back at Paddock Wood at 8.36pm where the engine came off, before running light to Tonbridge where it returned to the shed. On Saturdays an extra mid-afternoon run was made, presumably for shoppers and those desirous of reaching the area for hiking and other such pursuits. Perhaps surprisingly, there were no late evening trains, not even during the summer Saturdays when it would not be unreasonable to imagine that the locals might want a night out. Presumably the Regal cinema at Cranbrook and the local public houses provided sufficient entertainment.

Those who did avail themselves of a ticket in the 'ninepenny' or 'one-and-tuppennies' at the weekly filmshows, would have been made well aware by the newsreels of the worsening situation in Europe. The events taking place throughout Germany at that time might well have seemed many miles away, yet from Kent the continent could appear uncomfortably close. When, at last, the declaration of war came over the wireless that Sunday morning, the inhabitants of the High Weald were no less ill at ease when the air raid sirens were first tested, causing many to panic. Outwardly, the country-side remained almost unchanged, the surroundings seeming as secure and as lovely as ever. The timeless beauty of this part of Kent, with its sleepy villages and hamlets, its rambling market towns and ancient churches, epitomized the enduring image of England. Yet, how secure was this way of life now that hostile forces might soon be gathering upon the French coast just across that narrow stretch of water?

The outbreak of the war coincided with the height of the hop-picking season, a busier than usual time for the SR. Prior to the news, which most people had half-expected, the Southern Railway had made preliminary plans for emergency services to deal with such matters as troop movements and the transportation of war supplies. The Hawkhurst branch service was drastically cut, the normal timetable being immediately withdrawn. From the beginning of September 1939 there were only three down trains; at 7.35am, 12.40pm and 6.40pm, while up trains ran at 7.45am, 8.25am, 1.50pm and 7.25pm.

A few days into the war there occurred the first of three deaths upon the line in a spate of accidents in almost consecutive summers. The first happened on 16th September, when a sixty-one year-old man named Chamberlain was struck by a train near Cranbrook and instantly killed. He had no business to be trespassing on the railway and the coroner subsequently recorded a verdict of death by misadventure. A year later, on 17th July 1940, Mr. J. Foreman, aged 65, was run down and killed by a train at Smugley Farm crossing, south of Goudhurst. The driver stated he'd blown the whistle 200 yards before the crossing as required. Apparently the old chap suffered from deafness and had obviously heard nothing since he'd walked straight in front of the approaching train. This unhappy episode was concluded on 25th June 1942 when 71 year-old Mr. E. T. Turk also stepped in front of a train, the 12.40pm to Hawkhurst, at Church Farm accommodation crossing between Horsmonden and Goudhurst.

Further trouble with landslips between Goudhurst and Cranbrook came about towards the end of 1939. In the early morning of Tuesday, 28th November, a slip occurred on the down side, blocking the line between mileposts 43½ and 43¾. All services had to be suspended for the rest of the day, with trains running only between Paddock Wood and Goudhurst. A special 'bus service was laid on for Cranbrook and Hawkhurst until the engineers re-opened the line at 6.45 that evening.

With the sharp reduction in train services throughout the Southern, many passenger engines were stored away. Due to the increasing danger of air-raids, with railways being a favoured target, it was considered prudent to move as many locomotives as possible from the larger sheds. Remote locations were chosen and Don Bradley revealed that two of Wainwright's 'E' class 4-4-0s, Nos.1157 and 1516, were stored at Hawkhurst. Even though not specifically stated, it might be reasonable to assume they were housed inside the redundant, but perfectly useable, engine shed. It is noteworthy that the 'E's were ordinarily prohibited from travelling over this particular Wealden branch and the restriction was certainly reintroduced after the war since both engines are specifically listed in instructions issued in 1949. While dealing with engine restrictions, it is appropriate to mention that the ruling: 'Tender engines running to Hawkhurst should only proceed tender first' was rescinded as from 13th January 1944.

The operation of any railway can be a difficult and sometimes dangerous job in ordinary circumstances. The very nature of the conditions requires diligence to duty at all times, yet some accidents seem unavoidable.

HAWKHURST BRANCH—WEEK-DAYS.

	* a.m.		* p.m.		* p.m.	
Paddock Wood	7 35	...	12 40	...	6 40	...
Horsmonden	7 45	.	12 50	.	6 50	.
Goudhurst	7A 51	.	12 56	.	6 56	.
Cranbrook	8 10	...	1 5	...	7 5	...
Hawkhurst..............	8 15	.	1 10	.	7 10	.

	a.m.		* a.m.	* p.m.		* p.m.
Hawkhurst...............	7 45	.	8 25	1 50	.	7 25
Cranbrook	7 49	...	8 29	1 54	...	7 29
Goudhurst	7 58	.	8 38	2 3	.	7 38
Horsmonden	8 4	...	8 44	2 9	...	7 44
Paddock Wood	8 15	.	8 55	2 20	.	7 55

A—Depart Goudhurst 8.1 a.m.

Emergency timetable from September 1939.

HAWKHURST BRANCH.

UP TRAINS—WEEK-DAYS.

From	—		—					
	A.M. arr.	A.M. dep.	P.M. arr.	P.M. dep.				
		Q.						
Hawkhurst	...	10 0	...	5 50	...	...	...	...
Cranbrook	10 5	10 15	5 55	6 46	...	...	...	...
Pattenden Siding ...	...	...	C.	S.				
Goudhurst	10 25	10 37	6 56	7 15	...	...	...	...
Horsmonden	10 45	10 55	7 25	7 55	...	...	...	...
Churn Lane	11 0	11 7	8 0	8 15	...	...	...	...
Paddock Wood	11 15	...	8 25	...	...	...	...	...
To								

DOWN TRAINS—WEEK-DAYS.

	—		—	
	A.M. arr.	A.M. dep.	P.M. arr.	P.M. dep.
				S.X.
Paddock Wood ...	...	5 50	...	12 42
Churn Lane Siding	...	...	12 50	1 0
Horsmonden ...	6 5	6 15	1 10	1 50
Goudhurst	6 31	6 44	1 57	2 40
Pattenden Siding	...	...	C.	S.
Cranbrook	6 55	7 10	2 55	3 55
Hawkhurst	7 18	...	4 0	...

Freight timetable from 3rd July 1939.

Perhaps railway servants are no more superstitious than anyone else, yet they could be forgiven for supposing that luck has a habit of running out when a colleague is involved in an accident, or maybe even killed. Occasionally, men might have worked for years, then, all of a sudden, it seems the odds are stacked against them, as along comes a calamity which leaves workmates stunned. One man who fell into this category was driver J. J. Diplock of Tonbridge. It all began on 29th October 1941, a particularly foul and miserable day, with strong and bitterly cold winds, driving rain and sleet. At 1.7pm the up service pulled out of Hawkhurst, the engine running bunker first, with driver Diplock and his mate no doubt glad of the warmth emanating from the firebox. It was the sort of day when most people stayed indoors, venturing out only if they had to, so the train made good time and was not delayed at any of the stations on the way up. At 1.25pm it left Horsmonden, at the time when the crossing keeper at Churn Lane kept one ear on the bell at his hut. A tractor was busy at work in the sidings there and, with the high wind blowing and gusting, the keeper didn't hear the bell code rung through from Horsmonden, so he assumed the train was running late. Eventually, he thought he'd better stop helping out with the work and attend to the gates, or at least ring up on the circuit to find out what was happening. Just as he stepped from sleeper to sleeper he heard the train approaching. On board, driver Diplock had already observed the Churn Lane distant still at 'caution', whereupon he'd eased up. When he spotted the gates barring his path he promptly made a full application of the brake. Likewise, guard Blunden, who was travelling in the leading compartment, applied his handbrake when he looked out to see what was up. Ordinarily, the train would almost certainly have stopped in time, even though the weight of the train was pushing down on the engine on the 1 in 66 falling gradient. However, the sleet had made the rails quite treacherous and, at this time of the year, autumn leaves had covered the topside of the rails with a slimy, substance as slippery as grease. The crew must have thought they'd get away with it but the 'R1's wheels locked and skidded, whereupon the locomotive went straight through both gates at the very last moment, coming to a stand only ten yards the other side.

Driver Diplock was coming up to 65 years of age and due to retire very shortly. It is not difficult to imagine how he felt about this annoying incident which blotted his copybook. No doubt he expected his workmates to pull his leg over the incident, since a driver with a lifetime's experience might be expected to have done better. The combination of such cold weather in autumn was partly to blame, but the crossing keeper was still criticised for his lack of attentiveness. For driver Diplock, though, there was far worse to come. In all likelihood he could have expected little more than a warning in view of his pending retirement, yet fate was about to deal the cruellest of blows. Only two days after the incident, on Friday 31st October, Diplock entered the shed at Tonbridge where, at 6.20 in the morning he set about oiling up his engine. The rulebook stated that before any work commenced on locomotives, lighted warning lamps should be in position as a caution to other drivers and firemen. Perhaps the Churn Lane incident was still on his mind, but, for whatever reason, he simply didn't bother and climbed into the motion with his oilcan. Curiously, his fireman, who likewise should have noticed the error, failed to protect his driver. Minutes later another locomotive entered the shed and, although travelling only very slowly, came into contact with Diplock's engine and nudged it forwards. It was sufficient to trap him in the motion where he died almost instantly.

At a subsequent enquiry, the SR criticized the driver of the second engine for failing to see that the road was clear before entering the shed. Diplock's fireman was also remiss for failing to protect his engine with lamps, even though he was under the instruction of his mate. It was a sad and tragic end for one of the regular Hawkhurst branch drivers, a man with 46 long years of service behind him. Denied his well-earned retirement through a combination of carelessness and quirks of fate, it doubtless served as a chilling lesson to all his colleagues to observe more thoroughly the railway's rules and regulations.

The unhappy episode involving driver Diplock undoubtedly stunned and saddened his friends and workmates and is, perhaps, the worst incident in connection with the Hawkhurst branch. Rarely, though, did anyone who worked on the operating side not 'come a cropper' at some stage in their career. Some of the upsets appear mildly amusing nowadays, although they were viewed as anything but at the time. Quite what was going on at Hawkhurst one summer morning in 1941 defies description and the scant details surrounding the incident fail to fully explain the affair. On this day, Tuesday, 15th July, the 5.50am freight from Paddock Wood, consisting of seven wagons and a brake van, didn't stop at the home signal which was at 'danger', whereupon it collided with the empty passenger stock in the bay platform. Five wagons and the first vehicle of the stabled train were badly damaged in the accident which took place at half past seven. As a result, the first up train had to be cancelled, while hapless passengers were obliged to await the arrival of the later service. The driver of the goods lost a day's pay, while poor old signalman Saxby received a caution, although his part in the affair is not clear.

A year later, in the spring of 1942, it was the turn of the gates at Smallbridge to be renewed once again, by courtesy of Tonbridge locomotive depot! At 1.39pm, on what was rather appropriately April Fool's Day, the Goudhurst porter was deputizing as relief crossing keeper when, for some reason, both gates were made fit only for kindling wood. The driver was cautioned for not having his train under proper control, whilst the porter received a similar warning to be a little more attentive in future.

Another driver, later in that same year, had a surprise at Paddock Wood while on the trip up from Hawkhurst. On Thursday, 24th September, he'd just entered the bay platform with the 5.5pm when, it was later alleged, he misjudged his speed and consequently terminated the journey with a bang. Most drivers were well used to approaching the buffers here with more than a degree of caution since the rails in the bay road could often be very greasy and it was not a good idea to rely entirely on the engine's braking power!

The train service was gradually improved as the war dragged on into the 1940s. By September 1942 the timetable advertised six down and seven up trains on Mondays to Fridays, with the extra run on Saturday afternoons likewise restored. Nevertheless, it would appear that 'unnecessary' travelling was still being discouraged as the Minister of War Transport instructed that the entire range of cheap fare tickets should be withdrawn from 5th October.

During this period the freight trips were normally rationed to one outwards run in the morning, but during seasonal periods it was often requisite to organize a 'conditional' goods. This left Hawkhurst at 10am, picking up at all stations and Churn Siding, before arrival back at Paddock Wood at 11.15am. The average day began in the early hours when the signalman at Paddock Wood, which was manned all round the clock, would 'set the road' and descend his three flights of steps to hand over the first tablet to the driver of the down goods which departed at 5.30am. Breaking the early-morning stillness, the locomotive pounded through the quiet, empty fields with its string of empties and wagons loaded with inwards goods such as household coal, agricultural supplies, builders' merchandise, parcels, newspapers and milk. Apart from high summer, the mornings were dark, with only the odd light from the farmsteads twinkling across the hopfields and mist-strewn orchards. Ahead, the green light from Churn Lane distant signal indicated that the gates were open for a clear run through as the locomotive kept up the momentum for the climb into the Wealden hills. The echo from the exhaust and the resounding wheels over the rail joints provided a useful early-morning call for those who had to leave their slumbers and begin the day. Disappearing into Horsmonden cutting and the short tunnel, the train arrived moments later at the station where fifteen minutes were spent unloading before the 'right away' at six o'clock. After a leisurely ten minutes run down to Goudhurst, the day's business was sorted out with the station staff who booked on at 6am. At 6.27am the train steamed out, skirting the bottom of the hill, to pass through more hop fields, before pounding up the gradients through Bedgebury Forest. Pattenden siding was not called at on the outward journey, so the trip to Cranbrook was normally completed in eleven minutes. After unloading empty milk churns, parcels and the daily newspapers in the ten minutes allowed, the rails in Badger's Oak tunnel resounded to the sound of the 0-6-0 as it made the final lap to Hawkhurst. Beneath the canopy, the old SER longcase clock showed six minutes past seven, if the train was on time, as the last of the small consignments was unloaded. Having run round the train, the wagons were put into the sidings, before the engine backed onto the passenger stock left in the bay which formed the first up train of the day. This left at 7.40am, where it passed the first down train waiting in the loop platform at Goudhurst.

The afternoon freight ran on Mondays to Fridays, leaving Paddock Wood at 12.42pm, calling at Churn Lane for ten minutes, but setting off punctually in time to reach Horsmonden yard to enable the 1.10pm up passenger train to pass through. For the rest of the afternoon the goods crew had the branch entirely to themselves. A forty-minute period at both Horsmonden and Goudhurst, calling at Pattenden on request, followed by an hour at Cranbrook, was the usual roster, before arrival at Hawkhurst at 3.55 in the afternoon. Almost two hours was available for shunting until the scheduled departure at 5.50pm. During the time spent in the yard, the school train would have come down, invariably an 'R1' tank and a push-pull unit, and then returned to Paddock Wood. The freight followed behind, but went into the yard at Cranbrook for fifty minutes to fulfil its duties and to allow the early evening train of homeward-bound locals to pass through at 6.15pm. This particular passenger service had a quick turn-round period of six minutes at Hawkhurst in order to clear the branch for other trains. The freight at Cranbrook then followed fifteen minutes later, calling at Pattenden if there were wagons to pick up, whilst ten minutes was allowed at Goudhurst before setting off again at a quarter past seven. Half an hour at Horsmonden enabled the freight to be shunted out of the way while the 7.28pm from Paddock Wood could pass unhindered, dropping off its band of weary London office workers on the way. The 'right away' was then given to the freight which left at 7.55pm, running on to Churn Lane where only ten minutes were allowed to set down empties or pick up loaded wagons. Departure from here had to be at 8.15pm sharp, since the returning passenger train would, at that time, be between Cranbrook and Goudhurst. Arriving back at Paddock Wood at 8.25pm the afternoon shift for the freight crew came to an end. Twelve minutes later the last up passenger train arrived, running into the up local platform as, during this period, it was booked to continue and terminate at Tonbridge. Thus ended a typical day's service on the Hawkhurst branch.

Photographs of trains on the branch during the Second World War appear to be non-existent, perhaps for obvious reasons, notably that anyone seen with a camera or taking notes near railways was likely to be pounced upon by the authorities. However, locals speak of special trains run at intervals throughout these years, whilst Derek Reader recalls that he occasionally saw troop trains at Goudhurst comprising five carriages hauled by 4-4-0 locomotives.

It was only a matter of weeks after the relaxation of the restriction on tender engines always working smokebox first to Paddock Wood that instructions were given to remove the engine shed siding at Hawkhurst. This took place in March 1944 when, for some undiscovered reason, the points and siding to the rear of the water tower, as well as the second road only, leading directly into the shed, were taken out. Towards the end of the year the engineering department was again required to visit Hawkhurst following a collision with the buffer stops. On the 13th November driver Randall, having worked down the 9.7am, was in the process of running round his train when his engine 'came into sharp contact with the buffer stops, due he alleges, to the wheels picking up'. The impact was sufficient to crush the wooden buffer beam and move the stops slightly.

Throughout the rest of the war the traffic along this charming Kentish byway continued to gradually dwindle as the increasing availability and greater comfort of door-to-door road transport had a further impact on the railway's income. Not surprisingly, the branch escaped serious attack by the Luftwaffe since much of it was difficult to detect in its rural surroundings and there were no strategic targets, except for the railhead at Paddock Wood. The only occasions when 'Jerry' had a go was on a return from a sortie when ammunition was emptied into the hop fields, scattering pickers who dived for cover. 'Dog fights' in the skies above the Weald were often witnessed during the height of the Battle of Britain, when almost everyone risked the flying shrapnel to watch the events unfold before their eyes. The branch was not affected by the severest of the blackout regulations, enforced on lines which could be seen from the sea. Nevertheless, lights were extinguished where possible, whilst the station canopy supports and lamp posts were painted with white bands. Apart from these quite literal dark days, the area escaped the more evident signs of war which came in terrifying bombing raids to many Kentish towns and villages. The inhabitants were, of course, well aware of the deprivations, shortages and, worse still, the unease and sense of foreboding, especially in the first years of the conflict. Even so, springtime's cheerful carpet of primroses, which graced the sides of the railway cuttings, lifted the otherwise depressed spirits of travellers, while bluebells smothered the dank woodlands bordering the line. For the creatures who dwelt in the High Weald, the rabbits, foxes, badgers and others who scurried in the fields and woods, there was, of course, no sense of war. Nevertheless, each passing season, from autumn's mists and pungent smells, winter's crisp, sharp frosts and snow, to springtime's luxuriant re-growth and summer's languid drowsiness, brought fresh hope and determination. Somehow, knowing that the branch line's trains were still running as regularly as clockwork, through the hop gardens and along the valley floor, offered a sense of security and reassurance that all was well. When, at last, the end of yet another terrible war came to a close, the jubilation was no less felt in this area than anywhere else. Hand in hand with the feelings of exhaustion, came a deep yearning for change and hopes of better times ahead.

The ordinary weekday service remained at six down and seven up, handled by the remaining batch of 'R's and 'R1's still based at Tonbridge. Two of the 'R's, Nos.1668/9, had been scrapped during 1940, whilst the others were beginning to come to the end of their useful lives. The timetable schedules remained unaltered and there was apparently no attempt to improve matters by speeding-up the service, which would have been perfectly possible. A journey time of thirty minutes each way for a trip of just over eleven miles was hardly inviting, especially when compared with Edwardian days when it was normally five minutes quicker, as well as the trains, previously mentioned, which accomplished the run in only twenty minutes.

Complaints over missed connections followed, hardly endearing the service to those who used it on a regular basis. Cynics might well conclude that such a practice harked back to the days of fierce competition, continuing a time-honoured tradition among railway operators, perhaps even today. Certainly, the rivalry between the SER and LC&DR seems to have perfected the art of deliberately making matters as inconvenient as possible for each other's passengers. However, even on their own systems and, afterwards, the SE&CR and the Southern, it seems that the travelling public were expecting too much for booked connections to actually do just that. Transferring from branch line to main line was, by all accounts, equally fraught with anxiety in SR days as revealed by the frequent memoranda from the London East Divisional Superintendent. Evidently, the Hawkhurst line stations were regularly failing to give Paddock Wood notice of passengers intending to transfer when the up branch services were running behind time. Consequently, those on the train coming up from Hawkhurst had the habit of anxiously leaning out of the window on the parallel stretch of track at Paddock Wood, only to see their London connection steaming away into the distance. The luxury of having through carriages, in days gone before, must have been a sorely-missed convenience.

Further trouble occurred on the line's usual weak spot during 1945-6 when subsidence between Goudhurst and Cranbrook made itself known. Where the railway passed by Furnace Wood, at a point where the gradient stiffened from 1 in 85 to 1 in 60 in the direction of

Track relaying with concrete panels near Willow Lane Crossing, 20th July 1947. A 'C' class was on the train.

Southern Railway

Cranbrook, a farm track passed over the cutting on a brick occupation arch. This structure, numbered 1516 and known to the engineers as 'Arch bridge', was the only one of its type on the line. Recent land movements had caused large cracks to appear throughout its walls, causing concern to the 'civils' who recommended its removal. This single-arch brick overbridge, costing £640 in 1892, had originally been provided for the convenience of the Bedgebury Park Estate, as well as the tenant of Furnace Farm. Since its purpose had expired, the SR authorized its demolition at a cost of £420, of which £40 was recouped in recovered material. A further £175 had to be paid to the Commissioners for Crown Lands for extra land purchased in order to make the railway secure at this point. There was also an incidental saving on maintenance on the bridge of £3 per annum.

Even greater expenditure on the fabric of the railway was forthcoming during the summer of 1947 when major track renewal took place. Extensive relaying was carried out in the vicinity of Churn Lane when engineers had possession of the line over two consecutive weekends. Many lengths of worn-out rail on wooden sleepers were dragged out and replaced with new concrete-sleepered panels.

As 1947 came to a close, so the old order of private railway companies was finally eclipsed. The message of hope for a much brighter and more secure future for the railways went out from Sir Eustace Missenden, chairman of the new Railway Executive, at nationalization on New Year's Day 1948. A copy was duly pasted into the book containing parcels circulars by the porter at Cranbrook. Great changes would follow but, as always, the pace would be less detectable upon this delightful Kentish backwater.

In the last few weeks prior to the nationalization of the railways, 'R' class No. 1658 bearing its red tail lamp, is seen at Hawkhurst on Monday, 27th October 1947, before propelling the branch train back to Paddock Wood. *H. B. Priestley*

HAWKHURST BRANCH.—(SINGLE LINE.)
NO SUNDAY SERVICE.

Distances from Tonbridge.	DOWN TRAINS. WEEK-DAYS.		* a.m.	* a.m.	p.m.	* S.O. p.m.	* p.m.	* p.m.	* p.m.	
m. c.										
5 23	PADDOCK WOOD ... Ⓣ	dep	7 35	9 7	12 30	2 32	4 22	5 53	7 28	.
9 52	Horsmonden .... Ⓣ	arr.	7 45	9 17	12 40	2 42	4 32	6 3	7 38	...
11 53	Goudhurst .... Ⓣ	,,	7¶51	9 23	12 46	2 48	4 38	6 9	7 44	.
15 19	Cranbrook .... Ⓣ	,,	8 5	9 32	12 55	2 57	4 47	6 18	7 53	...
16 60	HAWKHURST .... Ⓣ	,,	8 10	9 37	1 0	3 2	4 52	6 23	7 58	.

Distances.	UP TRAINS. WEEK-DAYS.		a.m.	* a.m.	* a.m.	p.m.	* S.O. p.m.	* p.m.	* p.m.	* p.m.
m. c.										
—	HAWKHURST .... Ⓣ	dep.	7 40	8 20	9 43	1 10	3 12	5 5	6 28	8 7
1 41	Cranbrook .... Ⓣ	arr.	7 44	8 24	9 47	1 14	3 16	5 9	6 32	8 11
5 7	Goudhurst .... Ⓣ	,,	7 53	8 33	9 56	1 23	3 25	5 18	6 41	8 20
7 8	Horsmonden .... Ⓣ	,,	7 59	8 39	10 2	1 29	3 31	5 24	6 47	8 26
11 37	PADDOCK WOOD ... Ⓣ	,,	8 10	8 50	10 13	1 40	3 42	5 35	6 58	8§37

§—To Tonbridge. ¶—Depart Goudhurst 7.56 a.m.

Taken from Public Timetable for July 1946.

An up Kent Coast express thundering through Paddock Wood in Southern Railway days. Although there was less activity in the goods yard than in years gone by, the station retained its importance as a junction, whilst the SER's foresight in providing fast through tracks, local lines and bay platform roads may be appreciated.

CHAPTER SEVEN

LAND OF LOST CONTENT

PADDOCK WOOD owes its existence entirely to the South Eastern Railway. When the first trains began running in 1842, there was very little to be seen here except woodland and pastures, although nearby there was a solitary inn. Following the construction of the station and the branch line to Maidstone, this rural setting gradually began to grow. By 1892, when the new branch railway as far as Hope Mill was opened, Murray's *Hand Book for Travellers in Kent* spoke of the place as 'formerly a hamlet of Brenchley, now rising to the dignity of a town'.

At a little under thirty-five miles from London, the station grew into an important railhead for the developing agricultural business throughout the Weald of Kent. Facilities for handling livestock and a wide variety of fruit and vegetable produce came into being over the years as trade rapidly grew throughout the nineteenth century. However, perhaps its most well-known associations lie with the business of hop-picking, for the name of this particular station was only too familiar with the many generations of Londoners who were deposited here in the middle of the night.

Along the roads which were laid out to the south of the station, local builders erected rows of neat terraced houses and modest villas. Essentially, Paddock Wood began as a town of brick and slate houses, for there was no established settlement here containing dwellings fashioned from more primitive materials. Not unexpectedly, railway cottages sprang up, as did shops, inns and public houses, to serve the growing community required to work for, or in association with, the railway and its patrons.

From the outset, the station was extensively laid out in a substantial fashion which remains to this day. Because of its importance, loop platforms were laid in so that the through running lines would not be obstructed on this, the fast straight run between Tonbridge and the channel ports. The main building was thoughtfully designed along classical lines to an Italianate style of pleasing proportions. The view of 1872 depicts the station at its best, before the later addition of valanced canopies which rather spoiled its general appearance. Shamefully, this imposing building was torn down in the 1970s for no other reason than attempts to save on maintenance.

In the days of semaphore signalling there was always a good array of lofty posts and arms to control the movement of trains. Some quite extravagant examples were evident in SER days and the staff must have needed quite a head for heights when clambering to the top to

'H' class No. 31164, with the branch headcode, standing in the Hawkhurst bay platform at Paddock Wood on 23rd June 1958.
Rodney Lissenden

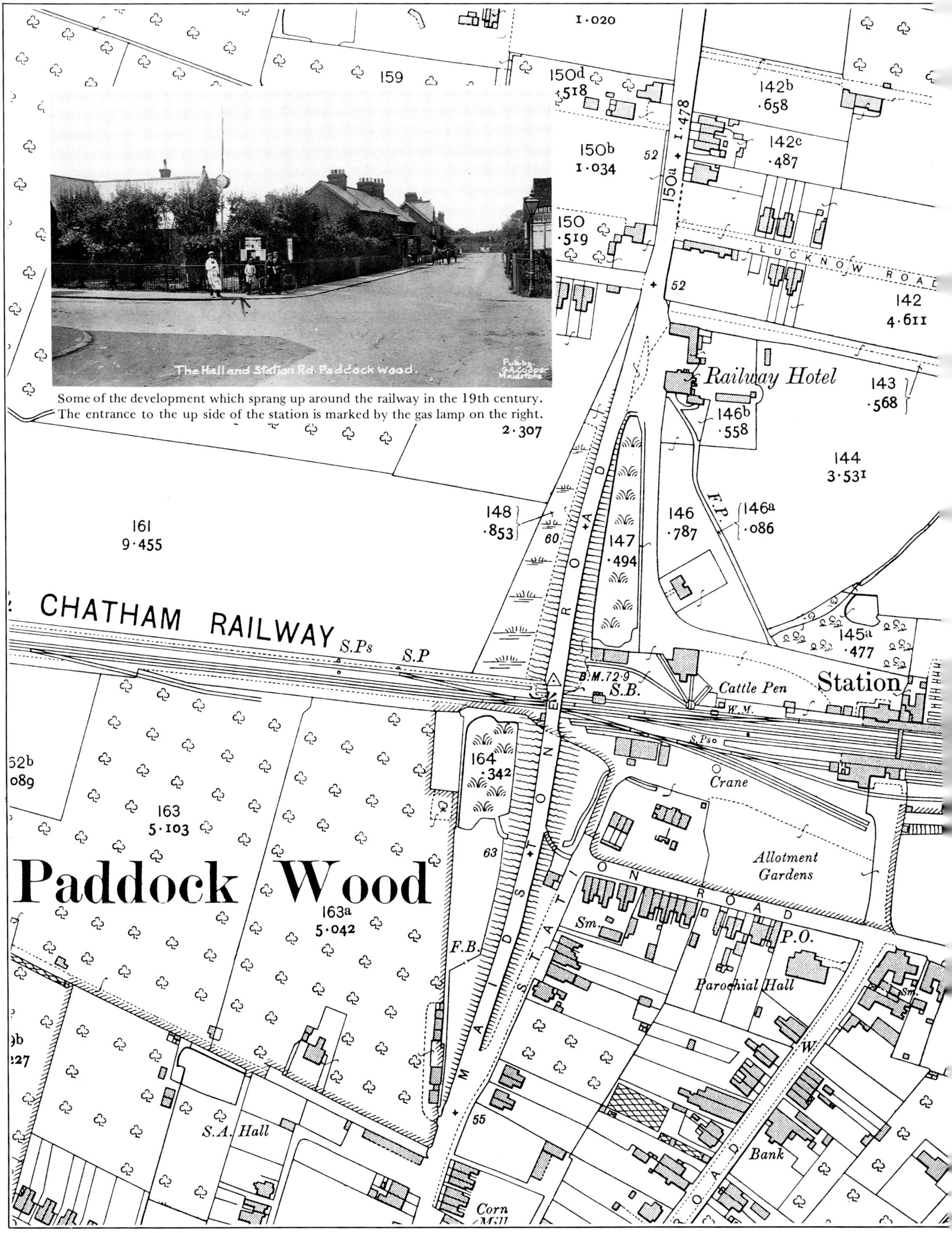

Some of the development which sprang up around the railway in the 19th century. The entrance to the up side of the station is marked by the gas lamp on the right.

The road running over the SER main line ran on to Maidstone whilst the one on the right led to the station.

e exterior of the up side buildings at Paddock Wood around 1905. The ak in the pavement was where the connecting siding between the east l west yards crossed the approach road.

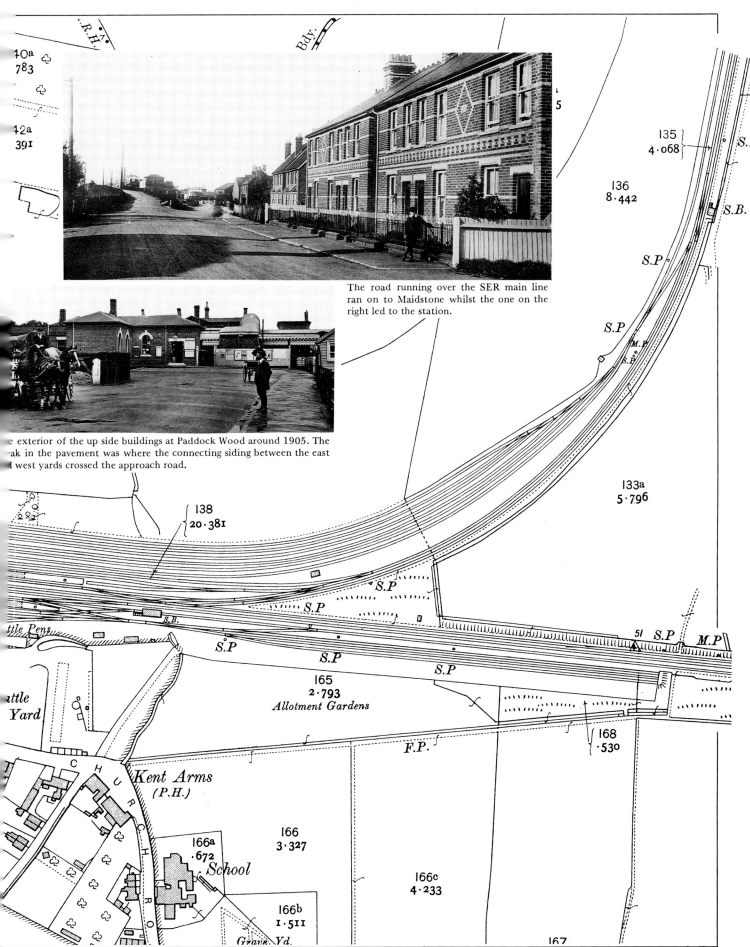

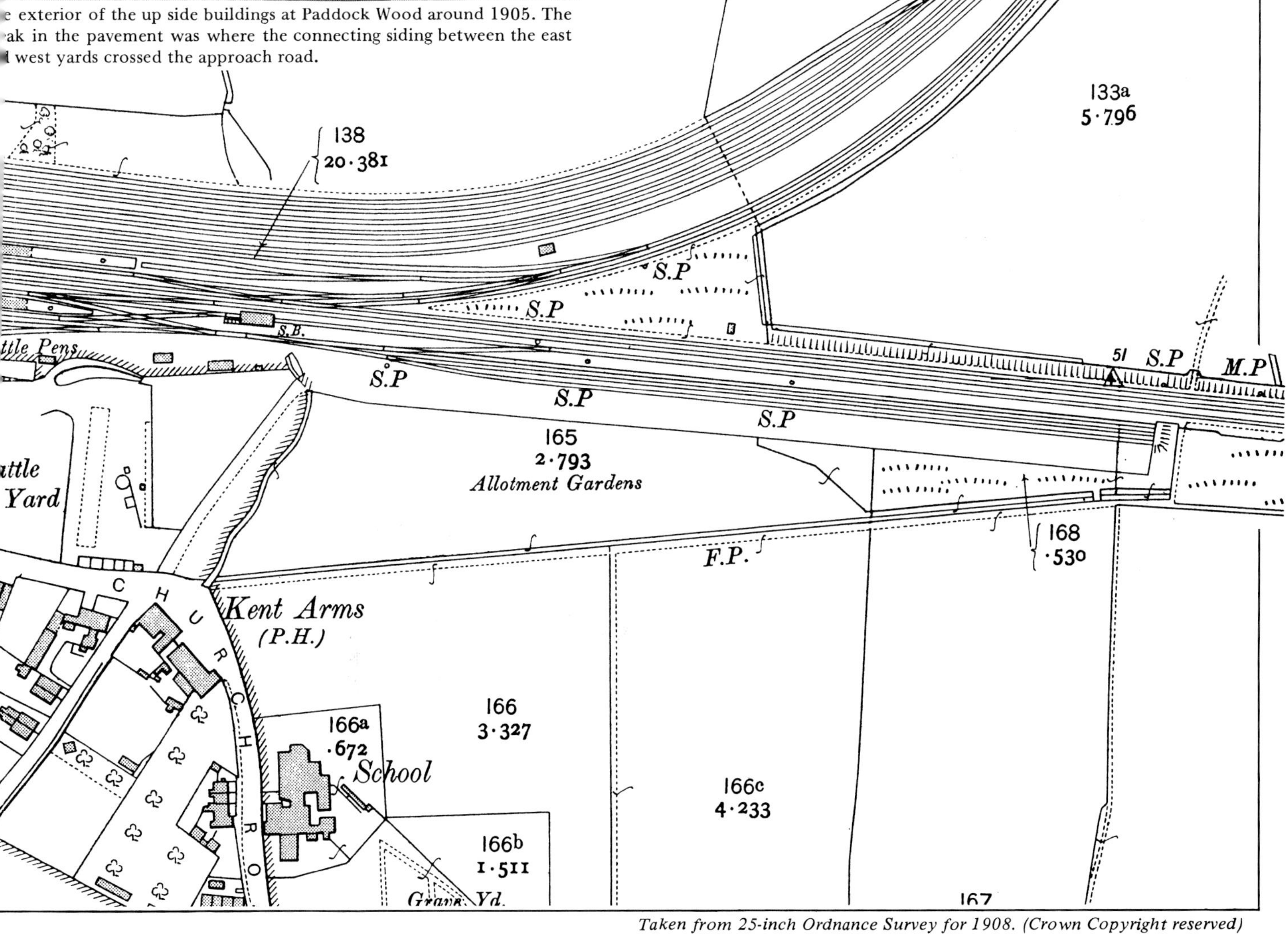

Taken from 25-inch Ordnance Survey for 1908. (Crown Copyright reserved)

This was the view from the footbridge at Paddock Wood for homeward-bound commuters changing for the Hawkhurst branch. It shows the SER's almost perfectly straight main line to Folkestone leading into the distance, the Maidstone branch bearing left, whilst Hawkhurst trains normally started from the bay platform on the right before running underneath the signal box. The push-pull unit featured here was the 'motor' from Maidstone West.
Collection R. S. Carpenter

'R1' class No. 31704 at the head of a typical branch train of the mid-1950s and seen here in the bay platform at Paddock Wood on Wednesday, 10th August 1955 with the 12.24 p.m. service. The the branch water crane on the left was once such a vital part of the railway system.
J. H. Aston

'H' class No. 31177 shunting a Maunsell auto-train at Paddock Wood on 9th June 1961. *Tony Wright*

change the oil lamps inside their casings. The wooden arms on the signals, which always rested at varying degrees above the horizontal when 'on', were rarely motionless as local and express trains, goods and the 'Tidal', all came this way. No doubt those with an interest in railways were quite content to stand and watch the comings and goings at this busy junction while waiting for their connections to either Maidstone or Hawkhurst branch line stations. However, those who had the misfortune to miss their local train, the hands on the large SER 30-inch double-faced dial clock beneath the up side canopy could not move fast enough as time hung heavily on these occasions.

Passengers who arrived from Tonbridge or London, on the down side, were directed by a large sign hanging beneath the footbridge which read 'Way Out for up trains and Horsmonden, Goudhurst, Cranbrook, Hawkhurst'. Once across the four lines of railway, the branch train was usually to be found waiting in the bay platform, the locomotive gently simmering at the head of the two-coach set. Throughout the 1940s and well into the next decade, an 'R' or 'R1' class invariably stood at the head of the regular push-pull unit. For these locomotives, the Hawkhurst branch was their last refuge, before the final trip to the works for breaking-up in the mid-50s. Although the 'H' class engines were more than suitable replacements and might well be most associated with the branch in most people's memories, the old 'Chatham' tanks somehow looked more at home on this line, especially when they appeared rather unkempt, with flat, faded and grubby paintwork.

There was always a sense of excitement when boarding the local train for those enchanted by rail travel. Heavy compartment doors swung shut with a dull thud, whilst the grimy windows could be carefully let down with the aid of a stout leather strap which was fastened onto a brass stud. Prints of local scenes, such as Dover Castle, or more tempting faraway places like the Isle of Wight or romantic Dorset, were tastefully framed upon the walls, but their colours had invariably faded with the sunlight of numerous summers.

Following the arrival of the connecting service, passengers spilled out onto the down platform, a few of whom came to join the branch train. The welcoming

'C' class No. 31588 heading away from Paddock Wood on Saturday, 10th June 1961 on the last day of regular services over the branch.
R. C. Riley

Striking away from Paddock Wood and under the signal box, 'C' class No. 31588, specially rostered for the day, hauling a Hawkhurst-bound service on Saturday, 10th June 1961.

R. C. Riley

A Paddock Wood signalman climbing the three flights of steps of this decaying structure which was in desperate need of a repaint. Photographed on 15th April 1961, within a matter of months the box was demolished when the Kent Coast line was resignalled. *J. J. Smith*

Watched by a couple of platelayers, a Maunsell 'King Arthur' class, No. 766 *Sir Geraint* speeding through Paddock Wood with a Kent Coast express in the 1930s. The single track of the Hawkhurst branch is in the foreground. *G. A. Stickler*

In the last six years prior to closure, the 'H' tanks were given almost exclusive charge of passenger duties. Here, No. 31512 is shown pacing alongside the line of trees bordering the main line. *Rodney Lissenden*

guard would eye his watch before giving the 'right away' to the driver, who would acknowledge with a short tug on the whistle, then ease the regulator open to start away. As the train gently creaked into life there was still time for any latecomer to run and hop aboard. At the end of the platform, the wheels would grind and rub against the check rails of the points guiding the train onto the branch proper. The signalman was obliged to descend from the soot and grime-encrusted cabin straddling the track, in order to hand over the single-line token to the driver or fireman as they passed by. For about half a mile, the branch track ran parallel to the main line alongside a row of swaying, whispering alders which bordered the company's boundary. Most times, branch trains quietly paced along this level stretch, but occasionally when a main line train was starting away from Paddock Wood at the same time, the drivers would race each other, blasting their smutty exhausts high above the trees. 'Letting her go' was a strictly unofficial pastime. Soon the toing and froing on the rarely quiet Kent Coast main line was left behind as the canted track of the Hawkhurst branch swung trains southwards, bearing their occupants into the heart of the Weald and towards those distant and romantic-looking wooded hills.

Thirkell's siding passed by just at this point on the down side, whilst beyond the view was often that of yet

'H' class No. 31512 heading away from the main line and commencing its journey down the branch on 18th March 1961.

Queen Street bridge with the branch leading away into the High Weald.

Willow Lane Crossing and keeper's cottage, which stood on the Horsmonden side of the lane.

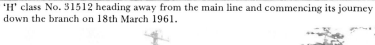

Hop gardens bordered the branch on the right along the approach to Old Hay crossing, as seen in this view from the 12.30 p.m. from Paddock Wood on 23rd July 1957.

A. A. Jackson

another main line express thundering down to Folkestone, jetting out a trail of white steam behind it. Queen Street bridge then passed overhead, marking something of a psychological boundary, since from here all thoughts of the busy outside world simply melted away. Now, the Hawkhurst branch had you all to itself, where it might begin working its charms on those who couldn't resist staring aimlessly at the broadening landscapes on either side. A reminder that this was unmistakeably Kent would come with the vista of hop fields with their serried clusters of bright green bines struggling to reach the top of the strings. Oast houses passed by in the distance, their homely, conical tiled roofs and white-painted cowls providing a familiar picture-postcard glimpse of this corner of the county. Where there were not hop gardens, the eye fell upon orchards, pastures or fields under cultivation. Here, farm workers would pause in the heat of the day, stretch their aching backs and watch the local train come gently swaying and rattling past.

At Willow Lane the gates would be dutifully set against road traffic whenever a train was due, while the railway continued to run almost on the level across these broad fertile plains. Reaching Old Hay, where a lane crossed over the line, numerous notices warned of trains, against trespassing and threatened financial penalties for not shutting the small gates which opened away from the railway.

The branch then skirted past the hamlet of Pearson's Green, seen from the up side compartment window, with its cluster of farm buildings, cottages and oasts against a background of orchards where the blossom of pink-dusted trees promised a fruitful bounty at harvest time. Here, an obligatory long blast upon the whistle warned those who tramped on foot along curiously-named Mousetrap Lane, while leaves on the wayside thorn bushes were tossed and left dancing in the the draught of passing trains. For a quarter of a mile the line then climbed at 1 in 78, while farmsteads at August Pitts and

Looking south to the occupation crossing at Old Hay, 1¾ miles from Paddock Wood.

Milepost 37¼ marks the distance from Charing Cross in this southwards glimpse of August Pitts occupation crossing.

Top: Churn Lane Crossing, looking south, with temporary ropes and red flags, awaiting replacement gates. *Above:* The sidings at Churn Lane became quite overgrown in latter years. Notice the warning bell on the telegraph pole.

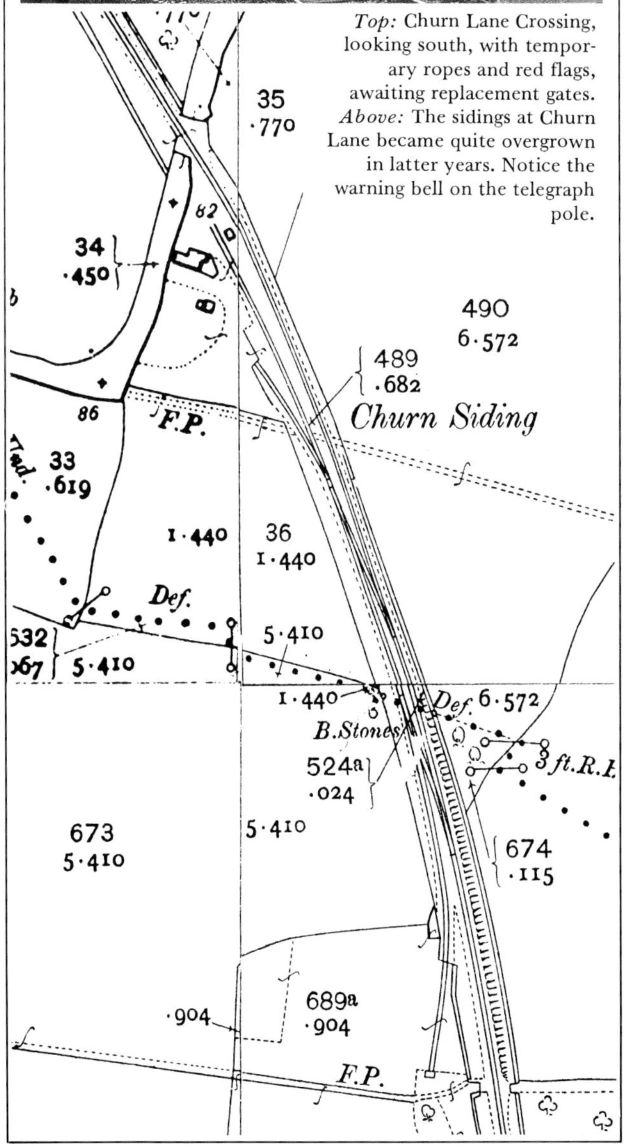

Taken from 25-inch Ordnance Survey for 1908. (Crown Copyright reserved)

Pittlands came into view on the down side. Immediately after an occupation crossing stood the down distant signal for Churn Lane siding.

At Churn Lane the crossing keeper's cottage nestled among the trees on the up side, whilst a few yards beyond were the useful sidings which were temporary home to at least a half dozen or more wagons, left there by the early morning goods. Here began the mile-long 1 in 66 gradient on the climb into the Wealden hills which always taxed the engines hauling heavily-loaded trains at hop-picking time. Simultaneously, the railway continued swinging on a long curve to the right, while the scenery began to change quite noticeably. Whereas Paddock Wood spreads across part of the flat, fertile vale between the North Downs and the ridges of the High Weald, the ascent into deeply-wooded countryside was soon made on the journey south. For the first couple of miles the Hawkhurst branch traversed an easy-going landscape, but it wasn't long before the views across open fields were replaced with enduring vistas of those beautiful and delightful hills, so tantalisingly glimpsed from compartment windows on the SER main line.

Entering a modest cutting at Yew Tree Green, a winding lane passed overhead, leading on to a variety of

Looking south near Poplar Farm towards Horsmonden.

Left: Ox-eye daisies lined the railway banks near Yew Tree Green on the 1 in 66 climb into the Wealden hills towards Horsmonden. *Right:* Churn Lane up distant signal, looking towards Yew Tree Green bridge.

Swigs Hole bridge carried the railway over this leafy lane.

Horsmonden's down distant signal stood at the entrance of the cutting leading towards the summit of the long climb from Paddock Wood.

places in these hidden, secret corners of the Weald, such as exotic-sounding Solomon's Temple, ancient Castle Hill and curious Wrangling Green.

Once clear of the cutting, the line immediately began to traverse a high embankment as the land dropped away on either side where Swigs Hole bridge carried trains over a delightfully leafy lane. Soon, however, the land rises sharply once more, whereby in order to keep the railway on a level stretch, another cutting was entered. Here passengers lost their views of the lineside hedgerows, hillside hop gardens and distant oasts as the railway ran into a cool and verdant wonderland of ferns, nettles, blackberry brambles and overhanging trees. It was reminiscent of one of those hidden glades from ancient Andredswold, complete with little rivulets stained rust-red which trickled out of the cutting sides and into the cess on either side of the track. At the commencement of Horsmonden cutting the distant signal gave prior warning of the following down home, although it is scarcely imaginable that any driver would need to check his speed having just climbed the bank from Churn Lane

At just 82½ yards long, Horsmonden, or the Dog House tunnel, as it was known locally, was numbered 1472 by the railway and was significant in that it marked the summit of the Hope Mill section. The tunnel was beautifully constructed throughout with a bore lined three bricks deep and incorporating a refuge on either side. Alternate rows of stretchers and headers, with indented courses formed the parapets and retaining walls in a perfect example of a single line tunnel. Apart from the great number of bricks which went into its construction, there must have been a great deal of toil and dedication on the part of the Victorian craftsmen. Perhaps, though, the showpiece in civil engineering on

The northern entrance to Horsmonden tunnel where the railway levelled out.

Although half hidden, the graceful appearance of Sandy Lane bridge is easily appreciated in this view towards Horsmonden.

the Hawkhurst branch came a few yards further on, where, from the dank pungent depths of this sylvan cutting, rose a graceful three-arched bridge. This carried Sandy Lane high above the line, with a drop of 45ft to rail level. Those aboard the trains wouldn't have been able to appreciate its elegance, but, surely, the men who created it must have stood back on its completion and felt a heart-swelling sense of pride and achievement. It must also have been a magnet for the children from the nearby school who, in their break times, or after lessons, scraped their shoes upon its parapets in order to peep at the trains which pounded away far below.

With the railway now falling at numerous gradients, in fact, all the way to Goudhurst, a gentle jolt would remind all those on board the trains that Horsmonden station was being approached. Just before leaving the cutting, the down home was passed by on the up side. This particular signal always seems to have been on the

Horsmonden's tall down home signal dominates the foreground of this view of 'C' class No. 31592 attaching wagons from the goods yard to the 1.45 p.m. Hawkhurst–Paddock Wood freight service on 19th May 1961. The grinding wheel, tail lamps, oil cans and platelayers' tools clustered around the trolley huts were all a familiar part of the scene. *J. J. Smith*

'wrong' side, so the very tall latticed-post replacement, complete with standard SR lower quadrant fittings, didn't alter accepted practice.

Horsmonden station had the enviable distinction of being relatively close to the community it purported to serve, a benefit unfortunately not shared by any of the other stations on the branch. Even so, the village was a short walk away to the west of the railway where the green formed the focal point of this pleasant place. Gathered around its perimeter at one time were the village smithy, inn, public house, general stores, as well as a cluster of houses, some of which are quite ancient and of a kind which so delight the wayside wanderer and the watercolour artist. The arrival of the railway not

Looking towards Paddock Wood on the quiet summer afternoon of Saturday, 29th September 1951. The goods platform erected for H. St. G. Ralling is seen on the right, next to the lever controlling No. 1 loop points. The stack of wooden trunks, bundled-up clothing and a pram at the far end of the station platform evidently belonged to homeward-bound hop-pickers. *Denis Cullum*

From the compartment window, a glimpse beneath the station canopy, showing the platform clock upon the wall.
Trans-Rail Publications

Horsmonden village on a warm, sunny afternoon in the 1920s.

The approach road to Horsmonden station, with the gate to the goods yard on the left. The extra window, installed in 1908, is seen at the far end of the building next to the signal box.

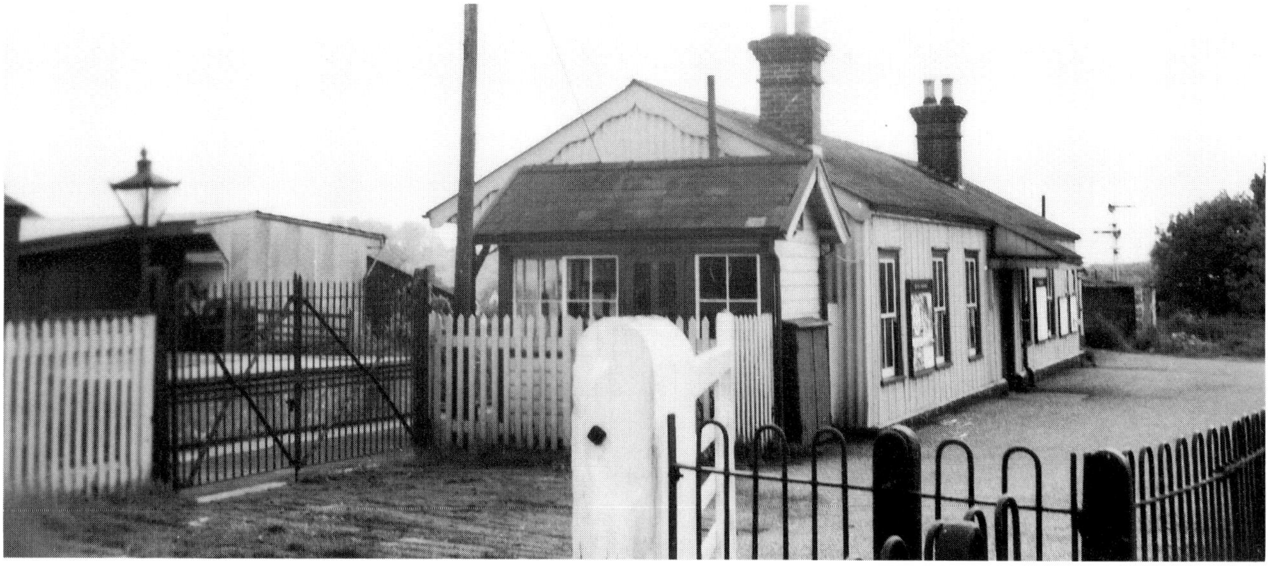

Horsmonden's signal box and station buildings from the goods yard dock. This pattern of signal box was once standard on the early SER system when signalling was more simple and limited to a few levers in small frames at every station. Even so, the choice of this type for a station box at this late period is rather curious, particularly given the lack of view along the line.

surprisingly encouraged further growth, but this was concentrated in the vicinity of the station and along Goudhurst Road where there already existed a few cottages. Agriculturalists, such as corn seed merchants, hop and fruit growers, arranged their businesses close to the railway for obvious reasons, yet, in spite of this commercial activity, the surroundings were actually enhanced. Oast houses, of both square and circular varieties, provided a most pleasing and extremely traditional backdrop for this particular Kentish station, in a setting that was nothing less than enchanting.

Locally-made bricks and tiles, and even those which were brought in by rail from further afield, were used sympathetically and harmoniously, along with weather-boarding which is commonly seen throughout the Weald. Surprisingly, the corrugated-iron cladding used in the construction of the station never seemed too out of place, perhaps because it was suitably fashioned in a manner that neither jarred the eye, nor looked in the least temporary. The building contained the usual offices and public rooms, whilst Horsmonden was unique on the branch in being provided with one of the early SER pattern signal cabins. This was positioned alongside the station building at the Paddock Wood end. The design was once quite commonplace throughout the SER, but the visibility of the signalman was undoubtedly severely impaired since most boxes stood back from the platform with little or no vision in either direction. Presumably this was not important at minor, intermediate, stations which might explain why this particular cabin remained

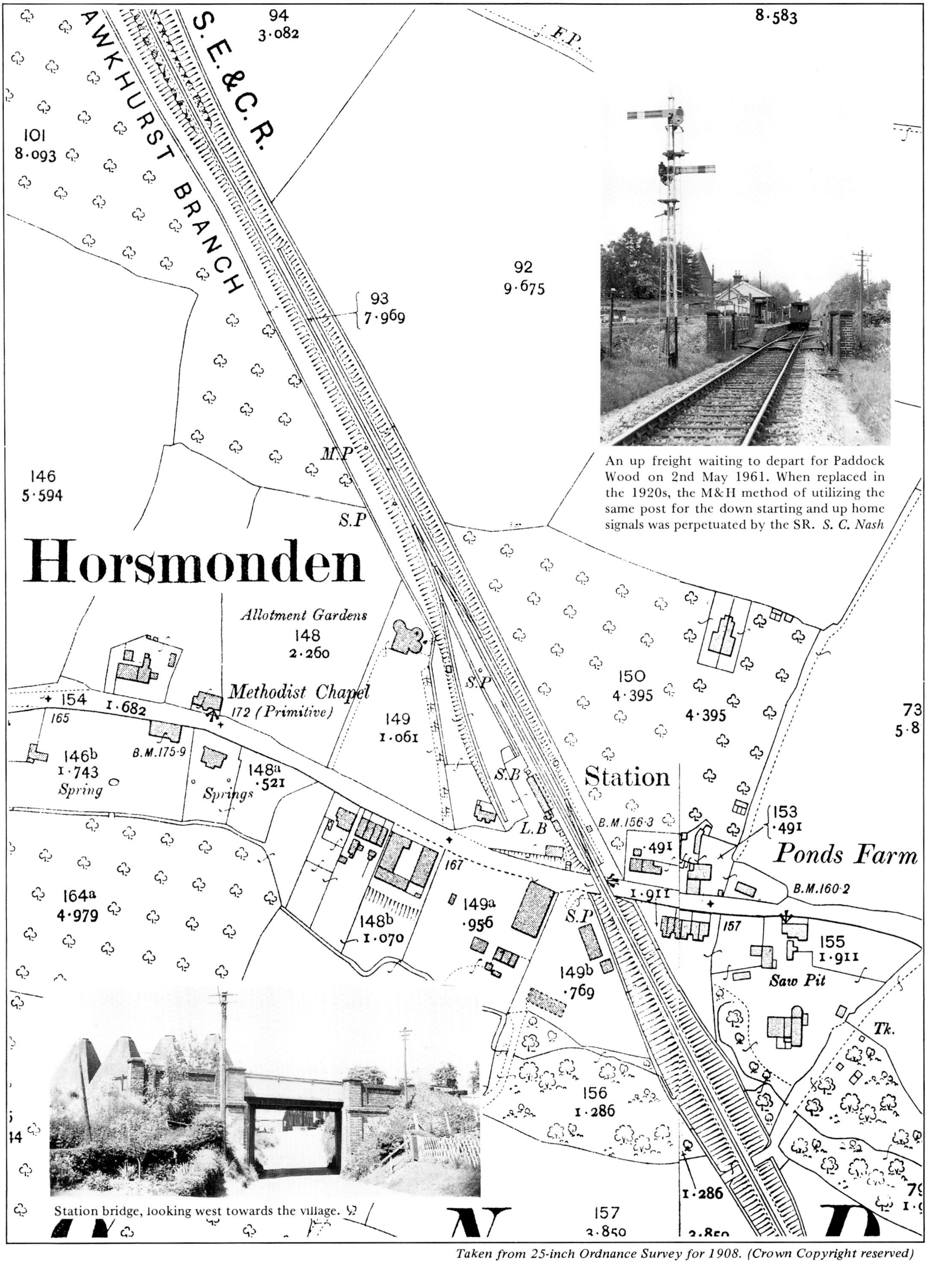

An up freight waiting to depart for Paddock Wood on 2nd May 1961. When replaced in the 1920s, the M&H method of utilizing the same post for the down starting and up home signals was perpetuated by the SR. *S. C. Nash*

Station bridge, looking west towards the village.

Taken from 25-inch Ordnance Survey for 1908. (Crown Copyright reserved)

'C' class No. 31592 momentarily disturbing the afternoon stillness amidst the orchards south of Horsmonden with the 1.45 p.m. goods train on Friday, 2nd May 1961. *J. J. Smith*

in use throughout the line's entire existence. Immediately opposite the platform a loop was installed to facilitate the handling of goods trains, but never intended, nor used, for passenger work. However, the loop really came into its own in later years with the addition of a dock platform and the establishment of the fruit packing depot. Behind the station buildings a modest goods yard spread out for the use of the local traders and farmers. Beyond that stood the station master's house which, although similar in style to those at Goudhurst and Cranbrook, differed most noticeably by not being located on the platform.

Having arrived at Horsmonden, the traveller was now well and truly in the High Weald of Kent. Here, it is still impossible to find a vista that is not favourable to the eye, so lovely is the landscape of this part of Kent. Tempting byways and lanes beckon from many directions, while to the south, Goudhurst sits majestically upon its hillside, encouraging those with a sense of adventure to press onwards. Obligingly, the down starting signal, which shared a post with the up home, would creak into the 'off' position by lowering itself to forty-five degrees. It almost seemed to be urging the train and its passengers to journey further into this magical land.

Pulling out of the station, trains would rumble over the plate girder bridge carrying the railway across

The height of summer in the High Weald, with the branch curving towards Horsmonden. The tall up distant signal was positioned on the 'wrong' side for sighting purposes. The hops on the right were almost ready for picking.

Goudhurst Road, before running almost silently as the engine settled down to an agreeable saunter, enabling everyone to admire the passing scenery. Swaying ox-eye daises, those familiar and cheerful blooms which thrive alongside railways, bordered both sides of the track and up to the boundary fence. Beyond, stretched lush pastures, meadows, and hop fields, whilst dotted all around were coppice woods, or shaws, as they are more commonly known in Kent. Lulled by the gentle motion of the carriages and the regular beat of the wheels over the joints, a shrill whistle would shatter daydreams as Starveden foot crossing was approached. A few yards further, Horsmonden up distant signal, with its warning fish-tailed yellow blade perched high upon a lofty latticed-post, came sailing by the compartment window on the down side, just as the decending line began to curve into the valley of the river Teise. Another lane, which wandered off towards Nevergood, passed beneath the railway where meadows, in summer's gentle wind, became a sea of rippling, bent grasses. More whistling usually followed at this point as Smallbridge crossing would come into sight. Here, the road rose up on either side, upon a small embankment, to enable it to cross the railway. Before very long, the line levelled out on the last lap to Goudhurst where, after crossing the swirling river Teise, down trains glided slowly into the loop platform.

'H' class No. 31177 sailing down the branch towards Goudhurst on Saturday, 29th September 1951. The hops had already been gathered from the field on the right.
Dennis Cullum

Nevergood bridge, looking southwards to Goudhurst.

Nevergood bridge, ¾ mile from Horsmonden, looking east. Road signs of that era seem far more pleasing and much less obtrusive in rural surroundings.

A view across the Teise valley from Goudhurst, with the railway running from left to right in the middle distance and Smallbridge crossing near the curving road.

An Austin van waiting for 'H' class No. 31518, bound for Hawkhurst with the auto train, at Smallbridge level crossing, on Friday, 11th September 1959. Notice the lorry load of hop pockets on the other side, adjacent to the crossing keeper's cottage. *Tony Wright*

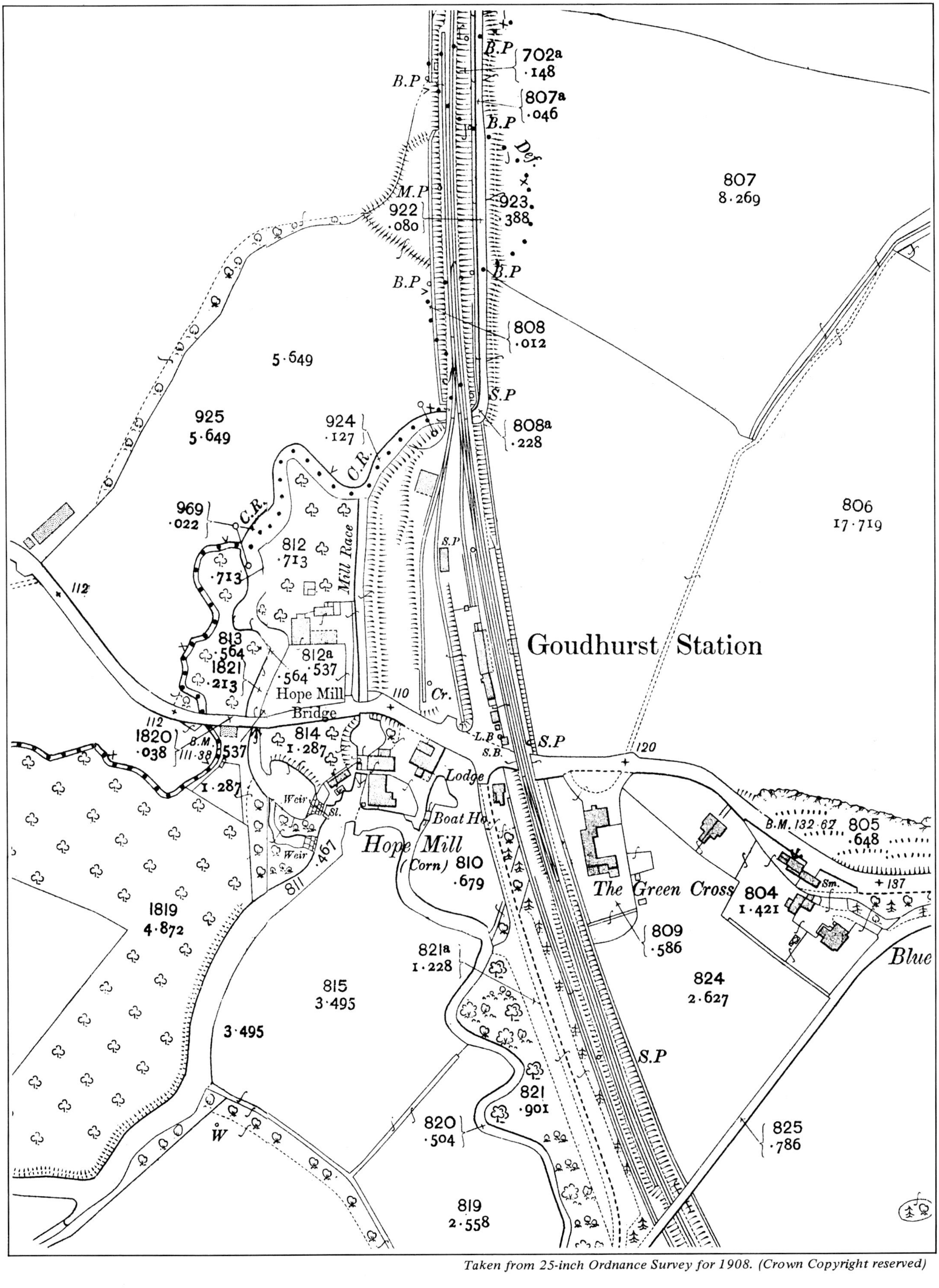

Taken from 25-inch Ordnance Survey for 1908. (Crown Copyright reserved)

Goudhurst station was the only passing place for passenger trains on the branch, but this event generally occurred only once in the morning and evening. The station buildings were situated on the up platform, facing eastwards and towards the village upon the hill. The tall, three-storey station master's house had a distinctly impressive appearance about it, with three gabled dormer windows which rather added to its sense of importance. Adjacent stood the station offices, similar to Horsmonden and comprising a timber-framed building on a brick base. The interior was boarded throughout with tongued and grooved cladding, whilst corrugated iron sheeting was fixed to the exterior walls. These structures were only to be found on the SER system on the Hawkhurst and Elham Valley branches. Whilst they were undoubtedly at the lower end of the scale in railway architectural terms, the criticism that they were crude and ugly seems a little unfair. They certainly lent themselves to the Southern Railway livery, for with their buff-coloured walls, rich green woodwork and white window frames, they looked very smart indeed. A testimony to their sturdiness is the fact that four out of the seven examples survive to this day, after well over a century of wear and tear throughout all kinds of weather.

On the opposite platform the SER provided one of its standard clapboard waiting shelters when the station

The 12.30 p.m. to Hawkhurst held outside Goudhurst by the down home signal until the level crossing gates had been closed across the road, permitting entry into the down platform, on 23rd July 1957. *A. A. Jackson*

Push-pull set No. 733, made from ex-L&SWR coaching stock, in the up platform at Goudhurst on the midday service to Paddock Wood, 23rd July 1957. *A. A. Jackson*

A panoramic view of Goudhurst station on a warm late spring day where the fresh growth of the surrounding countryside provides a perfect backdrop to this rural setting. 25th May 1961. *J. J. Smith*

opened as Hope Mill in 1892. This lasted well into Southern days, but the reasons for its eventual removal remain undiscovered, although subsidence might have been a possible cause. Another explanation may be that in later years the down platform was almost exclusively used by people arriving, rather than waiting to travel south to Cranbrook and Hawkhurst, which were more easily reached by 'bus. Rows of lamp posts, with the name in azure blue glass in the housings, were provided along the length of both platforms. In the early days it is likely that every single lamp was dutifully lit, providing at dusk not only a welcoming sight to passengers, but equally a comforting landmark of twinkling lights way down in the valley. Gradually, though, over the years, the more remote lamps were left unattended, making instead convenient homes for spiders who arrived on breeze-blown strands of gossamer.

Oil lighting was also the only means of illumination at the station master's house, likewise the signalman who, from his cosy, roomy and comfortable cabin with its stove, could obtain a good view of the line in both directions. It was, of course, also convenient for the level crossing, the gates of which were worked by hand. Behind the station spread the goods yard, along with a dock at the back of the up platform. Sidings were also laid parallel with the running line in both directions, giving the distinct impression to those who bounced over the crossing in motor cars that this rather humble branch was an important double-track railway.

Years ago a cattle market existed nearby, not far from the local hostelry which was originally called 'The Railway Hotel'. On the western side of the railway was Hope Mill, its huge wheel driven by the fast-running water of the River Teise which came noisily rushing through the mill race. This mill, the nearby oasts and the surrounding trees, created a truly rustic atmosphere which gave the station a naturally pleasant setting. It was a beautiful location, set in the lush valley of the Teise, with traditional hopfields, rows of orchard trees and rustling meadows all around. Goudhurst was certainly memorable for being one of those rural wayside stations which were suddenly stumbled upon by unwary motorists who came this way when touring the quieter roads of southern England.

Whilst the station and its environs were lovely, the village was even more enchanting but, alas, the prize had to be earned for those on foot. A mile away and along a road that twists and winds its way up hill, the weary stroller is eventually rewarded with a remarkable view. The panorama from the church tower remains one of the wonders of the Weald. The vista, across this most scenic corner of Kent, and beyond into glorious Sussex, is nothing less than breathtaking and exhilarating, whilst all around are huddled homely dwellings whose roofs of warm, red-rich, hand-made tiles are pure joy to behold. From this lofty vantage point the station and railway could be clearly seen in the valley far below, where the local train and its plume of telltale white vapour might be followed all the way to Horsmonden. In happier days the twisting roads around Goudhurst were uncluttered and unsullied by the present-day bane of intrusive and offensive motor traffic. Air which was the freshest that might be desired was often heady with little else but the scent from cottage garden blossoms, the smell of new-mown hay, or fragrant wild honeysuckle which ran amok and joyously tumbled out of wayside hedgerows.

The substantial branch line accommodation at Goudhurst is well illustrated in this view from May 1961. Square oasts next to Hope Mill may be seen on the right, whilst the former crossing keeper's cottage features across the road beyond the signal box. The down side waiting shelter had long since disappeared, whilst the raising of platform levels has rather buried the lower parts of the oil lamp standards. *John Scrace*

Goudhurst's up platform down starting signal was probably brought into existence in the 1920s, since it does not appear in pictures before then. The signal is shown on a 1931 diagram, and is known to have been renewed on Friday, 15th May 1942 when this upper quadrant semaphore arm replaced an earlier example. Its purpose was to enable goods trains for Hawkhurst to run into the up platform in order to shunt the sidings. Southbound goods (and passenger trains if need be) could then depart from the up platform. The provision of this signal necessitated the repositioning of the signal box steps as, originally, the wooden staging extended as far as the end of the concrete base, whilst the steps ran parallel with the platform. *K. G. Carr*

A hot afternoon in deserted Goudhurst where canvas shop awnings had been drawn and everyone apparently gone in search of shade. *Goudhurst & Kilndown Local History Society*

Steam from a down train in Goudhurst station can be seen rising in the distance, just above the oast-house cowl. All around, the Kent peg-tile roofs of buildings clustered around the church delight the roving eye, whilst on the far right the Goudhurst Coffee House beckoned passers by and visitors alike.

Tranquillity, peace and stillness once reigned far more than we can possibly imagine nowadays, whilst the contented wayfarer was left to wander around undisturbed, exploring the serene nooks within this delightful Wealden village. Large canvas blinds were drawn across narrow, crooked pathways, which led past shops of all kinds and where, on hot and sunny days, the brilliant light and perspiring heat of a high summer's afternoon sent everyone in search of a cool spot. Along uneven brick-paved alleyways, where clustered the vivid blue quivering bell-like flowers of campanula, the tiny ever-wandering toadflax and opportunistic fern, cooling breezes periodically wafted in the welcome shade. Beneath bushes of well-stocked comely gardens the household cat would slumber, too relaxed even to greet the passing stranger who might well envy her ability to accomplish a restful nap at whim. Here and there, fussing bumble bees would momentarily disappear into beckoning blossoms of foxgloves and welcoming hollyhocks, whilst showers of sweet-scented damask roses cascaded across rickety bowers. It was a sensation which never fails to bring to mind the immortal evocation penned by Matthew Arnold and set to music so exquisitely by Ralph Vaughan Williams:

> 'Soon will the high Midsummer pomps come on,
> Soon will the musk carnations break and swell,
> Soon shall we have gold-dusted snapdragon,
> Sweet-William with his homely cottage smell,
> And stocks in fragrant blow;
> Roses, that down the alleys shine afar,
> And open, jasmine-muffled lattices,
> And groups under the dreaming garden trees.......'

At regular intervals the chiming of the church clock was all that could be heard above the birdsong that filled the air. Here, among leaning gravestones speckled with yellow patches of lichen, a pensive spell contemplating one's own mortal state served only to encourage the desire to savour the moment. In corners of the churchyard smaller headstones commemorate little ones who died too soon, while sad memorials bear grim witness to the grief of Goudhurst for lost sons who fell in those faraway poppy-speckled foreign fields. Long grasses, the roving, dark green ivy and simple, dainty wild flowers which always take hold in unkempt corners may seem at first unwelcome. Yet, somehow, they are almost comforting, as though they are nature's way of healing, of taking back that which belongs to her, our mortal remains too.

A distant whistle far off somewhere would bring the mind back to more day-to-day matters and, in this lovely part of Kent, might remind us that the Hawkhurst branch was inextricably very much part of its surroundings and firmly belonged to an age which has slipped away. Its appeal and the very reasons behind its charm rested solely within the glorious tracts of countryside through which it meandered. Had it been built elsewhere, say, across a dispiriting marsh, or through cheerless industrial lands, then few would have mourned its passing. Who might then have spoken so wistfully and misty-eyed, of this lost railway into the High Weald? It was genuinely an intrinsic part of village life to the scattered rural communities who lived here and often looked upon with affection by visitors and hop-pickers alike. Nowadays it is no longer possible to hear the wailing call of the ordinary, everyday, local steam train, followed by the resounding clatter of wheels upon rail joints and the once-familiar clank-clank-clank of coupling rods gradually dying away into the distance. Yet it was once such a uniquely assuring sound, whether on drowsy summer afternoons, or conversely on wild winter nights when, by the dim light of a flickering candle, the bedtime book was wearily laid to rest as the last panting train scurried home into the howling darkness.

Judging by the sepia picture-postcards sent to friends and relations, it is apparent that the Weald once attracted many people to visit its many secret corners. The ever-popular teashop was always there to provide refreshments and recuperation for the aching limbs which tramped these dusty ways in shimmering midsummer. There was also a rare and precious stillness in the air, other than maybe the calming, steady beat of a longcase clock in the corner or the homely sound of

Appearing like a double-track railway, the branch crossed the A262 and curved through Goudhurst station in this view across hopfields to Horsmonden. The track in the foreground with the catchpoints was the south siding. Trains from Cranbrook would always cross over the set of points from the single line into the up platform. This marvellous view was obtained by Denis Cullum when he climbed to the staging of the up home signal on Saturday, 29th September 1951. *Denis Cullum*

crockery in the back parlour. Such was all that could be heard in an age when peace and quiet were qualities which were truly and rightfully treasured. Suitably refreshed by the teatime ritual, the casual wanderer would fold away the pocket map or close the handy, dog-eared, guidebook before emerging, blinking and squinting into the bright light and still-gasping heat of the day. Pottering around, peering into cluttered shop windows where the sun had bleached cardboard advertisements, fading and curling them so that their messages became barely decipherable, helped to idle away the spare time. However, it was the promise of an ice cream wafer which gave new spring to the heel and, with the butter-coloured treat melting fast in the hot sunshine, the saunter down to the station commenced. Above high banks of tall waving grasses, gently dancing red campion and cheerful milkmaids dotted about tousled verges, there floated in the haze all the sighing sounds of the season. Borne upon the gentle breeze, came the lowing of cattle, the bleating of sheep, while on late summer days there sometimes drifted the distant, intermittent songs and cries of hop-pickers in the fields.

On reaching the station once more, the scene was frequently one of complete desertion between the comings and goings of trains. So often, the only sound was the soft wind gently rustling leaves on lineside trees, or the distant drone of an aeroplane fading into the distance. At last, the 'ting-ting' and 'tang-tang' from bells within the signalbox preceded the emergence of the signalman who would walk down to the road and unbolt the gates. The heavy wooden barriers would swing across the road with only an odd creak or squeak from dry hinges until the sound of the bolt was heard, dragging itself across the last part of the dusty roadway before falling into its hole as the gate shut with its distinctive clack. Shortly afterwards there followed more bells, a heavy thudding of levers from inside the cabin and rustling signal wires. This inevitably instilled a sense of excitement as ears strained to detect the first telltale sounds of an approaching train. Within minutes it came gliding in, whistling on its approach as, for five minutes at least, the village station became all life. Those who'd alighted were perhaps driven away by car as the train steamed away, leaving the staff to return to their duties and silence to reign once more upon the empty platforms.

South of Goudhurst, the railway began to swing on a sharp leftward curve, skirting the hill beneath the village and at the foot of the long climb towards Cranbrook. This commenced at Bluecoats bridge, just within sight from the station platform and where a siding used for stabling hop-pickers' coaches came to an end. Continuing in a short cutting, the railway passed by Goudhurst pumping station, owned by the Cranbrook Waterworks Company, before running beneath Rise bridge. With open ground and fields on either side, the line soon reached Pattenden bridge which marked the start of a fairly stiff climb at 1 in 85. Pattenden siding then came into view on the down side, after which the whistle was

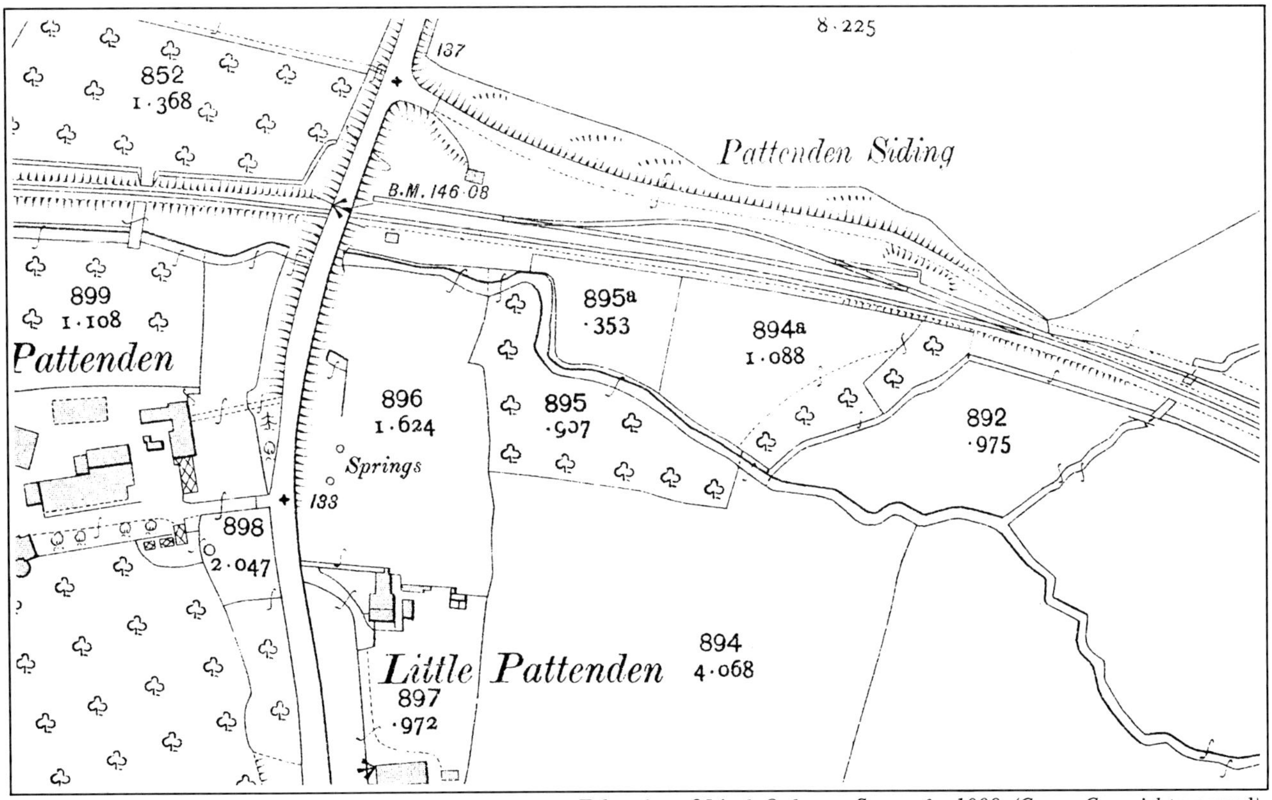

Taken from 25-inch Ordnance Survey for 1908. (Crown Copyright reserved)

Overgrown sidings at Pattenden, with the branch sweeping in the direction of Cranbrook, 10th June 1961. *J. H. Aston*

A mile south of Goudhurst and 'H' class No. 31530 had just passed beneath Pattenden bridge on its way to Hawkhurst with a Maunsell auto unit. The heavily-overgrown sidings on the right were once well used by local farmers and hop-growers. 9th June 1961. *Tony Wright*

'R1' class No. 31700 passing Pattenden siding before commencing the 1 in 60 climb through Furnace Wood to Cranbrook on Saturday, 29th September 1951. The two-lever frame, unlocked by the token, permitted entry into the sidings. The board on the pole near the gate gave notice of the private road leading to Smugley Farm. *Denis Cullum*

required to be sounded for Smugley Farm crossing. Because of the curvature in the line, it was also requisite for trains to slow down to 10 mph at this point so that they might be quickly brought to a stand if there were any obstructions. This was for good reason, especially at hop-picking time when workers in the fields constantly wandered to and fro at all hours of the day.

A breather of a short level stretch was soon superseded by the gradient stiffening to 1 in 60 near Forge Farm, where the railway ran on an embankment. Easing slightly again to 1 in 85, the railway then meandered through some of the most delightfully wooded sections as it traversed the leafy glades and hidden depths of Bedgebury Forest, one moment in a cutting, the next on more embankments. Through Furnace Wood, which had once resounded to the sound of the old Wealden forges, the trains thumped by, the beat of hard-working locomotives easily discernible from the winding trackways which led through the great sun-dappled canopy of broad-leafed trees. A little beyond Arch bridge, demolished in 1946, the gradient resumed at 1 in 60 for almost three-quarters of a mile. Edward Seaton was undoubtedly wise to have lessened the original gradients from 1 in 50 during the construction of the line. According to enginemen, the regular 0-4-4 tank and its train usually 'went up like a dose of salts', with no trouble except on particularly wet days in late autumn when the wheels occasionally slipped. However, the spectacular sights came at hop-picking time when fully-laden trains were hauled with the aid of 'D' class 4-4-0s, or 'C' class 0-6-0s. These Wainwright engines gave everything they could, pounding the track, their exhausts echoing back from the surrounding hillsides, before the welcome sight of Cranbrook down distant signal came into view. On the

Still climbing at 1 in 60, the line passed through Bull Wood on the approach to Cranbrook station. Remarkably, the original wooden M&H signal post lasted throughout the line's existence and was the sole survivor on the branch to retain its distinctive cast-iron M&H finial, even though the top part of the spike was broken off. Unfortunately, the lower quadrant arm and other fittings did not survive and this ugly modern BR replacement was bolted on in its place. *K. G. Carr*

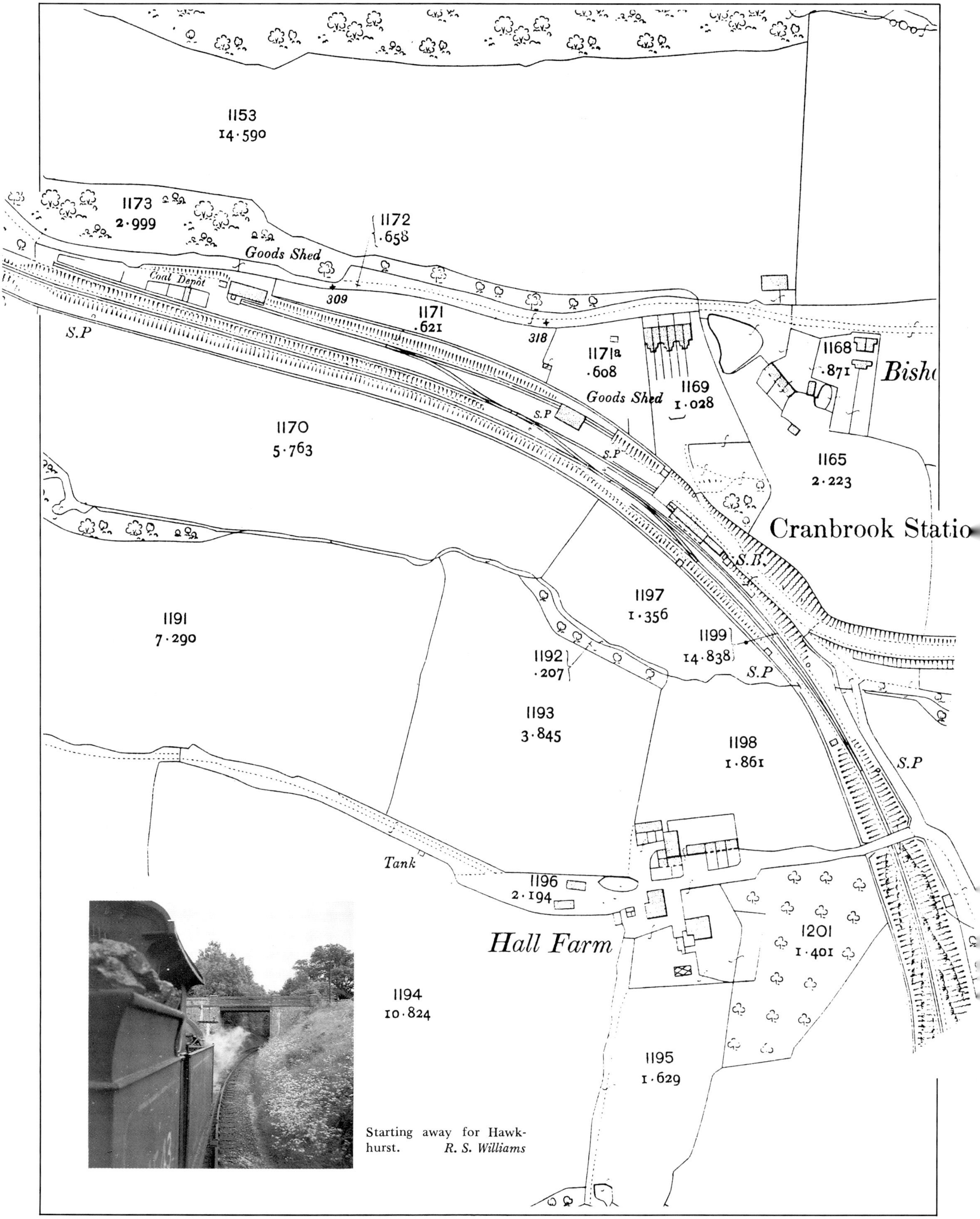

Starting away for Hawkhurst. *R. S. Williams*

Taken from 25-inch Ordnance Survey for 1908. (Crown Copyright reserved)

run in to the station, sidings came alongside on the down direction, where a coal depot and goods shed were provided. A second shed was also erected nearer the station which was convenient to the approach road and dock

The platform and buildings enjoyed a south-facing aspect which made it a particularly pleasant place to work since the entire station nestled in a well-sheltered valley. Similar structures to those at Goudhurst were provided, whilst a loop siding was laid down for shunting purposes only. However, it is rather tempting to suggest that this could have easily been lengthened and adapted to serve a second platform had the line extended beyond Hawkhurst and necessitated a more intensive service. Among those who knew the line well, this station invariably seems to have been everyone's favourite, yet, it must be said, each had its own particular appeal. Cranbrook certainly blossomed throughout the summer months, thanks to the efforts of green-fingered staff whose lovingly-tended flowerbeds and allotment gardens provided a variety of colour. Climbing roses also once graced the sun-baked walls of the station master's house, while other specimens were encouraged to entwine themselves around the odd lamp post.

A long and seemingly never-ending approach road led up to the main highway which runs from Maidstone to Hastings. Here, the scattered hamlet of Hartley, which boasted the important-sounding 'Railway Hotel', once enjoyed a rare peace and quietude before the days of mass car ownership. Almost two miles further up the road lies Cranbrook, the largest of the towns in the

A late-1940s view, showing the goods loop. *H. C. Casserley*

When visited on 22nd September 1951, it was still possible to capture one of the last M&H signals in esixtence, although this, too, disappeared within a couple of years. From the end of the platform the gradient fell away at 1 in 260 towards Goudhurst, hence the difference in the levels of the track leading into the goods yard. Here, a long line of wagons were stored, whilst Cranbrook's other goods shed can be seen in the distance. *R. F. Roberts*

The SR occasionally used concrete posts for signalling purposes which were cheaper to manufacture and did not require painting. The branch was also a haven for many SE&CR miniature arm shunting signals which lingered long after they had disappeared elsewhere on the Southern. One is seen next to the point lever, whilst another can be seen perched halfway up the concrete post of the down home signal. This picture also shows the main goods shed, with heavy sliding doors, and a large lorry parked at the goods yard entrance where large trunks were being stacked on the platform in connection with the schools' term traffic. *J. J. Smith*

district. It is truly ironic that the 'capital of the Weald' and its inhabitants were rather let down by the C&PWR when the decision was made to continue instead in the direction of Hawkhurst. It was, perhaps, a fateful move, which abandoned original aspirations and simply led to the railway failing to properly serve either town.

Cranbrook boasts a rich variety of traditional Kentish houses. Here, weatherboard abounds, intermingled with hand-made brick and tile-hung dwellings, shops and other buildings of various ages, hues and designs. It is one of those marvellous, indiscriminate, higgledy-piggledy jumbles of a place that has been gradually added to

'H' class No. 31263 propelling push-pull unit No. 661 out of the lengthening evening shadows at Cranbrook on Saturday, 10th September 1960. This train was the 5 p.m. Hawkhurst to Paddock Wood.
J. H. Aston

This quiet road was the main highway between Maidstone and Hastings, yet the hamlet of Hartley in the 1920s saw so little traffic that this small lad could ride his tricycle in the road outside his house in the drowsy late afternoon summer sunshine. The large billboard was situated to the left at the entrance to the approach road leading to Cranbrook station, whilst the Railway Hotel opposite was a popular haunt of hop-pickers during the season.

A sunny morning in Cranbrook in the late 1940s with large canvas awnings, once such a common sight in the High Street, drawn across to shield windows and passing customers from the hot sunshine.

over the years and which matures like a much-loved garden. How far removed it is from the cramped, bland and homogeneous 'country style' developments today's speculators erect in a contemptible parody of so-called rural life. Worse still, these estates, with their contrived rustic-sounding names, only destroy acres of bordering countryside and irrevocably spoil the unique character of our once simple towns and villages.

The town is also blessed with one of the most magnificent windmills in the country, the Union Mill, erected in 1814, surely a shrine to the devotees of these once-familiar rural artefacts. As a centre for exploring the High Weald, Cranbrook is ideally suited and many visitors regularly came here by train during the early years of the twentieth century. Perhaps Cranbrook folk eventually forgave the railway builders for not serving them as they'd once hoped, for in spite of the long haul to and from the railway, the station receipts were always among the healthiest on the line. However, it is a shame that today's visitors must arrive in cars which, even in their static condition, disfigure and clutter our lovely old towns simply by their gaudy presence, let alone their perpetual noise and odious fumes.

Whereas the goods yard at Cranbrook was laid out on the level, the running line and station were on a rising gradient of 1 in 80 to Hawkhurst. Thus the climb to the

If the weather was fine in the quiet hours between trains, what more enjoyable task then keeping the station flowerbeds at Cranbrook well tended? This view was taken on 22nd September 1951.
R. F. Roberts

Young Norman Rusbridge enjoying a spot of cycle speedway practice – a popular pastime with lads at that time – in the station approach at Cranbrook. Notice the small balcony and French windows on the first floor of the station accommodation.
Hazel Rusbridge

In this glimpse beneath the station canopy we see the key token in its leather pouch and iron hoop – not an item to mislay! *Trans-Rail Publications*

Cranbrook station basking in summer sunshine. *K. G. Carr*

Cranbrook down starting signal, of SE&CR origin, beckoned continuation of the journey to Hawkhurst as the railway swung southwards beneath Hall Farm bridge on the 1 in 80 climb towards Badger's Oak and the summit of the whole line. 22nd September 1951. *R. F. Roberts*

The distinctive 'arrowhead' iron finial of the SE&CR signal is highlighted against the bright sky in this pleasing portrait of the station captured in September 1951. *Denis Cullum*

'R' class No. 31675 rolling in to Cranbrook with an up afternoon service on Saturday, 29th September 1951.
Denis Cullum

This fine SE&CR bracket signal was put up around 1910 when it replaced the original McKenzie & Holland up home signal seen in earlier pictures. Cast-iron brackets embossed 'SE&CR' supported the wooden platform which was shared by a miniature arm shunt signal (see page 134) and controlled the entry to the loop siding. In later years the shunt signal was renewed with this rather less-inspiring modern design, whilst the original wooden up home arm was sawn off and a steel arm bolted onto the stub. This signal arm with its heavy cast-iron spectacle plate, rod and counterweight (all marked SE&CR) were salvaged prior to the line's demolition and now belong to a collector on Romney Marsh who has restored and re-assembled them upon a new wooden post.
K. G. Carr

summit of the entire branch was recommenced upon pulling away from the platform. This was on a fairly sharp curve of 21 chains in order to enable the railway to head directly southwards for Hawkhurst. Soon after passing beneath Hall Farm bridge a level stretch for about a quarter of a mile was reached where the railway was now some 200 feet above sea level. From this point a thickly-wooded cutting marked the commencement of a mile-long descent at 1 in 80 towards Hawkhurst. Ahead yawned Badger's Oak tunnel, a structure similar in design to that at Horsmonden, also constructed on a slight curve, but twice as long at 178 yards. It was much wetter inside however, its blackened bricks frequently streaming with water, especially during spells of pro-

Having reached a main ridge of the High Weald, the line fell in both directions on a gradient of 1 in 80. Looking out of the northern portal of Badger's Oak tunnel, Cranbrook's up distant signal is glimpsed in this highly atmospheric view of the branch and its surroundings. *John Scrace*

Hawkhurst's down fixed distant on the approach to the southern portal of Badger's Oak tunnel. *K. G. Carr*

longed rain. Emerging from the hillside, the railway passed through Lemon Wood where the fixed distant for Hawkhurst warned engine crews. A few hundred yards further, the line ran onto a very high embankment near Yew Tree Farm where a curve of 19 chains, the sharpest on the entire branch, led directly into Hawkhurst station. A pair of bracketed home signals announced whether the bay or platform road would be taken, whilst here, after crossing Mill Road bridge, the railway cottages could be seen on the right, followed by the engine shed, water tower and signal box. Slowing to running pace, trains

Top: Trenley Road bridge, looking north towards Badger's Oak. Drivers were warned at this point to avoid emitting sparks due to the surrounding woodland. *Above:* Guarding the approach to Hawkhurst station was this fine bracket signal of SR origin. On the right are glimpsed the railway cottages, and beyond them the handsome brick engine shed, water tower, signal box and goods shed.

R. F. Roberts

Slip Mill Road bridge which was rebuilt in reinforced concrete.

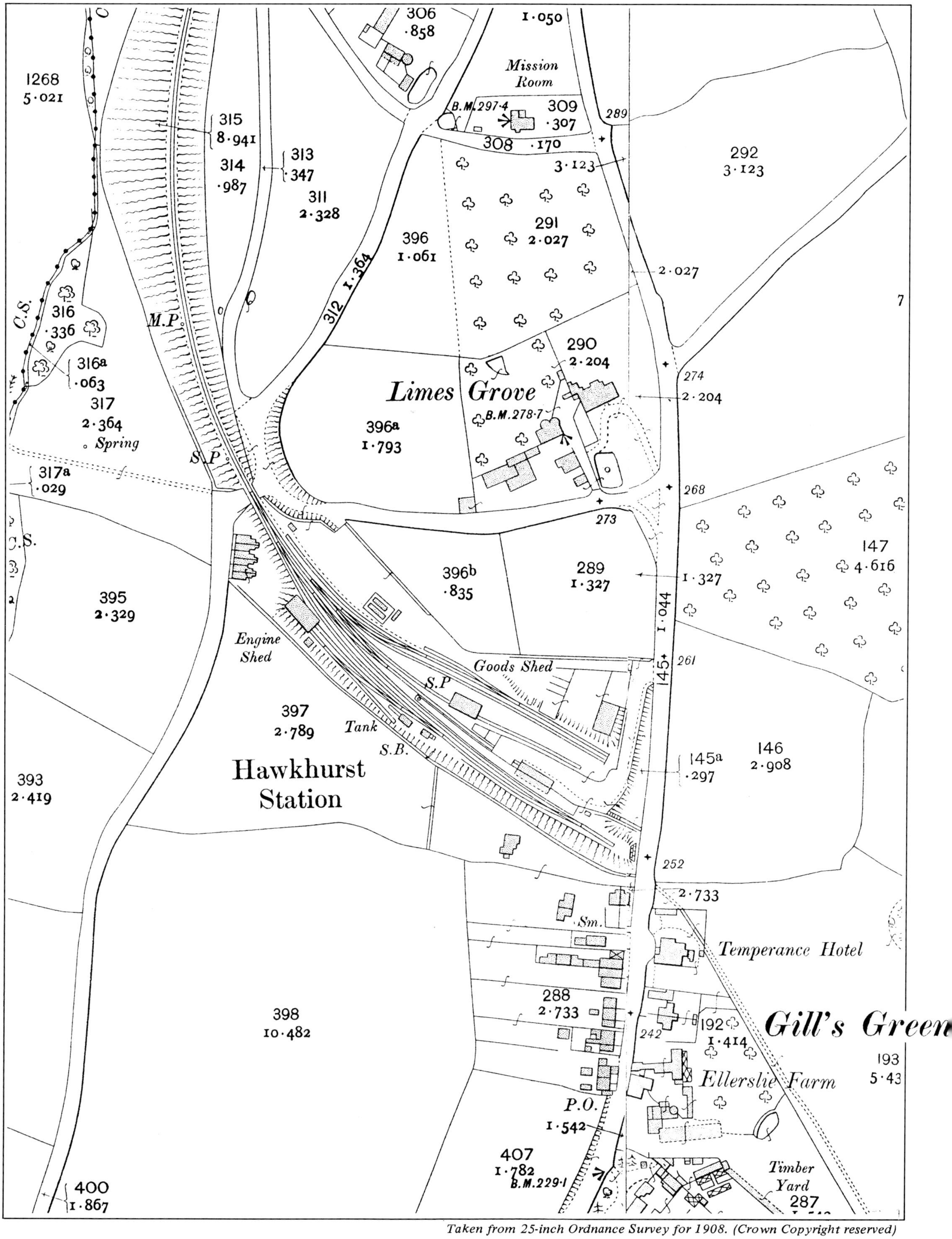

Taken from 25-inch Ordnance Survey for 1908. (Crown Copyright reserved)

The entry to Hawkhurst station from the down home signal gantry, featuring a substantial quantity of hop poles stacked in the yard, the late afternoon goods on the shed road, and coaching stock in the bay. Hawkhurst's handsome brick engine shed dominates the scene, whilst the water tower was another fine feature of this pleasant country terminus.

slowly cruised gently to a stand, 46¼ miles from London and just over eleven miles from Paddock Wood.

Alas, it was only the idle gaze which might continue onwards from the buffer stops perched high above the road that runs below. Perhaps the lie of the land from here on and the formidable earthworks which would have been required to reach Appledore were in themselves sufficient disincentives for the SER to even seriously contemplate the line's extension. Denied further adventure into this wonderful district, we may only ponder upon what fortune might have held in store had the course of history been otherwise. Standing at the end of the platform, a tantalizing view encompassed a wide tract of Wealden downland where distant farms, half-hidden oasts, barns and centuries-old cottages peeped from behind trees and led on to far horizons of hazy ridges.

Hawkhurst had the most extensive goods yard on the branch, spreading out to the rear of the station buildings upon a large, substantially-engineered plateau. Opposite the platform, half-hidden behind a line of fir trees and bushes, the station master's dwelling followed the more traditional style of a detached house. Complete with its own large garden, it enjoyed a sunny, warm and sheltered south-facing aspect, with a commanding view towards the village. Upon the single platform stood the familiar corrugated-iron station building, behind which a wide approach road swept down to the main highway. The distance to the town, lying a mile away and across a wide, deep valley, must have proved a wearisome plod at times for those who had no choice but to walk. There can have been little pleasure in winter when contemplating leaving the relative warmth and comfort of the steam-heated compartment, only to face an unpleasant trek home in cold winds and driving rain. However, the office commuter in summer can surely only have relished the fresh, clean air of Kent after a day in London when the cool evening air would be full of birdsong to gladden the heart and revive flagging spirits.

Hawkhurst similarly possesses many traditional buildings and boasts a fine colonnade of shops with a pleasant sunny aspect. Parched visitors were no doubt delighted to find the Colonnade Café where tempting luncheons

This aerial panorama was taken on the morning of Sunday, 28th August 1949, at the height of the hop-picking season. Tents, huts and caravans to house the pickers can be seen in the field near Slip Mill Road bridge.
Collection Brian Piper

A lovely sunny day in Hawkhurst, with the Colonnade Café advertising luncheons and teas on its gaily-striped awning, and the once common Hovis sign with its gilt letters announcing the presence of the local bakery.

and teas proved irresistible. In a little more than two miles from Highgate crossroads the way to the south and west leads over the border and into dreamy Sussex where yet more leafy byways ever beckon.

During the lifetime of the Hawkhurst branch this corner of Kent was in most people's affections a land full of springtime scented orchards, summery flower-strewn meadows and autumnal mists which settled in the valleys among pungent hop fields. Quiet villages along the wayside were disturbed by little else than the sound of the church clock hesistatingly striking the passing hours and the delivery boy's bicycle rattling over the rough roads as he busily went on his rounds, his cheerful whistling caught on the wind.

From these high, tree-topped hills the eye may still yet wander out across the lush and thickly-wooded valleys and into the dim bluish distance where beyond stretches the pale gentle form of the faraway South Downs. Here indeed is one of the most enchanting districts of the 'Fair Land of Kent', where the magic of the countryside may still weave a spell upon the receptively impressionable who wander through these evocative byways. Sometimes, images of places such as these are so strong that they provide the inspiration for poetry, literature and art. Great writers and painters have all paid homage to this district, whilst even Mary Tourtel of Canterbury, creator of much-loved Rupert Bear, is said to have found her magical land of Nutwood in these parts. Reputedly she was so utterly enchanted and inspired by the landscapes she found in the High Weald and the faraway downs of Sussex that she based her creation on these impressions. Maybe the romance in all of us often leads to a yearning to find those long-lost lanes of our childhood, where we wandered with a skip in our step, carefree in spirit, happy and contented in the simple pleasures of our young lives. How even more precious they seem as the years roll by and although the memory is dimmed, the impression never fades, while the longing to return to those seemingly never-ending happy days rarely fails. How perfectly this desire was captured by A. E. Housman when he penned:

'Into my heart an air that kills
From yon far country blows:
What are those blue remembered hills,
What spires, what farms are those?

That is the land of lost content,
I see it shining plain,
The happy highways where I went
And cannot come again.'

Taken on 22nd May 1955, this view shows the lifted siding to the engine shed and locomotive's coaling stage. The huge number of hop poles were stacked in the yards prior to despatch.
Collection Brian Piper

Two views taken in 1951 of the fuel depot adjacent to the goods yard at Hawkhurst. *Ken Garrett*

This shot affords an unusual view of the station environs, as well as a glimpse of the rear of the water tower and signal box. *Collection Brian Piper*

The yard crane at Hawkhurst saw much activity in its working life and, happily, was eventually presented to the preserved Kent & East Sussex Railway.
Ken Garrett

From the platform of the starting signals, a good view was obtained of the station and goods yard in 1951. *Ken Garrett*

The loading gauge and goods shed entrance. *Ken Garrett*

Busier days at Hawkhurst with a string of wagons and vans in the goods shed road at Hawkhurst. *Ken Garrett*

The nationalized British Railways set up a door-to-door service for goods and parcels traffic which provided an efficient and cheap means of transporting merchandise all over the country. This view shows one of the railway lorries parked outside Hawkhurst goods shed during the day's business. *Ken Garrett*

The only known photograph of the interior of the goods shed with its magnificent Victorian crane, cleverly geared for each manual operation to load and unload all manner of merchandise sent by rail. Nowadays politicians love nothing more than to eulogize about integrated transport systems and shifting freight onto rail, when the truth is that they were responsible for its destruction in the 1950s-60s! *Ken Garrett*

This view, taken on 11th June 1950, shows the bay platform which was mostly used for the school trains and for stabling empty stock during the day. It is easy to appreciate the charm and rural beauty of this Kentish terminus.
Derek Clayton

An aerial shot showing the end of the Hawkhurst branch at Gill's Green and the raised land upon which it was built. The station master's handsome detached house is seen just to the south of the station buildings. *Collection Brian Piper*

The other side of the goods shed, with the siding leading to the adjacent cattle dock. *Ken Garrett*

An aerial view of the station and yard from above the Kent Woodware Company. The round oasts were a later variation on the older form of square oasts which are found mostly in Kent. *Collection Brian Piper*

The very neat timber signal box photographed in 1951. Although looking rather dilapidated here, it was thoroughly smartened-up with a fresh coat of paint by BR only a few years before closure. Unlike the handsome and very solid brick water tower, the signal box survived the railway and is now looked after by the adjoining Kent Woodware Company which owns the site. *Ken Garrett*

This fine view of the station was obtained by bravely scaling the iron ladder to the top of the water tower. *Ken Garrett*

Crates of plants and other items awaiting the next service from Paddock Wood in this pleasant trackside glimpse of the country terminus.
Ken Garrett

The driver of push-pull unit No. 732 sitting in his driving compartment prior to the departure from this outpost of the Southern, 46¼ miles from Charing Cross on 8th August 1959.
Frank Saunders

Set No. 723 waiting to leave Hawkhurst as the 5.5 p.m. to Paddock Wood on the afternoon of Wednesday, 10th August 1955. The engine blowing off excess steam was 'R1' No. 31704.
J. H. Aston

The station building well highlighted in the pleasant light of late afternoon sunshine. The platform facing of wooden sleepers is also shown.
K. A. Stone

The large 18in dial longcase clock witnessed the arrival of the first and last trains to Hawkhurst, faithfully and accurately recording the time for passengers and staff for 68 years. Many SR stations remained illuminated by oil lamps well into the 1960s, and this fine bracketed example beneath the canopy at Hawkhurst served the station well.

'H' class No. 31543, fitted with tail lamp, waiting to propel its train back to Paddock Wood on a sunny day, 27th May 1961. *John Scrace*

The porters' humble accommodation which was provided for their use following the alterations to the main station building. Warmth was provided by a stove, the chimney of which may be seen emerging from the roof. The 12in x 6in black & white 1-inch striped card upon the door was temporarily placed there by Ken as an aid to scaling these photographs for modelling purposes. *Ken Garrett*

The station seen from the signal box steps.
A. W. Burges

Afternoon sunshine highlighting detail on the porters' accommodation, permanent way trolley hut and corrugated-iron oil store. *Ken Garrett*

The end of the branch, where the buffer stops marked an end to further journeying by rail into this lovely part of Kent.
Tony Wright

Looking from the wide approach road to the station buildings at Hawkhurst, with a local service about to depart for Paddock Wood in 1951. *Ken Garrett*

Looking across the approach road to the porters' accommodation.
Ken Garrett

This fine oil lamp once cast a wan but welcome light upon the flight of twenty-four steps leading up from the Maidstone to Hastings road at Gill's Green.
Ken Garrett

Waiting for a hop-pickers' special at London Bridge station on Tuesday, 27th August 1935.

Hulton Getty

CHAPTER EIGHT

THE HOP-PICKERS' TALE

ALTHOUGH the Romans are believed to have first introduced the hop to Britain, commercial cultivation did not begin until the sixteenth century. For many years though, there lingered resistance to their widespread planting, even superstition, when it was described as a 'wicked weed'. Nevertheless, its ability to improve the qualities of beer soon dispelled such notions, whilst eventually everyone acknowledged its importance. Thus, the 'weed' not only found many farmers keen to establish hop gardens, as they are properly termed, but in due course the humble hop became synonymous with Kent. It is also worth mentioning here that a hop motif was appropriately chosen as the seal of the Cranbrook and Paddock Wood Railway Company.

The hop-picking season lasts for approximately three weeks, generally beginning around the very end of August and finishing in mid-September. The work was once extremely labour-intensive, requiring as many hands as possible to bring down the bines and gather the clusters of bright green hops into bins. Here they would be tallied, before being carted off to the oast houses for drying. With the growth of the industry there was significantly far more work than local people could manage, hence the influx into the fields of Kent in late summer of thousands of Londoners, gypsies and anyone else looking for the means of earning a few shillings. Initially, many came by foot, tramping thirty or forty miles over two wearying days, whilst others travelled down in horse-drawn wagons. Places such as Peckham, Deptford, Bermondsey, Rotherhithe, etc., witnessed something approaching a mass exodus, whilst thousands more came from the East End, crossing the Thames at Greenwich where they continued on foot.

With the coming of the railways to Kent, the companies were well aware of the lucrative trade in hops and the necessary human cargo of attendant pickers. Railway rates were calculated per mile; for

With the exception of babies and toddlers, every member of the family was expected to help out with the gathering of hops. Here, young children watch the menfolk empty hops from wicker baskets in readiness for 'pocketing-up' and loading into railway wagons.

Hulton Getty

instance, in 1853 it cost 1s 9d to send a pocket of hops from Marden to London, whereas the tariff was 2s 0d from recently-opened Smeeth station, just the other side of Ashford.

There was, of course, little point in expecting hop-pickers to pay the ordinary fares, so the first 'specials' were organized in the 1850s. Conditions at this time were quite appalling. Cattle trucks are reputed to have at first been used, whereby the pickers were left to make themselves as comfortable as possible on the straw, or whatever they could manage to bring with them. Eventually, the oldest and roughest carriages were laid on, with the SER charging from a florin (2s 0d) to half-a-crown (2s 6d) for the journey. Babes in arms were carried free and, not surprisingly, this led to many of the poorest families wrapping up their older children in shawls, or cramming them into handcarts as a means of avoiding fares. Those who were quite obviously too grown-up were customarily smuggled past the barriers and secreted underneath compartment seats. Many adults also did their best to avoid paying their way and dodge the ticket collectors at the end of the journey. Some ran off across the tracks as the train pulled in and there were instances of pickers being killed or horribly injured by passing trains. Those whom the railway authorities managed to apprehend were often made to forfeit personal belongings; for example, the station master at Paddock Wood had a reputation for confiscating shoes.

By 1865, over 11,000 hop-pickers were annually being taken into Kent by train. However, in a little over a decade, this more than trebled, although fluctuations naturally occurred from year to year. Journeys normally began very early in the morning, so that by 4am the area around Bricklayers Arms goods station was heaving with the throng of many hundreds of Londoners. It was a scene described as nothing short of pandemonium as this swarm of humanity, huddled in the darkness prior to dawn breaking, jostled and crowded onto the lines of waiting trains. These spectacles made a deep impression upon contemporary observers who described how the light from the gas globes lit up a sea of wan faces, including many children who clutched fearfully onto the ragged clothing of their impoverished parents. All around a deafening chorus of railway engines filled the air as safety valves lifted on those awaiting departure, while others noisily steamed out into the darkness.

The 'hoppers', as they were colloquially known, originally came from the most wretched sections of society, many dressed quite literally in tatters. Such dire poverty is scarcely imaginable today, but during the nineteenth century the conditions in which many of them lived was astoundingly grim. There was also much habitual drunkenness, fighting and outbreaks of rowdyism. In an often vain attempt to control the arriving crowds, the Kent constabulary regularly posted its policemen at stations when hop-pickers' trains were due. It frequently proved to be an unenviable duty for these men since many of the rougher elements on board had neither fear nor respect for the law, let alone its enforcers. Where there were no policemen it was common practice for the railway staff to lock themselves in the station for their own safety. As the trains pulled into normally quiet, rural wayside platforms, doors would burst open as crowds poured forth, seething out onto the approach road to the accompaniment of much shouting, swearing and hullabaloo. Children inevitably became separated from their parents, leading to varying amounts of screaming and crying, while in the general chaos attempts were made to organize the rabble into parties for their respective destinations

The journey down to Kent was rarely direct and normally most trains travelled over the quieter routes to the main railhead at Paddock Wood. Sometimes this was via New Cross Gate, Croydon and Redhill, other times via the North Kent Line to Strood, before running south along the Medway Valley. During the last century many of the hop-pickers' specials were invariably run at night and it was not uncommon for the occupants of these trains to unexpectedly find themselves ejected from the relative warmth of the compartments to await connections. Here, on cold, miserable and draughty platforms, they would huddle together, often for hours at a stretch, awaiting dawn and the train which would carry them to their final destination. The plight of these wretched people did not go unnoticed and in September 1890 a correspondent to the *Post* made the following plea on their behalf:

> 'STAPLEHURST: A Hop-picker's Journey.
> Sir, Can you afford a short space to narrate a very sad experience I have just had in connection with the poor hop-pickers who had the misfortune to leave London Bridge on Sunday night for the above. After arriving at Paddock Wood about twenty minutes to two a.m. about 150 men, women and children were kept standing for six hours on an uncovered platform. To see the poor little children shivering with cold was heart-rending. Surely the company could arrange to do the journey from London to Staplehurst in under eight hours, or provide some shelter for the poor in the dead of night? But then, I suppose, they were only poor hoppers in the train after all.'

The opening of the C&PWR, first to Hope Mill in September 1892 and then to Hawkhurst in the following year, made the hop fields of the High Weald more easily accessible. Whether the inhabitants of the area actually welcomed this fact is indeed a moot point, but they all appear to have done their best by putting on a brave face.

With two branches now connecting into the main line, both serving large areas of hop fields, the station master at Paddock Wood saw a substantial increase in his workload during the autumn. It was customarily a time of little sleep and constant awareness, since it was rare indeed if a season went by without an injury. Curiously, many pickers seemed to show scant regard for their own safety, apparently quite oblivious to the dangers associated with the railway. In September 1893 there was utter disarray when hop-pickers at Tonbridge overflowed from the platform and rampaged across the quadruple lines, whilst in 1891 the Paddock Wood station master bravely risked his own life by springing onto the busy main line to save one drunken hop-picker from the wheels of a fast approaching train. This particular inebriate, blissfully unaware of his predicament, had attempted to stagger across the four sets of tracks rather than use the footbridge. Less fortunate was a picker who arrived here at the commencement of the season in 1895. He came with a party of East Enders who'd journeyed by special midnight train before disembarking to await the local connection. Shortly afterwards a woman stumbled off the platform and into the path of an approaching goods train, whereupon the man concerned jumped down in a heroic attempt to drag her to one side. Tragically he was too late, whereby both of them were horribly mown down by the engine which, it was later claimed, had displayed no lights, nor sounded its whistle, even though it was pitch dark. Both 'sustained frightful injuries' and it must have been a truly dreadful experience for everyone else involved. They were hurriedly taken by train to Maidstone Hospital, but the man died not long after his crushed legs were amputated, while the woman lingered for some time in a 'dangerous condition' before finally expiring.

A repeat of this terrible incident seemed about to take place only three weeks later when a group of pickers were waiting to return home from Marden station. A woman, who in this instance was in a drunken stupor, suddenly pitched forward onto the up track. Even though the line was already signalled for a through train, a booking clerk and porter courageously leapt after her, much to the horror of the signalman who hollered at the top of his voice 'Look out! - the express!'. Miraculously, they managed to drag her off the rails and into the 'six foot', between the running lines, as a mere split second later, the train thundered through. No doubt there were cheers from the crowd on seeing them all safe after such a close shave, whilst it was reported that the woman 'sobered up remarkably quickly' after her brush with death.

Fatalities were not always confined to deaths on the railway and there were often violent outbursts which ended brutally. One of these was a fight which broke out among hop-pickers staying at Horsmonden and involving a twenty-six year-old man named John Stevens, described as a 'costermonger and pugilist'. He was stabbed by an opponent, Billy Maher, who hurriedly made off, but was later tracked down and arrested. Before he expired, Stevens cried out: 'Hold me up, goodbye old girl, goodbye wife, I'm stabbed through the heart, I'm done for Moggy'. He was carried bleeding badly from the knife wound to a nearby oast at Hale Farm where he 'died before brandy could be administered'.

Stabbings, affrays and drunkenness among a minority of hoppers were sadly all too commonplace in these times. The church and temperance associations did their best to provide non-alcoholic refreshments and entertainments for the pickers, but it was difficult to coax them away from the inns and ale houses. The well-meaning individuals who trundled their tea and coffee barrows around the hop gardens probably imagined that they were performing a worthwhile and reforming task, since everyone took advantage of the free beverages. However, by the end of the season, with three weeks 'pay-off' in hand, the consumption of beer and gin resumed to excess, bringing with it the bouts of bad behaviour. Quite a multitude willingly attended the magic lantern shows, set up in the fields and put on by the local evangelists, no doubt pleased to enjoy a spot of entertainment, although many were affronted when it was accompanied by the distribution of hymn sheets. The Bishop of Dover visited hop gardens at Goudhurst and Lamberhurst in 1893 in an attempt to see what could be done, not only towards modifying the behaviour of the rowdier elements, but generally improving living conditions which remained extremely crude. Even so, many years would pass before any real advancements were forthcoming.

At the end of the 1893 season work finished in the second week of September, whereby the SER issued notices that special trains for London would be put on at two shillings per head. Overall, the conduct of the pickers had not been too bad that year, even though several had attempted to dodge paying fares at East Farleigh and, when challenged, had beaten up both the station master and ticket collector. Consequently all the offenders ended up in Maidstone gaol for a fortnight. Similarly, petty pilfering was particularly rife, especially in the early days and it was no wonder that local people greeted the season with a degree of trepidation. When, on a Wednesday morning during the last week of August 1895, the first hop-pickers' train arrived at Cranbrook station, the crowds made straight for the Railway Tavern at Hartley. In a moment's absence of the landlord, 14s 0d was stolen from the till, a substantial sum of money in those days.

For the children who were brought to the hopfields for the first time, the experience must have been one of sheer wonderment. From the overcrowded, filthy slums of London with only a back alley, yard or grubby street in which to play, and air foul with the smoke from countless domestic and factory chimneys, they were suddenly let loose in what must have seemed paradise. Here was open space, soft ground that was covered in scented, dewy grass, a gentle landscape which comprised hay fields, great and many-boughed trees, sparkling crystal-clear rivers and distant hilltops with windmills and oast houses. There were unfamiliar animals, new smells and tastes, strange things to touch and explore, birdsong, humming and buzzing insects, indeed, a whole unknown world. It must have come as a complete surprise and although it was generally a very hard-working period for all concerned, it was also an enjoyable break, provided that the weather and conditions weren't too bad.

Some of the farms were better than others, with the more fortunate allowed to set up home within barns or outhouses. There was often plenty of fresh straw for bedding and a well from which to draw clean water, whilst the better hop gardens began to provide small wooden huts. However, there was little that could be done to control the weather which, on occasions, could be quite soul-destroying and miserable. It was certainly not uncommon for pickers to die of exposure, since many took to simply sleeping under hedgerows, or in fields under nothing more than flimsy tents or canvas awnings. When there was a dry autumn it was simply beautiful and there was singing in the fields to accompany the glorious weather, but when it was wet it was quite awful. The season of 1896 was particularly bad, with violent thunderstorms during the second week of September and non-stop torrential rain for over three hours during one night. The *Post* commented that it was:

> 'Not a comfortable night for [Hawkhurst] householders, what it must have been like for the dwellers in tents and hopper huts is easier imagined than described! Work has been rendered very unpleasant as a result.'

Equally hazardous were the sporadic fires which broke out when a camp fire spread out of control, or a candle or oil lamp was knocked over in a hut. In 1898 there was much commotion one evening when a row of wooden hopper huts at Smugley Farm was destroyed when tinder-dry straw on the floors accidentally ignited. Many hop-pickers lost all their personal belongings as well as their clothes as a result of this conflagration.

Occurrences of drunkenness, disorderly conduct, breaking windows, stealing money and groceries, raiding washing lines for clothing, pilfering fruit, vegetables, chickens and other livestock, indecent behaviour, using foul language in public, etc., happened annually as a

Another scene from the Kentish hopfields taken around 1900. The hop bines were pulled down from their supporting twines, whereby the bright green and uniquely fragrant 'flowers' could then be harvested into wicker baskets. Although it wasn't a particularly difficult job, the work was generally intensive, whilst the hops were very coarse on the skin and blackened hands. *Hulton Getty*

Hop pockets, brought by horse and cart from Brenchley, being loaded onto railway wagons in the west yard at Paddock Wood.

matter of course at this time. Offenders were regularly hauled up before Cranbrook magistrates to face the consequences, sometimes a fine, but invariably a spell in prison since most were either quite unable or simply unwilling to pay up. In September 1899 a hop-picker by the name of Elizabeth Vincent was charged with smashing a window, valued at two shillings, at Horsmonden. This in itself is certainly not worthy of note; however, the ghastly incident which took place the next day merits relating. In spite of her misdemeanour, Elizabeth Vincent was compassionately discharged, owing to the tragic death on the following afternoon of her step-brother, likewise a hop-picker from London. The circumstances surrounding the demise of this man remain shrouded in mystery, with no proper explanation being given as to exactly how or why he met with such a gruesome end. The event upset the whole village and culminated with the discovery of badly mutilated remains of a man inside the Dog House tunnel. Mr. Charles Roberts of Horsmonden had the unpleasant misfortune to come across the mangled corpse, whereupon he hurriedly fetched constable Goldup who immediately summoned the coroner. At the inquest Mr. Roberts testified that he'd found the body 'Lying on its back, part way in the tunnel, and perfectly cold'. Another witness, Alfred Humphrey, stated that earlier on that afternoon he'd been holding a pony for the deceased hop-picker when a row had broken out, at which he'd been suddenly threatened with a cut-throat razor. In defence, someone else had struck out at the hop-picker, whereby the assailant promptly made off in the direction of Sandy Lane. Constable Goldup reported that he'd made a thorough search of the area, discovering a large clot of blood at the foot of the cutting beneath Sandy Lane railway bridge and concluded that the man had somehow fallen the fifty feet from the parapet. It could not be ascertained if the fall had caused his death, or whether he'd lain insensible. However he'd then been hit by the engine of the last up train of the day. The front guard irons in front of the locomotive's driving wheels had evidently struck the man, dragging him along the railway line for about 150 yards and into the mouth of the tunnel where he finally went under the wheels. Isaac Jeffries, station master at Horsmonden, said he'd called through to Paddock Wood on being told of the affair, whereupon the crew examined their train. Whereas blood was found on the engine's guard irons, neither driver nor guard had felt anything unusual, nor heard any noise.

No other witnesses came forward, nor could any person at the hearing explain why the hop-picker should so mysteriously have fallen to his death from Sandy Lane bridge. In the event there was no alternative but to record a verdict of accidental death, whilst there remained an air of suspicion and mystery surrounding this grim event.

An equally distressing accident befell a hop-picking family in 1902, involving a five year-old girl, Clara Anderson, who came down with her mother from Canning Town to Mr. William Levett's farm at Glassenbury. A traction engine and two coupled wagons had been sent down to Cranbrook station to meet this particular happy band of pickers who were then conveyed the two miles north to the farm. In the general excitement on arrival at Glassenbury, the unattended child wandered between the two trucks where she stumbled and fell beneath the wheels which passed over her little body. Tragically, the little mite expired before a doctor could attend. Accidents such as these were fortunately rare and the worst upsets most parents had to contend with were everyday cuts and bruises or wasp stings.

A small group of hop-pickers and children setting out from the down side at Paddock Wood on their way to nearby farms, with the family belongings loaded into an old pram, in August 1910. *Hulton Getty*

At the end of picking and following paying-out, the less reputable hoppers immediately headed for the local pubs and promptly swilled away much of their hard-earned cash. The usual fights and arguments broke out on the way home and it is small wonder that the railway staff breathed a collective sigh of relief when the last special was to be seen steaming off into the distance. In 1904 a dispute broke out at Hawkhurst station between a band of hop-pickers and the station staff. William Saxby, who was at that time a porter, was involved in a skirmish to which the local police constables were hurriedly called. The offender was hauled off and eventually sentenced to fourteen days hard labour by Cranbrook magistrates.

The regular seasons of picking the millions of hops came and went as the agricultural calendar turned full circle. Some years were better than others, depending on the unpredictable English climate, disease and fungal blight among the bines, as well as fluctuations in the market price which could be equally disastrous. 1908 was a particularly grim time for both the hop-picker and grower, so bad in fact that it was reported as the worst year in living memory. This was brought about by a collapse in the commercial value of the commodity, with prices 'ridiculously low', whereby whole acres at Lamberhurst were simply left to rot on the bine. The knock-on effect depressed the takings on the Hawkhurst branch, but fortunately matters quickly improved so that by the following year the traditional embarkation for the hopfields of Kent was in full swing during late August. One of the most vivid portrayals of the time appeared in the *Courier* when an observer witnessed the multitudes arriving at London Bridge station on their way down:

'The main army of hop-pickers started at midnight on Monday on its annual invasion of Kent. The advance guard has been feeling its way in negligible quantities during the past week and before next Sunday the East End of London will be depleted by more than 30,000 of its inhabitants. London Bridge is the starting centre and belated business-men stopped for a moment to watch the arrival of whole families and the household goods at the SE&CR Company's station. At first they came in twos or threes; but towards 11 o'clock there was one seething mass of humanity crossing London Bridge, laden with parcels of all descriptions. There were grey-haired women pushing dilapidated perambulators laden with bundles and boxes. Younger women staggered along with heavy burdens - animate and inanimate - of varying degrees of cleanliness and men and boys laboured till their faces glistened wet in the lamplight. The approach to the station resembled some primitive camp. At the foot of each iron pillar supporting the roof, baggage was piled many feet high and each pile was invariably surmounted by a heavy-eyed child, whose little head had drooped wearily in spite of the babel of cries. Other children of maturer age sprawled at the base of the pile, while in one dark corner several youths gathered together for a game of 'pitch and toss'. There were babes scarcely a month old, blinking and wondering at the huge arc lights, or sleeping peacefully in the folds of an immense shawl and there were old men and women upon whom the tale of many years was plainly evident. The South Eastern Railway authorities had made arrangements for carrying some 3,000, not including children. Eight special trains were in readiness and shortly after eleven, the first train steamed out into the darkness, crowded to the uttermost. It is a heartless thing to rob the poor, yet the railway company has been compelled to issue porters warning the hoppers against buying their railway tickets from unauthorized people. When the officials have their train in readiness the barriers are thrown open and a rush is made. Every member of every family grabs hold of his or her bundle and makes a dash for the ticket office. No matter to what station the picker is going the fare is but 2s 0d. Then there is a rush for the first train and, despite the fact that seven more are waiting, everybody tries to crowd into that one. Baggage is stowed in the vans, on the floor, under the seats; mouth organs and concertinas come out and the station is full of melody - or its equivalent to the happy travellers. An extra staff of police and porters is on duty but there is little need of their services unless it is to find a missing baby at the last minute.

These special 'roundabout' trains, as they are called for hop-pickers, run between London, Tonbridge and Snodland via Chislehurst and Sevenoaks on the North Kent line. Tickets are usually collected at Spa Road station and then they go on to Snodland where the first stop is made, a little over an hour after leaving London. When travelling via Sevenoaks, Tonbridge is the first stop. Aylesford, Maidstone, East Farleigh, Wateringbury, Yalding and Paddock Wood are the chief centres to which the pickers travel. The carriages used are not, of course, those in daily use by the general public, but old stock. As showing how the grubbing of the hop fields affects the East Ender, the figures for last year and for 1905 are given below:

1905 : Trains - 66	Passengers - 23,008
1907 : Trains - 53	Passengers - 20,693

The twentieth century brought with it significant improvements in the lot of the humble hop-picker and his family. Local authorities began stipulating minimum conditions, insisting upon a modicum of decent accom-

Most hop-pickers came from the poorest families, as depicted here. The women were probably glad to earn extra shillings during these three weeks which supplemented their meagre income throughout the winter – provided their husbands didn't swill away most of their hard-won cash down at the 'local'. At the start of another crisp, clear morning, an elderly woman is pictured brewing tea on an open fire, which was then poured into glass bottles before being taken into the hopfields.

modation and a standard of hygiene. Farmers were required to provide shelter which was clean and dry, properly ventilated and secure from the elements. Screens were also required to separate the sexes. However, judging by the number of three month-old babies which regularly came down the following year, this requirement doesn't seem to have been effected, or if so, respected! Separate lavatories for men and women were also deemed essential, but these rules were hardly ever enforced and most pickers had to make do with a communal latrine which consisted of nothing more than a corrugated iron hut over a smelly pit. More up-to-date models were positioned over a trench which could periodically be moved along as the waste was buried. Water for drinking, cooking and washing was also required to be provided, but most were lucky to have access to a solitary tap, whilst cooking facilities were centred around a group of camp fires. Few people complained about roughing it, indeed, it made little difference to many of them since they were well-used to the conditions of their cramped, dingy and damp homes, which were little better in the worst of the slum areas of the capital. However, events on a national scale were now changing fast and these would have a direct effect upon the lives of those who toiled in the hop gardens of Kent.

The Great War heralded many changes. For the first time there was an acute shortage of labour as most of the men volunteered, or were later conscripted, to fight in the battlefields of Europe. Simultaneously, the women-folk found convenient and far more lucrative employment nearer home, working in the munitions factories, driving trams and stepping into jobs which were once the sole preserve of men. As a result, there was a need to attract others to come along and gather the harvest. This could only be achieved by providing many of the facilities demanded by local authorities in order to woo volunteers from other walks of life. An admirable example was set by Mr. Isaac Lewis of Bedgebury, upon whose estate were set up 'model dwellings' at Three Chimneys Farm. He also had the brainwave of offering prizes for the best-kept huts, which instilled a sense of pride among those who took up temporary residence. Two classes of prizes were offered. Firstly, the best kept dwelling for those pickers with children and, secondly, those without children. Quite evidently there was much pride and good-humoured rivalry among the Londoners for in 1917 the prize-winners were as follows:

First category:	
1st prize (10s 0d)	Mrs. Jones, Bermondsey
2nd prize (7s 6d)	Mrs. Darling, Hammersmith
3rd prize (5s 0d)	Mrs. Shepherd, Hammersmith
4th prize (3s 0d)	Mrs. Tucker, Brighton
Second category:	
1st prize (7s 6d)	Mrs. Gardener, Walworth
2nd prize (6s 0d)	Mrs. Wood, Kennington
3rd prize (4s 0d)	Mrs. Kellner, Bermondsey
4th prize (2s 6d)	Mrs. Wilson, Whitechapel

Further improvements came with the setting up of small mobile shops, selling bread, vegetables, groceries and provisions. It was also reported that paying-off took place that year on 15th September, after which the pickers were conveyed in open wagons to Goudhurst station where trains were already waiting to take them back to London.

After the war it was necessary to enforce rather than attempt to encourage minimum standards of hygiene in order to counteract the instances of infection and disease which broke out at the worst farms. The local medical health officers were frequently critical of conditions, particularly the foul-smelling latrines, lack of washing facilities and the squalid state of the older wooden huts where overcrowding was described 'worse than the most dismal slums of industrial Britain'. Living accommodation worsened at weekends with the arrival of trainloads of hop-pickers' friends who came down into the countryside for a couple of days' break. Nothing was thought of simply cramming themselves into the already overflowing huts. The voluntary services and the Red Cross in particular did much to improve the health and well-being of the youngsters, some of whom were undernourished and had never been medically examined in their lives. However, it was difficult to more than scratch the surface of the problem. There were no proper baths of course and, apart from a wash down in an enamelled basin or a swim in a nearby river, the accumulated smell of some sections of unwashed mass humanity was simply tolerated. It would be wrong, nevertheless, to conclude that everyone was dirty. This was far from the case and most families managed to keep themselves clean and their admittedly limited temporary housing spick and span.

The day began while the early-morning mist and dew were still covering the cold quiet fields. The hop-pickers emerged from their dwellings at between six and six-thirty, usually just as the first goods train for Hawkhurst was making its way down and acting as a rather convenient alarm call. Breakfast consisted of fried bread and potatoes, with large, flat field mushrooms included if they could be found in the local paddocks. More fortunate families frequently had local eggs, rashers of sizzling bacon and sausages to add to their plate. Tea was then brewed and bottled-up to be taken with packed food into the hop gardens where the morning's picking commenced. Around midday, small fires were lit to warm up the tea, while sandwiches, thick chunks of fruit cake and bread pudding were hungrily consumed. There was nothing like hard work and the fresh air of the Kentish countryside to bring about an appetite. Work continued all afternoon until five or maybe six o'clock. The evenings were then free to enjoy a communal meal around the camp fire. It was at these times that nostalgia for those days is at its greatest among the one-time pickers. Faces would be lit up by the flames of flickering fires as a rousing sing-song sounded far off into the dusk. Individuals would perform a solitary turn, or perhaps a duet and a dance around the fire, while laughter rang out across the darkening, silent fields on these most memorable occasions.

The new Southern Railway Company organized the movement of the hop-pickers by train to a greater degree of efficiency. For example, in 1924 they coped with 37,774 pickers on the outward journey, of which more than 7,000 detrained at stations on the Hawkhurst branch. A 'Hop Control Room' was set up at Paddock Wood, which was the main railhead for dealing with the thousands of people and the many trains - eighty-five in 1925 - needed to shift this human cargo from London. Farmers, who would judge when the hops would be ready for gathering, sent out cards to the Central Liaison Officer who would then be able to assess the number of trains required and when they'd have to run. These cards were then posted individually to the pickers who would arrive at London Bridge at the appointed time. Here they would be directed to a platform and whichever train was waiting to convey them into Kent. Special luggage labels, identifiable by a larger initial capital letter, were pasted onto the assortment of baggage. Even so, there invariably arose varying degrees of confusion and mayhem at the other end.

Towards the culmination of picking, the farmer would once again contact the railway authorities to arrange the trains home. In order not to interfere with other services, these trains were regularly routed along some of the secondary lines, causing some pickers to curse at being sent on a 'bleeding mystery tour'! The old South Eastern route from Tonbridge to Redhill was a useful pathway, with trains able to head north for London by running via the Crowhurst spur line west of Edenbridge. This provided access onto the Lewes - East Grinstead - Oxted route, thus avoiding Redhill and the busy Brighton main line. Incidentally, it was here that in 1925 the signalman on duty at Crowhurst Junction North cabin found himself in trouble. At around 4.45pm on 23rd September, he cleared his signals for a homeward-bound hop-pickers' special from Paddock Wood, allowing it to come off the ex-SER line and spur, before continuing onward to Hurst Green Junction. At the time, a passenger train

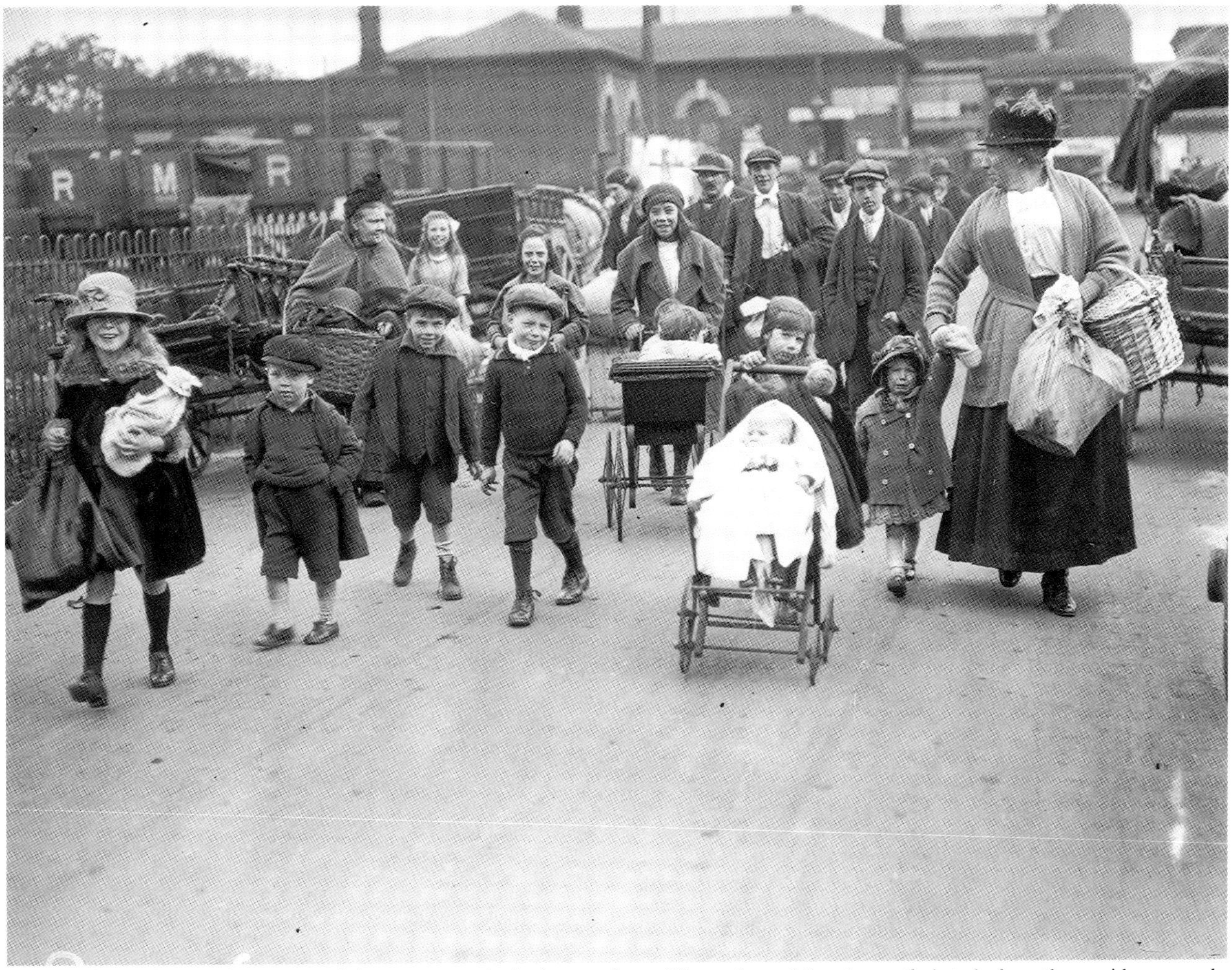

Looking forward to earning some useful extra money in the hop gardens of Kent, these pickers began their trek along the up side approach road at Paddock Wood in September 1922. *Hulton Getty*

Outside the Railway Hotel at Hartley, near Cranbrook, on a Sunday lunchtime, hop-pickers, dressed in their Sunday best, would enjoy pints of the Kentish ale which had benefited from their labours. A barrel (just by the Shell-Mex pump) had been set up on the trestle table to supply the Londoners who had congregated here.

These huts were home for three weeks of the year, when everyone 'mucked-in', intent on having a break from everyday life in London while gathering the annual harvest of hops. *Hulton Getty*

With a pair of fowl and all their wordly possessions for the fortnight's duration, two families of hop-pickers are pictured here on their way across London Bridge on the homeward journey from the hopfields of Kent on 3rd October 1936. *Hulton Getty*

from Uckfield to Victoria was already 'in section' on the nearby ex-LB&SCR line between Edenbridge Town station and Hurst Green. The Block Regulations forbade two trains to approach a converging junction at the same time, even if the signals at the junction were set against both. This was because of the danger of an overrun, causing the junction to be fouled. For his error in not having first obtained authority with a 'Line Clear' message from his colleague in Hurst Green Junction Box, he was accordingly cautioned over the incident.

Another mishap, also around this time and likewise connected with the hop traffic, occurred during September 1924. On the morning of Saturday, 13th, a line of wagons in Cranbrook yard had been loaded with pockets of dried hops from the local oasts, but the tarpaulins used to cover the cargo had not yet been fully secured. At lunchtime an exceptionally heavily-loaded train of hop-pickers' friends arrived, the locomotive having to work especially hard on the bank into the station. Shortly after it had left for Hawkhurst, the staff noticed smoke and flames coming from the siding which ran adjacent to the running line. Before they could isolate the wagon, which belonged to the Great Western Railway, the fire quickly took hold, having obviously been started by a stray spark from the special train. Cranbrook fire brigade was quickly summoned, but by the time they arrived, a second wagon, also containing hops, was well alight. Since there was no hydrant in the vicinity, it took two and a half hours to finally extinguish the blaze using buckets of water from the station tap and a chain of men; as a result both wagons were severely damaged.

The days of ill-behaved pickers were now, by and large, a thing of the past and most local people welcomed the familiar faces who came down each season. Many London families made a habit of returning to the same farm each year, becoming firm friends with not only the farmer, but also the villagers. Most of the shopkeepers, however, remained wary of this influx and did their best to prevent pilfering, but there are honest and unscrupulous individuals in all walks of life. While some pickers were quick to take advantage of a moment's unattendance in a shop, on the other hand some store owners quite shamefully 'fleeced' the visitors by over-charging at stalls set up in the fields. Generally speaking, however, the three-weeks 'holiday' was good-natured and enjoyed by all. In a letter to the *Southern Railway Magazine* in 1929, Mrs. K. M. Miller, wife of the chief goods clerk, explained how everything was organized:

> 'The shops in hop-picking time are all stripped and wire netting is fastened from the counters nearly up to the ceiling and little pigeon holes are made to put your money through. Most of the trades-people have small stores in the fields adjoining the hop gardens; two men are generally put in charge and they live in the back until hop-picking is over. On every available space stalls spring up for the sale of coffee and tea, old clothes, fruit, fish and vegetables. Lots of the villagers have stalls in their gardens and sell all their surplus vegetables and fruit. Big tents are put up in the market field and fish and chips are fried. Tricycles with an oil stove and oven run round with hot meat pies, also ice cream, in fact our little village of about 2,000 is turned into a noisy town of about 8,000 and at weekends with the hop-pickers' friends, about 20,000 to 30,000. At night time from the window it is a pretty sight to see all the camp fires, but they have to be all out by 10 o'clock. Most of the big growers have a room where a nurse can be consulted, also a reading and writing room. Hundreds of bunches of flowers are sold to the friends

to take home, in fact quite a little business is set up each year in cut flowers. I sometimes get a customer at my door - one asked me for "a pound of that cheese with the red rind on".'

During 1930, the Southern Railway inaugurated a new 'Farm to Station' scheme, in which SR lorries were provided to carry the hop pockets from the farm or oasthouse to the nearest station. A special charge of 5d per pocket was made and this arrangement was obviously very successful, judging by the returns. Whereas the 1930 season was a bad year for the Kent hop gardens generally, the SR actually increased its share of the traffic to 53%, compared with 33% the previous year.

A valuable insight into the antics and behaviour of hop-pickers, as well as the work that was required to carry everyone by train, was given in an article in the *Southern Railway Magazine* of January 1936. Chief Travelling Ticket Inspector Henry Thrower related his first-hand experiences over the years:

THE HOP-PICKERS TRAFFIC
Some Reminiscences by Chief Travelling Ticket Inspector Henry Thrower

I have for the past 33 years done duty dealing with the Outward and Homeward Hop-pickers traffic at London Bridge and Paddock Wood district, and I don't think I can do better than to relate some of the incidents that have happened during these years when dealing with this traffic

In the first place, no other Railway Company in England has such a passenger traffic to deal with as the hop pickers. I have been on duty with other special traffic for a number of years, but nothing in comparison calls for more tact than this kind of traffic.

But what a difference has been brought about during the past few years in regard to the cleanliness and behaviour of these passengers. Twenty-five to thirty years ago, on the outward traffic, women wore shawls over their heads, and dozens of children were without shoes. Unfortunately the public houses were open till midnight and they were generously patronised. The heaviest night for passengers travelling to the hop-district usually fell on a Saturday, 18 to 20 special trains being run from London Bridge, dispatched from 10pm till 7am.

One of these nights referred to there were over 20 specials run. The booking of tickets commenced at 10 pm; the first special left about 10.30pm and others left as soon as loaded; at 6.30 in the morning the mass of people in front of the station was nearly as great as it was at midnight, and it was found necessary to send for extra Metropolitan Police to clear the front of the station. All people not travelling by train were forced to go over London Bridge, or down the Borough High Street, and it was not until 8.30am that all was clear. Fourteen costermongers' barrows, that had been hired by the hoppers were found left outside the station and were taken to the Police Station (Lost Property). The Company's dust cart, after cleaning up the front of the station, was filled with rubbish, pram wheels, smashed boxes, clothing, etc.

FRAUDULENT PRINTING OF HOPPERS' TICKETS 1905

After a heavy night of traffic, I was with another Inspector sorting collected hoppers' tickets, when I found a ticket I detected was not of our print. The case was immediately reported and the next evening a sharp look-out was kept. On arrival of the special train at Spa Road Station, where all tickets were collected, a woman was found in possession of one ticket, Company's issue from London Bridge to the hop-district, and two forged tickets. She was questioned and informed me that a man (giving a description of him) had purchased the tickets for her at London Bridge.

Next evening, I was detailed off with two other Inspectors and a detective to keep observation at London Bridge. I dressed myself representing a Hop-picker as near as I could, my make-up being cap, jersey, old suit and muffler. On arrival at London Bridge I sat on some Hoppers luggage near the Booking Office outside the station keeping a sharp lookout for the man described.

After some time and having no luck, I decided to visit the public bars of the public houses down Tooley Street and Borough High Street, but did not meet with any success. I returned to the station, and then ascertained that a man answering the description had been followed by our Inspector and Detective over London Bridge and was stopped by them by the Monument, questioned and searched, but no tickets were found in his possession. It was surmised that on crossing London Bridge, he had thrown the forged tickets in the river. However, no more forged tickets were found in the collection.

It was decided afterwards to print tickets in a different colour as previously they had always been one colour.

I shall ever remember this night on account of being almost choked by a Metropolitan Police sergeant. I wanted to enter the station and on trying to do so the sergeant seized me by the muffler and before I could explain who I was he pulled it tightly round my neck, taking me for one of the rough old hoppers.

An apology was afterwards tendered to me and accepted with thanks.

EVADING PAYMENT OF CHILDREN'S FARES

It was common practice for hoppers to put their youngsters, which were chargeable, in sacks and box wheel carts to pass the barrier. In most cases they were detected and their parents made good the fares. If they escaped at London Bridge they were then told to get under the seats in the train. On arrival at Spa Road Station the collecting staff would find them and the parents made to pay. To-day these incidents scarcely ever happen. The hop-pickers are far cleaner and an interest has been taken in them by the farmer and the Company, and they have special trains, run to time. There is also not so much 'rough element' among them now as formerly.

HOMEWARD JOURNEY

What a great difference exists now to that of years past. Special trains now run to time in conveying these passengers home. Years ago these trains ran as required from Paddock Wood and district. Farmers paid off their pickers at any time of the day and they did not care what became of them, after the farmers had done with them. What chaos it was! Some of the special trains were sent Main Line to London via

Sevenoaks, others via Maidstone, Gravesend. The latter route was hated by the Hop-pickers and they would shout out of the window "Where are we going, round the world, governor?" when a train was sent that way. The roughest stations in the Hop district were East Farleigh, Marden, Horsmonden, Yalding, and Paddock Wood. The worst evil, I think, was the public house being open all day. The Hoppers, coming from the farms, had in some cases to pass two or three on the road to the station and these pubs were "red lights" to them; after having a good drink up you may guess the condition of a good many when they arrived at stations. Beer was cheap and strong; there was fighting among them all day.

The usual practice of hiding youngsters under the seats prevailed, the same as on the down journey, and many adults were found in the same positions. After they were detected, a lot of argument and bad language was used; and the fares were paid. On one occasion, I found a gipsy woman lying the whole length of the compartment, under the seat; with some trouble I got her out of the compartment on to the platform. She then struck out at me left and right, but fortunately I missed her blows. She then ran across the line at Paddock Wood, and just missed being cut to pieces by the down Folkestone Express; next I saw her seated on the up platform, and I went to her and asked for her ticket; she made no reply. A mission worker paid her fare to London and she was dispatched with all speed by the next up Special.

PRESENT DAY BEHAVIOUR

The Homeward journey now of the Hop-pickers is far better. They are more sober and, although one has to be very tactful in dealing with them so as to avoid trouble, they are far better behaved. This has, in my mind, been brought about by better conditions. Everybody connected with them have taken interest and they are treated better by the farmers. The mission workers do wonderful work in assisting in the Hopfields, also as regards helping us at the stations in the transport.

For the past few years, the control traffic has been worked by controllers, Messrs. Ball and Corney at Paddock Wood, and myself and staff have worked with them to maintain a perfect transport. In my opinion great credit is due to both Messrs. Ball and Corney for the able way they have dealt with this traffic and I can honestly say, in conclusion, I wish I could have all the time I have worked for the Railway over again. Taking the "rough with the smooth" I have had a most happy time dealing with this traffic and serving the Company of which I am so justly proud.

The number of hop-pickers travelling by rail began to steadily decline around the 1920s and continued falling in the '30s. In 1924 almost 38,000 came down by special and ordinary trains but, six years later, this had plummeted to just 13,500. Throughout the 'thirties the loss was stemmed, numbers averaging out at around 14,000, but it was evident that many were now coming down by road, packed in lorries and vans which provided cheaper, if less comfortable, travel than by train. Road transport was also easier for carrying as many household comforts as could be piled high onto the back of a lorry. However, the railways were to enjoy a brief Indian Summer during the Second World War, brought about by a combination of petrol rationing and the widespread desire to get away from bombed-out London.

Throughout this period many hoppers were only too glad to escape and leave behind the shattered streets and houses which were the result of Hitler's terrifying 'Blitzkrieg' on the civilian population. Many stayed on as long as they could in the relative safety of the countryside, but the fields of the frontline county were frequently in the firing line and casualties invariably came about. This was not only through deliberate bombing, which claimed lives, but also from shrapnel and aircraft breaking up, as well as machine gun bullets when the hop gardens were strafed by mean-spirited marauding members of the Luftwaffe. In 1940, the local newspaper reported that 'hopping was in full swing' in the Cranbrook area and went on to state that full provision had been made for the sheltering of the pickers during air raids. Sandbags and sheets of corrugated iron were positioned around trenches dug into the fields, while younger members of the hopping families were sometimes engaged to keep a lookout in the skies. The bravery and stoicism of the Londoner was frequently admired, as revealed in the Hawkhurst press:

> 'One doughty veteran of the hop gardens remarked as she arrived by train: "I've been 'op-picking for twenty years ducks, and ol' Hitler ain't gonna stop me this year." - That's the stuff to give 'em!'

The blackout had to be observed every bit as strictly in the hop gardens as in the local towns and villages. Each hut was provided with the means of covering the windows to ensure that not a chink of light escaped to aid the enemy's aim. Likewise, all camp fires were extinguished after daylight. On moonless nights the pickers were therefore left to grope their way back from the pubs in the pitch blackness. For many of them this was a totally new and strange experience and it transpired that quite a few were scared of the dark country lanes, having been so accustomed to the perpetual lights and noise of city life. Sometimes an encouraging chorus of 'Ol' Muvver Riley', or 'The White Cliffs of Dover' dispelled these fears, but there was many a harmless cow in a neighbouring field which startled them on their nocturnal treks back to the camps as they tripped and stumbled in the dead of night. The depths of Kent presented a stillness never before experienced, as well as providing many alarming new sounds. Most adults could recognize the screech of an owl, and would reassure any inquisitive children. However, anyone who has witnessed the unexpected sudden scream of a vixen will know only too well how it can make the blood run cold.

1942 brought a good crop of hops and railway receipts were well up all over Kent, with more than 36,000 pickers arriving by train. In the following year all records were broken with almost 57,000 passengers, necessitating a grand total of 96 special trains. During this season, Bert Bassett was transferred to Goudhurst station and he vividly recalls those days, now well over half a century ago:

'In April 1943 I was sent to Goudhurst as a clerk for the fruit and hop-picking season. In those days Goudhurst came under the jurisdiction of the station master at Horsmonden (the late Mr. Percy Prescott) who resided there. The staff at Goudhurst station comprised two class 5 signalmen, as well as a female porter who resided in the station house. At first all was tranquil; the usual country scene, a few passengers, but a lot of goods, war department materials and a variety of parcels traffic to and from the local community. Plenty of soft fruit was despatched. However, from the end of August things began to change, - the hoppers' luggage began to arrive, as PLA [paid luggage in advance], consisting of metal trunks, boxes, cases, tea chests, tables etc., in fact everything bar the kitchen sink. This was sorted out for the various farms, but the volume was such that it filled the goods shed. Parcels vans were placed in the dock siding and later overspilled onto the platforms where it had to be covered with wagon tarpaulins. Every item was entered into the 'Inwards Parcels Counter Book' with the hope of obtaining a signature for every item as evidence of receipt.

The day eventually arrived for the first of the 'Hoppers' Specials'. Prior to its arrival, the local farmers came down with their farm carts and other transport. The train arrived in the down platform and, although too long for the platform, the hoppers could not wait to alight. They clambered down from both sides of the train and swarmed over the tracks, seeking their luggage. They rummaged through the piles, carrying away their bits and pieces to the waiting transport.

Having abandoned the idea of trying to obtain signatures, I, a bewildered youth, sought sanctuary behind the bars of the booking office window, but an elderly woman came to complain that the leg of her table was broken and wished to make a claim. She was invited to fill in a claim form, which she did, claiming thirty shillings! She indicated where the table was to be located and I said I would examine it later. Meanwhile, things had quietened down and most of the hoppers had drifted away, but there were a few groups still waiting around for transport. The signalman suggested we went to the cafe opposite (behind the present hotel) for a cup of tea before the arrival of the next train. On the way, I explained that I needed to examine a broken table which was on the down platform. We found it and, unbeknown to me, the woman complainant had come up behind me. I examined the table, which had a large metal trunk tied between the legs, the weight of which had broken one of them. I remarked to the signalman that, in my opinion, it wasn't worth more than five bob [5s 0d]. Unfortunately, the woman overheard my remarks and I was subjected to the most abusive cockney language - indicating I hadn't a proper father! I tried to apologize, but hot and red-faced I beat a hasty retreat!

On Sundays the line opened specially and their 'friends' came down on the specials. This meant a welcome Sunday duty. The friends obviously enjoyed their day out, for on their return home, in the evening, there were many drunks, - a time to stay behind the bars of the booking office window.

Towards the end of September the specials took the hoppers back to London Bridge and other destinations - mostly in East London and Essex. The same procedure, booking up luggage and issuing tickets in return for vouchers from the Hop Marketing Board who were charged the fares. After their departure things began to get back to normal. This left the job of despatching numerous pockets of hops and quantities of fruit - mostly plums and apples.'

With 1944 came another hazard for the pickers in the form of the fearsome V1 flying bombs, or 'doodlebugs' as they were more commonly known. Almost two and a half thousand fell on Kentish soil, more than on London, as a result of being either shot down or knocked off their original deadly course by courageous pilots of the RAF. Although some fell harmlessly into the countryside, there were inevitable casualties as many found a target in the fields and towns on the flight path to London.

Needless to say, the end of the war was a time of great rejoicing, but the changes in the hop-picking industry, which had begun to manifest themselves in the 1930s, simply accelerated.

Inevitably, mechanised hop-picking was becoming more widespread, ever since its first demonstration in 1937 at Smugley Farm near Goudhurst. It was also encouraged by yet another severe shortage of manual labour. Whilst the responsibility for gathering in the annual hop harvest had mainly fallen upon the shoulders of womenfolk during the war, the return of their husbands and loved ones didn't guarantee a resumption of life as normal. Even though the SR carried close on 21,000 pickers during 1947, the following year the numbers slumped dramatically. The newly-formed Southern Region of British Railways saw only 10,000 patronize its trains. Those who still came down carried on the same traditions, whilst Joseph Braddock, in his book *Footpaths of the Kent-Sussex Border*, reminds us of those scenes which were fast disappearing at that time:

'When there is a red sunset over the Weald, seen from North Hill, or from lower down by the green, nothing could be more impressive than the fading panorama with its slowly darkening blue-veiled distance.
....after dark the sight of the hoppers' camps will make an unforgettable picture: the doors of the huts stand half open, while the oil lamps within give a glimpse only of the interior; but most of the pickers are outside, huge in the firelight, the flames falling on wild faces and rough hair; many are dancing; more, gathered round stick fires every fifty yards or so, are singing raucous choruses, to the accompaniment of an accordion, the flames leaping twenty feet when new sticks are added.'

The drift away from this traditional holiday for Londoners continued as mechanization spread, but it wasn't solely down to the machines, which noisily ripped and stripped the fragile bines, tossing and sorting the frail green hops into metal containers. Working families, who began to experience a gradual rise in their living

Roadside stalls and a mobile fish and chip van catered for the hop-picking families who had come down to the farms around Goudhurst. A sign on the wall by the woman pushing the pram read 'Nurse for hop-pickers'. The splendid four-armed road sign, once a common sight in Kent, is also worthy of note. *Gordon Batchelor*

standards, came to expect more than just toiling in the hopfields as their only means of an annual holiday. Instead, many sought more orthodox breaks from the drudgery of everyday work and chose to take themselves off to numerous seaside resorts such as Clacton, Southend, Margate and Brighton. Throughout the 'fifties the numbers coming down by train dwindled even further. In 1950 there were 8,000, but by 1957 this had shrunk to just 2,500, with only two special trains being required. The number of 'friends' coming down had likewise diminished and whereas in 1948 there were close on 30,000 travelling on Southern Region trains, a decade later it was barely 6,000. The SR's traffic department annually commented upon the figures and generally attributed the decrease to the greater use of machines. Tellingly, the 1958 summary noted:

> 'It was reported that the number of hop-pickers conveyed by rail, which has been falling in recent years, showed a further decrease this year; there was a similar fall in the number of hop-pickers' friends. This was attributed to greater use of private transport, the counter-attractions of other kinds of holiday and the bad weather this year, particularly the storms on Friday September 5th, the damage from which dislocated train services to and from the hopfields over the following weekend.'

In spite of this gradual shift and the fact that everyone probably knew that the great days of hop-picking were coming to a close, many regulars still came down as faithfully as had their parents and grandparents before them. Former pickers to whom I have spoken wistfully recall those crisp clear mornings, fresh with dew upon the grass, the long rows of bines stretching high up, like the nave of some great cathedral to Mother Earth. As for the journeys by train to and from the gardens each season, these were equally memorable for the sing-songs along the way, as well as the odd incidents which invariably cropped up. One of the most memorable operating upsets for the Southern Region during this time took place on the Hawkhurst branch and was related by Denis Cullum and Ken Carr in an article for *Trains Illustrated:*

> 'An example of what can happen at hop-picking time might be recalled from some workings on Saturday, September 29th, 1951. The picking season was coming to the end and a 'Hop-pickers' Return' special was to be run from Hawkhurst to London Bridge at 1.15pm. The train consisted of part of set No. 335, comprising two SE&CR 'birdcage' corridor brakes and four other ex-SE&CR compartment coaches, with the customary two luggage vans at each end. The stock was despatched from Paddock Wood with class 'D' 4-4-0 No.

31729 running tender-first, the intention being that the engine would run round the train at Hawkhurst and work it back. (A pull-off engine is provided at Hawkhurst when extra trains are running.) The down journey was not run as empty stock, but as one of the extra connections provided at this time from Paddock Wood to Hawkhurst.

It was a sunny morning following earlier rain and on the open section the sun had dried the rails; but towards Horsmonden tunnel the track was still in shade and the surface wet. Here the driving wheels began to slip and speed dropped, the train finally coming to a stand a short way from the tunnel. The trouble would have been averted by sanding the rails, but the engine was not fitted for sanding when running tender-first. The fireman applied sand manually for a distance ahead and a successful restart was achieved, but as soon as the driving wheels reached unsanded rail they slipped once more, the train coming to a stand.

This time attempts to restart were in vain, and the fireman proceeded through the tunnel to Horsmonden station in order to summon assistance from Paddock Wood, while the guard duly observed Rule No. 179 by placing detonators to protect the rear of the train. Paddock Wood despatched a 'C' class 0-6-0 No. 31717, also tender-first, which coupled to the rear of the train and after an exchange of whistles progress was resumed. At Horsmonden station No. 31717 ran round the train by the goods loop and coupled in front of the train engine for the remainder of the journey to Hawkhurst. The two engines remained together double-heading the return working as the 'Hop-pickers' Return' special, but reversed their order so that 31717 could come off when the train reached the main line.'

It was common to see double-headed trains on the Hawkhurst branch at hop-picking time and these trains were certainly a thrilling spectacle, winding their way

Hop-pickers enjoying the last of the day's sunshine on a warm evening in September 1949 and towards the end of a particularly glorious summer. The bundles of sticks were ready for the fires around which they gathered as dusk descended. With their children put safely to bed in the nearby huts, families and friends would sing their favourite songs well into the star-dusted night. *Hulton Getty*

This picture, taken at the end of the 1951 season, on Saturday, 29th September, shows homeward-bound hop-pickers watching from the platform at Goudhurst as their special train drew into the station, hauled by 'D' class No. 31729 and piloted by 'C' class No. 31717. Earlier in the day, the Tonbridge-based 'C' class had come to the aid of the crew of 31729 which was slipping badly on Horsmonden bank.

K. G. Carr

through glorious scenery, their exhausts blasting away in unison on the climb up from Churn Lane, till they were swallowed up into Horsmonden tunnel. On arrival at Hawkhurst they were either manoeuvred in the manner previously mentioned, or at Goudhurst they were reversed out of the up platfrom to be stabled in the siding south of the level crossing so as not to interfere with normal business on the branch. Here, the locomotive was left quietly simmering at the head of its train, while the crew had a brew-up at the station. At the appointed time, when there were long lines of people arriving and crowding onto the platform with their old prams and personal belongings, the train was slowly drawn forward where a rush was made to secure the best seats for the homeward journey.

Driver Frank Glazebrook of Tonbridge clearly remembers the days of running the hop-pickers' specials from London to the heartland of Kent. Beginning his career in 1944 at Bricklayers Arms, he recalls seeing some of the oldest coaching stock rostered for these duties, some of which even retained their long-disused gas lamps. Incidentally, many of these trains were quite without electric illumination, so their occupants were completely left in the dark through the long tunnels penetrating the North Downs. The entire carriage stock was exposed to the elements, being stored in the open all year round at Rotherhithe Road sidings. Since they were only ever taken out for the 'hoppers, presumably it didn't matter'. If it had been a dry summer they weren't too bad, but a wet July inevitably led to penetrating damp through the more exposed woodwork, which left them with a rather unpleasant, lingering odour. It need hardly be said that the stock was the roughest of all, with peeling paintwork, grimy windows, as well as torn, threadbare upholstery with the horsehair stuffing poking out in places.

In those days Bricklayers Arms was a very active place indeed, where shunting took place right round the clock. However, come the middle of August, extra time had to be found to prepare the special trains for hop-pickers and their friends. Apart from slapping plenty of grease into the axle boxes and checking that the vacuum brake hoses were still sound and hadn't perished, nothing else was ever done to the carriage stock. The locomotives rostered for these yearly late-summer outings fared only marginally better in regard to maintenance. Remaining ex-SER/SE&CR 4-4-0s were purposely held in reserve, usually James Stirling's rebuilt 'B1's, known to the men as 'Square Cabs', but sometimes 'F1's, affectionately nicknamed 'Jumbos'. These rosters really were the last chance for these elderly engines, the worst and ultimate ignominy of all being the removal of wheels and motion for stationary boiler duty! Here they rested all year in a corner of the shed, with rusty handrails, cobwebs and dirty cab glasses, awaiting their annual outing. Under normal circumstances these engines would certainly have been scrapped years earlier, but the declaration of war in 1939 had not only caused shortages all round, but had quite literally stopped the SR's programme of electrification in its tracks. Having survived a stay of execution, most were still able to prove that they had plenty of life left in them. In an attempt to spruce them up a little, the cleaners did the best they could, giving them a wipe round with oily rags to disguise the worst of the rust and obtain some sort of gleam on the remaining flat paintwork. However, there was only so much that could be achieved with cotton waste rags soaked in gas oil, whilst a little more attention was paid to the cab's

'D' class No. 31488 starting away from Cranbrook with an HPF (hop-pickers' friends) special in 1950. Some of its passengers were making their way up the approach road. The fresh paint on the lower half of the smokebox indicates recent repair work. *R. S. Williams*

A pair of 'C' class engines starting away from Cranbrook with an HPF special in the late summer of 1949. *R. S. Williams*

instruments and spectacle glasses. After this spruce-up, the depot's boilersmith would come along to give them the 'once-over', checking that they were entirely fit to be taken out, and not about to come to grief somewhere along the line. His reputation depended upon his skill and knowledge at detecting defects which might cause a locomotive's boiler to result in a failed engine, along with all the operational headaches that would entail. After his 'O.K.' the firelighters or 'steam-raisers' were given the task to fill the boilers, stock the tenders with whatever coal was currently available and fire them up. They would then be handed over to the crews whose job it was to move many thousands of Londoners into the hopfields of Kent over the next couple of days.

In later years, as the old Stirlings were sent for scrap, the Wainwright 'D' class, referred to as 'Coppertops' and the once-imperial 'E' class took their place. Even so, some of these younger engines were latterly neglected and ended up in just as bad a state. In his book *Engineman SR*, Michael Jackman recalls: 'Our first trip was with No. 1746 and a real rusty state she was in. The cleaners had had a go, but she did not look much better'. He also mentions that it remained a mystery why the hop-pickers' specials were so tightly timed, with no margins being allowed for engines that had not been run-in after such a lengthy period of storage.

By all accounts, the old 'Wainwrights' proved to many railwaymen they yet had plenty of life in them with the heavily-loaded hop-pickers' specials. The usual formation of nine coaches, made up of ex-SE&CR 'birdcage' stock, was shifted with ease as the 'D's and 'E's engines steamed well, whilst, with their 6′8″ and 6′6″ driving wheels respectively, they could maintain a good speed to their destinations 'given the road' and an experienced driver who knew precisely how to get the best out of these 'old-timers'.

In the early hours of the morning, the Hawkhurst branch special, along with the others, would be put together with the rake of elderly carriages being eased out of the sidings and round to London Bridge (Low Level), usually platform 8, 9, or 10. Here, the hop-pickers would customarily surge forward into the compartments well before the train had come to a halt as, in the general mayhem, a dash was made to secure the best seats. The luggage vans were loaded with the huge piles of suitcases and rusty metal trunks which they'd carried with them, whilst hand luggage, old carpet bags and refreshments for the journey down were stuffed into the string-mesh racks above the seats.

A choice of relatively quiet routes to the hopfields and away from the busy main lines was available to the SR, and for the Hawkhurst run it was usually via Oxted and Tonbridge. Following the 'right away' from London Bridge, the train passed above the chimney pots of Bermondsey, before swinging southwards on the 'old road' via New Cross Gate, where a stop was made for more passengers. Then, on through the leafier suburbs of Penge and Norwood, to East Croydon where the last of the pickers boarded. From here the Lewes line via Oxted and Sheffield Park took them down as far as Crowhurst Junction where the rails climbed eastwards to meet the old SER Redhill-Tonbridge route. Within a short while the activity at Tonbridge West Yard came into view, where a pause was inevitably made until the down platform in the station had been cleared. After the semaphore signal had bounced skywards, the old Stirling would drag its heavy load across the main Kent Coast running lines and into the station. The stop at Tonbridge was always brief and had to be performed efficiently in order to clear the busy platform. Since there was a need to take on water, the fireman would clamber onto the tender well before the train drew in. The moment the engine came to a halt, he would manoeuvre the horizontal pipe to the mouth of the tanks and hurriedly spin the wheel on the stand. Opening the valve too quickly would cause the leather sleeve to go rigid with the sudden high pressure of water, thus forcing it out, whereby a torrent of water would engulf the platform. This was bad enough if any unsuspecting passengers happened to be standing around, but perhaps worse was the fact that the refreshment room doors happened to be exactly opposite the water column. Frank recalls that on odd occasions the buffet floor was copiously washed down by courtesy of the loco' crews!

Very little trouble was ever experienced with the SER/SE&CR engines and whilst the 'B1's and 'F1's still had plenty of 'go' left in them, the 'D's were generally preferred. All had fairly large driving wheels, 7′ 0″ on both the Stirling classes, but this meant they occasionally 'danced about a bit' on the branch lines and slipped more easily, particularly after a shower of rain. Assistance was usually on hand in the form of a trusty 'C' class from the early morning Hawkhurst trip. Once coupled on, the 'C's 5′ 0″ driving wheels soon provided the necessary adhesion and extra pulling power. This Wainwright 'maid of all work' came off at the terminus and ran back light to Tonbridge when additional services were laid on. Whilst most of the hop-pickers' trains were double-headed, occasionally there were instances of engines banking at the rear. Although this practice had initially been prohibited by the Board of Trade upon the opening of the line and no photographs are known to exist, Derek Reader clearly recalls seeing such spectacles during the late '40s and early '50s

In spite of the fact that the locomotives kept in reserve for hop-pickers' specials might have normally gone to the scrap road earlier had different circumstances prevailed, relatively few problems were experienced with either the 'Square cabs' or the 'Jumbos'. However, Frank Glazebrook remembers one hair-raising experience which caused him and his mate to wonder if their luck was about to run out. On this well-remembered morning, nothing untoward happened at the start of a fine autumnal day as 'B1' No. 1445 was backed onto its train at London Bridge with a plentiful head of steam. Although the loco' had been given the usual once-over and a wipe, it was not in the condition they might have hoped, with signs of scale spattered down the boiler casing where the tubes hadn't been thoroughly washed out. Despite this, the heavy train was given a good 'heave-ho' out of the platform and in lively fashion the Stirling steamed merrily off towards New Cross Gate. However, on pulling up at the station, the water surged and, as the safety valves lifted, filthy water blew out instead of steam. On these SER 4–4–0s the fireman normally kept the boiler pressure at around 150lb per sq. in., the safety valves lifting above 160, but the water being carried with the steam not only kept the valves open but also damaged the delicate mechanism of the ageing pressure gauge, the needle of which began to rise.

'E1' class No. 31497 standing at the head of the 5.45 p.m. service to London Bridge on Sunday, 21st September 1952. *J. J. Smith*

Corridor stock in the south siding at Goudhurst on 14th September 1952. *S. C. Nash*

The morning of Sunday, 20th September 1953, saw 'D1' class No. 31735 and 'C' class No. 31244 double-heading empty HPF coaching stock to Hawkhurst on the approach to Horsmonden tunnel. *S. C. Nash*

As each tense second ticked by, it crept up to 180, then 200 and eventually bent against the stop at 220! This was a frightening experience until the safety valves closed and the crew realised the reading was false. The needle remained well and truly wedged round the dial and they had to complete the rest of their duty without a pressure gauge.

The arrangements for dealing with hop-pickers' traffic were handled with military precision and thoroughly planned, with Special Notices circulated among staff in all departments. To begin with, it was important that the vans on the Hop-pickers' Specials were loaded correctly for Paddock Wood, Maidstone West Branch, Hawkhurst Branch and stations between Marden and Pluckley. Staff at London Bridge, New Cross, and New Cross Gate stations had to sort each item of luggage, allocate it to the van marked accordingly, as well as making certain that luggage was never mixed. Four vans were provided on each special train and coupled on at the rear. Each van was clearly labelled, whilst every item of luggage had its own printed paper label pasted on. These different coloured 'hop-picking' labels were distinguishable from ordinary luggage labels by the extra large initial letter for each station. Instructions were given that all van labels should be removed at destinations prior to the despatch of empty trains.

With regard to the Hawkhurst Branch, passengers were ushered to the front portion of the Specials. Tonbridge motive power depot provided a pull-off engine at Hawkhurst which backed onto the first down Special from Paddock Wood and always provided lineside spectators with cameras some good shots. This train was brought to a stand at the Down Home signal at Hawkhurst where the leading pilot engine detached and ran into a siding. Trains terminating at Goudhurst were similarly double-headed from Paddock Wood owing to the heavy gradients leading up to Horsmonden and the often greasy state of the rails after rain.

The weekday specials bound for Paddock Wood took about 2½ hours to complete the journey from London Bridge, no matter whether they ran to Tonbridge via Otford and Sevenoaks, or via Oxted. On Saturdays the Oxted Line was used exclusively, some trains even avoiding Croydon by running down through Elmers End and Selsdon, whereas on Sundays the Kent Coast main line via Sevenoaks seems to have been favoured, albeit that the journey took even longer - almost three hours. The Ashford portion departed first, followed by the Maidstone Branch and then the Hawkhurst Branch which had to be shunted as, of course, there was no facing connection from the main line. This operation could sometimes take up to an hour to complete, whereas

Having arrived at Hawkhurst on the afternoon of Sunday, 18th September 1955, 'C' class No. 31272 came off the empty stock, running round in order to pull the train off 'D' class No. 31737. The 'D' then hauled the 5.15 p.m. to London Bridge, whilst 31272 shunted stock before departing with the 7.45 p.m. to London Bridge made up of six coaches. At Tonbridge 31272 came off, its place taken by Maunsell 'U' class 2–6–0 No. 31639 (prohibited from working the Hawkhurst branch). The six-coach set numbered 920, in the goods shed road, formed the 6.40 p.m. to London Bridge, worked by 'E1' class No. 31165 which had arrived at Hawkhurst at 5.5 p.m. *J. J. Smith*

'D' class No. 31737 at Cranbrook with the 5.15 p.m. Hawkhurst–London Bridge hop-pickers return special on Sunday, 18th September 1955. No. 31737 was eventually preserved as part of the national collection. *J. J. Smith*

around ten minutes was allowed at each stop on the way down to Hawkhurst to allow for unloading.

On the return journeys at the end of the season, all Hawkhurst Branch stations were asked to advise Hop Control at Paddock Wood when there were passengers for main line stations so that connecting services would not be unduly delayed. The empty trains to Hawkhurst which came down via Maidstone West were provided with a turn-over engine at Paddock Wood as revealed in a Special Traffic Notice for 1950 which also states that carriage sets 896, 918, and 906 were berthed at Blackheath, with sets 335, 519, 696 and 921 at Maze Hill. Each train during this period was formed of six bogies and four vans, whilst a spare train was provided at Paddock Wood from 10am to 8pm for Hawkhurst branch working when main line services were running late.

In the period following the war, the shortages were felt in all sorts of ways and not just in the availability of suitable locomotives. Whereas most drivers I've spoken to have talked enthusiastically about their days working with steam, few, it seems, would relish a return. The hours were long and hard, whilst conditions were often miserable and nothing like the warm, air-conditioned, push-button comfort which is increasingly coming in nowadays.

Up until 1957, the trains mostly comprised pre-grouping rolling stock of SE&CR vintage. These coaches, although rapidly ageing by that time, were far more comfortable than the long trains of decrepit, mouldering ex-LC&DR six-wheelers with which previous generations had to contend. These are understood to have disappeared after the Great War. The railways also provided luggage vans, normally at either end, in order to cope with the vast quantities of household baggage which the pickers insisted on bringing with them. According to Joseph Braddock:

> '....the huts are not allowed to remain bare for long. The Cockney knows all about home, and the families bring their own treasures with them - bedspreads, pictures, lace curtains, ornaments - and in the evening by the light of an oil lamp the huts look quite cosy.'

The colourful chapter of the hop-pickers' trains came to a close in 1960 when the last special ran, thus ending more than a century of carrying the poorer sections of the community to something resembling a holiday. It may have been arduous and sometimes cheerless work in the wet seasons, but there were ample rewards, not least in the friendships struck up. Older generations, who are still able to recall such happy times understandably look upon those distant days with much nostalgia. It was also the end of an era since the Hawkhurst branch saw a large proportion of this human traffic and the story of this railway would be much diminished were it not for the jovial Londoners who rode over its metals. Nowadays, it seems scarcely possible that such events could have taken place, but, rather than dwell upon such a loss, it is perhaps better to conclude with the reminiscences of John Pullan of London. His eye-witness account of those rapidly-disappearing scenes in the High Weald of the 1950s, perhaps sums it all up in a nutshell:

'From the tower of St Mary's Church at Goudhurst, Kent, 500 feet above the level of the sea, Queen Elizabeth's subjects watched the warning fires burn on the Kent and Sussex heights as the Armada sailed into our English Channel. From this same vantage point, on a clear September night, I looked out on another ring of fires circling the hillside village - the camp fires of the great Hop-Pickers Army.

As August ends, for more than two hundred years, the Cockney Cohorts and the Lambeth Legions have marched into the Kent hop fields and 'occupied' the ancient villages of the Weald. And behind this forty-thousand strong army come the East End barrow boys following their customers from Bermondsey, Peckham, Whitechapel, Stepney and Poplar. Always in the front ranks are the Tadgells, Hicks, Coodes, Smalls and Smiths who for generations have yearly pitched their camps in the selfsame fields. Many have spent more than fifty 'holidays with pay' among the hops and in this essentially family affair it is not unusual to see four generations at work round a 'bin'. 'This year' Mr. Coode remarked to me, 'there's only 38 of the family here. A lot of them couldn't get away.'

Goudhurst has a population of 2000. Crowning the hilltop stands the Early English Church and the 15th Century 'Star and Eagle' Inn. The main street winds down the hill, past the little bow-windowed shops until it comes to the four cross roads and the village pond. No more peaceful prospect could be imagined than the sight of these old houses leaning lazily against the hill. Then, suddenly into the quietness of this immemorial scene, on the first September Saturday, with a tempestuous wave of Cockney vitality, burst ten thousand hop-pickers. Stalls ring the pond, whelks, jellied-eels, spun sugar, fruits and cake, prams and queues, a singing, jostling, dancing crowd transform the village into a miniature of London's East End. As night falls each pub is jammed solid with hilarious humanity and the crowd spills over into every nook and cranny of the village. They squat on doorsteps, pavements, roadways, perch on the top of cars and, sitting among the tombstones of the churchyard, mothers feed their babies and brandish bottles of beer while tired children sleep propped against the headstones. By the light of the street lamps and the flares of the stalls they dance the age-old 'Knees Up Mother Brown' and the whole vivid scene irresistibly shouts Hogarth! Rowlandson! When quietness falls again on the littered village, the sound of singing floats up from the valley camps where, the children packed away in bed, the grown-ups continue to sing and dance round the well-stoked fires to the music of an accordion. In the small hours of the morning the strains of 'Red Roses for a Blue Lady', 'Candy Kisses' and 'When you go down Hopping' announce yet another hopping season in full swing.

What do the villagers think of this annual invasion of their peace and quiet? Well, to begin with, the hop-pickers bring a lot of money to the village. A skilled picker can earn upwards of twenty-five shillings a day; at weekends the pickers, mostly women and children, are reinforced by thousands of their wage-earning menfolk brought down by special trains from London, and the Cockney is a generous spender. To earn this money the publicans, butchers, grocers and bakers have to work a fourteen-hour day. Two Goudhurst butchers will sell ten thousand pies on a Saturday, cut up as many rations, stay open till midnight and serve again on Sunday morning. Four inns will be serving 18,000 pints of beer to the gloriously thirsty hoppers who help to make it. By charging a shilling on every pint glass, sixpence on a half, and employing an army of washers-up they somehow manage to keep pace with the demand. Peter Weekes, the baker, will be making his thousands of cream buns until, as he puts it, 'I haven't an ounce of cooking fat left in the bakery'.

I called on Canon MacMichael, Vicar of St. Mary's, to ask him what he thought of this sudden addition to his parish. He told me that the hop-pickers did not go to his church and that he did not really feel responsible for them. The Cambridge Mission, and others, did excellent work in the hop gardens, and he considered the pickers to be, for the most part, a jolly and well-behaved crowd. Naturally he regretted the litter which they left in the village and added that a number of his parishioners chose this time to take their holidays. 73 year-old George Haylor, born and bred in Goudhurst, agreed with the Vicar about the good behaviour. He recalled the times when all the windows in the village were smashed and twelve policemen failed to stop the fighting. 'They're quieter now' he said, and added, half-regretfully, 'a couple of fights with them there Diddikies [a Kentish term for pseudo-gypsies, pronounced *diddy-kye*] is all you're likely to see of an evening nowadays.'

Mr. Dick Noakes, who grows fifteen acres of hops at Spratsbourne Farm, was less sympathetic. 'In 1947', he told me, 'after employing two hundred pickers for two weeks the damage they did on my farm was assessed at £450. I'm going up to Worcester to have a look at a picking machine and if I'm satisfied, there will be no more pickers on my farm.'

Most of the villagers look forward to the annual three weeks of life and laughter and, although they wouldn't care for it the year round, enjoy the dramatic change of tempo wrought by the Cockney pickers with their high spirits and quick humour. For the few inhabitants who do not wish to fraternize with the 'occupying troops' each inn provides a back parlour which is for the use of 'locals' only. The final verdict seemed to be voiced by George Standen of the Post Office Garage who said 'We're pretty quiet here for most of the year. They make a bit of fun and we're sorry to see them go.'

Leaving Goudhurst, at the end of the 'hopping' season I was thinking of Dick Noakes and his search for the perfect machine. The village would sleep for eleven months. Could it be that I had seen the last enactment of the traditional scene? I felt grateful to have seen the human pickers.'

CHAPTER NINE

SWANSONG

'R1' class No. 1707 pausing at Goudhurst with the 2.32 p.m. from Paddock Wood on Saturday, 24th July 1948. *J. H. Aston*

WITH the creation of British Railways, the former private companies were amalgamated into the unified national system. The new Southern Region also absorbed a few small, independent lines, most notably in this area, the Kent & East Sussex Railway. There naturally followed a review of the system, in which Kent, like so many other English counties, lost branch lines which were perceived surplus to requirements. In this period the first casualty had been the Elham Valley Line although, strictly speaking, it closed purely a matter of months before the railways were nationalized as from January 1948. Then, in the following December, the East Kent Light Railway lost its passenger service, followed by the Sheppey Light Railway in 1950. In 1951 the Hythe branch saw its last train, whilst the historic, goods-only Canterbury & Whitstable finally succumbed at the end of 1952. Mention of these lines is purely to make a comparison between their fortunes and the prospects for the Hawkhurst branch. In doing so it may be appreciated that during this period the line was still proving remunerative. Equally, it may be seen that Watkin's scepticism in the 1880s as to its commercial value was ill-placed. There should be no illusion that the Southern Railway, or the emergent BR Southern Region would have shut the line without hesitation had its returns been otherwise. For the forseeable future, though, the 'Wealth of the Weald' continued to spring forth, sufficient to sustain its railway.

Just one facet of the business which maintained a healthy balance book was the annual lamb sale at Horsmonden which took place around the end of July. Indeed, 1948 proved to be no exception and the goods yard over the 28th and 29th overflowed with sheep as trucks arrived to a chorus of bleating and the shouts from farmhands who attempted to organize the loading. Temporary barriers were erected on the platform and in the yard to prevent straying while the sheep were herded into the waiting wagons on the running line. The whole day necessitated much previous planning and needed to be timed almost to the minute so as not to cause delays to the ordinary passenger services. Around 9,000 lambs were sold and despatched that season, the majority being conveyed by rail over the Hawkhurst branch.

A more constant source of income to the line was the fruit and flower traffic, most noticeably at Horsmonden where H. St. G. Ralling Ltd had a small depot. The company regularly sent out large quantities of crated apples and pears each season, but wished to improve upon the methods of loading. An agreement was therefore drawn up between British Railways and

Employees busy during the seasonal fruit packing at Horsmonden.

Ralling's to construct a concrete loading dock alongside the goods loop line. This was financed by the company which also paid an additional £5 per annum for ground rental. Fruit was packed by a team of women in the adjoining warehouse before being loaded directly into wagons just a few yards away. These wagons, bound for Covent Garden market, would then be collected by the evening goods returning to Paddock Wood which would shunt the loop as well as the yard.

It was on one of these evening duties that the crew of the 5.50pm freight from Hawkhurst had a rather frightening experience, as did the station staff at both Horsmonden and Goudhurst. The drama began at 8.24pm on Wednesday 25th August, shortly after the goods train had arrived at Horsmonden and was engaged in its shunting operations. It was normal practice for the guard to be travelling in the brake van at the rear, so he might be in charge of securing this portion of the train when it was propelled by the engine during manoeuvres. However, on this occasion the guard wound down the brake as he thought sufficient before walking up to the station. Unfortunately, the brake was not fully secure, with the result that this portion of the train, comprising twenty wagons and the brake van, continued rolling after the engine had pulled up. Since the line fell away on a gradient of 1 in 108-242 all the way to Goudhurst, everyone realized that the runaways would not come to a stand for some considerable distance. Worse still, there was also a passenger train scheduled to follow up behind which, had it been running on time, would have already left Goudhurst. Fortunately, the 8.20pm from Goudhurst had not yet started away from the platform when signalman East at Horsmonden hurriedly sent the bell signal 2-5-5 'vehicles running away...' before telephoning his colleague. He also alerted the crossing keeper at Smallbridge who managed to open both gates seconds before the wagons came rumbling past. Meanwhile, signalman Francis at Goudhurst did some smart thinking and promptly arranged a safe haven for the passenger train which he sent forward into No.1 siding, north of the up platform. He then ran down to the level crossing to open the gates before setting the road for the runaways to enter the up platform and roll into No.2 siding which would act as a trap. Not content with this, he then set off towards the oncoming train where, sprinting alongside, he pluckily managed to scramble aboard the brake van. Screwing down the brake, he succeeded in slowing the runaways so that they finally came to a stand alongside the platform, thus preventing a pile-up in No.2 siding. At a subsequent investigation the guard was reprimanded for his carelessness, whilst signalman Francis was rewarded for his quick-thinking and bravery.

The dramatic events of that evening were out of the public gaze and probably very few villagers ever came to know about it. Not so the spectacular derailment which had taken place earlier in the year, when the 7.40am passenger train came to grief on Wednesday, 18th February 1948. This was the first up train of the day and conveyed schoolchildren, as well as office and factory employees who worked in Paddock Wood and Tonbridge. On the footplate of 'C' class No. 1225 was Ian Russell, at that time a young fireman and he related to Gordon Batchelor what took place:

> 'We left with the old 'Hawkhurst Flyer', as it was known locally, and we departed in good time, although it was a rotten, cold morning. We'd already worked the early morning goods down to Hawkhurst and had put that train

away, before backing on to our little 'flyer'. Well, off we went, on to Cranbrook and then down the bank to Goudhurst. On arrival we made the usual tablet exchange with the signalman, while passengers boarded the train and the guard occupied himself with loading up a few parcels. As I say, it was a bitter cold morning and my old driver, Billy, had got this old army overcoat on, a dyed-black one, and he was tucked-up in a corner of the cab, keeping out of the cold wind and I was looking out along the platform. 'How we looking behind?' asked Bill, at which I said: 'The guard's given us the green flag', and he was – he was waving the flag, so we'd got the 'right-away'. Well, neither of us looked at the signal – we had the key to the road – the tablet – but with the signal set at danger, the points were set for the siding and that's of course where we went, instead of going up the line! Anyway, away we went and I was busy throwing coal on the fire and we'd gone about 300 yards – enough to get a fair speed up – when we hit the stops and neither of us knew what had happened. All we knew was that the coal was tumbling about on us and we were rock-a-billying around. The engine was off the road, and it was going down and, I tell you what, I was *scared*. Well, it came to a stop and we were picking ourselves up out of the coals and old Billy said: 'We made a pancake landing!'. We were pretty panicky then, there were lots of school kiddies milling around and young ladies from the factory at Paddock Wood. Bill said:

'C' class No. 1225, wrongly despatched into the north siding at Goudhurst on the morning of Wednesday, 18th February 1948. *Gordon Batchelor*

'You'd better throw the fire out' – that was to save the firebox, otherwise we'd have probably ended up getting the sack. Anyway, I got on with that while in the meantime Bill and the guard went down to the signal box to make arrangements with District Control for a 'bus to take us, the children and other passengers to Paddock Wood. So we all had to troop down the track to the station to get on the 'bus, and there we sat in our dirty old oily overalls. Old Bill sat next to the window and said: 'Hold your head in shame' – he had a great sense of humour!

We had to go to the head offices in London – I received a caution, but I believe poor old Bill got two day's suspension as, of course, he had to be responsible for his engine. Afterwards he often used to laugh and joke about it, but I was always very sensitive, I saw it as a stain on my record and I was embarrassed to talk about it for many years because neither we, nor the guard, had looked at the signal. On my duty the following day I saw they'd had the steam crane down there, whilst the 'C' class was taken into Ashford works for an overhaul. They were wonderful years though'.

Gordon Batchelor regularly cycled down to catch this train each morning and recalls 'many times did I leap aboard, just as the train was pulling out, though of course Mrs. Giles, the 'station mistress', would hold a roll-call!'. Fortunately, Gordon had a habit of always carrying his camera with him and, on this occasion, was suitably rewarded. Although one old lady ended up sitting on Gordon's lap, most passengers on board recalled only 'a slight jolting', whilst many of the schoolchildren became quite excited, not so much by the accident, but the prospect of not having to attend lessons that day. However, their hopes were eventually dashed. Within seconds Gordon was out of the carriage and was able to use up the last four frames on his film, whereupon he ran back to the Old Forge where he used to leave his bike during the day. From here he cycled the two miles

Cranbrook station in 1948 with hop bine growing up the straining wire of a telegraph pole. *Collection N. A. Rusbridge*

Station staff at Cranbrook in 1948, with from left to right, back row: Bill Potten, lengthman; Frank Goodsell, yard foreman; Fred Masters, chief clerk; Arthur Collier, porter/signalman; Peter, the junior clerk; Ernie Christmas, Benenden carrier; Tom Griffin, porter/signalman. Left to right, front row: Mrs. Palmer; Len Palmer, goods porter; Mrs. Hobbs; Stan Hobbs, outgoing station master; Len Rusbridge, incoming station master (yet to receive uniform). *Collection N. A. Rusbridge*

Auto-set 739 being propelled into Cranbrook by 'R' class No. 1675 on a returning up service in 1949. Guards were still in attendance at this time, and this picture shows one accompanying the driver. *R. S. Williams*

up to the main A21 road where he caught a 'bus into Tunbridge Wells. Arriving at the offices of the *Kent and Sussex Courier*, he produced his film saying: 'I've got a scoop for you here!' and waited while they quickly developed it. A car was then sent down specially to Hastings where their printing blocks were made. Accordingly a picture appeared in the Friday morning edition with the caption: 'Coo, Our Train's Gone Wonky!' – doubtless to the irritation and embarrassment of the new Southern Region administration of British Railways.

Another error of judgement was to blame for the calamity which took place on 17th September 1949 at Hawkhurst. Here, though, it is not made clear whether the blame rested with the signalman or the engine crew. It was the end of the hop-picking season and an empty eight-coach train had been brought down by 'D' class No. 31057. Waiting in the yard was 'C' class No. 31686 which then coupled up to the rear before drawing the entire train out of the platform road. Whether the driver misjudged the length of his train, or thought he was propelling the stock into a longer siding, isn't known. Perhaps the signalman sent the train into the wrong siding. For whatever reason, it was a mistake which led to the empty train being pushed, at quite some speed, into the bay road. Unfortunately, this was already occupied by a three-coach set, believed to have been Set No. 913, as well as vans Nos. 2331, 2205, 1951 and 694. A resounding crash followed as coach No. 3298 derailed and telescoped itself into the leading luggage van. Significant damage was also caused to the berthed set, the vans and six other coaches of the morning train. Coach No. 3298, forming part of Set 899, was so badly wrecked that it was subsequently sent for scrap.

The rolling stock used on the Hawkhurst branch throughout its lifetime was certainly varied and interesting. In his book *The Hawkhurst Railway*, Roger Crombleholme described the coaches which greeted travellers in the 1890s and went on to outline the eventual replacements:

> 'A typical vehicle of this period used on the Hawkhurst branch and elsewhere would have had four narrow compartments, each pair sharing one dim lamp, divided by partitions extending only up to the tops of the seat backs. These bone-shaking four-wheelers provided all the shiny hygienic bareness of varnished pine boards as seats, though the six-wheel coaches that replaced them were little better in this respect, having only a narrow red cushion stuffed with horsehair on the seats. In 1912 the Hawkhurst train was made up of eight of these six-wheelers and this formation remained standard until the introduction of much-needed bogie stock in the early twenties.'

Perhaps the Hawkhurst branch is best associated with the two-coach push-pull units which were commonly used throughout the 'fifties. These comprised sets made up from the Southern's pre-grouping constituents, with a brake third and driver's control compartment paired up to a first and third class trailer. The working of these units and the duties shared by the Tonbridge locomotive crews is worth summarizing. Two groups of men were required to work duty No. 326 which was combined passenger and freight, whilst two other groups were

'R' class No. 1675 waiting at Cranbrook with the auto-train on a down service in the early spring of 1949. *R. S. Williams*

rostered for duty No. 312. The first clocked on at 3.45 in the morning, prepared their engine, usually a 'C' class 0-6-0, and departed Tonbridge shed at 4.30am. On arrival at Paddock Wood the early morning Hawkhurst freight was assembled before departing at 5.25am to arrive at the terminus at 7.06am. Here, the engine came off the freight before coupling up to the push-pull set berthed overnight in the bay. On the way up, it passed a down train at Goudhurst, worked by crews on duty No. 312, before arrival at Paddock Wood where this push-pull set was put into a siding adjacent to the Hawkhurst bay. The first crew then shunted the yard here, until they were relieved by their late-turn colleagues on duty 326 who took over around midday. The afternoon freight was marshalled together and left Paddock Wood at 1.40pm (12.24pm on Saturdays), taking with it the empty push-pull unit from the morning working. On the way down all the yards were shunted, with arrival at Hawkhurst scheduled at 4.25pm. The coaches were propelled back into the bay, in preparation for the following morning, whilst the return up freight was made ready for a 5.50pm departure, again shunting and picking up wagons along the way. Paddock Wood was reached by 8.25pm, where the engine came off at 8.50pm and ran light to Tonbridge shed.

The two crews on duty 312 worked the passenger service with an 'R1' and a push-and-pull two-coach unit which had been berthed at Tonbridge overnight. Departure from the locomotive yard was normally around 6.55am, the men having booked on at 6.10am. After running down to Paddock Wood, the train was propelled back across the main line to the Hawkhurst platform in readiness for the the first down trip, the 7.35am. It was this train which was required to wait for five minutes at Goudhurst for the 'C' class and up passenger train to arrive from Hawkhurst. Two further trips down the branch were made by this crew, culminating with the 1.05pm up service from Hawkhurst, whence they were relieved at Paddock Wood by the late shift. On Saturdays the late duty involved taking down an extra passenger working, scheduled at 2.24pm, returning from Hawkhurst at 3.12pm. Three more runs were made until arrival back at Paddock Wood at 8.39 in the evening. This train then carried on to Tonbridge where it terminated, before being stabled once more in the yard, the crew booking off at 9.30pm.

The push-pull units were worked without guards, whilst the driver was by himself when the unit was being propelled by the locomotive at the rear. Staffing levels at the stations had slowly decreased over the years, although the requirement to employ two signalmen at each station signal box remained constant.

In 1950 a relief signalman at Cranbrook found himself in hot water when, on Monday 23rd October, he allowed the 5.05pm from Hawkhurst to proceed without having exchanged tablets. Whilst the erstwhile Southern Railway had improved upon Tyer's token system in an attempt to obviate errors of this nature, the system could never be entirely foolproof. This particular incident came about due to the signalman hanging the loop on the door handle of the brake compartment while dealing with mail and parcels traffic. He forgot to make the exchange and only realized his mistake once the train had left, so a road journey to Goudhurst station had to be made in order to complete the changeover. As a result both he and the errant driver were subsequently disciplined.

As mentioned elsewhere, the rules enforced by the railways were there for specific reasons and were expected to be strictly observed. Even more rigorous were the schedules brought into force when royal trains were involved, as demonstrated when Queen Elizabeth (the present Queen Mother) journeyed to Cranbrook by train. The visit took place on Thursday, 6th July 1950, when Her Majesty visited Benenden Hospital, before continuing to Tenterden. The train was hauled by 'E1' 4-4-0 No. 31067 and comprised a corridor third brake

Len Rusbridge, station master at Cranbrook, 1948-1952, was a popular man with a keen sense of humour. What little spare time he had available was spent on a game of bowls when he'd cycle into Cranbrook. In later years he became a county player representing Berkshire. *R. S. Williams*

(brake leading), corridor composite, Pullman car *Malaga* (kitchen trailing), corridor composite, and corridor third brake (brake trailing). At 11.10am the stock was taken empty from Stewarts Lane to Victoria by an 'H' class 0-4-4T which was directed to uncouple and remain until the departure. At 11.45am a pristine 31067 arrived 'supplied with the best quality coal' and backed onto the waiting train. Instructions were given to all locomotive crews to avoid emitting smoke or causing any avoidable noise. Other 'E1's and crews were held on standby, Stewarts Lane had 31019, Bricklayers Arms held 31511 at Orpington, whilst Tonbridge stood by with 31497 at Paddock Wood. All engines were required to be 'in good order, well-cleaned and thoroughly examined'. However, 31067 performed admirably and at 12.35pm departed punctually from No.12 platform at Victoria. The journey was routed via Sydenham Hill and Beckenham Junction, joining the Kent Coast Line at Petts Wood, before arrival at Paddock Wood fifty-five minutes later. Here it was propelled into the up local platform and within five minutes, at 1.35pm, set off for Cranbrook. The royal train passed through Horsmonden station ten minutes later, before running through Goudhurst at 1.51pm, dead on schedule for arrival at Cranbrook at two o'clock. Not unexpectedly, the visit caused considerable interest and local people turned out all the way down the branch to wave and raise their hats, either at the stations or the crossings as the train glided past. At Cranbrook, signalman Bert Furnell lowered his down home signal, while station master Len Rusbridge and the divisional superintendent Percy Nunn waited on the platform with other dignitaries. During the morning the station had been suitably decorated, draped with bunting and flags, but in the run-up to the visit had been

A Royal train at Cranbrook with HRH Queen Elizabeth, the Queen Mother.
Collection N. A. Rusbridge

A Maidstone & District 'bus waiting at the bottom of the High Street before continuing its journey across the Weald. A wonderful variety of brick, weatherboard and tile-hung buildings is prominent in this glimpse of a quieter and far more leisurely age.

generally spruced-up. This involved a complete repaint, replacement of broken platform coping and 'tarmac' to substitute the worn slabs at the entrance. As a footnote, these old paving slabs were quickly acquired by station master Rusbridge to replace the rotting sleeper steps leading up to his garden. Also, the awning support in front of.the booking hall doors was deemed obstructive for the royal party, so it was removed, with two temporary posts substituting either side. After the visit it was reinstated.

Her Majesty was warmly greeted on her arrival at Cranbrook station, the locomotive, under the careful charge of driver W. Philpot and fireman S. White, pulling up at the chalk mark on the platform, thus aligning precisely with the red carpet. The boys and staff of nearby Swattenden school who lined the station approach, cheered and waved as the royal cavalcade set off for Benenden, much in the same manner as Princess Christian had done half a century earlier.

The high spot of Len Rusbridge's career was over all too soon, but being introduced to the Queen had been a great honour for him. As soon as Her Majesty had left, 31067 departed for Hawkhurst where, at 2.15pm, it came off and ran round, stopping at the water tower on the way to fill the tender. At 2.35pm the train left the terminus, arriving back at Tonbridge at 3.28pm whence the stock was returned empty to Stewarts Lane.

Whereas the Hawkhurst branch was understandably featured in the local newspapers following the royal visit, it made the national press a few weeks later when a truly horrific fatal accident occurred between Horsmonden and Paddock Wood. It happened towards the end of the hop-picking season and at a time when trains weren't normally running. Sunday, 17th September, started off much as any other, when the hop-pickers were up rather later than usual. During the morning an empty passenger train from Margate to Goudhurst had been brought down by a 'D' class, No. 31731, in preparation for the late afternoon return special to London Bridge. At Old Hay farm, pickers, their families and friends, were enjoying the brighter weather after the early morning showers. Some were preparing Sunday lunch on open fires in the fields, while others leisurely wandered over to the ice cream van which habitually turned up to sell wafers, confectionery and cigarettes. The van, belonging to Divito Bros. of Deal, was in the charge of George Huelin aged 40 and his young companion Ben Wicks, 23, who rented lodgings in Strood and had come down to the farms since business could often be brisk on these occasions. At one o'clock they packed-up and set off, retracing their tracks along the narrow road which led onto the hop and fruit farm. Tragically, just two minutes later both men were killed when their van was struck on Old Hay crossing.

Running light on its return from Goudhurst, 31731 was in the experienced hands of driver Waghorn who was watching the line up ahead from the down side. At hop-picking time all crews were diligently observant for they were well-aware of the habitual lineside wanderings by pickers and suchlike. At the same time the fireman kept a look-out from the opposite side and periodically sounded the whistle as the engine paced along at around twenty miles an hour. Only yards from Old Hay, a van suddenly appeared from the down side whereupon driver Waghorn spontaneously made a full application of the vacuum brake, slammed the regulator closed and held open the whistle even though his fireman had only just ceased sounding it. However, the rails were greasy, the wheels skidded and 31731 ploughed into the vehicle with a loud bang. Mrs Elizabeth Hutchings of Finsbury subsequently told a reporter she was cooking dinner on an open fire in a field alongside the railway: 'I heard the crash, then saw a shower of wood and metal'. The van broke up immediately on impact, most of it was tossed aside, whilst the roof and one door remained wedged in front of the 'D' class which halted 275 yards beyond the crossing. One body was trapped inside the wreckage, whilst the other was found next to the track on the up side. Witnesses stated they had clearly heard the locomotive approaching and its whistle being sounded, but it was concluded that the van's occupants were oblivious to the danger. The blame for the accident was deemed to rest entirely with the deceased who had attempted to cross the railway without first ensuring it was safe to do so.

At a subsequent enquiry it was stated that the large iron gates provided at Old Hay opened outwards from the railway and had originally been provided with self-

A driver's view of Old Hay Crossing, between Churn Lane and Paddock Wood, on the approach from the south.

Looking east towards the farm. As seen here, the substantial wood and iron gates were intended to normally remain closed against the lane, whilst 'Beware of Trains' notices warned those using the lane to be vigilant when crossing.

British Railways

An up goods train being taken out of Cranbrook on its journey up the branch in September 1950. Within a few years the signalling here was also modernized; the original M&H up starting and SE&CR down starting signals were replaced by the rail-built variety. Most surprisingly, the SE&CR bracketed up home signal escaped renewal, although the little SE&CR shunt signal sharing the staging was not so lucky. The wooden arm of the up home presumably decayed, hence bolting-on of a modern BR steel arm to the sawn-off stump of its predecessor. Whenever the signal was pulled 'off', the rising iron counterweight on the lever below clouted the arm just below the white band with a loud 'clang', causing it to chip and eventually buckle. *Derek Clayton*

closing devices. However, these were always being tampered with by hop-pickers, whilst padlocks, although provided by the railway, were habitually never used by the farm owners. Consequently the gates were invariably wedged open. Warning notices instructing the proper use of the crossing and penalties for failure to close the gates were always ignored, hence there was little else the Southern Region could do. It emerged that the vendors had not been given permission to enter the farmlands and, therefore, pass over the level crossing. Accordingly, a verdict of 'death by misadventure' was recorded by the coroner.

As a result of the accident the SR installed a telephone at Old Hay which gave direct communication with the signalman at Paddock Wood. Fears over the safety of these occupation crossings had already caused the newly-formed Southern Region, in the summer of 1948, to reconsider the arrangements at Smugley. During hop-picking the crossing was heavily used by vehicles, as well as large numbers of pickers and their sometimes unattended children passing to and fro. The crossing keepers, who were allocated there during a five-week period, drew attention to the fact that there was no

'R1' No. 31706 simmering quietly beneath familiar SER wooden valancing in the bay at Paddock Wood, before setting off for Hawkhurst in September 1950. *Derek Clayton*

communication or warning system when a train was approaching. Very often, with the wind in a particular direction, they were almost silent, especially coming down the bank from Cranbrook with the engine propelling. Trains were required to whistle and reduce speed on the approach to Smugley, but they didn't come into view until they were 300 yards away in the up direction and only 200 yards in the down. Percy Nunn, divisional superintendent, recommended that a block repeating bell, which could be switched out at other times of the year, be provided in a cupboard in the hut. Accordingly, from that year, warning equipment was installed and the following instructions were issued annually to the keeper, as well as the signalmen at Cranbrook and Goudhurst:

> 'From 6.15am to 8.30pm daily commencing . . day the . . of August and until . . day the . . of September, a Crossing Keeper will be provided at Smugley Occupation Level Crossing, the large gates of which are normally closed and locked across the roadway and must be worked in accordance with Rules 99 to 102 and 104 to 107 inclusive. A telephone, with a code of 3 pause 3, has been provided at the crossing and upon an up train leaving Cranbrook Station or a down train leaving Goudhurst Station, the Signalman concerned must so advise the Crossing Keeper. On being advised that a train is approaching the crossing the Crossing Keeper must maintain and lock the gates across the roadway until the train concerned has passed clear of the crossing.'

Because many of the farms were on remote byways, often the most direct path to reach them on foot was to follow the railway. Hop-pickers and the 'friends' had a habit of trespassing along the track, often quite recklessly sauntering from sleeper to sleeper with little regard for their own safety and causing a hazard and a perpetual problem for the train crews.

HAWKHURST BRANCH. (SINGLE LINE.)

NO SUNDAY SERVICE.

Distances from Tonbridge.	DOWN TRAINS. WEEK-DAYS.		* a.m.	* a.m.	* p.m.	* S.O. p.m.	* p.m.	* p.m.	* p.m.	
m. c.										
5 23	PADDOCK WOOD ... Ⓣ	dep.	7 35	9 7	12 24	2 24	4 25	5 50	7 28	.
9 52	Horsmonden .... Ⓣ	arr.	7 45	9 17	12 34	2 32	4 35	6 0	7 38	...
11 53	Goudhurst .... Ⓣ	,,	7¶51	9 23	12 40	2 40	4 41	6 6	7 44	.
15 19	Cranbrook .... Ⓣ	,,	8 5	9 32	12 49	2 49	4 50	6 15	7 53	...
16 60	HAWKHURST .... Ⓣ	,,	8 10	9 37	12 54	2 54	4 55	6 20	7 58	.

Distances.	UP TRAINS. WEEK-DAYS.		* a.m.	* a.m.	* a.m.	* p.m.	* S.O. p.m.	* p.m.	* p.m.	* p.m.
m. c.										
—	HAWKHURST .... Ⓣ	dep.	7 40	8 24	9 43	1 5	3 12	5 5	6 35	8 7
1 41	Cranbrook .... Ⓣ	arr.	7 44	8 28	9 47	1 9	3 16	5 9	6 39	8 11
5 7	Goudhurst .... Ⓣ	,,	7 53	8 37	9 56	1 18	3 25	5 18	6 48	8 20
7 8	Horsmonden .... Ⓣ	,,	7 59	8 43	10 2	1 24	3 31	5 24	6 54	8 26
11 37	PADDOCK WOOD .. Ⓣ	,,	8 10	8 54	10 13	1 35	3 42	5 35	7 5	8§37

§—To Tonbridge dep. 8.39 p.m. ¶—Depart Goudhurst 7.56 a.m.

25/9/50

Whereas it was obviously requisite to keep a watchful eye on the road ahead as much as possible, occasionally it was very difficult to observe this rule. Such was the case before dawn just after Christmas, on 27th December 1951. It was a thoroughly horrible morning, the sort of day when most men might wonder why they'd ever chosen to work on the footplate. A stiff gale was blowing at the time, it was bitingly cold, with squally showers of driving rain, the kind which seems to fall almost horizontally, drenching everything. Five minutes out from Paddock Wood a 'C' class, No. 31716, was running tender first, its tarpaulin offering little protection from the weather which was simply throwing itself at the early morning goods which comprised thirteen vehicles. Unfortunately for the crew, the crossing keeper at Churn Lane was still sound asleep in his warm bed, thus the gates remained firmly across the railway and weren't seen until it was too late. Following the inevitable crash, a delay of fifteen minutes was incurred while pieces of splintered wood and mangled wire were removed from the coupling hooks, brake pipes and extracted from beneath the tender's wheels. The bleary-eyed crossing keeper likely heard a few choice expletives from the crew who could expect to be disciplined over the incident.

At the subsequent investigation, the driver claimed he'd not seen the yellow warning light of the down distant signal in the pitch darkness, nor observed the red 'bull's eye' on the gates. However, the station master at Horsmonden, who'd stoically braved the appalling weather and walked all the way to Churn Lane, noted that both distant signals were still alight, but couldn't give any evidence as to the condition of the gate lamps since 31716 had smashed them to pieces. The 'C's regulator had been closed, with a speed of fifteen miles an hour being maintained, but neither fireman nor driver had spotted the distant still 'on'. Likewise, the guard stated he'd seen no light in the signal, although he had observed a red light on the gate, at which he'd promptly applied the brake in his van. Driver Dear was let off with a caution bearing in mind 'his excellent past record' and the appalling weather that morning, but the crossing keeper was suspended for a day with loss of pay. He was also admonished when the lamps on the

HAWKHURST BRANCH.

Distances M.	Distances C.	DOWN WEEK-DAYS	— A.M. arr.	dep.			S.X.Q. A.M. arr.	dep.			S.X. P.M. arr,	dep.			S.X. Q. P.M. arr.	dep.
.	.	Keylands Yard	.	5 25	.	.	.	11 40	.	.	.	1 40	.	.	.	6 0
0	00	Paddock Wood Ⓣ	5 28	5 30	...	...	11 43	11 45	...	...	1 43	1 45	...	...	6 3	6 5
2	64	Churn Lane Siding	...	...	.	.	11 53	12 8	.	.	C.	S.	.	.	6 13	6 23
4	29	Horsmonden Ⓣ	5 45	6 0	...	...	12 18	1 32	...	...	2 0	2 20	...	...	6 33	6 55
6	30	Goudhurst Ⓣ	6 10	6 27	.	.	1 39	2 10	.	.	2 27	3 7	.	.	7 2	...
7	33	Pattenden Siding	.	.	...	...	C.	S.	...	...	C.	S.	...	...	.	.
9	76	Cranbrook ... Ⓣ	6 38	6 58	.	.	2 25	3 25	.	.	3 22	4 20	.	.	...	...
11	37	Hawkhurst Ⓣ	7 6	.	...	...	3 30	.	...	...	4 25	.	...	...	.	.

UP WEEK-DAYS	Q. No. 7 A.M. arr.	dep.			— P.M. arr.	dep.			S.X. Q P.M. arr.	dep.					S.X. Q. P.M. arr.	dep.
Hawkhurst ... Ⓣ	.	10 0	.	.	.	5 35	.	.	.	5 50	.	.	.	.	.	.
Cranbrook ... Ⓣ	10 5	10 15	...	...	5 40	5 55	...	...	5 55	6 46	...	...	...	...	...	...
Pattenden Siding	.	.	.	.	C.	S.	.	.	C.	S.	.	.	.	.	.	.
Goudhurst ... Ⓣ	10 25	10 37	...	...	6 5	6 25	...	...	6 56	7 10	...	...	...	...	...	8 40
Horsmonden... Ⓣ	10 45	10 55	.	.	6 35	7 50	.	.	7 20	7 40	.	.	.	.	8 50	9 10
Churn Lane Siding	11 0	11 7	...	...	C.	S.	...	...	...	...	...	...	...	...	9 15	9 25
Paddock Wood Ⓣ	11 15	.	.	.	8 5	.	.	.	7 55	.	.	.	.	.	9 35	

Extract from 1951 freight timetable.

temporary gates were inspected a week after the incident and were found to be 'in a filthy condition'.

The replacement gates which duly arrived lasted barely a few months before they too were destroyed. On this occasion it was the 8.24am Hawkhurst to Paddock Wood which, on Thursday 22nd May 1952, failed to pull up in time. Unlike the mishap of the previous December, it was a fine spring morning with good visibility when 'H' class No. 31523 propelled push-pull unit No. 719 through the beautiful Kentish orchards at the start of another day. On arrival at Horsmonden the obligatory bell codes were exchanged with Goudhurst, after which the young signalman offered the train to Paddock Wood who immediately accepted it. However, he forgot to tap out the follow-up code 'Train entering section' which, in the usual manner, alerted the crossing keeper at Churn Lane to close the gates against the road and set his distant signals to 'off'. During the two and a half minutes it took a train to reach Churn Lane, the keeper remained unaware of its approach and carried on cleaning the gate lamps inside his hut, expecting a message at any moment. In the meantime, 31523 had just entered Horsmonden tunnel, where the driver rang the bell in his driving compartment to instruct his mate in the engine's cab to close the regulator. The fireman then turned on the blower before preparing the fire for the return trip. Up ahead, the driver observed Churn Lane distant still at 'caution', whereby he applied the brakes and blew the whistle. Moments later he caught sight of the gates, but, because the crossing stood at a peculiar angle, he mistook them for being open for his train. It was only when he'd run a few hundred yards further on the curve leading up to the roadway that he realized his path was barred and promptly made a full application of the brakes. The fireman, alerted by the sudden jolt, attempted to work the sanding gear, but the boxes turned out to be empty. Simultaneously, he slammed the 'H' into reverse, but these desperate measures came too late whereby the unit sailed through both barriers.

The crossing keeper was taken completely by surprise by the arrival of the train and ran out from his hut knowing he'd no chance of altering the gates, besides, he was more concerned with flagging down the approaching coachload of schoolchildren. Not surprisingly, Kent Education Committee raised the matter with British Railways when it learned 'with deep disquiet' of the events at Churn Lane that spring morning. It appeared to them that a potentially tragic accident had only been averted by the presence of mind of the crossing keeper. Naturally, they sought an assurance that this type of incident should never happen again. In view of the seriousness of the situation, the Southern Region interviewed all the staff concerned, as well as other regular drivers and firemen rostered on the branch duties. Beginning with the driver of 31523 that day, he was asked to simply state why he hadn't been able to stop in time. He replied that although the up distant signal was often 'on', he'd never once been stopped at the crossing and therefore had only slowed his train, expecting the gates, as usual, to be open. Because of the curvature in the line from the southerly direction, it was, he claimed, virtually impossible to judge which way the gates stood until the train was within yards of the crossing, a point of view corroborated by other drivers. He thought the only reason he'd been unable to stop in time was because the regulator had been slightly open when he released the brake, thus giving the train an extra push. Colleagues based at Tonbridge confirmed the difficulty experienced when approaching this particular crossing from Horsmonden. A disused hut near the gates obscured proper vision, but nothing compared to the line of wagons which, on frequent occasions, filled the sidings there and blanked out all sight of the gates and warning lamps until the last moment. They also considered that the distant signals were far too closely positioned.

Following this evidence, the Sighting Committee visited Churn Lane and recommended that home signals be provided and controlled by a new ground frame of nine levers. In effect, the Southern Region was being asked to replace what had been removed in 1926, for it would seem that distant signals alone were insufficient. The estimate for the work amounted to £1,250, but in spite of the fact that all the various departments approved the plan, the chief regional manager, S. W. Smart, refused to authorize such expenditure, retorting that it could hardly be justified 'in view of the unremunerative character of the passenger traffic carried on the line'. This comment is the earliest discovered indication that declining receipts were causing the SR to question the line's future. Soon after, both the driver involved and the Horsmonden signalman were given a stern warning to be far more cautious in future. Eventually, three years later, in the spring of 1955, both up and down distant signals were replaced with modern,

A friendly smile from the driver and fireman of 'R' class No. 31675 as it was heading away with a Saturday afternoon train from Cranbrook on 29th September 1951. Not only was it the end of the season for the hop-picker, but also the allotment holder's trackside patch, as yet another year had run full circle in the life of this rural byway. *Denis Cullum*

The pastoral setting of Cranbrook is easily appreciated in this view from the staging of the down home signal in 1951. *L. A. Rusbridge*

rail-built upper quadrant examples sited at a greater distance from Churn Lane.

Other railway staff were similarly in trouble during 1952 when, on the afternoon of Thursday, 24th January, the 1.05pm from Hawkhurst continued to Horsmonden with the tablet for the Cranbrook-Goudhurst section. Accompanying the driver 'up front' was a relief signalman who was due to take over at Goudhurst cabin. On arrival, he was handed the correct tablet for Horsmonden by his colleague who'd just signed off. Here, the station master decided he would also join the driver in the push-pull unit for the journey to Horsmonden, so they set off, as usual, with the engine propelling. It was only after they'd left that the driver noticed he'd been handed back the surrendered tablet by the relief signalman, at which the station master suggested he should continue to Smallbridge crosing. Here, the off-duty signalman, who was also riding in the driving compartment on his way home, was able to jump down and head back along the track to Goudhurst to make the proper exchange. In the meantime the train was taken on to Horsmonden to avoid being delayed any longer. Whereas there were probably odd occasions when errors were successfully hushed-up, this was not one of them and all concerned found themselves in trouble. Both Goudhurst signalmen were reprimanded for their inattentiveness to duty, as well as being criticised, along with the station master, for travelling in the unit with the driver. Primary blame was deemed to rest with the driver for allowing himself to be influenced by the station master who should have known better than to advise him to take the train forward without the tablet. All were accordingly dealt with in the 'recognized disciplinary procedure'.

Whilst documented instances such as these provide a useful insight into the working of the branch and the day-to-day duties required of the staff, only first-hand experiences can effectively illustrate what life was really like at that time. A most valuable account is provided by Norman Rusbridge, whose father was appointed station master at Cranbrook soon after nationalization, and his fascinating recollections of the period between 1948 and 1952 are uniquely informative:

> Prior to my father being appointed station master to Cranbrook, we were living at Hastings. After being offered the job my father naturally wanted to view the situation with my mother and therefore set out by the easiest and quickest route, this being by Maidstone and District No. 5 service to Maidstone. Unfortunately, with Cranbrook station not being visible from the main road, they missed their stop and remained on board the bus until Cranbrook town itself was reached. Directions were then obtained and, there being no convenient bus back, decided to do it the hard way and walk back, not realizing quite how far it was, not only to Hartley, but also down the long approach road. This road was so long that anyone could be forgiven for doubting a station existed. Not a very good start; however, it was promotion.

My mother was not very happy at leaving a modern home at Hastings for a remote house that had no electricity or gas! Lighting was provided by Tilley lamps and candles, cooking by coal-fired kitchen range. The family have since always smiled about this when my mother innocently recalls that 'Your father used to get up Sunday morning and clean the flue in his pyjamas'. Washing of clothes was by a wood-burning copper which also supplied hot water for baths. Many Sunday mornings were spent on the railway bank with the station cross-cut saw, cutting up old sleepers etc., for this purpose. For the younger members of the family, though, it was all very novel and exciting.

Although there was no electricity, the station house had, in fact, been wired-up prior to the outbreak of the war and all the fittings were in place. Within a short space of time my father had become friendly with Mr. Martin, the owner of a nearby farm. The farmer owned an electricity generator and my father, with the Railway Board's approval, came to a private arrangement with Mr. Martin to supply electricity for lighting and running of a small hotplate only. To this aim, poles were purchased and erected from the house, along the railway bank towards Badger's Oak and over the bridge to the farm. The poles can be seen in photographs of the period. Because of the farm's demand for electricity during the hop-picking season it was agreed that our use would be kept to a minimum.

The railway cottages were also without connected power, but weren't included in this private arrangement. They were unusual in as much that the frontage faced an adjacent cinder-surfaced lane to the north east which led from the main road to the lower end of the goods yard and on, over the railway, to Furnace Farm. A pathway from the rear of these premises led to the station and approach road which was more often used by the residents. The lower entrance to the goods yard was always locked and little-used. Needless to say, in view of the remoteness of the area, we all soon acquired bicycles.

The station master whom my father replaced was Stan Hobbs. He left to take up duties at Merstham [near Redhill] and there was already a family connection since Merstham had been my uncle Reg's second appointment. The station master at Hawkhurst until about 1950 was Mr. Henbest who left to take a position at Sheffield Park and subsequently Uckfield. His successor was Mr. Curling who, I believe, had the distinction of being the youngest appointed station master. At that time both Horsmonden and Goudhurst came under the charge of Mr. Hargreaves.

Although Cranbrook was probably the busiest station regarding goods traffic, as time passed the staff dwindled. First to go was young Peter, the junior clerk, and then Fred Masters, the chief clerk, who was sent on relief work. Neither was replaced; instead, Len Palmer, the goods porter, took on more office duties and was subsequently given a higher grade. Tom Griffin, one of the porter/signalmen, left after gaining promotion to relief signalman and was replaced by Bert Furnell, whilst the other porter/signalman, Arthur Collier, was to remain until closure of the branch.

Sometimes the silence of the area is hard to imagine today. On Sunday mornings the church bells at either Goudhurst or Cranbrook were within earshot, depending on the direction of the wind, as were trains on the Tonbridge-Hastings line, pulling away from Etchingham. On still winter evenings the branch trains could be heard starting away from Hawkhurst, right from the moment of departure until steam was shut off on the Cranbrook side of Badger's Oak tunnel.

In winter there was the friendly hum and warmth of the Tilley lamps in the booking hall and office, with their distinctive smell, particularly when they had just been lit up using the starter corks soaked in meths. The signal box always had a smell of cleanliness about it as it was kept spotless, floor scrubbed regularly and steel lever handles glinting in the sunlight. The sound of bells ringing, the Tyer's tablet machine operating and levers being pulled are very memorable, especially the bells when the box was closing down for the day. For some years and in keeping with the area, a hop bine was grown up the straining wire of the telephone post outside the box.

At seasonal times of the year distinctive smells around the station were strawberries, which usually went off to Covent Garden on the last up train of the day. There were also apples, which would be loaded into a special goods van shunted into the dock road prior to attaching to the rear of the last up train. Passengers often wondered where they were going when the complete train seemingly started away for Goudhurst, but ended up in the goods yard. Young trees encased in straw had a pleasing scent about them and many of these were sent off in large numbers by passenger train. The large pockets of hops perhaps had the most distinctive and memorable smell. These were packed into very heavy pockets and normally loaded onto wagons in the dock road. With most staff members lending a hand to manhandle them into the wagons, I remember this was very arduous and hazardous work. During one such loading, porter/signalman Arthur Collier was up top on the final layer using the usual docker's hook which, unfortunately for him, did not dig into the pocket, resulting in him losing his balance, falling backwards off the load and being impaled on the adjacent platform railings. A nasty accident which came very close to a fatality.

The unpleasant smell of hop manure coming in by truckload seemed to hang around for weeks, as did the strong odour of fish which arrived early morning in the usual crates. The empty fish containers would be returned to the station and stacked near the goods shed until there were sufficient to warrant a truckload for return. In the meantime we had to endure the pong.

On the bank opposite the platform, spring brought with it an abundance of primroses, whilst in summer a mass of ox-eye daisies lined the railway. Wild strawberries were plentiful just north of Badger's Oak tunnel, pheasants were a common sight and, naturally, rabbits could be seen in large numbers. An owl that nested nearby was often seen at dusk, regularly working its territory around the station and goods yard in search of the railway's mice and voles. Once, on a very dark night, beside the station approach road, a remarkable sighting of glow worms gave us much pleasure. On Sundays, weather permitting, and as there was no train service, the family would often go for long, wonderful walks in this lovely area. These outings invariably included a section of the railway line.

For a few years the disused mission hut still stood about halfway up the station approach road. On a dark night this old building was rather eerie and we would be glad to complete the ordeal of passing it when walking alone. A vast amount of coal came in by rail. There were two local coal merchants, one being Williams, Miles (two surnames), the other Banks. Of the two, Banks was the smaller company and possessed only two vehicles and was later bought out by Williams, Miles. They had a larger fleet, mainly Austins and all had a board fixed over the cab top with the words 'Miles coal - miles better'. Williams, Miles also handled the cartage of parcel traffic in the Cranbrook area. Initially this was a Commer 2/3T van which was also fitted out with longitudinal hinged bench seats each side and licensed as a public service vehicle. School children were conveyed to and from the station in this. The vehicle was eventually replaced by a new Austin with a body of similar arrangement. As the vehicle was licensed as a PSV, it could be hired out for trips. In the season a regular weekly excursion was made to Hastings speedway. Obviously the vehicle was not very comfortable for a lengthy trip such as this and it is difficult to imagine people tolerating travelling in such a fashion these days.

The parcel deliveries to the Benenden area were contracted to the firm of Stan and Ernie Christmas. The brothers used larger vehicles on occasions, especially when required to transport cattle to and from Maidstone market etc. Any goods traffic that could not be collected by the consignee was, on the rare occasion, handled by the railway's vehicles. I remember one such instance being a large delivery to a farm in the area when a Scammell and trailer came down on loan from Tunbridge Wells goods depot.

In recalling vehicles in the area, when we first moved to Cranbrook the local milkman delivered his rounds by World War Two 'Jeep'. Eventually this was replaced by a brand new Trojan (à la Dinky toy).

A few weeks prior to the end of term, special trains were arranged for the use of Benenden girls school. The head would send a taxi to convey the Cranbrook station master to and from the school wherein he would spend much of the day selling railway tickets, lunch also being courteously supplied. This would no doubt determine the strength of train required and I remember my father rather enjoyed this day out. Since the boys from Cranbrook school were less in numbers, they would purchase their tickets in the normal manner. The girls were, by and large, well-behaved. However, the boys were rather more boisterous and would travel by the normal train service which sometimes had to be strengthened to four coaches. On arrival, when returning to school, a great stampede would ensue in order to obtain the first taxis that would be ready and waiting in the approach road. On one occasion my father, in good humour, decided to momentarily close the normal exit and move it instead to the side wicket gate, thus the first off were last and the last off first for the taxis. They all took it in good part and had a good laugh about it.

In the days when Cranbrook had a small but modern cinema, 'The Regal', a billboard used to stand opposite the station exit, displaying posters of films being shown. Whether any advertising monies were paid to the railway is doubtful; however, a free pass for one was provided for the station master or family member to use once a week and advantage of this perk was often made by either my sister Hazel or myself. In the dark winter months we would invariably cadge a lift into Cranbrook with the local post office van that would be returning to the post office after sending mail off on the 6.15pm. Incidentally, the post office also despatched mail on the 1.09pm. Obviously, it was strictly against GPO regulations to carry passengers, but since it was so dark everywhere we could, with care, get away with it. It's interesting that in those days the films for the local cinema would be sent by rail in the customary large metal box - and they always arrived in time. Another very handy perk, but this time being for any one member or relation of the local station staff, was a rail pass to Tonbridge for shopping purposes.

Inevitably I should mention the hop-picking season. Shortly prior to this, a local farmer, Mr. Lawrence, engaged the services of young students, male and female, to assist with the season's harvesting. They were known to us as 'Young Harvesters' and did this work in their holidays. They would arrive by train and be met by tractor and trailer and lived for the next few weeks in some wartime Nissen huts. They all appeared to have a jolly good time and returned home looking a perfect picture of health. These harvest camps, as they were known, only lasted a couple of years or so. Hop-picking time was treated very much with mixed feelings among the railway staff. As the season drew near, my father would often sing the harvest festival hymn 'All is safely gathered in', but substituting 'Ere the winter storms begin' with 'Ere the hop-pickers begin'. Many hop-pickers sent their luggage as P.L.A. [Paid Luggage in Advance], addressed with their home and 'care of' the farm to which they were contracted. At times it piled up considerably and the staff had a difficult time finding space for it all until collected.

The special services laid on throughout this period were always of great interest. Because trains had to be strengthened, which often resulted in locomotives struggling with heavy loads, lineside fires were commonplace. When an incident was reported we all willingly lent a hand to extinguish the blaze, the best method being to beat out the flames with an old coal sack which was an easy thing to carry to the fire which could be some distance away from the station. The hop-pickers were always willing to lend a hand in this respect should they be near by. On one occasion we had the use of water while attending a fire near the down distant signal when a 'D1' 4-4-0 running light down the branch stopped and gave assistance with the footplate hose.

As some farms were on remote tracks the most direct method to reach them on foot was often via the railway line which, of course, meant hop-pickers and friends did, in spite of warnings and thus caused a hazard to the railway operating staff (rather like railway enthusiasts today). All in all, though, the period did bring a certain amount of excitement, especially of an evening when we could see their camp fires and hear their sing-songs at the nearby farm. For some reason they always sang at the very tops of their voices when returning from the pubs at night. Many locals were of the opinion that they were often more nervous of the darkness than merry with drink. Needless to say, when the season had finished it all seemed a bit dead everywhere. I remember one occasion when a family was returning home to London and waiting for the local pull and push from Hawkhurst. As the leading coach was propelled into view through the bridge near Hall Farm, the youngest lad exclaimed 'Cor! it's an electric' - an understandable mistake perhaps. Equally amusing were some others who, after purchasing their tickets, would ask in all innocence 'What time and which platform is it?', and my father, without batting an eyelid would answer 'Platform number one'.

Looking back, everyone appeared to be friendly and co-operative in those days. The first up train of the day was often a struggle to catch for some passengers. It was not uncommon for some of the regulars to arrive by car at Hawkhurst only to see their train steaming out, so they'd hop back in the car and motor on to Cranbrook. Meanwhile, the Hawkhurst staff would obligingly telephone through to Cranbrook where the train would be held for a couple of minutes to await their arrival.

During our stay at Cranbrook my father was unhappy with the chair in the station master's office since it was made entirely of wood and not very comfortable. Having a better chair with arms in our own furnishings, my father did a temporary exchange; however, on leaving Cranbrook, we inadvertently forgot to swap them back. No more was thought about this until many years later when you might well imagine my delight on turning the chair upside down one day and finding the magical letters branded underneath 'SE&CR.' Now it is my most prized possession from Cranbrook station. On recollection, I wonder how the railway authorities reconciled the station furniture inventory when the line closed?

One of the more interesting special trains which ran on the branch was organized by the education authorities for a schools' visit to Windsor. I remember our train terminated at Windsor and Eton Riverside and returned late in the evening. It was remarkable in that I have never seen so many people meeting a train at Cranbrook as on our arrival home that day.

Until the demise of guards on the branch, the train which came down at teatime was strengthened to two sets. The rear set was then detached at Hawkhurst, remaining there to form the first up train the following day. In later years the stock came down empty with the afternoon goods. Normally the local passenger trains, worked by 'R's or 'R1's, went smokebox first to Hawkhurst and propelled the stock back to Paddock Wood, whilst the 'C's, on goods trains, worked tender first to Hawkhurst. The first train of the day was the down goods with a 'C' in charge which then hauled the first up passenger service. This same engine also took down the afternoon goods, at which time the yard would be thoroughly shunted. Afterwards it returned early evening as a pick up goods. I recall on one rare occasion this train being handled by a St. Leonards 'D' class. On a Saturday there was a slight variation and whilst there was the usual early freight trip down, no afternoon goods was operated. Instead, the 'C' class engine worked the midday down passenger and return. After this my memory is not too clear, but I believe this same engine worked an extra mid-afternoon passenger train running down to Hawkhurst only, thus neatly placing the stock in readiness for the first up Monday morning train. Returning to Paddock Wood it would then work the evening pick up goods as normal. In the period we were at Cranbrook I think that the tank engines on the passenger trains changed Saturday afternoons. I don't recall an 'H' class tank working the branch, only 'R' and 'R1's, plus an occasional 'E4' working an extra mid-morning train in the hopping season on a Saturday. Other engines I observed on specials were members of the 'C', 'D', 'D1', 'E' and 'E1' class.

The staffing of the line continued to gradually dwindle until one station master, Mr. W. H. Lawford, was given charge of all four stations. It was very much a different picture compared with, for example, 1931 when the SR employed twenty-five men, excluding drivers, firemen and permanent way staff. At that time Hawkhurst had a station master, two booking clerks, a goods guard, a porter, one signalman and a porter/signalman. Cranbrook employed two booking clerks, two signalmen and a goods porter, whilst at Goudhurst there was a station master, two signalmen, a booking clerk and a porter, as well as a crossing keeper (Smallbridge). Two booking clerks were required at Horsmonden, as well as two signalmen, one porter and two checkers who had charge of Churn Lane siding and crossing. All the positions are believed to have been held by men up until the Second World War when it became necessary to engage women to fill the vacancies. Miss Jessie Russell worked for seven years, from April 1940, as a clerk at Paddock Wood goods office, before transferring to Horsmonden as a clerk for both passenger and goods business, with supplementary duties at Goudhurst. She recalls that at hop-picking time they were all obliged to work Sundays in order to deal with the 'Friends' trains which, as previously mentioned, proved a busy time. Miss Russell relates that 'all the clerks were taken off the branch in October 1948, thus ending my days on the railway, but I thoroughly enjoyed my term of service'. Booking office duties then passed to the porter/signalmen, or the former goods-only clerks who were accordingly upgraded.

The traffic figures and fortunes of the stations varied quite considerably over the years and a very brief summary of passenger receipts illustrates this to some extent, comparing the years 1938 and 1949. Whereas all stations show an increase in season ticket holders over the period, Hawkhurst saw the largest rise, which may reveal something about the employment trends, social habits and increasing mobility of the population. There was also a marked increase in the sales of ordinary tickets, whilst all four stations showed a significant leap in income:

Year 1949	(figures for 1938 in brackets)		
	Seasons	Ordinary Tickets	Total (£)
HORSMONDEN	50 (31)	7,599 (3,160)	10,175 (1,214)
GOUDHURST	43 (24)	5,001 (2,819)	2,333 (983)
CRANBROOK	58 (45)	4,764 (3,708)	5,587 (1,184)
HAWKHURST	102(49)	2,400 (1,856)	3,647 (2,088)

There were obviously fluctuations throughout the seasons, most noticeably at hop-picking time. For example, in one typical year at Goudhurst the staff issued 213 ordinary tickets in February, but this soared to 689 during September. Income from goods traffic also varied, but Horsmonden was especially profitable, mainly brought about by the variety of agricultural business handled there. Over 2,000 tons of general merchandise was sent out during 1949, whilst Cranbrook saw well over 8,000 tons of coal coming in to the yard. Livestock, milk, foodstuffs such as meat and fish and a variety of marketable commodities flowed in and out, thus sustaining the railway.

Such a happy state of affairs was not to last, however, as much of the goods traffic was diverted to private road hauliers. Government policies in the 1950s did little to help the railways or work towards any coherent, integrated transport plan, whilst unhelpful industrial disputes only served to aggravate the situation. Derek Reader considers the four-week rail strike of 1954 did much damage and virtually sealed the fate of the branch: 'We were good customers, but after having to find alternative arrangements we kept with them'. Also, meagre staffing levels did little towards engendering patronage. Although cheap day tickets could be purchased at Goudhurst on the first up train of the day, Derek would try to buy his post-dated, after the 'rush hour'. This was because the beleaguered porter had two trains to attend to at that time of the morning, as well as the duty of operating the level crossing gates. Thus, he was seldom in the booking office to sell tickets.

Whereas these factors in themselves did little to encourage people to use the trains, there were other upsets which deterred patronage, even though British Railways could not be blamed. The most notable occasion began on the 25th January 1955 when culvert No.1482 collapsed and caused subsidence of the railway embankment near Never Good bridge, a mile south of Horsmonden. It happened suddenly and without warning since only a brief while beforehand the early morning Hawkhurst goods had passed over this particular stretch of line, although sign of deflection had been detected by the crew. Following the slip, the entire train, in the charge of ex-LB&SCR E4 0-6-2T No. 32580, became marooned on this part of the branch. Within a short time an emergency 'bus service was laid on between Goudhurst and Horsmonden, which lasted for three days while engineers had possession of the line. The Southern Region was able to maintain a full service on either side of the closed section since 32580 could be stabled overnight in the redundant engine shed at Hawkhurst. Water was, of course, available from the nearby tower, whilst coal had to be purchased from local merchants' domestic supplies. This was because the original coal staithes and siding at the rear of the water tower had become redundant with the closure of Hawkhurst engine shed some twenty-five years earlier when crews were transferred to Tonbridge depot.

Throughout the duration of this minor emergency, crews were brought down from Tonbridge by road and worked in two shifts. The first arrived at Hawkhurst while it was still dark and cold on these winters mornings and left at 5.30am to run light to Goudhurst in order to pick up the load of newspapers, milk, fish and other supplies. On returning to Hawkhurst the push-pull unit was taken out in preparation for the day's Hawkhurst-Goudhurst shuttle. These temporary workings, which ran to the normal timetable as near as possible, must have seemed quite like a holiday in view of the extended tea breaks at Goudhurst. However, all was soon back to normal by the 28th January when through working resumed with the 4.25pm from Paddock Wood.

The 'E4s' were fairly frequent visitors to the branch during the mid-50s, normally working the mid-afternoon goods, although they were occasionally used for the earlier rosters when a 'C' was unavailable. As mentioned previously by Norman Rusbridge, a 'D' class 4-4-0, No. 31734, was sent down on at least one occasion to work the goods and Derek Reader also remembers seeing this elegant, Edwardian express engine relegated to performing such a lowly duty. Not only were the last remaining 'D's disappearing fast by the middle of the decade but, likewise, replacements were being found for the 'Bob-tails'. The Hawkhurst branch became the last refuge for 'R' class No.31666, but its time ran out at the close of 1955 when it worked its last push-pull set on 17th December. Within a few days, 31666 was sent from Tonbridge shed, across the lovely Sussex Weald on a last journey to Brighton for breaking up, but at least it was granted the dignity of running under its own steam. Cutting-up commenced on 24th December and was completed after Christmas. As for the remainder of the 'R1' 0-4-4Ts which had worked the line for so many years, only 31698, 31703 and 31704 remained by 1954, all based at Tonbridge for the Westerham, Maidstone and Hawkhurst duties. 31703 was the first of the trio to go for scrap, being withdrawn in February 1954. Then 31698 was declared to be in very poor mechanical condition, in spite of recent repairs and was consequently taken out of service in October 1955. 31704 had a little more luck and went on to outlast its sister engines, undergoing a 'general' and even a repaint at Ashford. Treated to a fresh application of gleaming BR black livery, which suited them particularly well, it re-appeared on the Hawkhurst branch in the summer of 1954 where it worked almost continually until the spring of 1956. Sadly, a fracture in its frames condemned it and brought its career to an abrupt end. Thus, with more than a million and a half miles clocked-up, it too left Tonbridge on a last journey to the Brighton scraproad. Replacements for the 'R's and 'R1's came with the introduction of Wainwright 'H' class 0-4-4Ts. As previously mentioned, these locomotives were rarely seen on the branch until the final years when, thereafter, they were used almost to the exclusion of anything else, apart from the 'C's handling the goods.

Whilst much of the motive power had seen better days, the rolling stock was even worse. Leaking steam pipes in the heating system led to considerable condensation in winter which, in turn, made the upholstery damp and extremely malodorous. The compartments were also draughty and generally uncomfortable and were hardly an incentive to travel by train. It was one of these units which, due to a defective brake piston, led to a collision with the buffer stops at Paddock Wood. The train, the 9.43am from Hawkhurst, was entering the bay on 7th March 1955, but when the driver came to make a final application of the brake, it proved ineffective. Two passengers sustained cuts, but there was little damage and the driver was held blameless.

Such was not the case the following year when the same driver found himself in trouble over a tablet irregularity. At 5.35pm on Tuesday, 18th December, the 5.5pm from Hawkhurst left Horsmonden without having exchanged tablets. On reaching Churn Lane crossing his train was flagged down whereupon he was informed of his error by the checker who'd received an anxious call from Horsmonden signal box. It was decided to return to make the exchange and this was achieved with only ten minutes delay. The driver explained that at Cranbrook some saplings had been loaded into the brake van whereby, on arrival at Horsmonden, he'd been required to assist in moving them in order to make room for a perambulator. He'd then put the tablet hoop back on the hook, completely forgetting to insert the new one in its pouch. Both driver and signalman were reprimanded, as was the goods guard on the train who, it was pointed out, should not have permitted the irregular return to Horsmonden. In many respects it's not difficult to feel some sympathy for those who were 'hauled over the coals' when such incidents as these took place. On reflection, most of the irregularities appear to have happened when the men were obliged to assist in other duties because of a shortage of staff brought about by managerial attempts to save money. In any dispute there are always two sides and it seems unfair that on occasions cost-cutting measures led indirectly to mistakes being made and disciplinary procedures.

Footplatemen have always been traditionally conscientious and diligent, whilst most treated their job seriously, realizing only too well the tremendous responsibility upon their shoulders for the safety of the passengers riding behind them. Branch line duties were less burdensome of course; nevertheless, the same rules applied. The graduation to driver was a long and sometimes difficult path in any young man's career and, quite apart from the technical knowledge and practical experience, all drivers had to 'learn the road'. Ken Hodson, like all drivers, began his railway career as a locomotive cleaner. Entering service in August 1954, he was based at Tonbridge where eventually he graduated to 'passed fireman'. His first duties were on the push-pull units which Tonbridge used for the Maidstone, Westerham, Hawkhurst and Oxted services, the latter operating to Tunbridge Wells West and through the beautiful Upper Medway valley via Hartfield and East Grinstead.

The Hawkhurst branch was still worked in two shifts. Men for the early morning rosters booked on at Tonbridge in the small hours, before taking out the 'C'

'C' class No. 31761 waiting in the dock siding at Hawkhurst with an afternoon freight working in the mid-1950s. *Peter Winding*

class, or very occasionally the 'E4', depending on availability of motive power and the trainload. The goods, which included all the newspapers and milk for the villages along the way, was made up at Paddock Wood before a normally prompt departure at 5.30am. It was a pleasant roster, especially in the summer months when it was good to be up before most people on a bright morning, enjoying the fresh air and early sunshine. There was always a slight sensation of excitement too when, after running alongside the main line at Paddock Wood for a short distance, the rails slowly eased the train southwards, whilst ahead stretched the well-maintained single line leading into the Wealden hills. On arrival at Horsmonden there was often time for a tea break in the signalbox once the papers and milk had been dropped off. This was because Goudhurst signalbox had yet to open. At six o'clock the bell code 5-5-5 came through on the circuit, whereby the Tyers tablet for the next section was taken out of the machine and, as Ken remembers, was hung around his neck by the driver to avoid the wretched thing being left behind! Pulling away from Horsmonden, the descent into the valley of the Teise was always a lovely ride on still mornings, with Goudhurst upon its hilltop on the bright eastern skyline. Sheep nibbling grass in the quiet fields bordering the railway stared momentarily as the train came pounding along, whilst rabbits playing on the track scattered in all directions. Dropping off merchandise along the way, the arrival at Hawkhurst was made almost without exception on time and here the engine came off before coupling up to the push-pull unit. During the wintertime some crews tried to do this as soon as possible so the locomotive might generate the steam heating with the intention of warming compartments. However, Hazel Rusbridge, who used to travel daily to Tonbridge on the first up train, remembers that the compartments were invariably bitterly cold for the whole journey.

On the late turns the afternoon freight was sometimes taken down by the 'Brighton' tank. At Hawkhurst it was the habit of the driver to nip across the tracks to the signalbox for a 'cuppa', leaving the fireman to shunt the train. On one of these occasions Ken was given charge of the 'E4' for the first time but, being accustomed to the brake on the 'C's, he wasn't prepared for the sharp pull-up on the tank engine. This resulted in the wagons pushing forward, whereupon the leading truck's coupling disengaged from the brake van next to the engine. Since the line at that point fell on a 1 in 80 gradient into the station, it was only a matter of seconds before the wagons gained momentum. Hurriedly securing his engine, Ken set off in pursuit and just managed to pin down the brakes as the runaways entered the platform road, otherwise they might have gone straight through the buffers and onto the highway below. There was little sympathy displayed by his colleagues who watched in amusement from the signalbox and were pulling his leg over the event weeks later.

During the mid-1950s the quantity of freight dwindled alarmingly, in fact to such an extent that the locomotive on the early morning trip was often taken down light, solely to work the first up train of the day. It was on one of these duties that Ken remembers a near miss with the infamous level crossing gates at Churn Lane. The day was perishingly cold, in fact so bitterly freezing that the air almost stung. Ken and his driver were due to take a 'C' class down to Hawkhurst, tender-first as usual but, as he recalls, there was no 'sheet' available. Tarpaulins had a habit of being 'nicked' by other crews, although Tonbridge shed hadn't a bad reputation, unlike Bricklayers Arms where an unattended engine was likely to have its tools, fire irons, lamps and anything else that was removable 'borrowed' during a tea break! However, on this day there was no alternative but to endure the cold, dressed as they were in only thin clothes and railway overalls. On leaving Paddock Wood they both naturally huddled up as close as they could to the firebox for warmth. The coal on the 'C's tender was piled high and there was no view of the road ahead from the cab without hanging out of the side. The biting draught sweeping past the engine was numbing in the extreme, but a look out had to be made from time to time. Rounding the curve near Churn Lane they were unable to see the distant signal due to the heap of coal and promptly sailed past it, noticing with alarm that it was still 'on'. This usually meant only one thing, whereby the brakes were hurriedly applied as, sure enough, the

This view shows the newly-fitted 'upper quadrant' starting signal pulled off for departure of the 5.5 p.m. service, whilst ex-LB&SCR 'E4' 0–6–2T No. 32580 (formerly *Shermanbury*) would follow behind with the 5.30 p.m. freight on Wednesday, 10th August 1955. *J. H. Aston*

This scene, taken on Wednesday, 10th August 1955, shows the signalman about to hand over the Tyer's token to the crew of 'E4' No. 32580 at Cranbrook with the 1.50 p.m. freight service from Paddock Wood. This included a push-pull unit, set 721, freshly painted and just ex-works. *J. H. Aston*

'R1' class No. 31704, simmering in the mid-day sunshine, at Horsmonden with the 12.24 p.m. down service on Wednesday, 10th August 1955. *J. H. Aston*

crossing gates were still closed against the railway. The whistle was then sounded, at which a light came on inside the crossing cottage, followed by the hurried emergence of the checker who, bleary-eyed and pulling on his trousers, opened the way for them.

For a period during the late 'fifties the relatively light freight loads were handled by a diesel-electric shunter. Ken reflects: 'It was like taking a holiday – anything to get off shovelling!'. This 350hp locomotive was based, fuelled and maintained at Ashford. From here it was rostered for various duties, involving shunting the Hump Yard at Ashford, the sidings at Dover Town and Dover Bulwark Street, Tonbridge East and West yards, as well as Maidstone West goods depot. Duty 389, commencing at 4.40am, embraced shunting at Paddock Wood and operating the Hawkhurst branch goods. Although capable of a much higher speed, the locomotive sauntered along the branch at a distinctly leisurely pace ranging from 15 to 20 miles an hour. The diesel was preferred by Ken at the time but, he added: 'Given the choice today it would be steam every time'. The Hawkhurst roster was always a favourite among the crews since it was varied and interesting. Generally enjoyable and fairly leisurely, with 'plenty of cups of tea along the way', it was quite unlike the Westerham duty which he considered 'intensive and boring'. The Hawkhurst branch wasn't difficult to work either, although care had to be taken on occasions. From February to May extra caution needed to be exercised when running through Bedgebury forest between Goudhurst and Hawkhurst, otherwise lineside fires could easily get out of hand. Few troubles were experienced with the 'H' class 0-4-4Ts, 'lovely little engines which behaved themselves perfectly', whilst any slipping on the gradients in wet weather was soon rectified with the sanding gear.

As mentioned earlier, the steam stock was deteriorating badly, particularly the ageing push-pull units which were in very poor condition towards the end and of equal discomfort to the drivers. Ken remembers that the driving compartments were 'pretty miserable', being extremely basic, cold and draughty. However, the best had to be made of them until such time as replacements were found. At hop-picking time the locomotive would be sandwiched between two units. Generally speaking, most firemen preferred having their drivers with them, rather than at the other end of the train. Throughout the rest of the year, though, they were able to enjoy each other's company, at least on the journey down to Hawkhurst which entailed running engine first. Then, at the terminus, the driver would walk up to the unit, leaving his fireman to look after the engine. Communication between driver and fireman was by means of a bell code. There were electrical and air brake connections between the engine and unit, whilst the apparatus was designed to give the driver sole control of the regulator in the locomotive's cab. However, it never worked, the valve would open wide and the regulator would fly over, thus causing all sorts of problems. All crews, therefore, adopted the unofficial method of working whereby the fireman would manually open up, shut off steam, or work the reverser on coded instruction from the driver. No doubt management knew all about this, but the men nevertheless had to keep an eye open for an over-zealous locomotive inspector. Irregular it may have been, but otherwise it meant failed trains and complaints from passengers.

Having worked the 5.05 p.m. from Hawkhurst on duty 306, the 'H' class had been brought alongside the water column where Ken Hodson is seen replenishing 31558. After a pause of twenty minutes, the train set off again with the 5.50 p.m. *Collection Ken Hodson*

The Westinghouse, or 'donkey', brake pump frequently proved troublesome, but it was nothing which couldn't be cured with a bit of skilled engineering - a hefty 'wallop' with a spanner or hammer which always did the trick!

Some of the most memorable occasions for Ken came with taking out the 5.50pm for Hawkhurst from Paddock Wood. This sometimes coincided with the departure of the 4.38pm from Cannon Street to Folkestone which was booked to move away from the adjacent down platform at 5.48pm. If the Folkestone train was a couple of minutes behind schedule it often resulted in a race between the two crews. The spirited 'H' tank would gaily set off with its two-coach set, passing under the signalbox before running along the side of the main line. Initially the branch train would outrun the unrebuilt Bulleid Pacific and its heavy ten-coach train. However, by the time Ken and his mate had almost reached the point where the branch swung away southwards, the immensely powerful 'spam can' would come pacing past to an accompaniment of good-humoured jeers and waves from its grinning crew.

The days of steam traction on Kent's railways were beginning to draw to a close and there were but a few years left until its complete eradication. The electrification schemes being planned during the mid to late 'fifties highlighted a number of problems in regard to the remaining branch lines which had not already been abandoned. In the late autumn of 1957 the Southern Region began to look tentatively into the possibility of using two-car diesel units on both the Hawkhurst and Westerham branches. The report dealing with the Hawkhurst service was circulated to all departments and provides one of those tantalizing might-have-beens had saner attitudes towards the railways prevailed. Two detailed estimates were undertaken, based on running either the existing (steam) timetable, or opting for a more ambitious hourly interval service. Both proposals required the provision of three sets of units, two sets running every weekday, with the third held in reserve at Tonbridge on a rotational basis. Two crews would be sufficient for operating the existing service, but four would be needed if the more intensive timetable was inaugurated. Each complete two-car unit would cost the Southern £40,070, whilst annual wage costs for every driver and guard was put at £630 and £518 respectively. Refuelling would take place at Tonbridge, thus adding some extra mileage, as would the daily empty run down the branch required to balance the 7.43am Hawkhurst service. However, it was noted that this unit could, in practice, make the return journey as a four-car train on the last trip down from Paddock Wood. It was calculated that a total of 52,176 miles would be run annually if the current timetable was adopted. Alternatively, a new hourly interval service would almost double the mileage, clocking up 101,917 with a service of 28 trains per day (one running empty) Monday to Saturday. Incidentally, there was no proposal or indication to reinstate the long-lost Sunday trains. The estimated total annual cost to the Southern Region of such a vastly improved timetable amounted to £17,995, compared with £12,899 if the existing pattern was maintained.

On the reverse side of the coin, other proposals under consideration at that time involved economies not only in staffing, but also equipment, as internal memoranda reveal, for example:

> 'The branch could be worked under the 'one engine in steam' arrangement with provision for the signalling to be converted to Train Staff & Ticket Sections during the hop-picking season and as other occasions demand, such as for special school traffic. The need for Crossing Keepers at Willow Lane and Smallbridge level crossings would not be so great and could be dealt with by a travelling porter or by the addition of relief staff as necessary during hop-picking.'

Clearly, the Southern Region was looking into all possibilities and, inevitably, it wasn't long before rumours of closure began to circulate among the staff. In spite of reassurances from Waterloo headquarters that the line would remain open 'for the foreseeable future', it was understandable that the railwaymen employed on the branch wanted to know where they stood. At that time the prospect of unemployment was remote since there were plenty of vacancies elsewhere and a list of positions to be filled on other lines and at numerous stations and signalboxes was regularly circulated. So, for a while, it certainly seemed that the branch was safe, particularly in the minds of the faithful travelling public when all the stations were entirely repainted. This smartened them up considerably, especially as they hadn't had a lick of paint since Southern Railway days. New station name signs in the form of British Railways 'totems' appeared beneath the canopies and on a few of the lamp posts, although for some undiscovered reason Hawkhurst was omitted. Improvements to the rolling stock came about, perhaps not so much through choice on the part of the Southern Region, but necessity. The increasingly deteriorating ex-L&SWR push-pull units were well past their scrapping date, their condition by 1958 being described as 'appalling'. Three of the regular Hawkhurst sets, nos. 733, 734 and 737 were withdrawn soon afterwards, to be replaced with new units made up from some of Maunsell's ex-Southern Railway carriages. In all, twenty sets were created, using these steel-bodied coaches, comprising corridor composite brakes and open second class saloons. They were infinitely superior in terms of riding, comfort and heating and their generous amount of leg room, luxurious springing in the cushions and availability of window space would pleasantly surprise today's cramped railway passengers. Numbered in the 600 series, No. 609 was often to be found on the 8.20am out of Hawkhurst and these re-conditioned

'H' class 31533 with auto-set 656 heading away from Goudhurst as a few passengers were making their way off the platform in this charming cameo captured on Friday, 10th June 1960. Having been neglected for many years, it was ironic that the recently-painted signal box would fall silent the following year. *Tony Wright*

A view from the train on the bridge across Goudhurst Road showing the approach to Horsmonden station on 15th July 1958. The front of the station master's house may be seen on the far left as well as the entrance to the station and goods yard. Note the stone retaining wall supporting the rear of the platform. *H. F. Wheeller*

trains, which weren't dissimilar to their diesel-powered counterparts in appearance from the driving end, must have encouraged the belief that the line had a future.

In spite of all these improvements, the ultimate fate of the branch had more to do with the political thinking of the day, social changes after the Second World War and, to some extent, a sense of increased 'affluence' which led to a popularity in motoring. The government encouraged this trend, ministers were easily swayed by the belief that a huge road building programme would solve everything, but it was really a dismal lack of planning towards a national, strategically integrated transport system which did untold damage. Of course, the Hawkhurst branch was only a minor casualty of this blinkered approach and it would likely have made no difference whatsoever had its financial returns been any better at that time. It appeared that the closure of the Kentish branches serving Hawkhurst, Westerham and the Hundred of Hoo was a prelude to the highly regrettable approach taken a couple of years later when Dr. Richard Beeching took the chair of British Railways.

On the brighter side, the work on planning the electrification of Kent's railways was making good progress and commuters could see for themselves the steady laying of the third rail in readiness for the gleaming green units which, it was promised, would

Maunsell auto-set 609 being propelled into Cranbrook on an up service on 18th May 1961. *G. A. Stickler*

whisk them to and from work. Many of the morning and evening services on the main line were increasingly being hauled by modern, powerful diesel locomotives, whilst the Tonbridge-Hastings line had recently received new diesel-electric units to improve the services. Elsewhere in the Weald other lines already scheduled for electrification, such as the Tunbridge Wells-Lewes and Oxted lines, were being worked more and more by diesel units, purely, it was stated, as a short interim measure. Likewise, the Hastings-Ashford line, bordering the southern edge of the Kentish Weald, went over to diesel operation with the end of steam traction. Meanwhile, a faithful 'H' class and its two-coach unit was always waiting to greet homeward-bound commuters in the bay at Paddock Wood each evening. Even so, the question in the minds of these regular patrons must have been for just how much longer would it be there? This was something which the Southern Region was investigating, as a decision over the future of both the Hawkhurst and Westerham branches needed to be made. Given the latter line's close proximity to the commuter belt, electrification seemed a distinct possibility. However, no such plans have ever come to light in relation to the Hawkhurst branch other than a statement of 'heavy capital expenditure' and it is doubtful whether senior management had entertained any serious thoughts other than complete closure.

Inevitably, the dreaded time and motion surveys were undertaken to ascertain passenger loadings on the branch. This demonstrated that the line was used chiefly by commuters to London, a small number of schoolchildren and some local workers during 'peak' hours. The morning 7.33 service out of Hawkhurst was the most popular, averaging the following numbers of passengers joining the train: Hawkhurst 6; Cranbrook 3; Goudhurst 15; Horsmonden 16. In the evening the 5.50 from Paddock Wood was most used, with the following average numbers detraining: Horsmonden 11; Goudhurst 12; Cranbrook 2; Hawkhurst 3. These figures, as well as other passenger numbers, were well down on previous years. A significant factor had been the decision of Kent Education Committee to contract private coach operators to transport the Weald's schoolchildren. Throughout the rest of the day, the passenger traffic understandably dwindled, but as many as 130 people were counted using the up trains during weekdays, whilst 140 travelled in the opposite direction.

In the spring of 1960 the Southern Region commenced the closure procedure with a circular to its various departments. From here onwards the only uncertainty seems to have revolved around the precise date of abandonment.

Accordingly, on Monday 23rd May 1960, Mr. C. P. Hopkins, General Manager at Waterloo, despatched his memorandum to the Southern Area Board, noting that he was 'in agreement with this proposal'. In arguing the case for closure it was disclosed that passenger receipts amounted to £12,000 per annum, parcels traffic was worth £22,000 and freight £46,000 - 'On this basis, the estimated loss of receipts is £13,400 per annum. Against this there will be the gross annual saving estimated at £61,000'.

Alternative arrangements using 'buses were then mentioned, although the Maidstone & District Co. already operated services to Maidstone and Tunbridge Wells which called at stations on the Kent Coast line. The Southern Region intended to ask the 'bus company to operate additional journeys in the morning and evening, but knowing full well that 'buses can never replace trains, added: 'The arrangements will be closely watched and the need for continuing to run these services will be examined at regular intervals'.

An additional road vehicle based at Tonbridge was thought necessary to deal with parcels and freight, whilst the GPO would provide two more vans for deliveries. Full wagon load traffic for Horsmonden and Goudhurst would be sent to Tunbridge Wells Goods Depot, Staplehurst would handle Cranbrook traffic, whilst Hawkhurst-bound merchandise would be sent to Etchingham, thus, in effect, reverting to the situation in the 19th century before the line had been built. Coal was more of a problem as the SR knew the traders wouldn't accept these arrangements. It was therefore proposed to set up a central railhead for coal at Staplehurst and carry it through British Road Services which would also serve the more rural area affected by the closure of the Robertsbridge-Tenterden line. Incidentally, loss of traffic from Churn Lane siding was apparently negligible for a note mentioned this as 'rarely ever used'.

Apart from the annual savings to be made in operating the branch, £13,894 on staff, rolling stock repairs £4,082 and train movement costs £10,743, the accountants appear to have done a perfectly splendid job in putting together an unassailable case for closure. Day-to-day repairs of track, bridges, signalling, stations etc., were costing £4,407 a year, whilst it was reckoned that if the line continued in operation until 1964, then the Southern Region could expect a staggering bill of repairs totalling no less than £140,000.

If total closure was accepted, this would displace many members of staff, which, at that time, comprised one station master, six signalmen, two porter/signalmen, a leading porter/signalman, one leading porter and three crossing keepers, whilst six staff under the chief civil engineer would have to be found employment elsewhere. On the operating side, three drivers and three firemen would no longer be required, making a total saving of twenty-six staff. Two push-pull sets would become spare, as well as one 'H' class locomotive, whilst under 'other items of importance' the rather damning comments concluded:

> 'When Phase II of the Kent Coast Electrification Scheme comes into operation in 1961/2 and steam traction is abolished in the South Eastern Division, the Hawkhurst Branch, if retained, would become an isolated pocket of

Ex-SE&CR No. 31263, leaving Goudhurst with the 3.12 p.m. up service on Saturday, 10th September 1960. Built at Ashford Works in May 1905, it was the only member to survive from a total of sixty-six 'H' class 0—4—4T locomotives designed by H. S. Wainwright.

J. H. Aston

This atmospheric photograph shows the station reflected in the shiny paintwork of an up train waiting at Goudhurst, and the shadow of the propelling engine cast upon the platform. Dentillated brick coursing on the station house is highlighted, as is the attractive diagonal woodwork of the front door with its cast-iron knocker. The bracket near the nameboard had lost its oil lamp housing, whilst the motorbike, parked next to the wheelbarrow containing the signalman's supply of coal, likely belonged to a member of staff.

Trans-Rail Publications

diesel operation which would involve difficulties in servicing and maintaining the trains. Any alternative arrangement for working the Branch would involve heavy capital expenditure.'

While the Southern Region was busily planning the closure of the branch, the house journal, the *BR(S) Magazine* was engaged in preparing an article which eventually came out in the issue of August 1960 under the title 'A Kentish station sends plants by the million'. Readers were told: 'From a small Southern station in the lovely Weald of Kent, 46 miles from London, more than a million pot plants a year are being sent all over the country by rail'. The feature briefly described the traffic being handled at Hawkhurst station, ironically business that would soon be lost to road hauliers, whilst its appearance and timing must have caused more than a few bitter comments from railway staff.

The proposal to close the Hawkhurst branch was approved by the Southern Area Board on 2nd June 1960, with a note that a formal submission would soon be made to the Transport Users' Consultative Committee and the news made public. Meanwhile, arrangements were finalised for a joint consultation meeting between management and staff departments. This took place on the 13th July at which the staff representatives raised more than a few objections. Mr. Wainman considered the railway's faithful patrons should not be treated in this disgraceful way by having their trains simply taken away and left to the mercy of the 'bus company. He suggested that the closure should, at the very least, be immediately deferred until the Kent Coast electrification scheme had been introduced. Arguing that it was a well-known fact that improvements, such as electrification, generated more traffic, he contended that Phase II might well bring people and light industry into the area. Already, there were sixty new houses going up at Horsmonden and he suggested a morning and evening only diesel service should be instigated between Hawkhurst and Tonbridge where connections would be better. He didn't think passengers should be expected to be satisfied with the alternative 'service' being proposed, which included changing 'buses at Horsmonden, nor did he consider the fact that some of the branch stations were some distance from villages sufficient reason for closure. He pointed out that many people were now driving to their local station and Paddock Wood had very little parking space. The Woolworth's pot plant traffic, too, was worth £1,000 a week and would inevitably be lost to road hauliers, whilst coal, amounting to over 125 tons a week, would have to be carted by road.

Representing the management, Mr. Robinson, who also chaired the meeting, dismissed these pleas, replying that a hundred passengers a day were not enough to warrant retention of the branch, whilst improvements wouldn't make any difference. Mr. Clarke, on the staff side, then asked if reducing the number of block signalling posts would help, but Mr. Robinson interjected that porter/signalmen would be needed to staff stations, adding that had it been a borderline case, it might have been possible. Mr. Poulter expressed his deep unease at the way the whole closure case had been put together and still felt that passengers who used stations such as Tunbridge Wells West only did so simply because the Hawkhurst branch service was so relatively poor. With an improved diesel service more passengers would be attracted. Unimpressed, Mr. Robinson retorted that the catchment area was rather sparse, adding that it 'wasn't worth the candle'.

In turning to the schools' traffic which had recently been switched to private coach hauliers, it was surmised that complaints from first class passengers over the behaviour of the children had been a major contributory factor towards its loss. Other traffic, such as the pot plants, would be despatched by road, using lorries based at Tonbridge. The management view was that most traffic would be retained in spite of the loss of the branch itself. Whilst Horsmonden and Goudhurst might well develop, or prove increasingly more attractive to those working in London, but wishing to live in the country, 'enquiries' had demonstrated that any growth would be 'insufficient to warrant the line's retention'. Heavy capital expenditure on the track would be needed over the next five years and this fact alone could not be justified. At this point Mr. Northfield then questioned why, if in 1955, the General Manager had agreed to the Hawkhurst branch remaining open, should policy now be changed? In reply, Mr. Bryant claimed that traffic had fallen off 'considerably' over the past five years and it had been necessary to review its position 'in the light of current economies'. The Southern Region was of the opinion that the isolation of the 'pocket', i.e. the High Weald, would not be so great with the loss of the service. Mr. Northfield, however, thought differently and maintained that a lot of the imagined savings so neatly put together by their accountants simply could not be achieved for some considerable time.

It seemed that the Southern Region was acting with an almost indecent haste to rid itself not only of steam traction, but 'unremunerative' branchlines. As always, opponents of closure found themselves against an entrenched position whereby reasoned argument appeared useless. A case for closure could easily be put together simply through claiming huge expenditure on a backlog of repairs and renewals, a tactic frequently used in the years that followed. In concluding the meeting, the chairman thanked the members for attending, whilst a copy of the minutes was prepared and duly circulated. However, the documented content and conclusion which eventually arrived caused more than a little dismay and anger, as witnessed by the letter of 11th August, from the District Engineer's Office at Ashford and signed by Mr. Northfield:

'Dear Mr. Holford,

Proposed Closing of Hawkhurst Branch Line.

Thank you for the copy of Memorandum of Meeting held on Wednesday, 13th ultimo.

In deepest Kent, amidst springtime's scented blossom near Yew Tree Green bridge, 'C' class 31592 is captured trundling past Churn Lane up distant signal with the 1.45 p.m. freight service from Hawkhurst on Friday, 19th May 1961. *J. J. Smith*

If, as I am told, 'brevity is the soul of wit', you must surely be a very wise man. I can agree that, after listening to such a gloomy story from the Management Side, the Staff Side representatives doubtless felt they could expect little to be done, in practice, toward keeping the branch line open, but, you can hardly expect me to agree with your statement that 'no objections were raised to the proposal in principle.' This is simply ludicrous, and I feel you must agree that every Sectional Council present did, in fact, object to the principle of closing the branch, particularly when it meant turning over a hundred, or more, passengers - every day - to the inhuman mercies of the present day 'Bus Companies' as well as handing over merchandise to Railway Cartage or B.R.S. without any guarantee that it could not quite simply slip away into the hands of private hauliers. I think also, cognizance should be taken of the fact that we all felt - on the Staff Side, with the comparatively early advent of electrified services on the Main Line, it was a pity the proposed closure could not be delayed long enough to enable it to be re-examined in the light of a feeder service to the new electric service, especially if the 'branch' trains could be extended through to Tonbridge in order to link with the fast diesel services from Hastings via Tunbridge Wells or the fast electric services via Ashford.

There were, in addition, other issues raised, e.g. - Possible loss of traffic from Benenden School, loss of Woolworth's traffic from the Greenhouses in the area, and loss of the horse traffic from the Stud Farm at Goudhurst also the failure - if the branch was closed - of our ever again being in a position to re-attract the 11-Plus age traffic to the Tonbridge Central or Grammar Schools.

If all these matters were not raised as objections to the closure, then I cannot imagine why they were raised at all, and I rather object to the issue of such a bland statement which, in my opinion completely ignores 'protests' and I feel tends to make a terrible mockery of so-called Joint Consultation.'

It was evident that the disagreement caused by the decision to close the Hawkhurst branch could hardly be resolved; nevertheless the Southern Region remained adamant that all services would cease as soon as the necessary arrangements could be made. Efforts to try and persuade the SR to have a change of heart were soon forthcoming from the public and council representatives. In October Mr. Len Fagg, secretary of the Kent Association of Parish Councils' Tonbridge Area Committee and a Labour candidate, went to London to fight BR's closure proposal. At an area meeting held a few days beforehand, the chairman, Mr. J. Packham, declared that they were 'vehemently in favour of its retention', adding: 'Branch lines must be preserved.

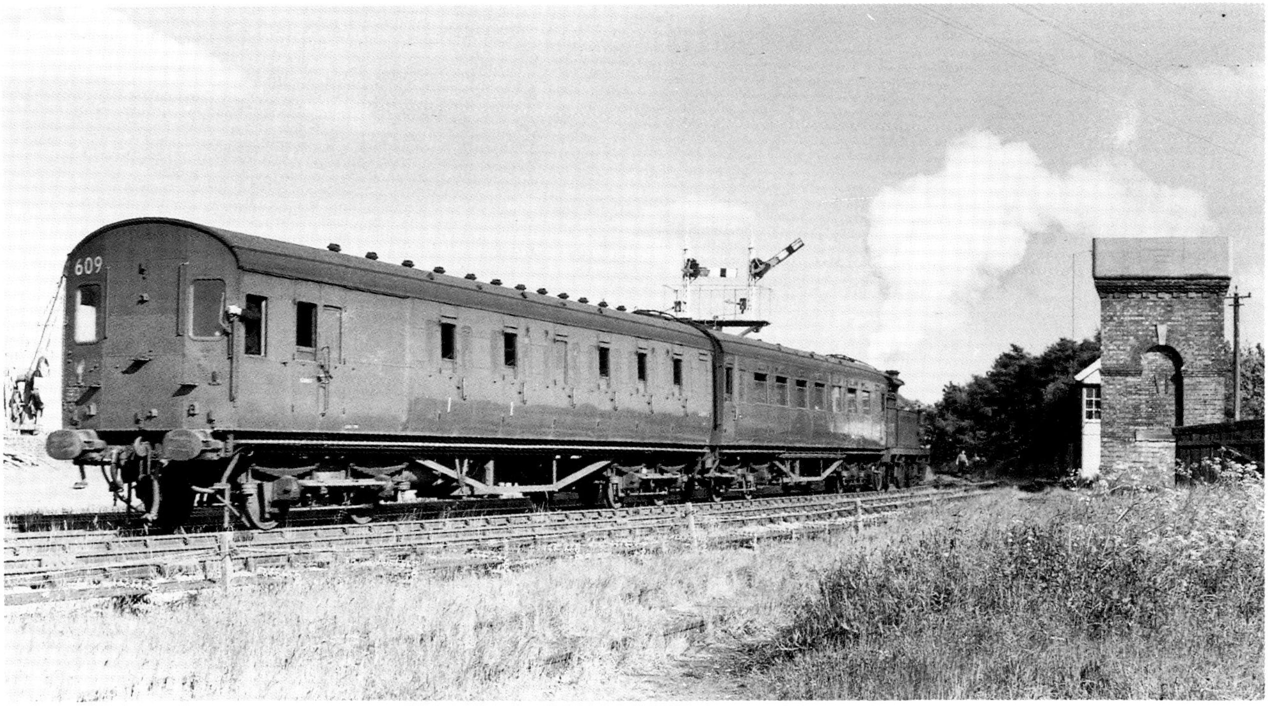

'H' class No. 31543 propelling Maunsell set 609, which formed the 5.3 p.m. to Paddock Wood, out of Hawkhurst on Monday, 22nd May 1961.
J. J. Smith

One of the closure notices, which appeared in March 1961.
R. Crombleholme

They must not be closed just because they do not pay and closure will only add to the congestion on the roads'. Mr. Fagg went further, saying: 'The closing of branch lines always infuriates me because it helps destroy rural life'. Representations were also made to the Transport Users' Consultative Committee, but the only compensation offered was that replacement 'buses would be laid on and subsidised by the British Transport Commission for a trial period of one year.

With the impending 'juicing' of the newly-laid third rail in connection with Phase II of the Kent Coast scheme, the branch was doomed to extinction in conjunction with the arrival of electric trains. Meanwhile, the withdrawal of steam stock from the Eastern Section gathered pace, and although most locomotives were still proudly tended by their crews and sheds, some engines in poor condition were often sent out, probably through a shortage of available motive power. There were also unusual workings, with former main line passenger engines working goods trains and vice versa. In regard to the Hawkhurst branch, this was likely the case on the dark, rainy evening of Friday, 13th January 1961, when an 'N' class 2-6-0, No. 31870, arrived at Tonbridge, having come off a train from Redhill. According to Guard W. Jackson's logbook, the 'N' was promptly despatched to Paddock Wood to take down the 7.28pm Hawkhurst service which comprised Set 656 made up of vehicles 5499 and 3442, both weighing 31 tons. This class of locomotive was normally prohibited from venturing onto the branch, but circumstances must have caused the waiving of this restriction, whereby driver

Streatfield was duly given his instructions. The irregular performance of 31870 is unlikely ever to be known, but the train was eight minutes late in getting away and by the time Hawkhurst was reached a further two minutes had been lost. Quite how the return service was worked is likewise a mystery, although it is logged that the train waited for only four minutes at Hawkhurst between arrival and departure. It seems probable the 'N' propelled the train on the down trip, especially as time was made up on the return journey to Paddock Wood, arriving, in fact, a minute ahead of schedule before continuing on to Tonbridge for the night.

In March, closure posters, which became so dreadfully familiar during that decade, were pasted up at all the branch stations and around the Tonbridge district. Not surprisingiy, the line suddenly became a mecca for

Top: On Sunday, 28th May 1961, the stillness of Furnace Wood was spectacularly disturbed by 'D1' 31739 and 'E1' 31067 pounding up Cranbrook bank with a heavy nine-coach Railway Ramblers' Special. *Above:* The same engines running light between Cranbrook and Goudhurst on their way back to Tonbridge. *S. C. Nash and J. J. Smith*

The rural charm of the Hawkhurst Branch and the delightful Kentish countryside it traversed is epitomized in this glimpse of 'H' class 31177 causing the railway's bankside ox-eye daisies to sway in the down-draught as it headed for Badger's Oak tunnel with an afternoon service to Hawkhurst on Friday, 9th June 1961. *Tony Wright*

railway enthusiasts, anxious to record the last weeks of operation before the usual final excursion trains. Invariably set 609 was sent up and down the branch, propelled by the familiar 'H' tanks, usually 31324, or 31517, whilst 'C's 31256 and 31592 were very much in evidence. All too soon, though, the last weekend finally arrived whereby on Saturday, 10th June, driver Blaber, with 'C' class 31256, handled the four morning trips on this fine sunny day. 31588 took over for the afternoon, but its poor external condition perhaps summed up the end of this era. By the end of the day the top of the boiler was heavily stained with white streaks of limed water which had been emitted when working hard on the gradients with heavily-laden trains. It seemed that

Top: Some of the last wagons idling in Goudhurst's overgrown goods yard being marshalled by 31256 which shunted both sidings before pulling away from the station a little while later. *Above:* Bursting out of Horsmonden tunnel with the last official freight working, 31256 looked rather the worse for wear as it made its way towards Paddock Wood on Friday, 9th June 1961. *Tony Wright*

'C' class 31588 relieved sister engine 31256 for the afternoon services on the final day of operation, Saturday, 10th June 1961. The trains were crowded with railway enthusiasts, and even BBC television cameramen, many of those present being keen to take their own souvenir photographs. *R. A. Stone*

Many local people took the opportunity to make a last sentimental journey, hence the extra coaching stock which was packed-out that day. Here, 31588 is seen entering Cranbrook with the 4.25 p.m. from Paddock Wood, having worked hard to haul its heavily-loaded train up the 1 in 60 bank. *R. C. Riley*

Blowing-off excess steam at Cranbrook, 'C' class 31588 preparing to depart tender-first with the very last 5 p.m. service from Hawkhurst on 10th June 1961. *J. H. Aston*

everyone was intent on riding over the branch, even though the weather had taken a distinct turn for the worse with a steady drizzle threatening to put a damper on the 'celebrations'. At Paddock Wood the last scheduled train to Hawkhurst was joined by an entourage of 'mourners' in Victorian-style fancy dress, whilst departure was subsequently delayed by around 90 minutes. Patiently, though, the villagers at Horsmonden, Goudhurst, Cranbrook and Hawkhurst waited on the wet platforms on this dull June night, as dusk set in, to await the arrival of their last train. On arrival back at Paddock Wood, the carriages were by then festooned with paper streamers trailing out of the windows, their lights blazing in the darkness. Then, with a final shrill whistle from 31588, the train was taken on to Tonbridge, while a solitary detonator sounded far off into the night.

On the following Sunday an enthusiasts' special was run, organized by the Locomotive Club of Great Britain and titled 'The South Eastern Limited'. It was a farewell tribute to steam and a last chance to ride over the Hawkhurst and Tenterden branches. A day of heavy showers dampened the events, but 'C' class 31592 and Stirling's last surviving locomotive, 'O1' No. 31065, soon gained everyone's attention as they were backed onto the rear of the special at Paddock Wood. The heavy train, which included a Pullman car, then set off for Hawkhurst with both engines performing beautifully, their combined exhausts resounding and no doubt delighting those on board armed with tape recorders. Locals braved the intermittent downpours, greeting the train at all the stations, whilst the events seemed more like a celebration than a farewell to a public service and way of life that had been in existence for almost seventy years.

Monday, 12th June 1961 finally came, a day when electric services were inaugurated as part of Phase II of the modernization of Kent's railways. On the Hawkhurst branch, though, all was silent. After 68 years of regular and faithful service, the early morning train for London commuters was no longer waiting at the platform. The stations were locked up, empty and deserted, whilst the staff who would normally have been there talking cheerfully, making tea and sorting out the day's business were gone. The signalboxes were quiet, the Tyer's electric mechanism silent, whilst within a fortnight the polished steel lever handles and bright, shiny brasswork would all be tarnished. Similarly, the silver gleam on the rails from Sunday's special train quickly turned a rusty brown in the aftermath of the downpours. Over the next few days or so, items of value were retrieved from the four station buildings and signalboxes, whilst the final train running under the authority of British Railways went down to Hawkhurst and back in the following week. Derek Reader made a note of this in his diary when a pick-up goods traversed the branch on Tuesday, 20th June, collecting the last of the heavy itineraries to be cleared out and despatched to stores.

The late author and keen railway photographer Derek Cross once mused: 'If ever a line called for preservation the Hawkhurst Branch was surely it, for it epitomised the lost charm of all our rural railways'. In his excellent book *Holding the Line*, Nick Pallant tells the story of the formative days of the Kent & East Sussex Railway Preservation Society and relates that, on two occasions in the summer of 1962, BR unsuccessfully attempted to persuade the fledgling K&ESRPS to relocate to the Hawkhurst Branch. Another reason why the line fell by the wayside was the intention at that time to preserve the Westerham Valley Railway, which had closed at the end of October 1961. Initially, prospects seemed bright for this society, hopeful of securing an entire ex-South Eastern Railway branch line. Everyone looked forward to the day when the last two examples of Wainwright's doughty 'H' class engines, earmarked for preservation, might haul restored 'birdcage' sets from Dunton Green to Westerham. However, it was not to be. By the time it became apparent that the battle was lost and the bypass and, finally, the M25 motorway-building bulldozers had moved in, the Hawkhurst branch had already been torn up, otherwise, who can say what might have transpired?

For two and a half years the branch stood disused, whilst the stations, with the notable exception of Cranbrook, suffered at the hands of vandals. Every piece of glass was eventually broken, not just windows and platform lamps, but even the red and green glass in the signal spectacles. The rooms within the buildings deteriorated quickly once exposed to the wind and rain, the floorboards becoming soaked and rotten, whilst rubbish was littered everywhere. Cupboards and doors were ripped off, whilst the plaster from ceilings was torn down in acts of senseless destruction. Hawkhurst suffered in particular and by 1964 had been totally wrecked. Great holes were made in the roof, whilst attempts were made to lever-off the sheets of corrugated iron cladding from the walls. Following the removal of the track, the proprietors of the adjoining wood yard bought the site and undertook the restoration of the signalbox. The water tower and station buildings were eventually demolished, but happily the old C&PWR engine house and goods shed remain intact. Cranbrook fared rather better and was sold off to become a pottery for a number of years. Today it is a comfortable-looking home and is still recognisable as a former railway station in spite of

The very last public train, 'The South Eastern Limited', organized by the Locomotive Club of Great Britain, heading back up the branch south of Horsmonden on Sunday, 11th June, a grim day of lowering skies, beset by heavy downpours. The two locomotives, 'C' class No. 31592 and 'O1' class No. 31065, both managed to escape being sent for scrap. Eventually restored, they continue to haul trains across the lovely Weald, not in Kent, but in Sussex, on the Bluebell Railway. The Hawkhurst branch was not so lucky and on the following day, Monday, 12th June 1961, fell silent after nearly 70 years of operation. Gone, too, was steam traction from this part of Kent as the sleek green electric trains had at last realised the prewar ambitions of the Southern Railway. *S. C. Nash*

extensive alterations. The three-storey station master's house has been extended, whilst the platform has been lowered in places to track level where a garden has been laid out. Less fortunate was Goudhurst. By 1968 only the corrugated building survived, standing forlorn and derelict upon what remained of the platform. Gone were the homely signalbox, the grand station house and all the other sundry buildings and artefacts which contributed to this lovely country station. Nowadays virtually nothing exists and even a trained eye for old railways would have difficulty in detecting exactly where the permanent way once ran. A garage proprietor took over the buildings at Horsmonden soon after the disposal of the line by British Railways, whilst the cutting beyond and the goods yard soon became very overgrown.

Not surprisingly, the route of the railway has been gradually taken back into cultivation along many stretches, so it is no longer possible to walk for any great distance. In some places it has disappeared completely without trace, whilst other parts are thickly swathed in brambles and quite impassable. Bridges have also been removed at a number of sites, whilst some years ago the Hawkhurst bay at Paddock Wood finally made way for a commuter car park. Up until the mid-eighties a fairly long section of the branch survived, running parallel with the main line until the point of divergence. From an accelerating Kent Coast train bound for Folkestone, it was possible to watch this last piece of the railway run alongside the boundary of alders and just detect the track begin to camber southwards, at which point a set of buffers abruptly marked the end of the road. Instinctively, however, the eye carried on, along a field boundary fence which led up to Queen Street bridge in the distance. With extensive remodelling in recent years, the old siding has been removed, but, at the time of writing, the buffers and just a few feet of track curiously remain.

The same autumnal moon rises in the eastern sky and beams down upon the empty, quiet meadows and scattered patches of woodland which are all that remain of long-lost Andredswold. Rust-coloured ore still taints the springs which gush forth from the fertile earth, but the land where nobody dwelt has seen many changes since the days of the swineherds and the iron forges. The westerly wind which sweeps up the valley of the Teise no longer carries the sound of the last train frantically hurrying back to Paddock Wood, the echoing beat of its exhaust and accompanying rail-ringing wheels slowly fading into the distance. The languid late summer days bring no more the wind-blown songs of hop-pickers, drifting up in the shimmering heat-haze to where long grasses rustle on the hilltops. The hopfields now stand silent and ghostly in the wan light of the September moon, whilst in the adjoining fields the darkness is almost complete, nevermore dispelled by the comforting flicker of camp fires which sent up bright red sparks into the cool indigo night. Lanes which weave between the 'dens' and the 'hursts' no longer witness the nervous laughter, nor the ribald choruses of tipsy Londoners, stumbling along in the dead of night. The village stations with their rows of glinting oil lanterns which welcomed the weary homeward traveller have vanished. Gone, too, are the moments of quiet contemplation when, from daisy-strewn banks, the local train came regularly clattering by, its trail of billowing white steam slowly dissipating through the greenery. The gravelled approach roads resound no more to the horse and carts, the delivery vans, nor the cheerful whistling of the men who went happily about their work. Alas, these days are gone forever.

It is very easy to become sentimental about railways, branch lines in particular, since they rather sum up a way of life which seems so gentle and appealing. Maybe we are guilty of being too retrospective, but there was a quality of life which sadly has been irretrievably lost. The Hawkhurst branch was simply one of those delightful undertakings which came about through the desire of the local inhabitants to better themselves and advance their corner of England. Happily, the railway rarely failed them and, through the dedication of its staff, provided a highly-valuable and indispensable service to the rural community. Neither did its purpose necessarily evaporate with closure in 1961. Instead, politicians and those in faraway offices who'd probably never even heard of the Weald, thought they'd found better forms of transport and ways of organizing our lives.

As generations grow older there will come a time when there are no living souls left who can remember the Hawkhurst branch, and that, to me, seems rather a pity. Already it is slipping into the realms of distant memory, its remains disappearing more and more into the landscape. Who, on board luxurious, air-conditioned *Eurostar*, gliding swiftly through Paddock Wood on their way to the continent, could ever know of this old line into the High Weald? Yet, what a characterful railway once ran towards those distant tree-topped hills.

David Lawrence

SOUTHERN RAILWAY - LOCOMOTIVE WORKINGS
2nd December 1946 and Until Further Notice

TONBRIDGE SHED - Weekdays

Arr	*From/To*	*Dep*	*Class*
Duty 312 - 'R1' Class			
	Tonbridge	6.55 a.m.	Passr
7.08 a.m.	Paddock Wood	7.35 a.m.	Passr
8.10 a.m.	Hawkhurst	8.20 a.m.	Passr
8.50 a.m.	Paddock Wood	9.07 a.m.	Passr
9.37 a.m.	Hawkhurst	9.43 a.m.	Passr
10.13 a.m.	Paddock Wood		
	Paddock Wood	10.20 a.m. (SO)	Lt Eng
10.30 a.m. (SO)	Tonbridge	1.35 p.m. (SO)	Lt Eng
1.45 p.m. (SO)	Paddock Wood	2.32 p.m. (SO	Passr
3.02 p.m. (SO)	Hawkhurst	3.12 p.m. (SO)	Passr
3.42 p.m. (SO)	Paddock Wood		
	Paddock Wood	12.30 p.m. (SX)	Passr
1.0 p.m. (SX)	Hawkhurst	1.10 p.m. (SX)	Passr
1.40 p.m. (SX)	Paddock Wood		
	Paddock Wood	4.22 p.m.	Passr
4.52 p.m.	Hawkhurst	5.05 p.m.	Passr
5.35 p.m.	Paddock Wood	5.53 p.m.	Passr
6.23 p.m.	Hawkhurst	6.28 p.m.	Passr
6.58 p.m.	Paddock Wood	7.28 p.m.	Passr
7.58 p.m.	Hawkhurst	8.07 p.m.	Passr
8.48 p.m.	Tonbridge		
Duty 323 - 'C' Class			
	Tonbridge	10.50 a.m. (SX)	Lt Eng
11.0 a.m. (SX)	Paddock Wood	11.45 a.m. (SX)	Freight
3.30 p.m. (SX)	Hawkhurst	5.50 p.m. (SX)	Freight
8.25 p.m. (SX)	Paddock Wood	8.50 p.m. (SX)	Lt Eng
9.00 p.m. (SX)	Tonbridge		
Duty 327 - 'O1' Class			
	Tonbridge	4.30 a.m.	Lt Eng
4.44 a.m.	Paddock Wood	5.30 a.m.	Freight
7.06 a.m.	Hawkhurst	7.40 a.m.	Passr
8.10 a.m.	Paddock Wood		
	Paddock Wood	5.0 p.m. (SX)	Lt Eng
5.10 p.m. (SX)	Tonbridge		
	Paddock Wood	12.30 p.m. (SO)	Passr
1.0 p.m. (SO)	Hawkhurst	1.10 p.m. (SO)	Passr
1.40 p.m. (SO)	Paddock Wood	As Req'd (SO)	Lt Eng
As Req'd (SO)	Hawkhurst	5.50 p.m. (SO)	Freight
8.25 p.m. (SO)	Paddock Wood	8.50 p.m. (SO)	Lt Eng
9.0 p.m. (SO)	Tonbridge		

NOTE Workings are daily, except where specified SX (Saturdays Excepted) or SO (Saturdays Only)

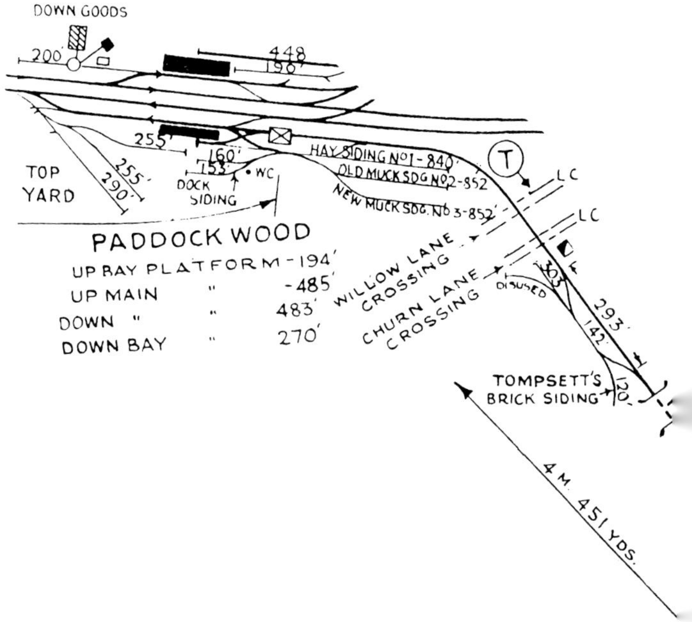

GRADIENT PROFILE

Southern Railway gradient profile including locations of bridges, tunnels and level crossings. Radius curves along route marked in chain lengths.

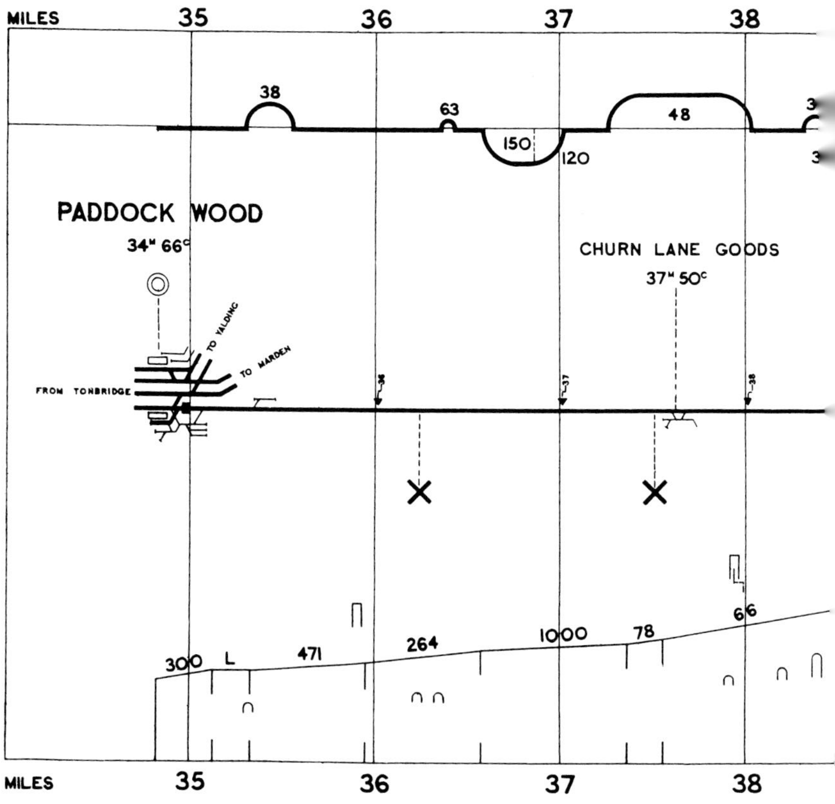

DISTANCE DIAGRAM

Southern Railway diagram of distances between signal boxes. Exact lengths of sidings measured in feet.

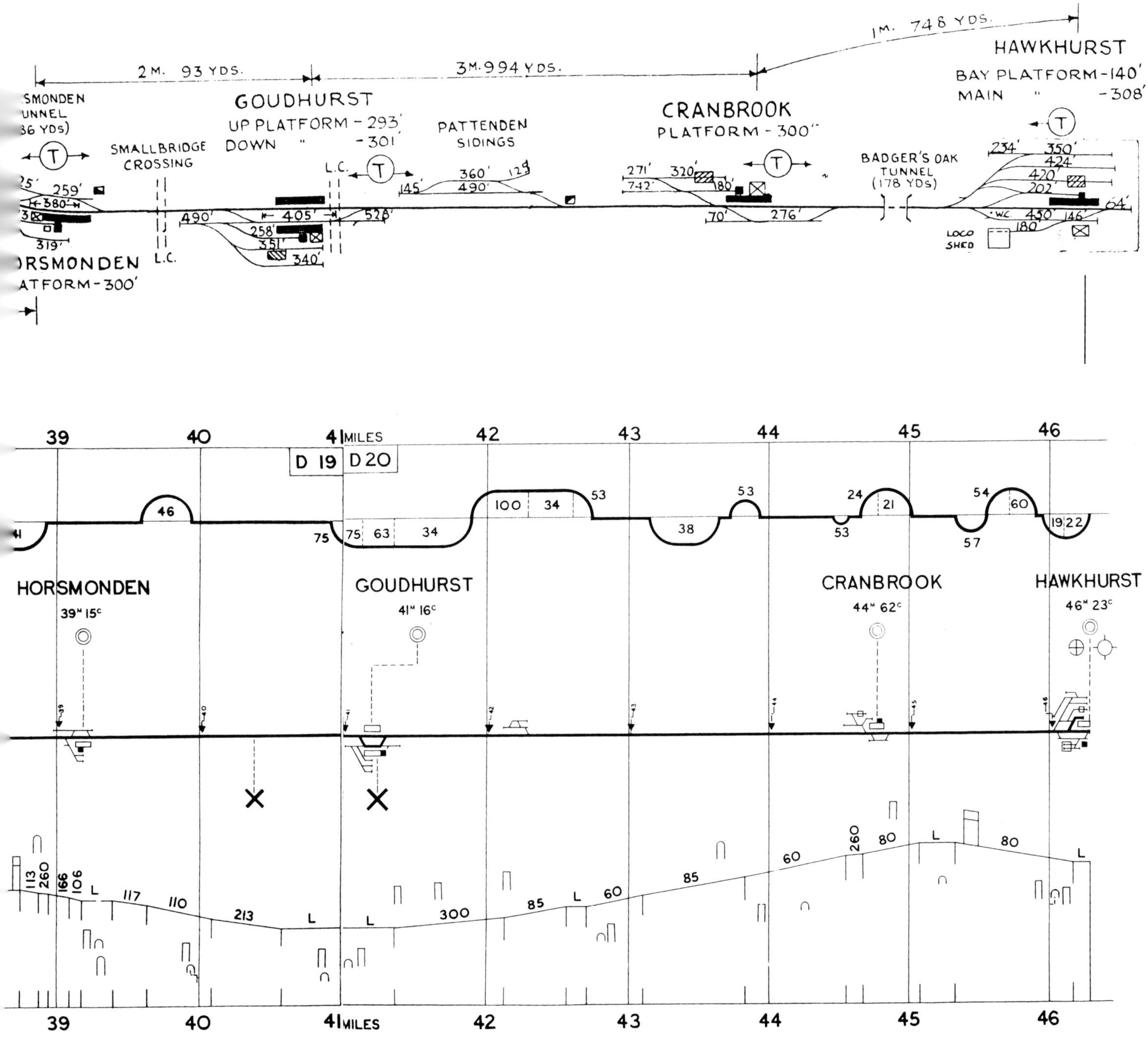

PADDOCK WOOD & CRANBROOK RAILWAY
HORSMONDEN STATION

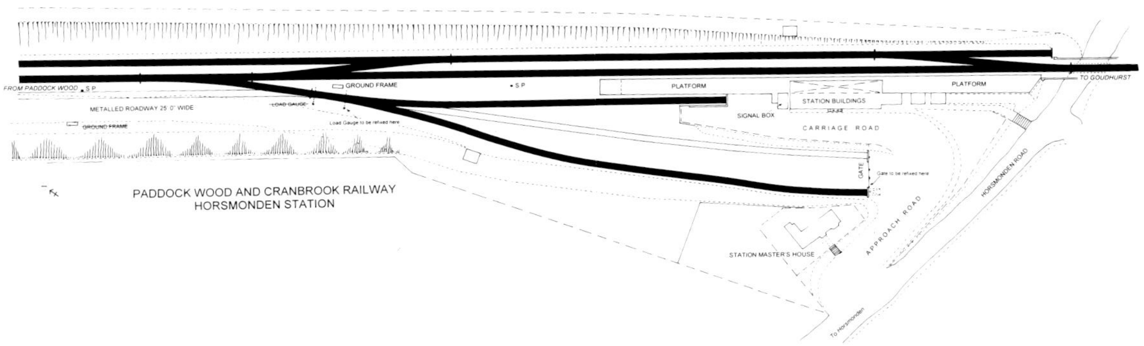
FROM PADDOCK WOOD
S P
GROUND FRAME
PLATFORM
STATION BUILDINGS
PLATFORM
TO GOUDHURST
METALLED ROADWAY 25' 0" WIDE
LOAD GAUGE
SIGNAL BOX
GROUND FRAME
Load Gauge to be refixed here
CARRIAGE ROAD
GATE
Gate to be refixed here
HORSMONDEN ROAD
APPROACH ROAD
STATION MASTER'S HOUSE
To Horsmonden
PADDOCK WOOD AND CRANBROOK RAILWAY
HORSMONDEN STATION

S. E. & C. R.
GOUDHURST STATION

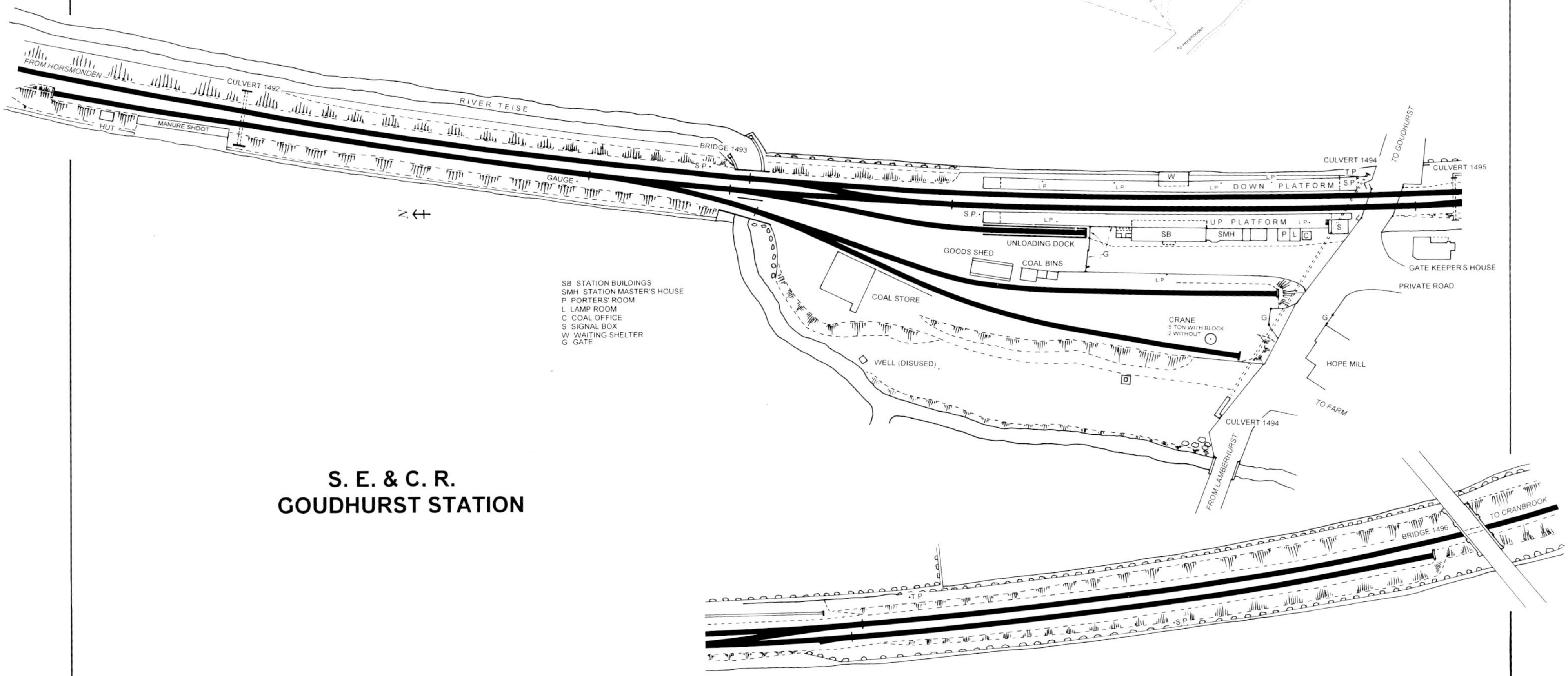
FROM HORSMONDEN
CULVERT 1492
RIVER TEISE
HUT
MANURE SHOOT
GAUGE
BRIDGE 1493
S P
N
CULVERT 1494
TO GOUDHURST
CULVERT 1495
T P
DOWN PLATFORM
W
LP
UP PLATFORM
SB
SMH
P
L
C
S
UNLOADING DOCK
GOODS SHED
COAL BINS
G
COAL STORE
CRANE
5 TON WITH BLOCK
2 WITHOUT
GATE KEEPER'S HOUSE
PRIVATE ROAD
HOPE MILL
TO FARM
WELL (DISUSED)
CULVERT 1494
FROM LAMBERHURST
SB STATION BUILDINGS
SMH STATION MASTER'S HOUSE
P PORTERS' ROOM
L LAMP ROOM
C COAL OFFICE
S SIGNAL BOX
W WAITING SHELTER
G GATE
BRIDGE 1496
TO CRANBROOK

S. R. GOUDHURST PATTENDEN SIDINGS

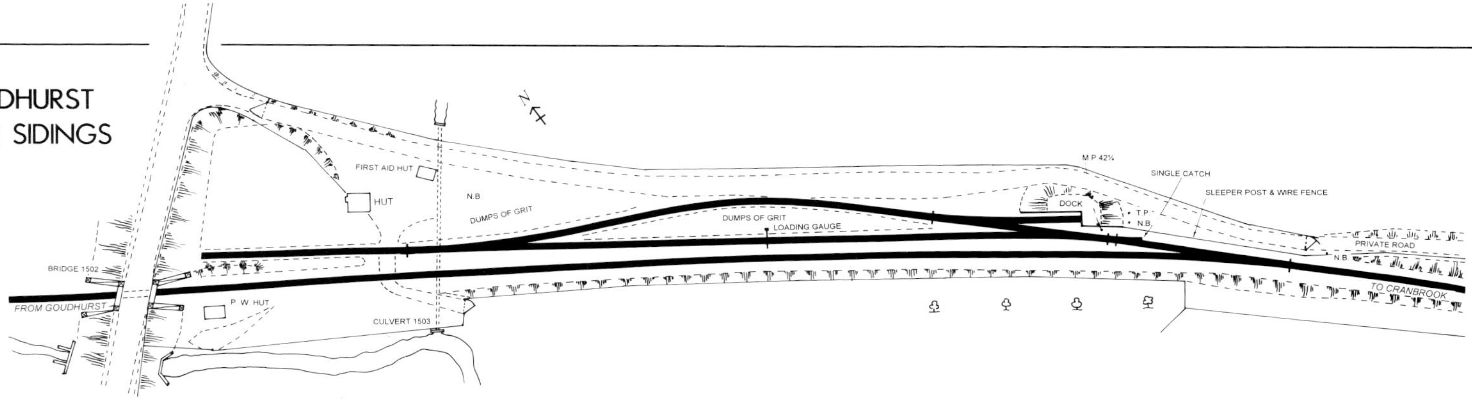

PADDOCK WOOD & CRANBROOK RAILWAY CRANBROOK STATION

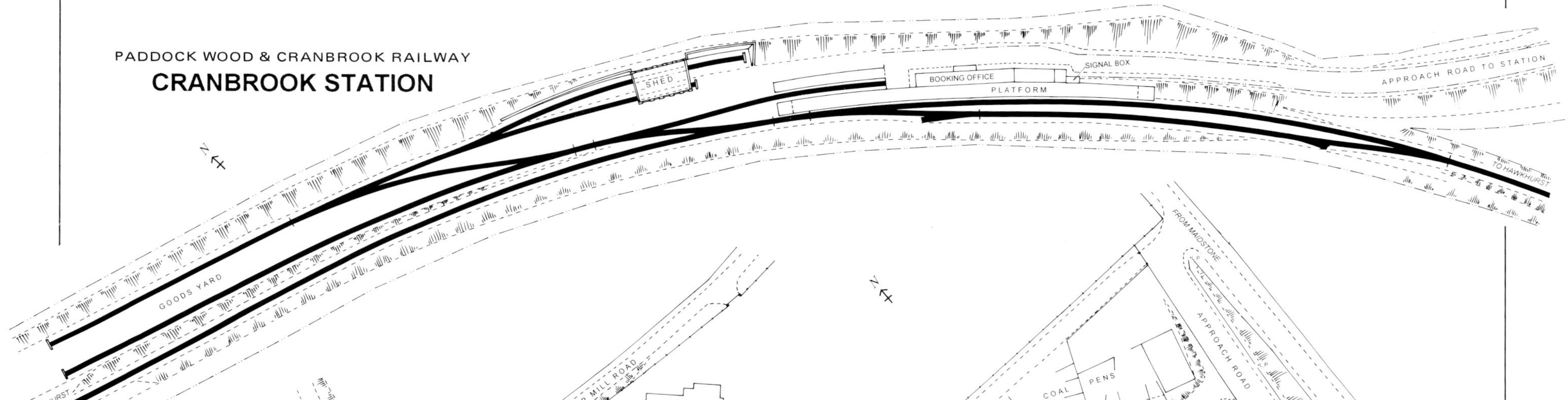

S. E. & C. R. HAWKHURST STATION

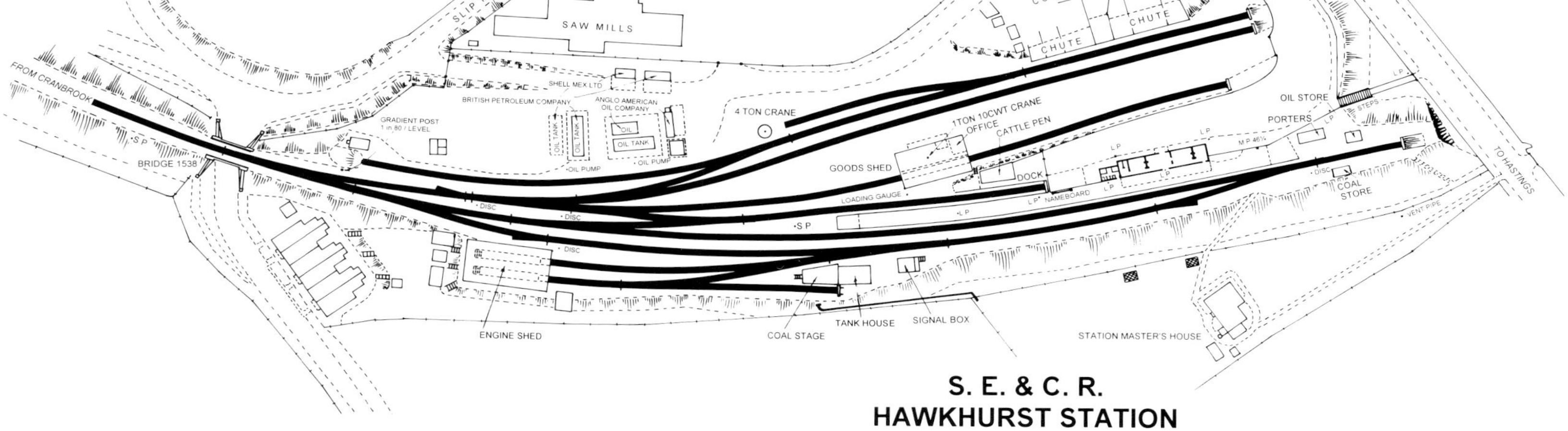

S. E. & C. R.

Paddock Wood & Hawkhurst Branch

CHURN LANE SIDING

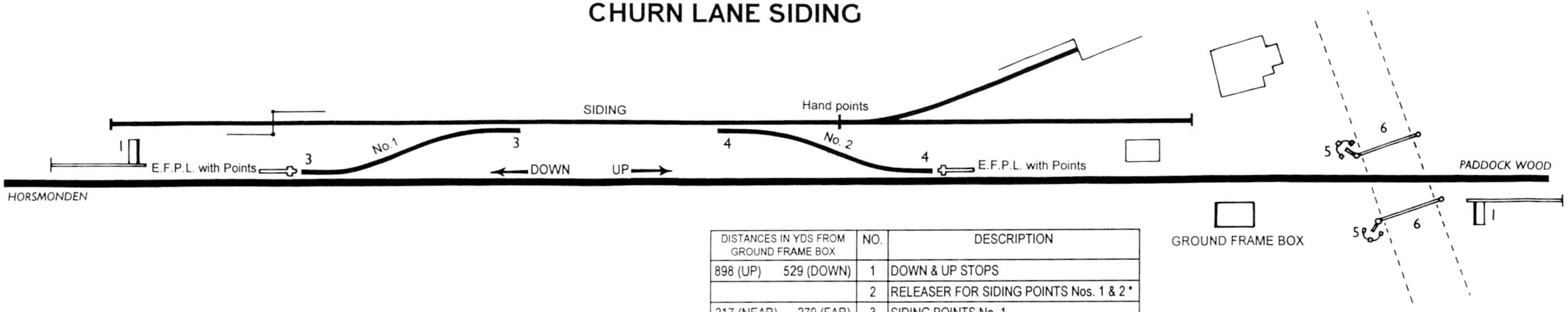

DISTANCES IN YDS FROM GROUND FRAME BOX	NO.	DESCRIPTION
898 (UP) 529 (DOWN)	1	DOWN & UP STOPS
	2	RELEASER FOR SIDING POINTS Nos. 1 & 2 *
217 (NEAR) 279 (FAR)	3	SIDING POINTS No. 1
100 (NEAR) 170 (FAR)	4	SIDING POINTS No. 2
30	5	WICKETS
30	6	GATE LOCKS

* (CONTROLLED BY TABLET)

BRITISH RAILWAYS - SOUTHERN REGION

HORSMONDEN

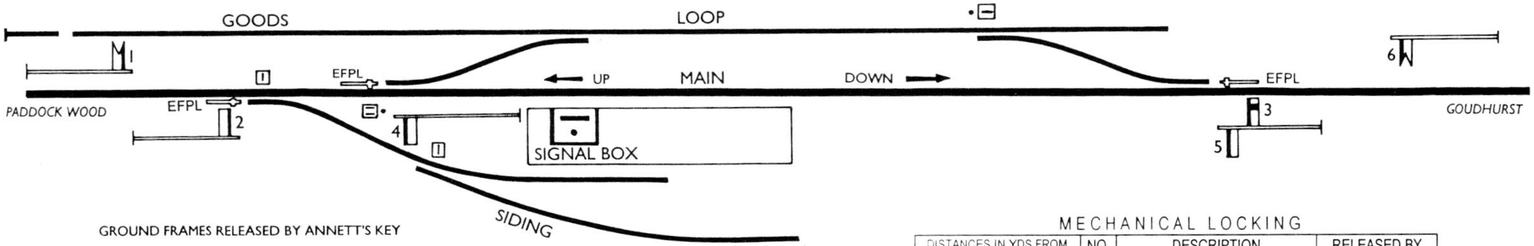

GROUND FRAMES RELEASED BY ANNETT'S KEY

MECHANICAL LOCKING

DISTANCES IN YDS FROM SIGNAL BOX	NO.	DESCRIPTION	RELEASED BY
1,035	1	DOWN DISTANT	2. 3.
161	2	DOWN HOME	
96	3	DOWN STARTING	
63	4	UP STARTING	
96	5	UP HOME	
900	6	UP DISTANT	4. 5.

BRITISH RAILWAYS - SOUTHERN REGION

GOUDHURST

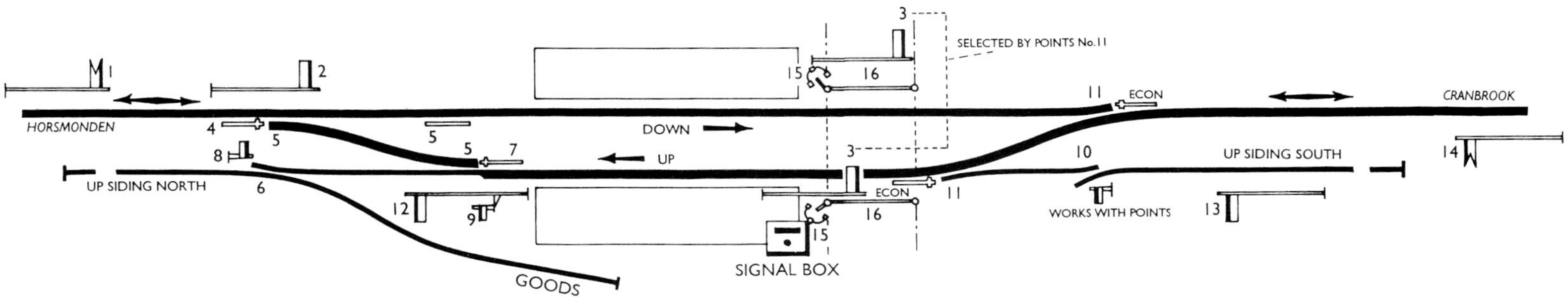

MECHANICAL LOCKING

DISTANCES IN YDS FROM SIGNAL BOX	NO.	DESCRIPTION	RELEASED BY	WORK	LOCKING
1,007	1	DOWN DISTANT	2. 3. 11.	1	
188	2	DOWN HOME	4	2	5. 16.
5. 5	3	FROM DOWN OR UP PLATFORMS DOWN STARTING		3	13. 16. (11 [11]) (9. 12. w 11)
176	4	F. P. L. ON 5 NORTH		4	12. (5 [5])
116. 176.	5	UP LINE POINTS		5	2. 6.
179	6	UP SIDING NORTH POINTS		6	5
116	7	F. P. L. ON 5 SOUTH		7	8. (5. [5])
180	8	FROM UP SIDING NORTH GROUND SIGNAL	6 (10 w [11])	8	7. 16. (11. [11])
105	9	FROM UP LINE GROUND SIGNAL	6. 7.	9	(10 [10]) (11 [11]) (3 w. 11)
76	10	UP SIDING SOUTH POINTS	11	10	
19. 80	11	DOWN LINE POINTS		11	13. 16
105	12	UP STARTING	5. 7.	12	4. (10 [10]) (11 [11]) (3 w. 11)
175	13	UP HOME	7	13	3. 11. 16.
944	14	UP DISTANT	12. 13.	14	
7	15	WICKETS		15	
8(up) 19 (down)	16	GATE LOCK		16	2. 3. 8. 11. 13.

ELEVATED FRAME
TYER'S No.6 TABLET
ARMS REPEATED. 1. 14.
LIGHTS REPEATED. NIL.
MECH. DETECTION.
BELL COMMUNICATION FROM No.2 SIGNAL TO SIGNAL BOX

Goudhurst's down starting signal with appopriate hop bine which had opportunistically made its way up the straining wire of the railway's telegraph pole. *Gordon Batchelor*

BRITISH RAILWAYS - SOUTHERN REGION

CRANBROOK

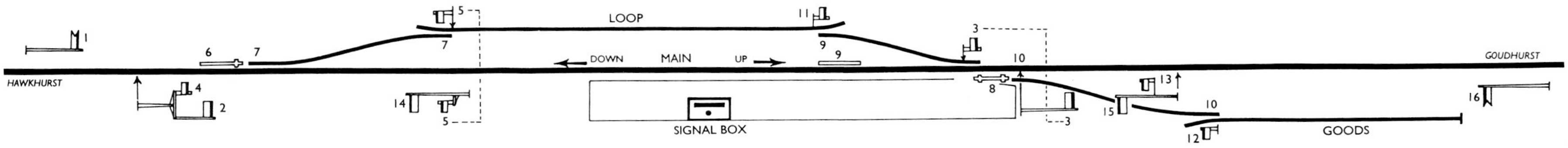

These shunt signals of SE&CR pattern were common on the Hawkhurst branch. This one, operated by lever No. 12, allowed access out of the goods siding onto the main line. *J. J. Smith*

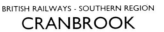

MECHANICAL LOCKING						DETECTION		
DISTANCES IN YARDS FROM CENTRE OF SIGNAL BOX	NO.	DESCRIPTION	RELEASED BY	WORK	LOCKING	WORK	DETECTION MECHANICAL	POINT BOLT 'IN'
960	1	UP DISTANT	2. 3.	1				
160	2	UP HOME	6. 8.	2	7. 9. 10. 15.	2	7	[6]
72 90	3	UP STARTING OR TO GOODS SHUNT OVER POINTS 10	8	3	12. 13. 14. 15. (5 w 7)	3	10 or [10]	[8]
160	4	FROM MAIN SHUNT OVER POINTS 7	6. 7.	4	12. 13. (9 [9])			
71 75	5	ALONG MAIN SHUNT SOUTHWARD OR FROM LOOP SHUNT OVER POINTS 7		5	6. 14. (7 [7] 9 [9]) (3 w 7) (11 w [7])	5	7 or [7]	
135	6	F. P. L. ON 7		6	5. 14. (7[7])			
77 135	7	LOOP POINTS SOUTH		7	2. 14.			
74 82	8	F. P. L.s on 9 & 10		8	(9 [9] 10 [10])			
15 74	9	LOOP POINTS NORTH		9	2. 15.			
82 144	10	GOODS POINTS		10	2. 13. 15.			
13	11	FROM LOOP SHUNT OVER POINTS 9	3. 9.	11	(7 [7]) (5 w [7])	11	[9]	
146	12	FROM GOODS SHUNT	8. 10.	12	3. 4. (7 [7] w [9])	12	[10]	
134	13	FROM MAIN SHUNT OVER POINTS 9	8. 9.	13	3. 4. 10. (7 [7])			
73	14	DOWN STARTING		14	3. 5. 6. 7. (8 [8] 9 [9] 10 [10])			
134	15	DOWN HOME	8	15	2. 3. 9. 10.	15	9	[8]
880	16	DOWN DISTANT	14. 15.	16				

ELEVATED FRAME
CLOSING SWITCH - NIL
TYER'S No.6 TABLET INSTRUMENT
ARMS REPEATED - 1. 16.
LIGHTS " - NIL
MECHANICAL DETECTION
F. P. L.s STAND OUT
BELL COMMUNICATION FROM No15 SIGNAL TO SIGNAL BOX

BRITISH RAILWAYS - SOUTHERN REGION

HAWKHURST

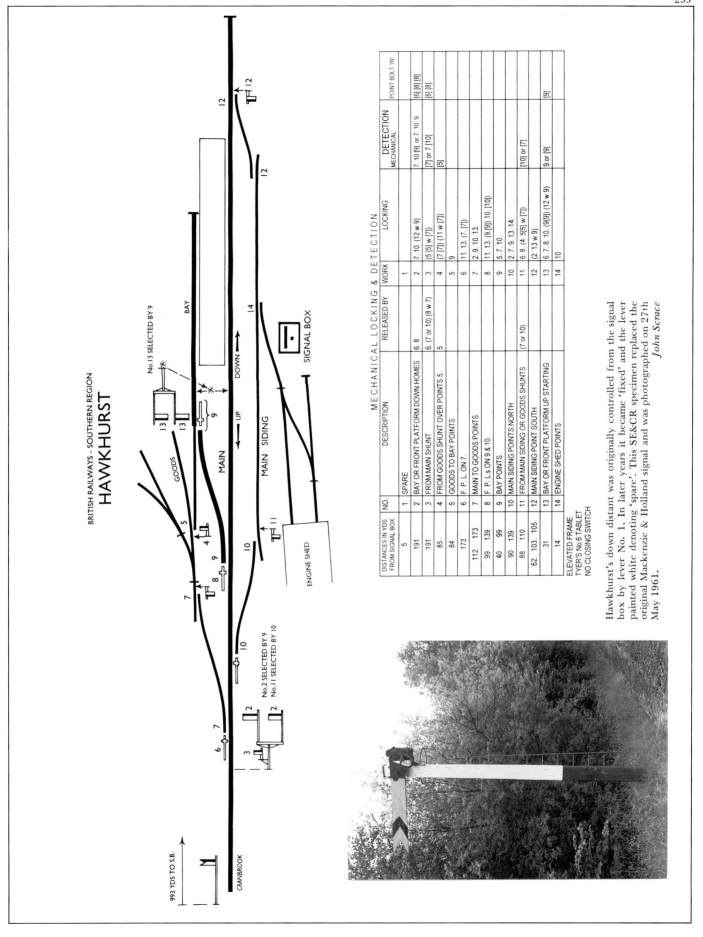

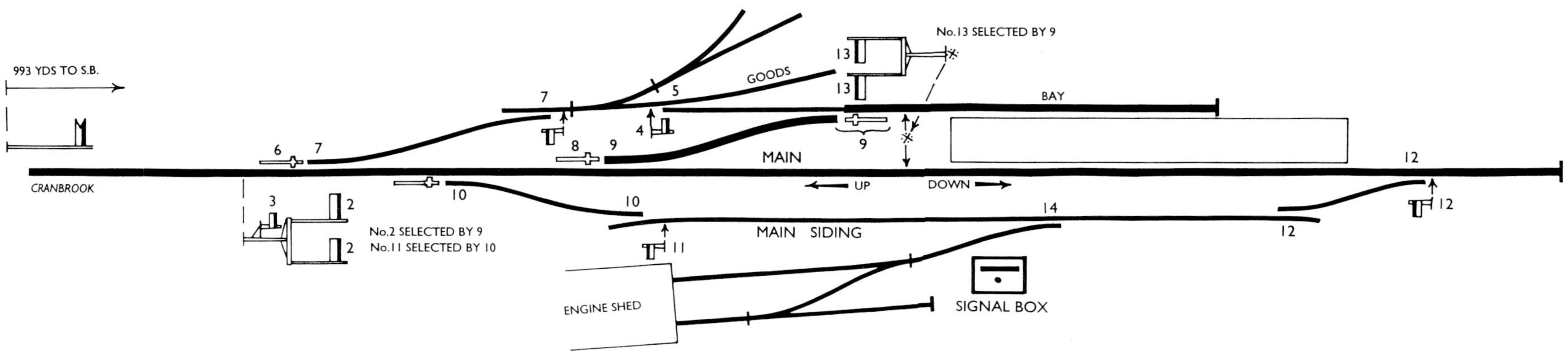

MECHANICAL LOCKING & DETECTION

DISTANCES IN YDS FROM SIGNAL BOX	NO.	DESCRIPTION	RELEASED BY	WORK	LOCKING	DETECTION MECHANICAL	POINT BOLT 'IN'
5	1	SPARE		1			
191	2	BAY OR FRONT PLATFORM DOWN HOMES	6. 8.	2	7. 10. (12 w 9)	7. 10 [9] or 7. 10. 9.	[6] [8] [8]
191	3	FROM MAIN SHUNT	6. (7 or 10) (8 w 7)	3	(5 [5] w [7])	[7] or 7 [10]	[6] [8]
85	4	FROM GOODS SHUNT OVER POINTS 5.	5	4	(7 [7]) (11 w [7])	[5]	
84	5	GOODS TO BAY POINTS		5	9		
173	6	F. P. L. ON 7.		6	11. 13. (7. [7])		
112 173	7	MAIN TO GOODS POINTS		7	2. 9. 10. 13.		
99 139	8	F. P. L.s ON 9 & 10.		8	11. 13. (9.[9]) 10. [10])		
40 99	9	BAY POINTS		9	5. 7. 10.		
90 139	10	MAIN SIDING POINTS NORTH		10	2. 7. 9. 13. 14.		
88 110	11	FROM MAIN SIDING OR GOODS SHUNTS	(7 or 10)	11	6. 8. (4. 5[5] w [7])	[10] or [7]	
62. 103. 105	12	MAIN SIDING POINT SOUTH		12	(2. 13 w 9)		
31	13	BAY OR FRONT PLATFORM UP STARTING		13	6. 7. 8. 10. (9[9]) (12 w 9)	9 or [9]	[9]
14	14	ENGINE SHED POINTS		14	10		

ELEVATED FRAME
TYER'S No.6 TABLET
NO CLOSING SWITCH

Hawkhurst's down distant was originally controlled from the signal box by lever No. 1. In later years it became 'fixed' and the lever painted white denoting 'spare'. This SE&CR specimen replaced the original Mackenzie & Holland signal and was photographed on 27th May 1961. *John Scrace*

HAWKHURST STATION BUILDING

Drawn by Ken Garrett. Scale: 3mm to 1 foot.

SOUTHWEST ELEVATION

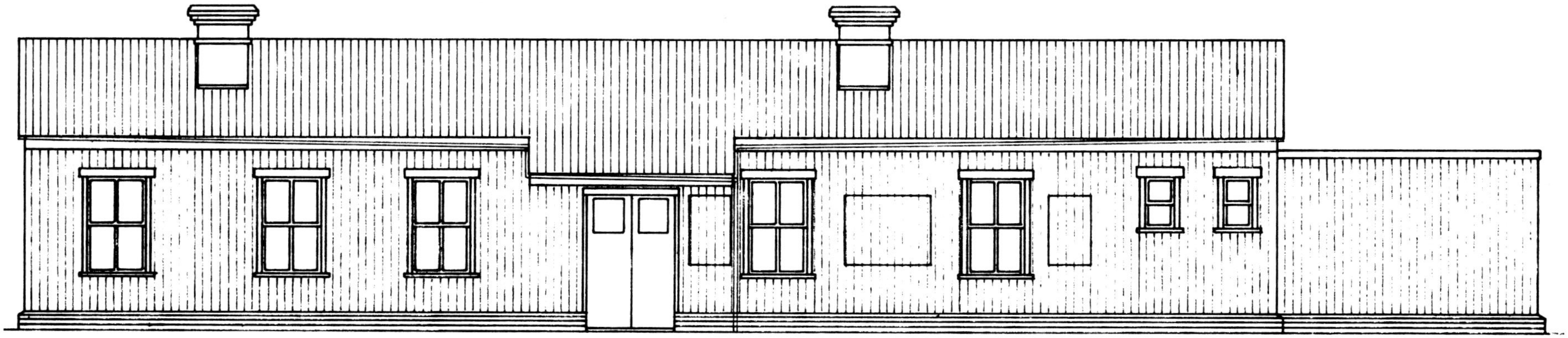

NORTHEAST ELEVATION

A 1951 view of the forecourt approach of the corrugated iron buildings provided at Hawkhurst station.
Ken Garrett

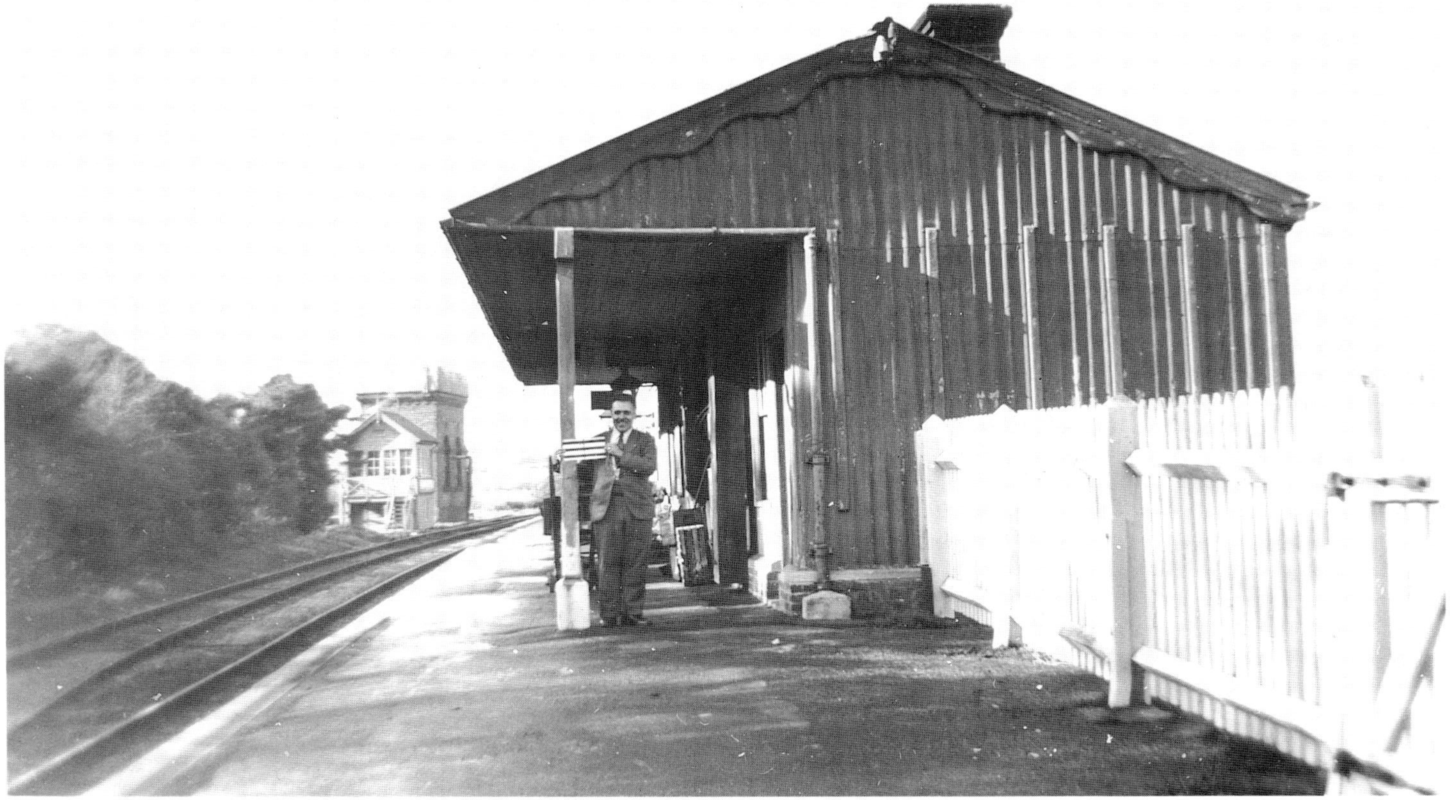

The south-east side of the station offices at Hawkhurst, with one of the photographer's colleagues holding a scaling board.
Ken Garrett

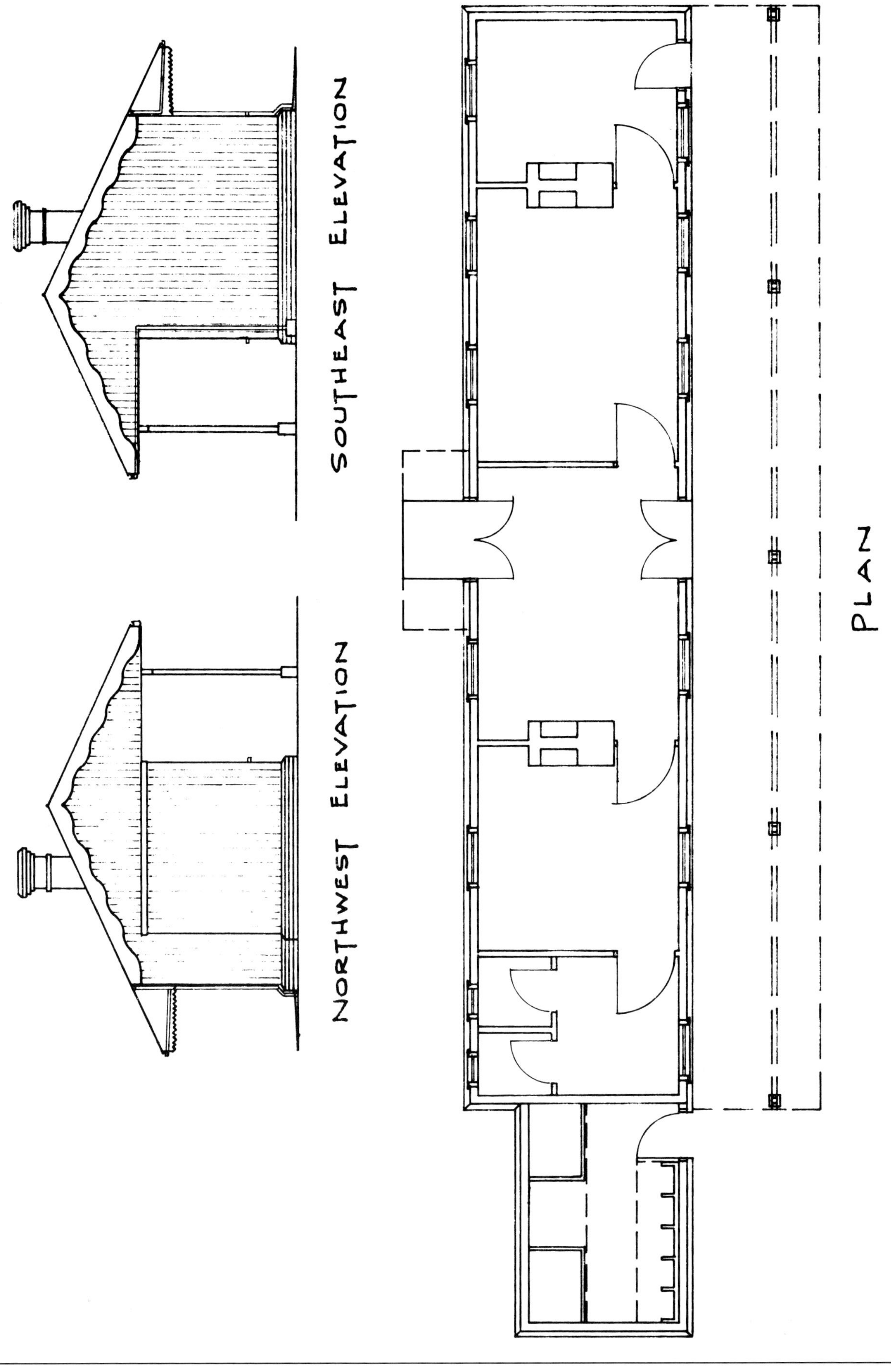

Drawn by Ken Garrett. Scale: 3mm to 1 foot.

HAWKHURST STATION

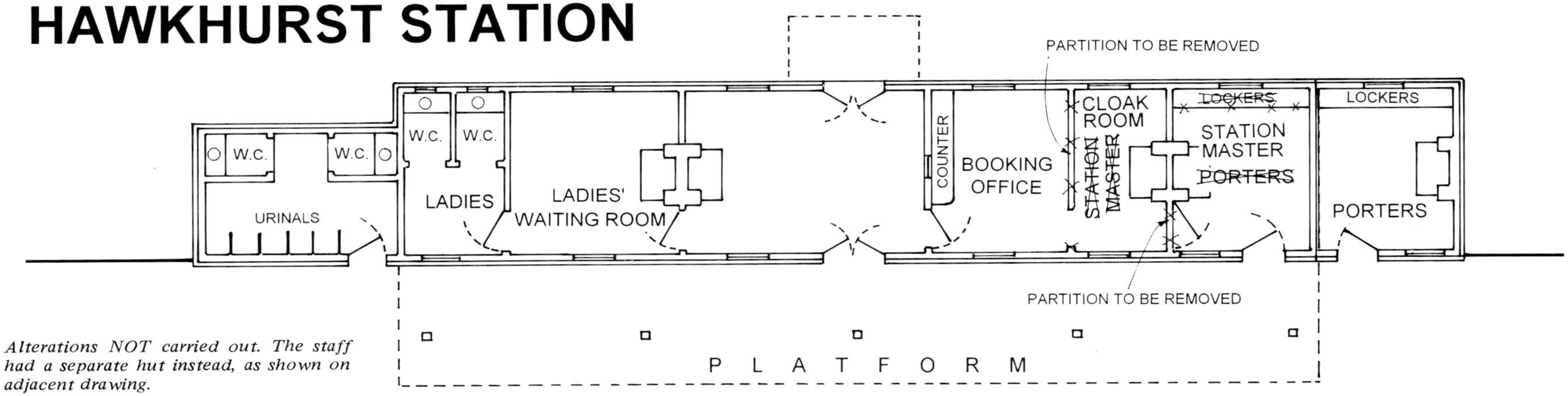

Alterations NOT carried out. The staff had a separate hut instead, as shown on adjacent drawing.

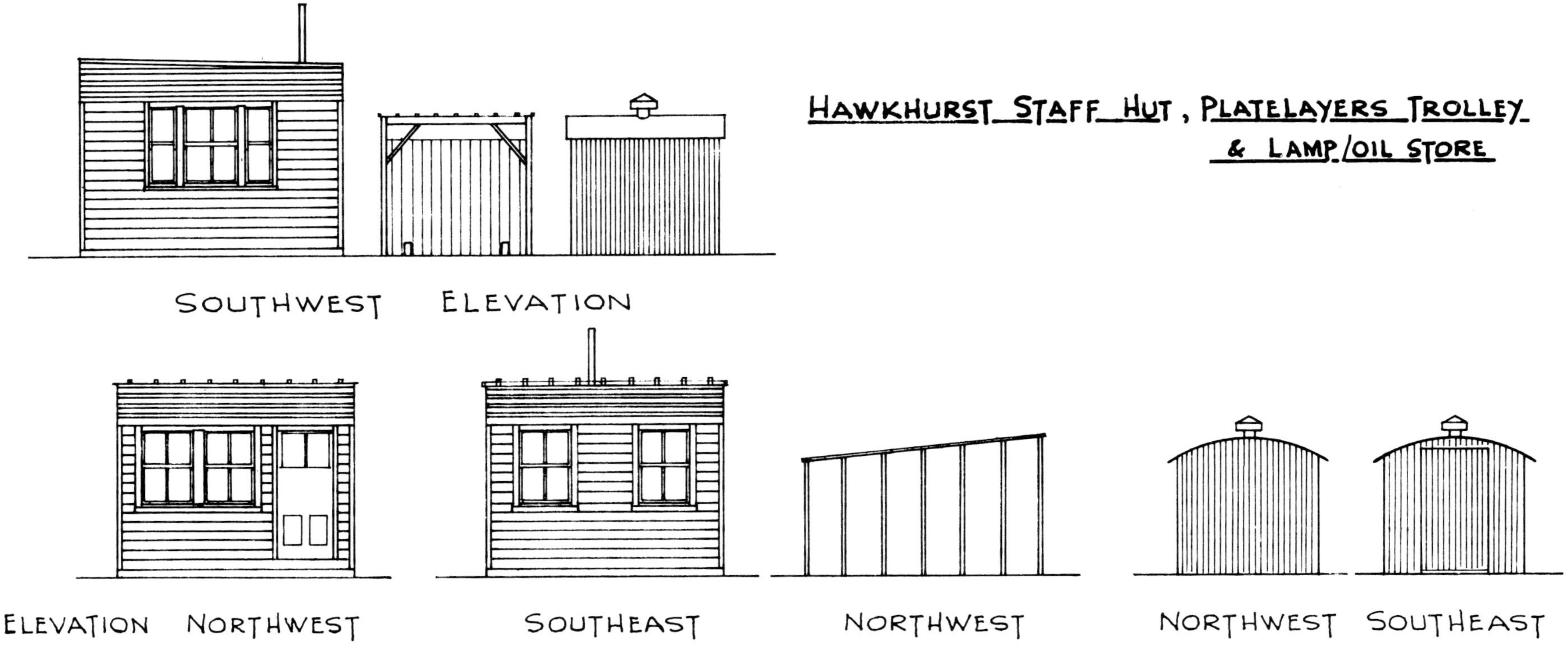

Drawn by Ken Garrett. Scale: 3mm to 1 foot.

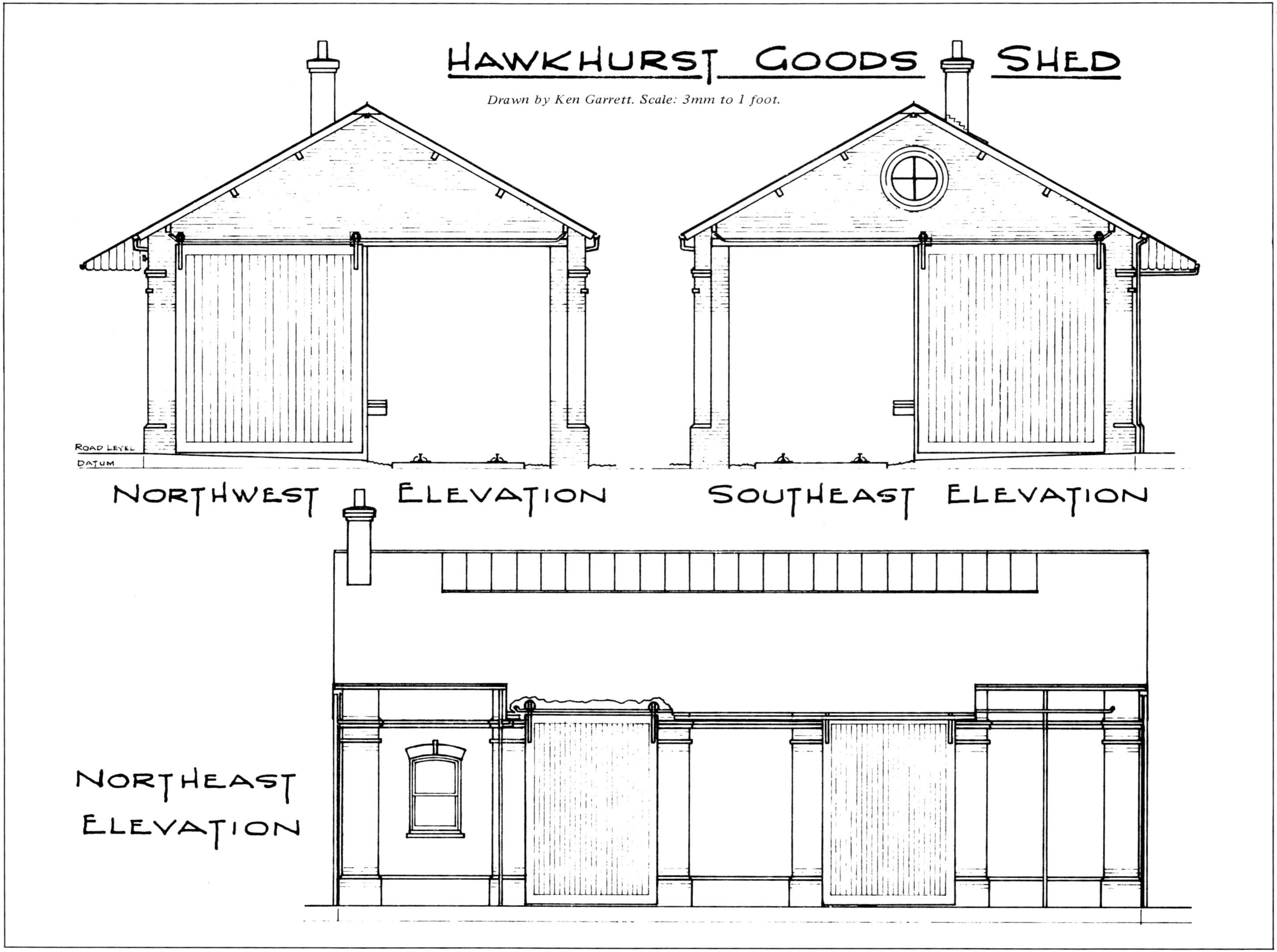
HAWKHURST GOODS SHED
Drawn by Ken Garrett. Scale: 3mm to 1 foot.
ROAD LEVEL
DATUM
NORTHWEST ELEVATION
SOUTHEAST ELEVATION
NORTHEAST
ELEVATION

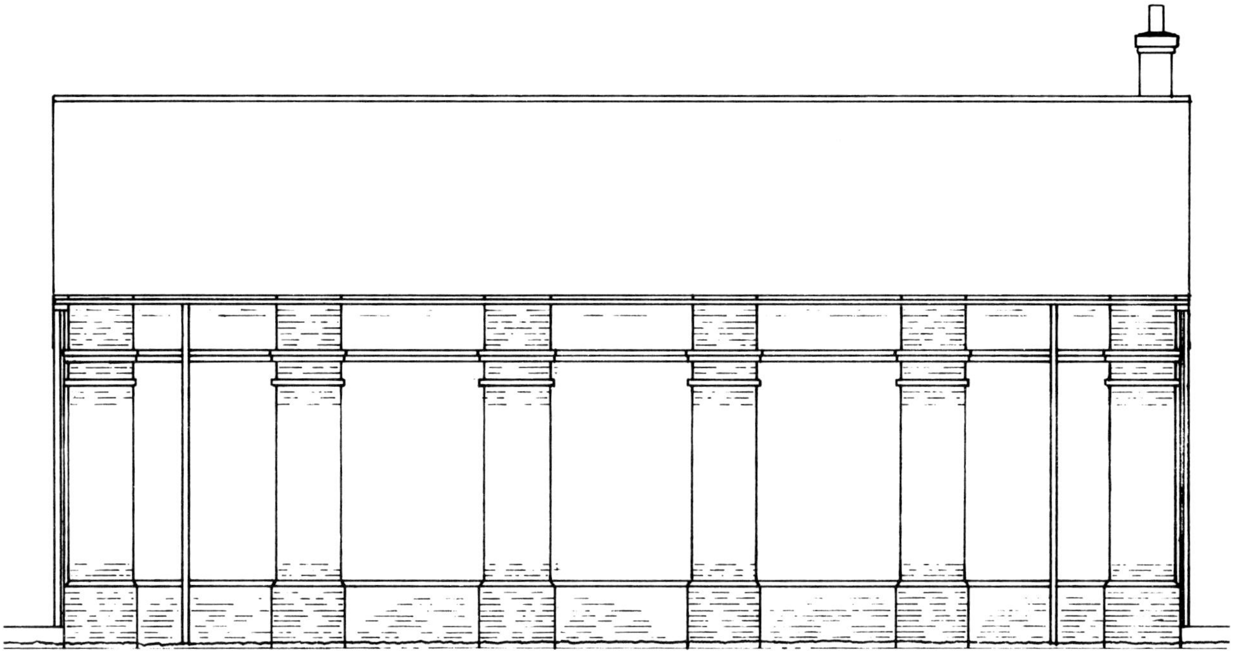

SOUTHWEST ELEVATION

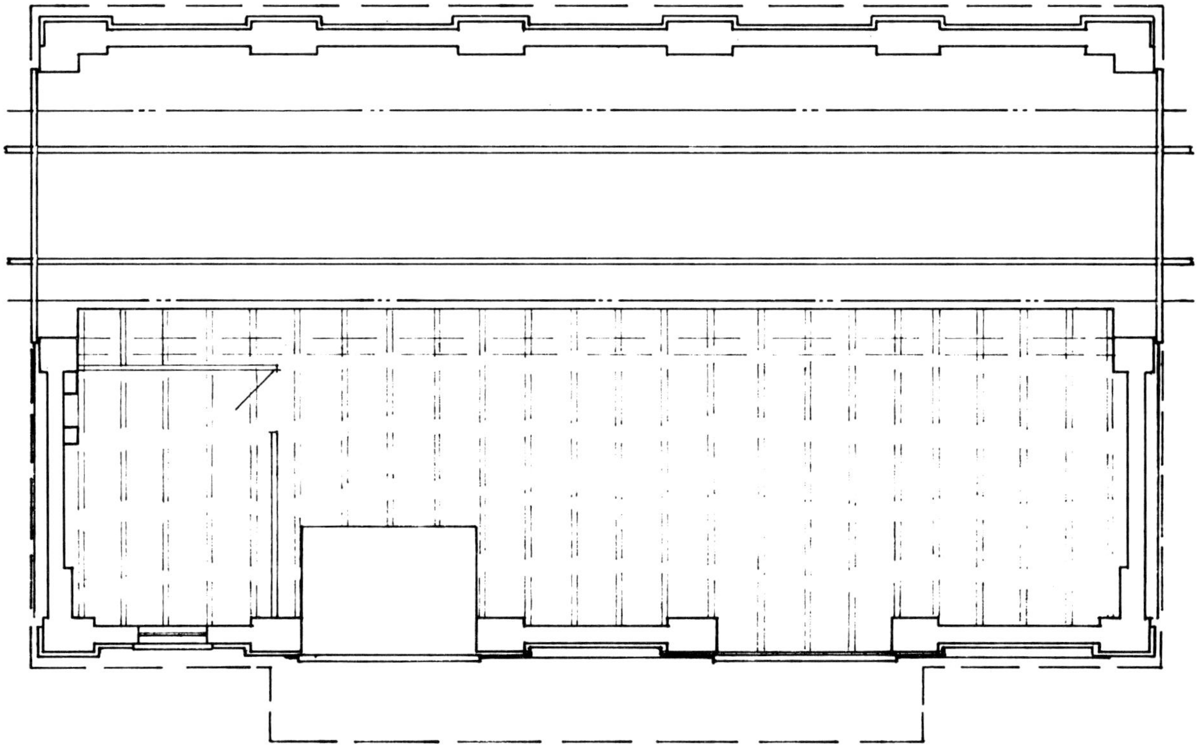

PLAN

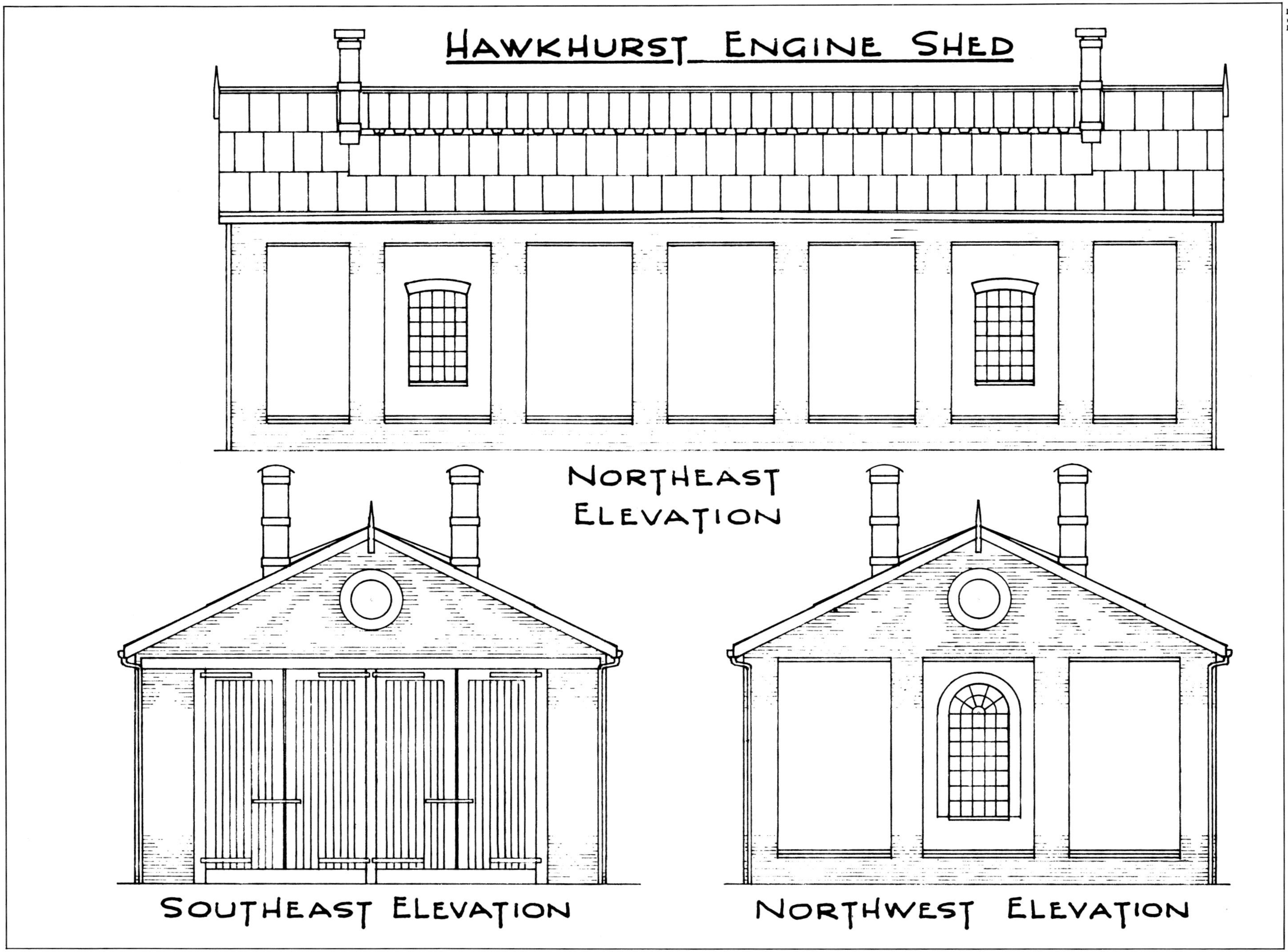

Drawn by Ken Garrett. Scale: 3mm to 1 foot.

The impressive entrance to Hawkhurst's two-road engine shed.
Ken Garrett

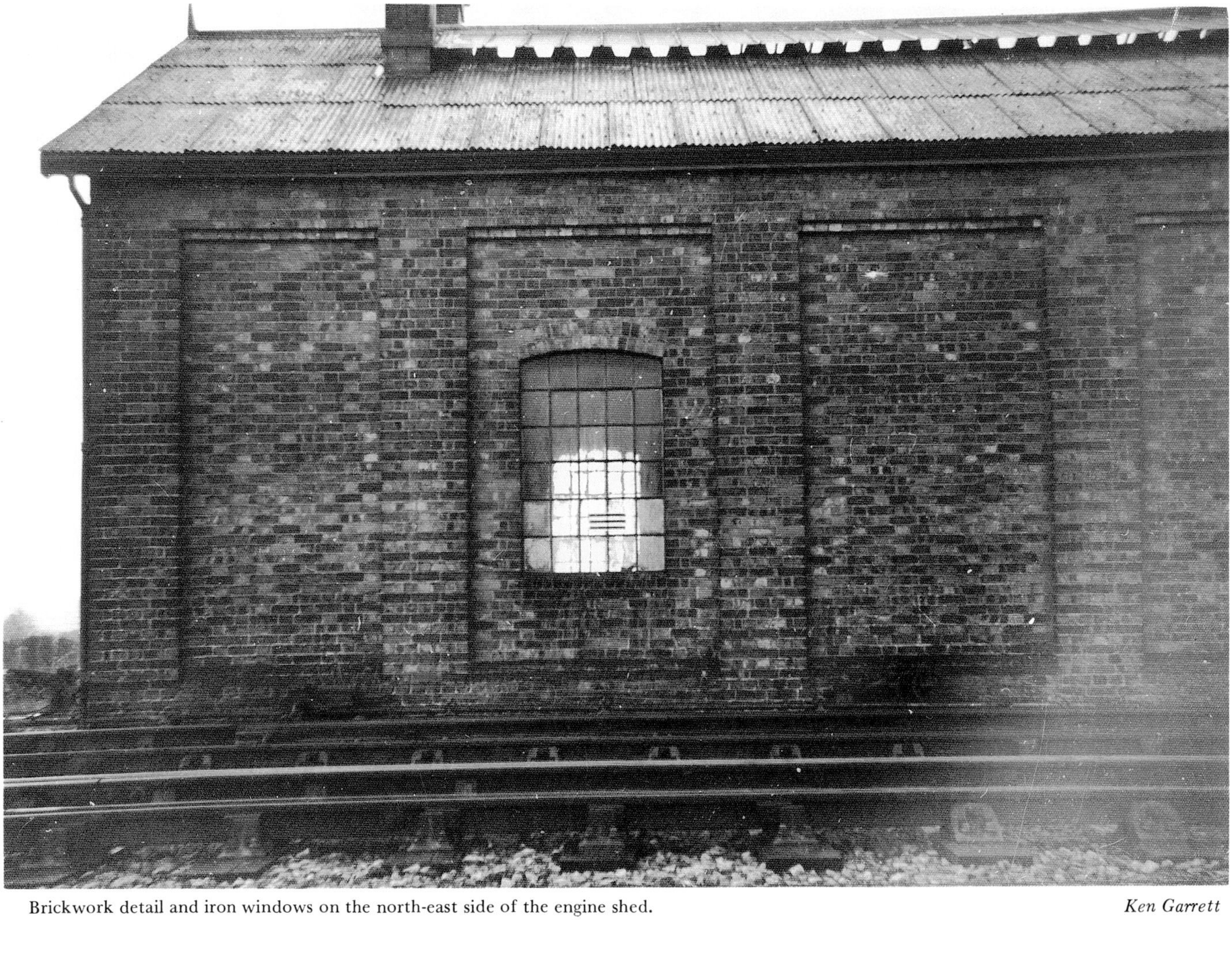

Brickwork detail and iron windows on the north-east side of the engine shed. *Ken Garrett*

Hawkhurst Water Tower

SOUTHEAST ELEVATION

NORTHEAST ELEVATION

NORTHWEST ELEVATION

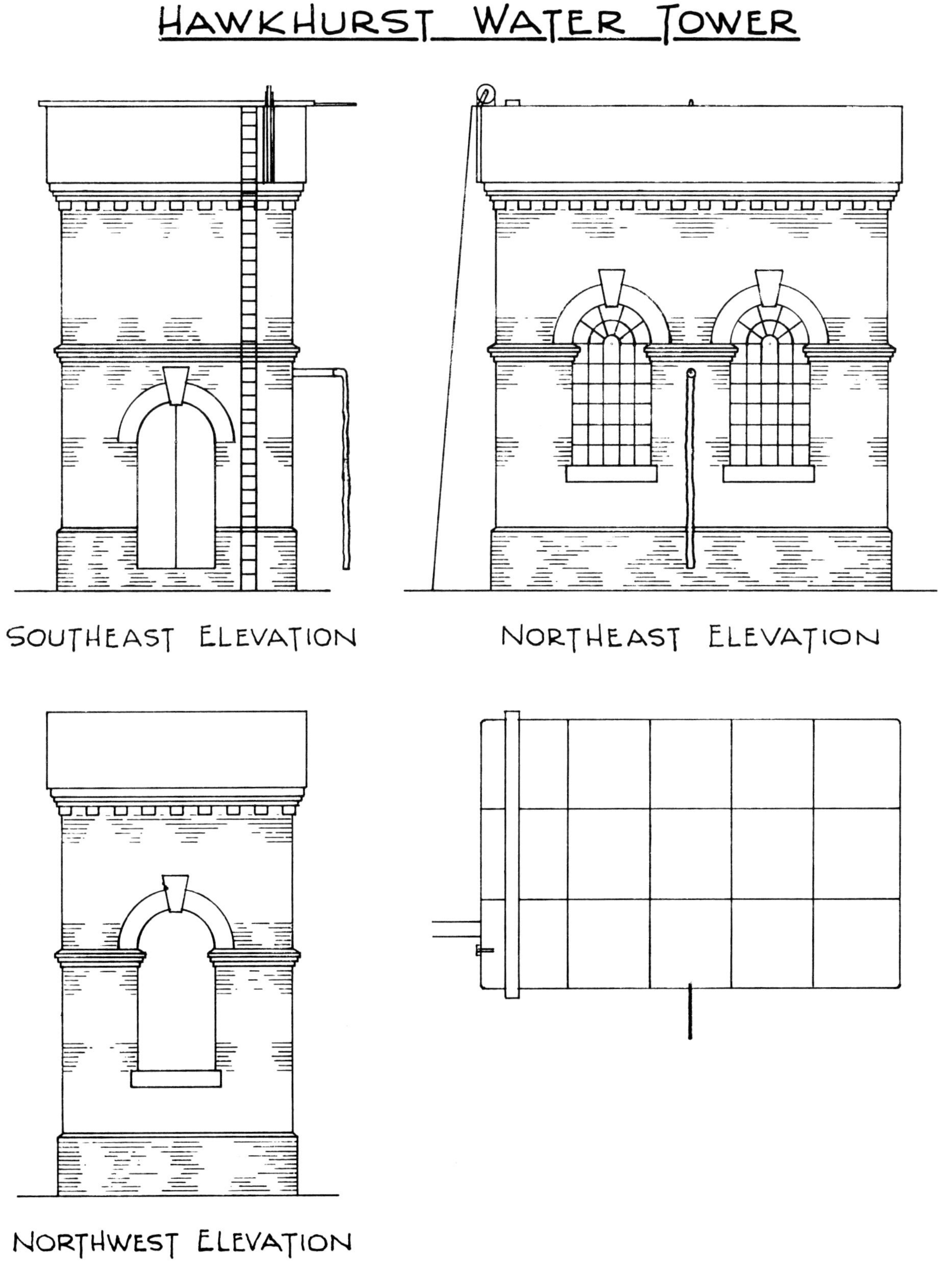

Drawn by Ken Garrett. Scale: 3mm to 1 foot.

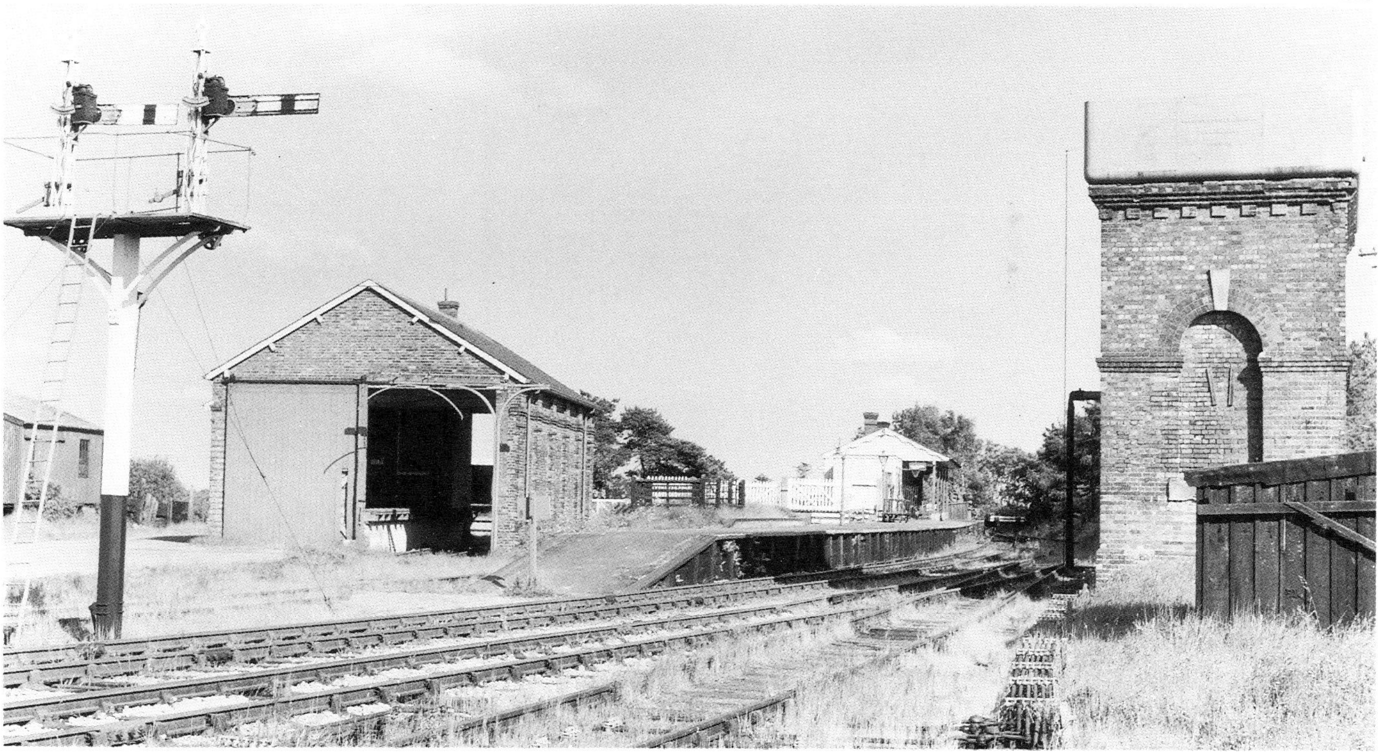

The north-west end of the water tower showing bricked-up window openings on 22nd May 1961.
J. J. Smith

The north-east side of Hawkhurst's water tower illustrating well the brickwork and type of construction. *Ken Garrett*

HAWKHURST SIGNAL BOX

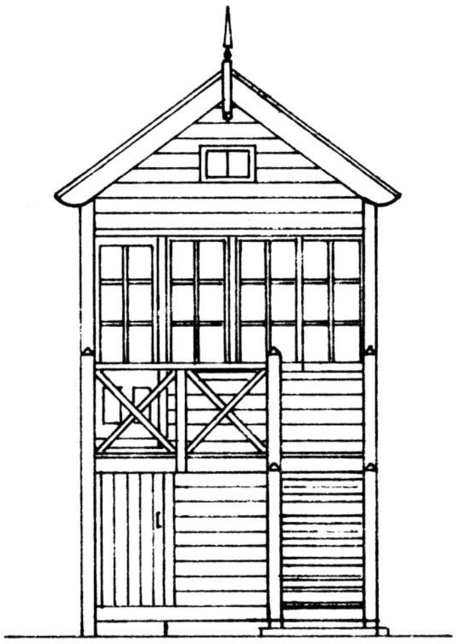

SOUTHEAST ELEVATION

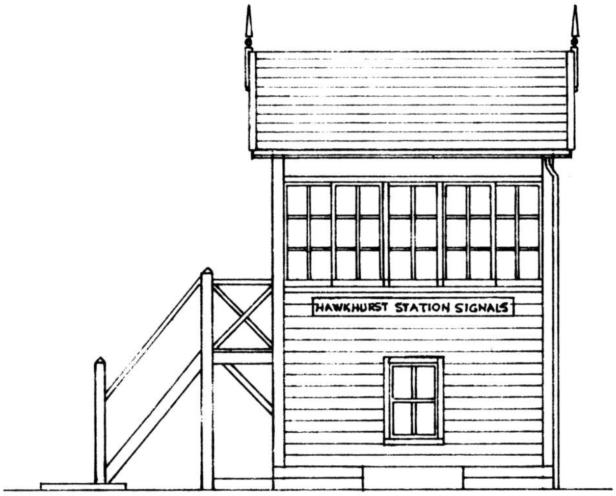

NORTHEAST ELEVATION

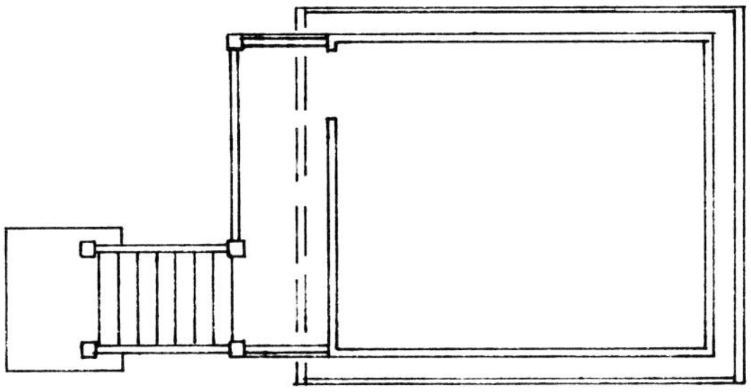

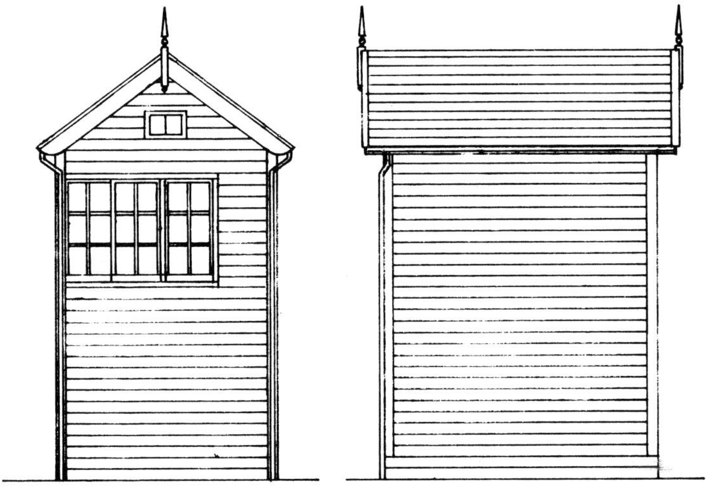

NORTHWEST ELEVATION

Drawn by Ken Garrett. Scale: 3mm to 1 foot.

Detail of the timber signal box, its steps and staging. The turned finials, typically Victorian, were an attractive feature and complete the overall symmetry.
Ken Garrett

This view of the front, or north-easterly side, shows the sliding wooden windows as well as other constructional details. Note the point rodding at the base. The Southern Railway enamel 'running-in', or platform sign was really much too large for the box and the original SER sign 'Hawkhurst Station Signals' on page 77 was aesthetically preferable. *Ken Garrett*

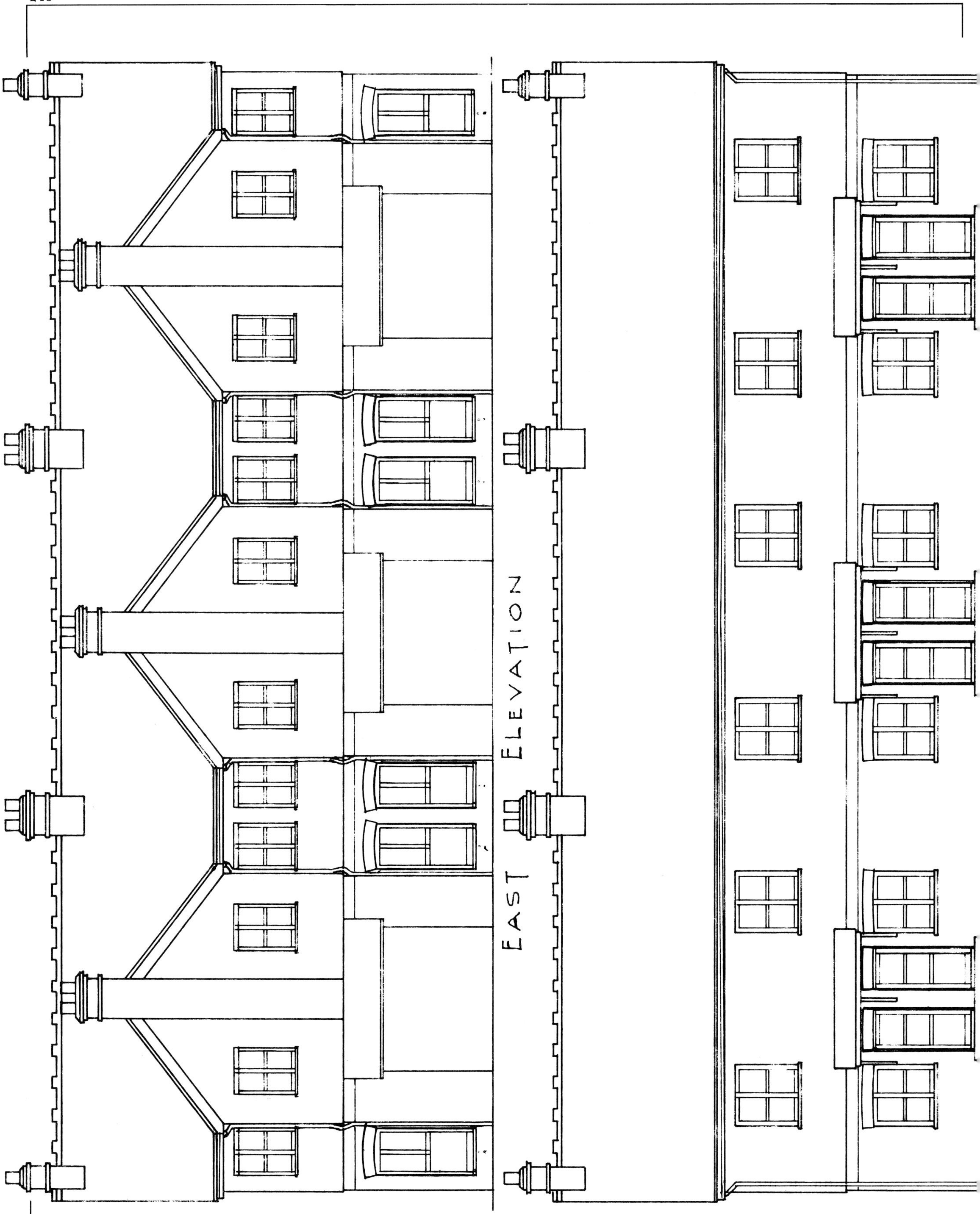
EAST ELEVATION

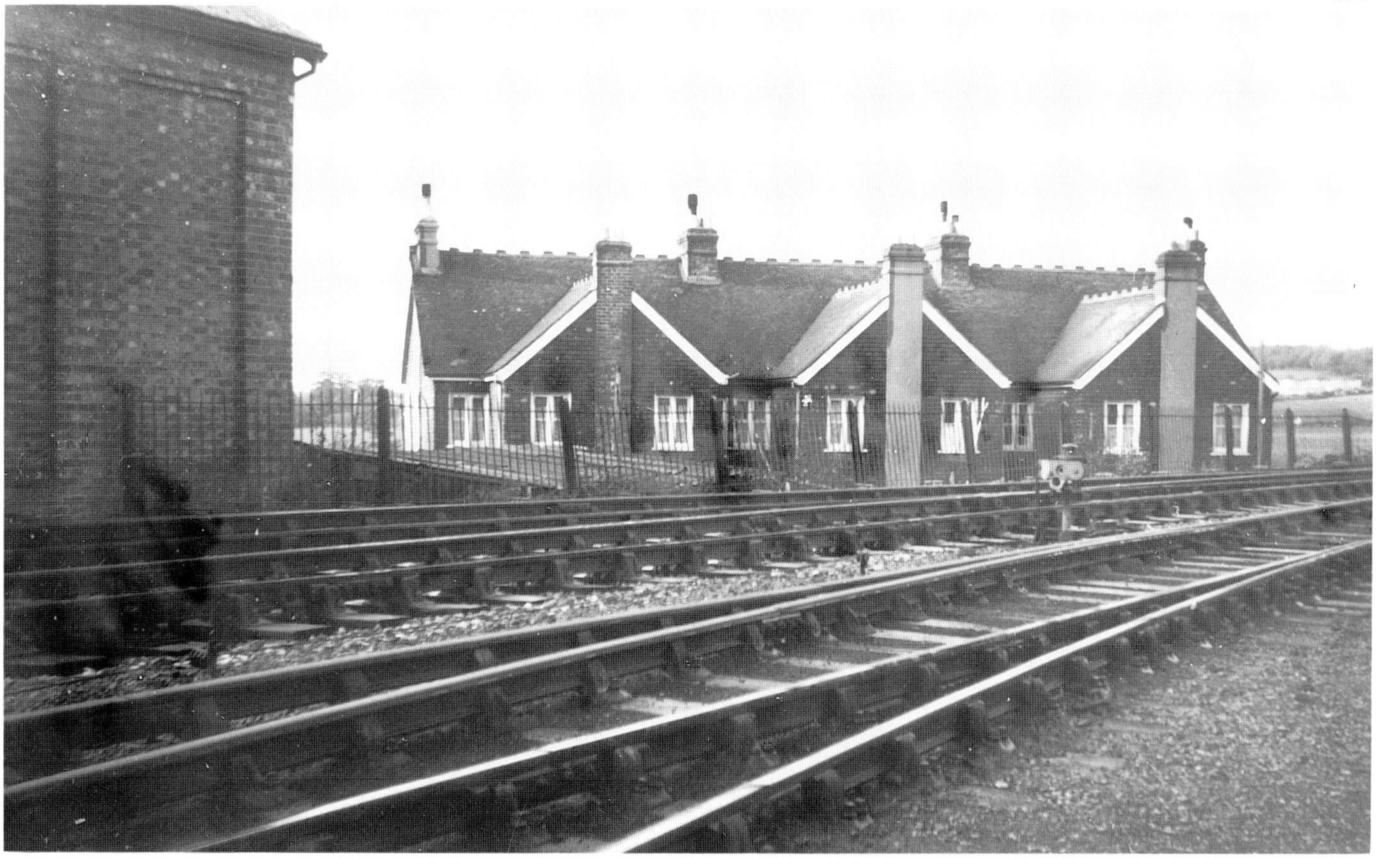

An unusual view across the running lines to the rear of the six railway cottages provided for the staff. *Ken Garrett*

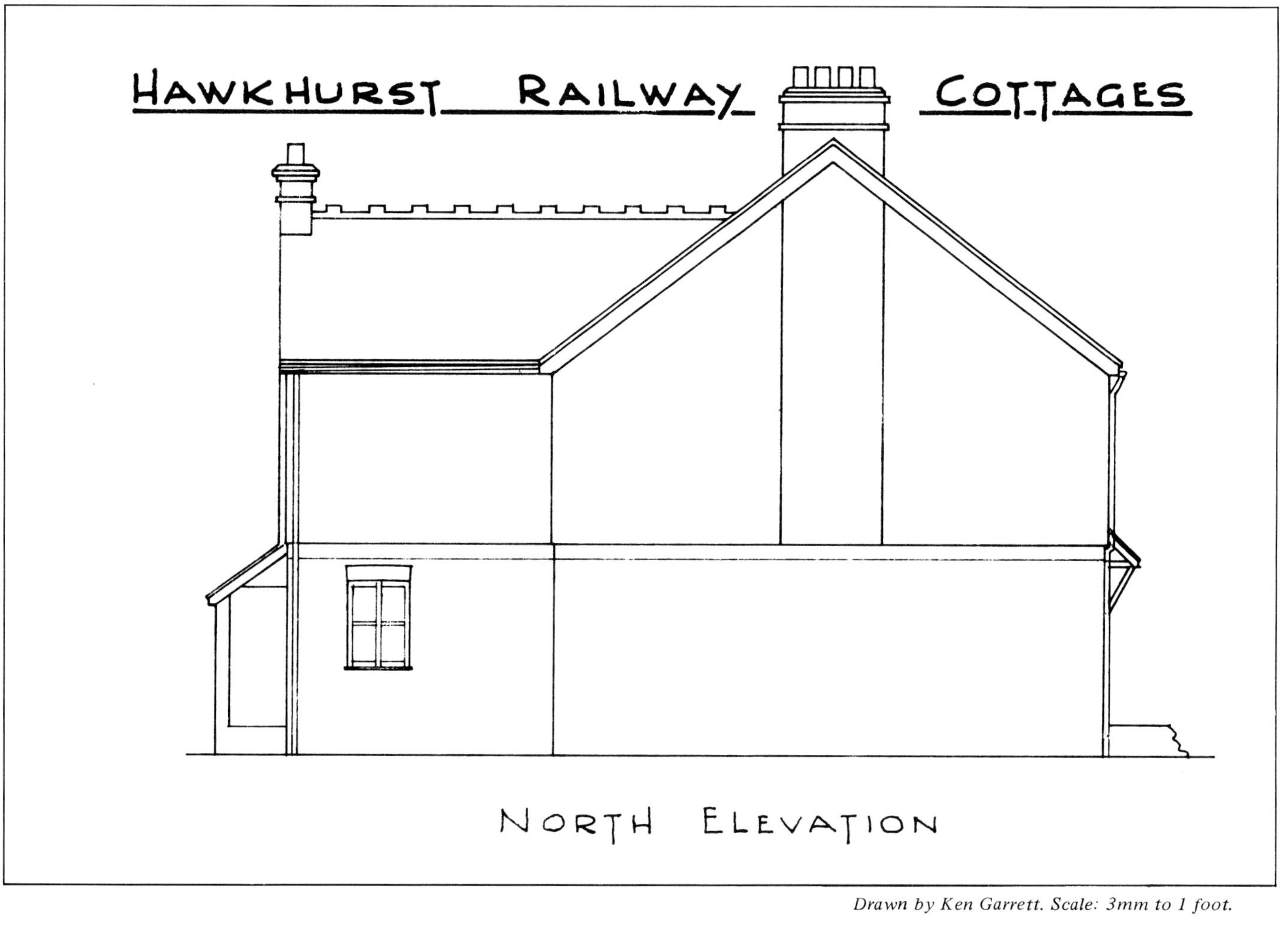

Drawn by Ken Garrett. Scale: 3mm to 1 foot.

PLAN

HAWKHURST OIL DEPOT

SOUTHWEST ELEVATION

SOUTHEAST ELEVATION

NORTHWEST ELEVATION

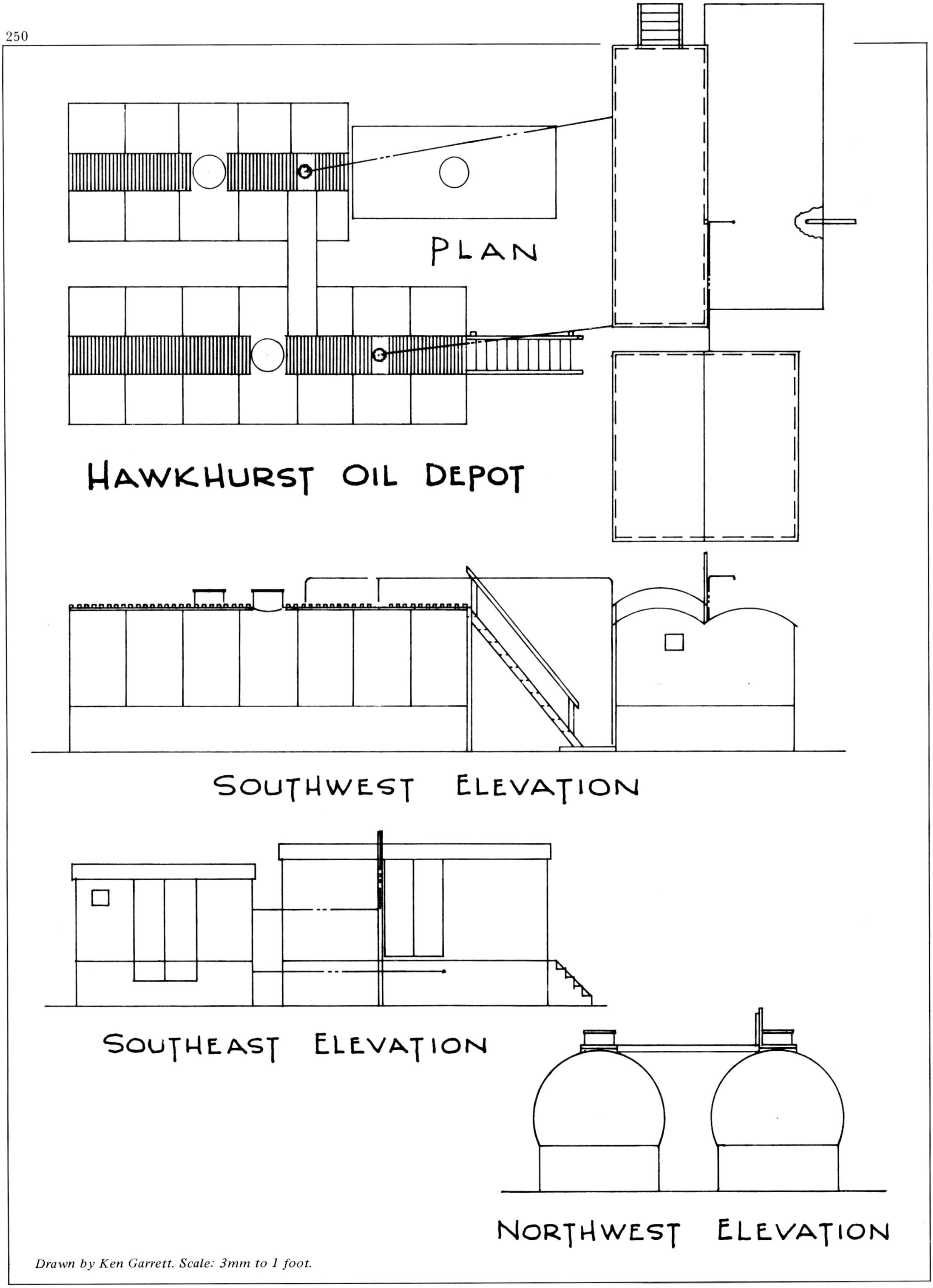

Drawn by Ken Garrett. Scale: 3mm to 1 foot.

S. E. & C. R. HORSMONDEN STATION

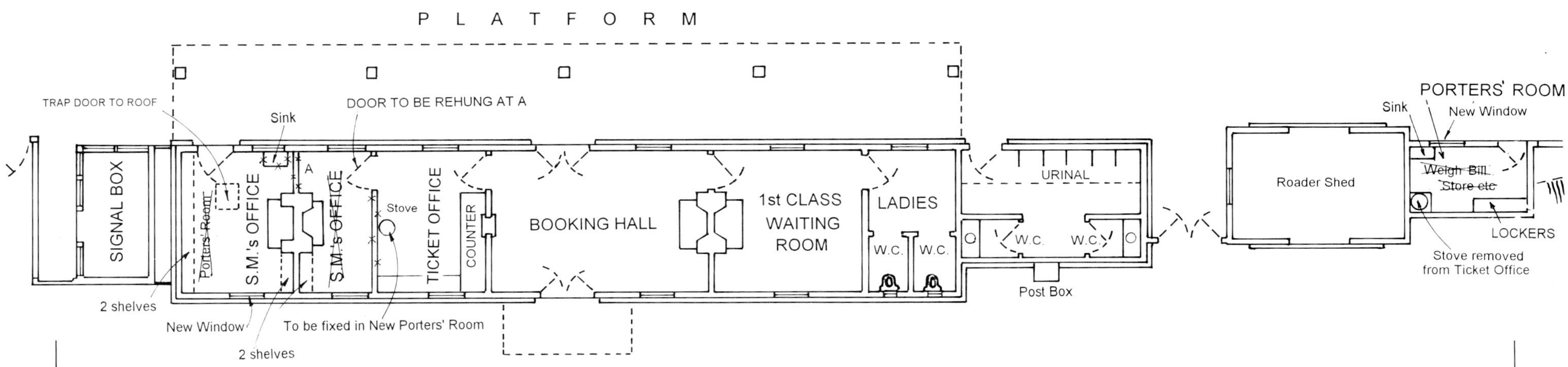

PLATFORM
TRAP DOOR TO ROOF
Sink
DOOR TO BE REHUNG AT A
A
SIGNAL BOX
Porters' Room
S.M.'s OFFICE
S.M.'s OFFICE
Stove
TICKET OFFICE
COUNTER
BOOKING HALL
1st CLASS WAITING ROOM
LADIES
W.C.
W.C.
URINAL
W.C.
W.C.
Post Box
Roader Shed
PORTERS' ROOM
Sink
New Window
Weigh Bill Store etc
LOCKERS
Stove removed from Ticket Office
2 shelves
New Window
To be fixed in New Porters' Room
2 shelves

S. E. & C. R. CRANBROOK STATION

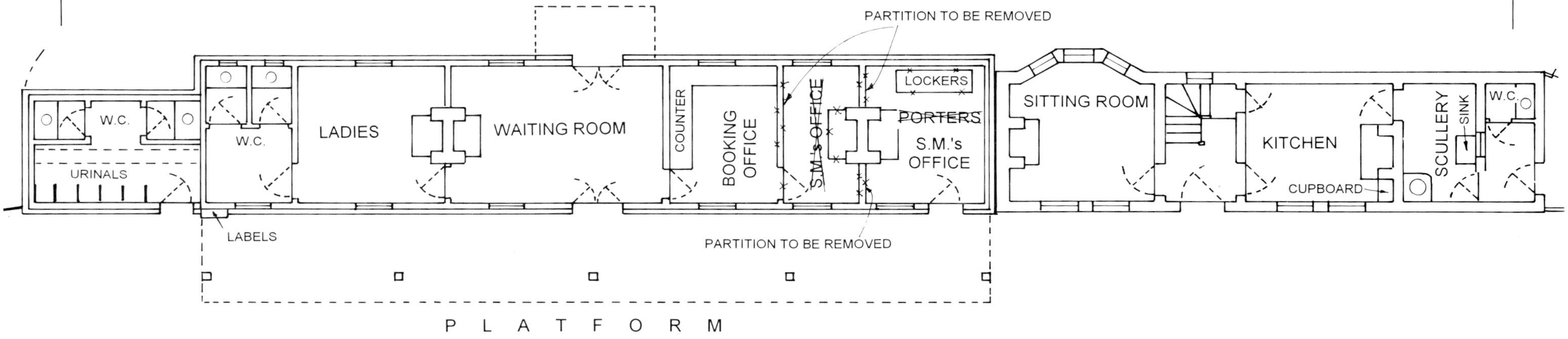

PARTITION TO BE REMOVED
W.C.
URINALS
W.C.
LABELS
LADIES
WAITING ROOM
COUNTER
BOOKING OFFICE
S.M.'s OFFICE
LOCKERS
PORTERS
S.M.'s OFFICE
PARTITION TO BE REMOVED
SITTING ROOM
KITCHEN
CUPBOARD
SCULLERY
SINK
W.C.
PLATFORM

ACKNOWLEDGEMENTS

Ron Williams

The Hawkhurst Branch has taken many years to compile, during which I have not only renewed old acquaintances, but made new friends along the way, in my quest to unearth the history of this lovely railway. Sadly, some of those have since passed on, but my feelings of gratitude are nevertheless just as strong.

I am aware that many people have waited patiently for this book to appear, so I hope it comes somewhere near to meeting their expectations. It has certainly been a pleasure to research and write about, whilst the pictures unfailingly give me endless pleasure. Throughout the countless hours I've spent in its creation, the special magic of this landscape has never been very far away. Other authors, infinitely greater than I, have similarly been entranced by the glorious hilltops, secret valleys and mystical woods which make up the ancient land of Andredswold. Sheila Kaye-Smith, who wrote lovingly about these parts, knew exactly what she meant when naming one of her books *Spell-Land*. Long may it remain so.

I must first thank the former staff of British Railways Southern Region, notably Reg Randell, Derek Clayton and colleagues at Waterloo. Thanks are also due to drivers Frank Glazebrook and Ken Hodson who made me so welcome on my visits and gave me valuable accounts of their days working the branch. Special thanks are due to Norman Rusbridge for not only providing a truly wonderful glimpse of life on the branch in the early 1950s, but for so generously allowing me to use his photographs (anyone who makes the journey by train from Wokingham to Uckfield via Redhill, East Croydon and Oxted to bring me his negatives deserves a round of applause!). Thanks are also due to Norman's brother-in-law Ron Williams for the loan of photographs. Without the considerable help from John Miller of the Colonel Stephens Railway Museum at Tenterden (if you haven't been there yet you've missed something wonderful) my account would have foundered in its third chapter. Likewise, I am grateful to Philip Shaw whose knowledge of 'The Colonel' is greater than anyone else I know.

I am also indebted to the following organizations and businesses: The Tonbridge Historical Society; Kent County Council's Centre for Kentish Studies; Tunbridge Wells Public Library; The Public Record Office; The British Newspaper Library; The National Railway Museum; Goudhurst & Kilndown Local History Society; Graham Thorn and staff at the *Wealden Advertiser*; The Industrial Railway Society; David Cole of Union Publications; Hulton-Deutsch Collection.

My dear departed friends are not forgotten: Derek Cross for his interest, encouragement and long, wonderfully penned letters; Bill Sparrowe, John Kite, Charles Evernden and George Gundry for their gentlemanly kindness on visits and in correspondence; Peter Winding for his perceptively wicked humour and ever-willingness to help; George Stickler's diligent photography and his wife Rita's help and hospitality; John Smith (Lens of Sutton) – a wonderful character, ever helpful and an irreplaceable loss to us all.

I am in debt to John Creed for diagrams and for explaining the intricacies of signalling regulations to me; Chris Turner for many items of material over the years; Gordon Batchelor for his contributions and generous help; Bert Bassett for his humorous memories; Derek Reader's eye-witness accounts and Brian Piper's valuable photographic contributions. Thanks are also recorded here to John Hendy; Ian Russell; Roger Dalleywater; Miss Jessie Russell; Dr. Edwin Course; Lewis 'Wag' Waghorn, as well as Robert Cromblehoime for so inspiring a 13-year-old with the first published book on the Hawkhurst branch.

Long-standing and valued acquaintances are not forgotten and whose friendship as the years roll by never wanes: Doug Lindsay; Barrie Clark; John Minnis; Tony Riley; Peter Harding.

To all the photographers and fellow authors – familiar names among Southern enthusiasts – whose dedication and skill never fails to amaze and inspire, we truly owe you all a great debt: John J. Smith; Sid Nash; Denis Cullum; James Aston; Dick Roberts; Dick Riley; John Scrace; Tony Wright; Alan Jackson; Ken Carr.

My thanks are also extended towards Henry Priestley, and to Richard Casserley for the kind loan of his father's superb photographs. I have been at pains to credit all known photographers where possible, but my apologies go to the person who, 34 years ago, provided the trackside views used in Chapter 7 and then disappeared, in spite of vain efforts over the ensuing years to trace him.

Ken Garrett deserves the warmest of thanks as his photographic survey captured so much of what has been lost. Without his determination, diligence and skilled draughtsmanship, our knowledge of this charming Wealden terminus would be significantly poorer. I know all members of the railway modelling fraternity will be eternally grateful to him for his dedication and attention to detail in what he has so generously and uniquely contributed.

The final acknowledgement comes not in order of appreciation, but perhaps saved till last so that I might emphasise the very great debt I owe to Paul Karau and June Judge of Wild Swan Publications. It has always been the greatest privilege to have a book published by Wild Swan and one I've never taken lightly, or for granted.

Brian Hart